Why You Need This New Edition

6 good reasons why you should buy this new edition of *Television and Radio Announcing*

As radio and television continue to adapt to and create public taste, necessary revisions of *Television and Radio Announcing* have strived to keep up with this dynamic field. This new revision is particularly relevant as contemporary broadcast media have lost their monopoly on audiences, and students and cultural tastes have changed more rapidly than any comparable time span since radio was first sent through the ether. To add a touch here and there to the book wouldn't serve. So, while this edition retains that which is ageless (e.g., voice and diction analysis and improvement), the text also moves directly into the ways announcers are affected by the digital age. The technological and societal revolutions have created new media and new generational perspectives. Aside from broadcasting and cable, such phenomena as MTV, YouTube, MySpace, iPods, and pirate radio are here and had to be addressed. A brief overview of some of the most important changes follows:

1. **New design** enhances the overall learning experience for visual learners.

2. **Student Voices** boxes are essays written by real students who offer a personal insight into key topics in today's industry.

3. Revised and expanded coverage **of job opportunities for announcers** are featured throughout the book.

4. New material about **changes in equipment and production procedures** are recognized and discussed in some detail in this new edition.

5. **New examples and illustrations** engage contemporary learners.

6. New and updated features focus on popular music practices such as **mobile DJs, karaoke,** and **working for a community radio station.**

PEARSON

Television and Radio Announcing

Eleventh Edition

Television and Radio Announcing

Stuart Hyde
San Francisco State University

Boston   New York   San Francisco
Mexico City   Montreal   Toronto   London   Madrid   Munich   Paris
Hong Kong   Singapore   Tokyo   Cape Town   Sydney

Editor-in-Chief: Karon Bowers
Acquisitions Editor: Jeanne Zalesky
Associate Editor: Jenny Lupica
Editorial Assistant: Brian Mickelson
Marketing Manager: Suzan Czajkowski
Production Editor: Claudine Bellanton
Editorial Production Service: Nesbitt Graphics, Inc.
Composition Buyer: Linda Cox
Manufacturing Buyer: JoAnne Sweeney
Electronic Composition: Nesbitt Graphics , Inc.
Interior Design: Nesbitt Graphics, Inc.
Cover Administrator/Designer: Kristina Mose-Libon

For related titles and support materials, visit our online catalog at www.ablongman.com.

Between the time website information is gathered and then published, it is not unusual for some sites to have closed. Also, the transcription of URLs can result in typographical errors. The publisher would appreciate notification where these errors occur so that they may be corrected in subsequent editions.

ISBN-13: 978-0-205-56304-3—ISBN-10: 0-205-56304-X

Library of Congress Cataloging-in-Publication data was not available at time of publication.

Printed in the United States of America

10 9 8 7 6 5 4 3 2 1 RRD-VA 12 11 10 09 08

To my teachers and students.
Looking back, I realize that I learned so much from each that I now understand that teachers and students are engaged in a reciprocal learning experience; anyone who believes that teaching learning is a one-way process is either naive or just hasn't thought about it. Thank you teachers, thank you students—my educators.

Contents

Chapter 1 ## Announcing for the Electronic Media   1

Chapter 8   Interview and Talk Programs   **170**

Chapter 9   Radio News   200

Chapter 10   Television News   227

Preface

The first edition of this book appeared in 1959, the second 12 years later. During those years, very little changed in broadcast technology or programming, so a revision wasn't considered urgent. Gradually, however, several changes did affect announcers, so these were reflected in a 1971 second edition. Developments included the rock-and-roll revolution, as well as slow but constant refinement of microphones, audio consoles, recorders, television cameras, and studio lighting. Even though many other changes occurred during these dozen years, they had only marginal effects on the preparation, performance duties, and job opportunities of most announcers.

The digital revolution changed all this. As you know—because you've lived through it—developments in recent years have brought about a radically new concept of electronics and a reconfiguration of electronic media production practices and distribution modes. In addition, the Telecommunications Act of 1996 resulted in drastic changes in station ownership and FCC regulations. Because both technical innovations and regulation changes affect announcers, a complete revision of many sections of *Television and Radio Announcing* was necessary.

But those issues are only part of the urgent need for a new edition. The Internet opened up new uses of the media, including "life-blogging," with such sites as MySpace, Facebook, YouTube, ConnectU, and Jazzed Up! Cell phones, which now do everything but cook breakfast, are used in a growing number of applications. Wikipedia cites these as examples:

> Mobile phones often have features beyond sending text messages and making voice calls, including Internet browsing, music (MP3) playback, memo recording, personal organizer functions, e-mail, instant messaging, built-in cameras and camcorders, ringtones, games, radio, Push-to-Talk (PTT), infrared and Bluetooth connectivity, call registers, ability to watch streaming video or download video for later viewing, video calling, and serving as a wireless modem for a PC.

Because of these developments, bringing this edition up-to-date required a recognition of the realities of the students who epitomize this new era. And that demanded a perception of their culture, interests, objectives, and attitudes toward electronic communication.

I believe that the greatest benefit of being a college teacher is the opportunity (and need!) to constantly be aware of the ever-changing culture of one's students. In my most recent teaching experience, I made it my top priority to investigate my students' interests, values, and beliefs. I quickly learned that today's college students (if I can project a sample of one to the larger college universe) are well educated and prepared to make a difference for the better in our society. True, they don't know as much about many things I always assumed "everyone" should know, but they do know things, important things, that I may never know. And wouldn't it be sad if every generation learned only what the preceding generation knew and passed on to it?

I asked these future media professionals to further my knowledge of their world by expressing, in their performances, anything they wanted to put forth. Their comments, made in assignments that they wrote or ad-libbed, introduced me to their world. I can't fully embrace that world, but I respect it. I now realize that to know today's students, to really know them, is to admire them.

Therefore, this, the eleventh edition, reflects the world of the students who will use this textbook. I have made many alterations and additions; here are a few of the most important changes:

- The writing style, which always aimed for clarity and precision, has been further sharpened to give it a more compelling, conversational texture. Updates in vocabulary, pronunciation, and usage have been made throughout the book. Our language, including the words we use and the way we speak them, is rapidly changing. MTV, BET, the Internet, text messaging, Podcasting, and many other conduits of communication have been widely adopted, and it would be alienating to ignore these changes.

- Eleven essays by students currently enrolled in media programs across the country were added to the eleventh edition. These "Student Voices" boxes cover topics from MTV VJs to YouTube; and because they are a student-to-student communication there is a relevancy, a cultural connection, that's very special.

- Other new features focus on relevant topics that include employment opportunities for announcers aside from broadcasting and cable. Careers discussed include employment by corporate and industrial media, performing as mobile DJs or karaoke hosts, and interning or working for community radio stations.

- Although this textbook is about performance, rather than production, changes in equipment and production procedures are noted throughout the book. The world of announcing is affected by the widespread use of robotic cameras, the reduced use of tape (although research shows tape is still widely used), voice-tracking, ear prompters, and performing without the assistance of floor managers.

- Many new examples of commercials, PSAs, news copy, and other scripts have replaced dated examples from the previous edition. Fresh copy with more appeal to today's students has been added.

When *Television and Radio Announcing* appeared in 1959, it included material not found in previous announcing textbooks. Detailed sections were devoted to improving every aspect of speech. Diagnostic readings helped instructors and students analyze the way they spoke and identify areas where improvement was needed. Exercises to improve pitch, inflection, tempo, volume, and vitality were given, and nasality, huskiness, excessive popping, and sibilance were explained. While the eleventh edition has retained all of this information and the exercises that address these concerns, content has been streamlined and explanations and diagrams have been improved to make the material more understandable and, therefore, more useful.

Chapter 7, "Commercials and Public-Service Announcements," is noticeably improved by the addition of an emphasis on announcers as actors. Distinctions are drawn between those who provide information without adopting a "role"—such as talk show hosts and documentary narrators—and those who employ characterization in dramatized commercials. Television and film voice-overs are discussed and suggestions given for preparing to work in those areas.

Chapter 13, "Starting Your Announcing Career," continues to offer advice on résumé writing, including scannable résumés, cover letters, audition (or résumé) recordings, finding job openings, applying for a position, interviewing for a job, joining a union, and much more.

In short, while the eleventh edition of *Television and Radio Announcing* remains solid in those areas that brought about its widespread adoption as a basic textbook, it also offers the material students need to become proficient announcers in today's ever-changing industry.

A Word from the Past

While there have been many alterations to this new edition, it's important to note that the text still boasts a strong lineage. This edition marks the 50th anniversary of the first edition, published in 1959—and to commemorate the event I've included for the enjoyment of students (and many of their younger instructors!) some of the practices of announcers "way back when."

News Aside from its own staff of reporters, local stations in 1959 were served by news organizations including the United Press International News Service and the Associated Press. These agencies sent news stories, and even complete news programs, to radio and television stations that had leased large machines with keys identical to those on typewriters. With a loud clacking sound, news was printed on lengthy paper rolls that were examined by newsroom personnel, torn off, and read by staff announcers, leading to the expression "a rip-and-read operation."

Sports When the first edition of this text was published, home games were covered on radio much as they are today, although with more primitive equipment. Away games were a different story. In the first edition, the PRACTICE of "recreating baseball games" was explained. Games played away from a home team's base were broadcast on radio in a manner that included not only the voice of the play-by-play announcer but crowd sounds, the voice of the stadium announcer, sounds of thrown balls hitting the catcher's mitt, and bats hitting pitched balls. These photos show an announcer and his engineer at work.

These photos, from the 1959 first edition, show Bob Bailey and his engineer, Clay Sanders recreating an away game for listeners.

Details of the game were sent over a Western Union circuit, and were very sparse: FOURTH INNING. DETROIT. MAXWELL UP. LIGHT DRIZZLE COMING DOWN. b1 LOW. S1. Here is how this was announced:

"Maxwell stands in there . . . left-handed batter, struck out in the first inning . . . Donovan into the wind-up . . . and the pitch is low for ball one. (LONG PAUSE, BACKGROUND CROWD NOISES) . . . Now the pitch: swing and a miss for a strike. Ball one and strike one. This is Bob Bailey and Clay Sanders with the game of the day from Comiskey Park where a light drizzle has begun to fall . . .

Music Radio For many years, songs were stored on 78 rpm vinyl records, and, occasionally, on 33 1/3 rpm LP records. DJs had before them an audio console, announce mic, and to the side, at least two turntables and reel-to-reel tape recorders. Tony King, a popular disc jockey at KSOL-FM, San Francisco, was among many DJs who ruled popular music on radio. He chose the songs he played, freely talked without time limits, and engineered his own programs.

Nearly all broadcasting was live. Some programs, including daytime serials (soap operas), were recorded on very large discs called E-Ts (for "electrical tran-

From the second edition in 1971, this photo of a prominent disc jockey was shown with this caption: "Combo operator at work. Tony King, disc jockey at KSOL-FM, San Francisco, operates a Sparta console, a QRK turntable, and an RCA 77DX ribbon microphone."

scription"), which were sent to stations and regional networks in all time zones for later broadcast. Because of the three-hour time difference between the East and West coasts, news programs, dramas, variety shows, and many other programs originating live in New York were broadcast twice. A program heard live on the East Coast at 8:00 p.m. was performed again at 11:00 p.m. for those in the far West.

Equipment was primitive by today's standards, but it served its purposes. It's now common to believe that such items as open-reel tape recorders, vinyl records, turntables, and even audiocassettes and VHS tapes are useless. But, to me, no item of equipment is obsolete as long as important archival material can be retrieved by it alone. I continue to maintain and use all of these equipment items. Recordings of announcing class performances from 20 or more years ago and interviews and skits I recorded on 1/2" Sony Portapack tape between 1970 and 1981 in my performance classes at San Quentin State Prison are of lasting value to me. My collection of rock-and-roll music on vinyl 78 rpm records is priceless, but only to me. In time, I will convert these to DVD, even though one day even that medium will be obsolete!

A Last Word from Me to You . . .

I close this trip into the past with a sincere wish that you enjoy and profit from this textbook. Things have changed quite a bit over the years, but regardless of new words or pronunciations, advanced technology, or the expanding options of media outlets, some things remain the same.

As mentioned earlier, you live in a world of great and rapidly changing technology, and I'm sure you're savoring and making creative uses of it. But always remember that information and techniques, important as they are, can't make you a good person or give you a happy life.

Your life's meaning ultimately will be written by you and will be determined by the values you hold and share. You have written your life very well so far, because you made it to college and will graduate with a splendid education. You will continue to write your own script.

The great Jackie Robinson, who suffered so much as he broke the color barrier in professional sports, wrote: "A life is not important except in the impact it has on the lives of others."

As an announcer, you can't avoid having an impact on the lives of others; if you use this privilege wisely, the future chapters you write will ensure a good career and a rewarding life.

I wish you well.

Stuart Hyde

Acknowledgments

Every edition of *Television and Radio Announcing* has been enriched by the contributions of so many individuals that to recognize them here would require a very lengthy chapter! So only individuals who made contributions to this edition are mentioned here. Those whose photos appear are identified in the captions, so their names need not be repeated here, but their cooperation is greatly appreciated and I extend my thanks to each of them.

Professor Tommy Booras, whose excellent article on sports reporting is the Spotlight for Chapter 12, was helpful in many ways including reviewing and commenting on the entire sports chapter. Ken Pries, Vice President, Communications and Broadcasting, and Debbie Gallas, Media Services Manager for the Oakland A's baseball team, made it possible for me to photograph and discuss sports announcing with play-by-play announcers Ken Korach and Vince Cotroneo of the A's and Ed Farmer and Chris Singleton of the Chicago White Sox. Hal Ramey, sports reporter and director at KCBS, described and demonstrated how he obtains, edits, and produces actualities for his daily sports reports.

Award-winning special assignment reporter Mike Sugerman for KPIX, Channel 5, described in detail how he chooses, investigates, records, edits, and reports stories that, while not breaking news, offer insights into people and events that enlighten and inform.

DJs Dave Sholin, Sue Hall, and Celeste Perry of KFRC-FM, put up with my intrusion into their on-air studio, answering questions, and permitting my endless taking of flash photos as they concentrated on their demanding work.

Special thanks go to colleague Dina Ibrahim who made her media performance class available for action photos taken during class sessions. Lyons Filmer, Program Director of Community Radio Station KWMR, made all station resources available to me, and she and husband, Gregory DeMascio, taught me most of what is reported here about community radio. Janice Lynch supplied information for the feature on Karaoke, and Roy McNeill provided material for the discussion of Mobile DJ work.

Peg Oberste, Broadcast Producer for ad agency Goodby, Silverstein & Partners, deserves very special thanks for spending a great deal of time and effort in gaining permission to use outstanding commercials produced by this creative agency. Rosy Chu, of KTVU, assisted me in many ways: opening up the news department for me to explore all aspects of its daily production of six newscasts, introducing me to key performers who graciously answered questions and posed for photos, and getting permission for me to sit through planning meetings and observe procedures in the studio and control room during newscasts.

Two students in my media performance class, John MacNamara and Andrew Kim, granted permission for use of commercials they'd written for class assignments. Several other scripts in this edition were written by students, including commercials, essays and "impressions," which may be found in Appendix A.

Jennifer Stanonis, a former student, now reporter, anchor, and weather reporter for the Buffalo, New York, NBC-affiliated station, sent photos of her at work that illustrate several aspects of news performance.

Students from colleges across the nation wrote their opinions about many facets of electronic communication, and deserve special thanks for bringing student voices to this book for the first time.

I am grateful to the following reviewers for their comments and suggestions for this edition: Mac Aipperspach, Del Mar College; Tommy G. Booras, Western Kentucky University; Ceilidh T. Charleston-Jennings, Collin County Community College; Howard Espravnik, Volunteer State College; Dale Harnett, SUNY, Brockport; Mark Labash, Oral Roberts University; Sam Lovato, Colorado State University–Pueblo; Beverly Love, Southern Illinois University; Riley Maynard, Southern Illinois University, Edwardsville; Patricia Williamson, Central Michigan University; and Evan Wirig, Grossmont College.

Finally, my very special thanks go to my Allyn & Bacon editors, Jenny Lupica and Jeanne Zalesky. I've had ten editors for prior editions, and while all were excellent, none was as supportive, responsive, knowledgeable, and dedicated as were Jenny and Jeanne. They worked with me almost daily during the twenty months of writing and rewriting, sending and captioning the photos, getting both photo and copy permissions, and much, much more, until the deadline was reached, and the manuscript was sent into production.

Stuart Hyde

Chapter 1

Announcing for the Electronic Media

Chapter Outline

This book is about how to get from where you are to where you want to be. It's a book for anyone who's intrigued by the mystery and magic of the media that send voices and pictures across tens of thousands of miles, connecting one individual to millions. In short, it's about a path you may follow and the dedication necessary to become a professional radio and television announcer.

Talent, Perseverance, and Preparation

In broadcasting, no one gets a free ride. Those who rise to the top earn their way there because they already possess or have developed three attributes: talent, perseverance, and preparation. *Television and Radio Announcing* was written to help you become prepared. Talent is a gift that can't be bought—although it can be cultivated—and perseverance comes from within. If you have two of these three qualities, you can go as far as your dreams can take you.

These attributes should be considered one at a time. First, **talent:** Many performers refer to themselves as "talent," but we know they mean "announcer." The word *talent* actually refers to a *possession*, not a *person*. Good looks and curly hair are possessions. So are inherited aptitudes, such as a gift for math, music, or language. Some people (Mozart, for example) are born with incredible innate talent that blossoms shortly after infancy. Does this mean we're born with announcing talent or without it? Not entirely. Most of us have potential gifts that don't become apparent until we discover and consciously cultivate them.

The American Heritage Dictionary defines talent as "a mental or physical aptitude; natural or *acquired* ability" (italics added). This says it all. Being endowed with a pleasant voice and an outgoing personality makes it easier to become an effective announcer, but there's more to success in this field than innate possessions. Good voice quality and a compelling presence can also be developed through hard and focused work. Many with excellent voices and precise articulation never make it as announcers, while others with lesser gifts who work systematically to develop their means of expression and a compelling personality may be heard on the air daily. Innate talent alone doesn't guarantee success as a communicator.

The second attribute is **perseverance.** The best-prepared would-be announcers will never see their dreams come true if they don't have a streak of stubbornness, which many call "drive" or "perseverance." To continue to believe in yourself through early disappointments is required of most who attempt to launch their announcing careers right out of college. Even if you're well prepared, you may struggle for years before you achieve significant career and financial rewards. Expect this and don't decide that initial setbacks are proof you lack what it takes. You deserve to have faith in yourself if you *truly believe you have something worthwhile to offer,* if you've *prepared yourself through sustained effort,* and if *you've taken advantage of performance opportunities* in classes, on campus stations, and in community-access cable productions. To succeed at the highest level, you also must have an urgent need to communicate worthwhile messages to others and have a passion for broadcasting.

At the same time, you should be aware that to charge blindly ahead hoping to become a success on the air is unrealistic if you haven't perfected your instruments of communication and acquired the knowledge, the sense of humor, and the poise required for success. Too many hopefuls, having heard about the money to be made in voice-overs (for example), believe they can join the ranks of professionals by taking a weekend course in commercial performance and then showing up for auditions. It really isn't that easy.

Preparation is the focus of this book. In its thirteen chapters you'll find hundreds of exercises for developing skills to help you be heard and appreciated by vast audiences.

About This Book

Overview of Chapters

This chapter of *Television and Radio Announcing* offers an overview of the announcing field and includes suggestions for studies outside your major department that are important for developing your abilities.

Messages sent through radio and television aren't about *broadcasting*. They're about news, history, economics, the arts, science, the weather—in short, just about any topic of importance you can think of makes its way to audiences through electronic media. To be successful, you must acquire a broadly based knowledge in many areas and an extensive vocabulary to help convey that knowledge to others.

Chapter 2, "The Announcer as Communicator," introduces several areas of performance, including script interpretation and ad-lib announcing, with many exercises and suggestions to help build effectiveness when speaking to others.

Chapters 3 and 4, "Voice Analysis and Improvement" and "Pronunciation and Articulation," are of primary importance and should be referred to regularly because they're guides to improving the most important instrument you possess: your voice. Diagnostic tests are included, in addition to many exercises for refining every aspect of your speech. Later chapters in the text may be read only once to obtain most of what they include, but you should become a regular visitor to these two chapters, 3 and 4. Using the exercises on a scheduled basis will, over time, bring impressive results.

Most of the remaining chapters go into detail about a number of specializations, including audio and video performance, commercial and public-service announcing, interviewing, radio news, television news, sports announcing, and music announcing.

The final chapter, "Starting Your Announcing Career," offers detailed information on job searches, résumés, audition recordings, job interviews, and much more.

What You Can Gain from This Book

The title *Television and Radio Announcing* describes this book's focus, but there's more substance to it than a narrow preparation for a career in broadcasting. Even if you haven't committed yourself to becoming a performer for the electronic media, improving your communication abilities can be of great value. Confident, effective expression has always been an invaluable tool. If you apply yourself, you can look forward to significant improvement in your ability to (1) speak with an appealing voice; (2) clearly articulate individual words and sentences; (3) vary pitch and volume effectively; (4) pronounce words according to accepted standards; (5) select and use words, phrases, similes, and metaphors effectively; (6) express yourself confidently; (7) interpret copy; (8) speak ad lib or impromptu; and (9) communicate ideas clearly, both orally and nonverbally. Aside from such specifics, your development as an effective communicator will enhance your rapport—your affinity—with others.

The Announcer for the Electronic Media

Media performers are products of the electronic age, but several related professions preceded them by centuries. Preliterate storytellers, troubadours, town criers, and early newspaper journalists were all forerunners of modern announcers. Each provided a service to the public. With some, the emphasis was on delivery of information; with others, it was to entertain audiences. Announcers are like storytellers in that they speak directly to their audiences. Radio announcers also resemble writers for the print media in that they describe events their audiences can't see. Because television reporters and news anchors describe events as their audiences simultaneously see them, they are unique in the entire history of human communication.

Think of the spectrum of newsworthy events—hurricanes, election returns, even wars—and then try to imagine their coverage without the investigations,

Figure 1-1
DJ Sue Hall stands as she delivers intros to a music sweep. Sue says that standing increases energy, allows unrestricted movement, and improves voice quality.
Courtesy Sue Hall and KFRC-FM.

comments, and explanations of on-the-scene broadcast reporters and analysts. All communication media, including the Internet, have important roles to play, but for direct on-mic or on-camera presentation of ongoing events, nothing can equal the impact of the broadcast and cable media.

Although announcers share roles with earlier news delivery professions, there are important differences. Both radio and television reach vast audiences scattered over thousands of miles, and both are instantaneous. Radio made it possible for the first time in history to describe to millions of people events as they occurred. Because radio presented real-time communication over great distances and because radio is a "blind" medium, announcers became indispensable. Radio couldn't function without those who provided direct oral communication by describing events, reporting the news, introducing speakers and entertainers, and alerting audiences to tornado, hurricane, or flood dangers.

The radio announcer is the clarifying link between listeners and what would otherwise be a jumble of sound, noise, or silence. On television the announcer is the presenter, the communicator, and the interpreter. Without such performers, neither radio nor television as we know it would be possible. Announcers are important to many types of programs and reach their audiences through many distribution systems. Their responsibility is substantial, and because announcers usually make direct presentations to their audiences, they are efficient and economical. No other means of disseminating information is so direct and swift as the word spoken directly to the listener. Small wonder, then, that radio and television announcers must possess native talent, acquire a broad educational background, and then undergo intensive training and consistent practice as they develop professional competencies.

An **announcer** is *anyone who communicates over the public airwaves, as on radio or television broadcasts; Internet radio (e-radio); through cable channels into homes, schools, offices, and the like; or over closed-circuit audio or video distribution by electronic amplification, as in an auditorium, stadium, arena, or theater.* Singers, actors, and actresses are considered announcers only when they perform that specific function. Because a great many commercials involve dramatization—or, at least, characterization—you should enroll in acting classes.

Sound Bytes

BACKGROUNDS OF SUCCESSFUL ANNOUNCERS

Many radio and television stations maintain websites, and most include brief biographies of on-air performers. Using these as your source, compile information about several announcers whose work you admire. You may want to look for these information items: Where did they attend school? In what academic area did they major? Where did they begin their announcing careers?

For a complete updated list of URLs for this textbook, please see the accompanying CD.

Areas of Specialization

Announcing includes many areas of specialization:

Broadcast Journalism

Anchors, or news readers

Field reporters—special assignment or general assignment

Feature reporters

Analysts

Commentators

Weather reporters

Consumer affairs reporters

Environmental reporters

Science reporters

Entertainment reporters

Farm news reporters

Business news reporters

Medical reporters (frequently doctors)

Traffic reporters

Sports

Radio and television sports reporters

Play-by-play announcers

Play and game analysts

Sports talk program hosts

Music

Announcers on popular music stations (referred to variously as DJs, deejays, or jocks)

Music video jockeys (VJs or veejays)

Mobile DJs

Community radio DJs

Internet radio (e-radio) music announcers

Classical music announcers (for both live and recorded performances)

Public Affairs

Interviewers

Panel moderators

Commercials

Voice-over announcers (radio and television)

Demonstration and commercial announcers (television)

"Infomercial" announcers (television)—who present lengthy commercials showing and demonstrating products

Salespersons on the Home Shopping Network or QVC

Narration

Documentaries, such as *Nova, National Geographic* specials, Ken Burns's *The Civil War, The War,* and *Baseball*

Informative programs, such as the History Channel's *Modern Marvels* and educational programs on NPR and PBS

Readers of scripts for industrial or corporate presentations

Readers of essays, editorials, feature reports, and "impressions" for both radio and television

Special Programs

Interview shows, including *The Oprah Winfrey Show, Larry King Live, Charlie Rose, Fresh Air,* and topical political sessions with current newsmakers—*Meet the Press, Face the Nation,* and ABC's *This Week*

Interview and phone-in shows (television and radio)

Magazine shows such as *Sixty Minutes, Dateline,* features on *Animal Planet* (television), and *All Things Considered* and *Science Friday* (NPR)

Food, gardening, home repair, and similar specialty shows

Dance and popular music shows (television)

Children's programs

Game shows

Introducers of feature films on television

Sound Bytes

Several lists of talent agencies may be found on the Internet. Here are some URLs:

www.futurecasting2000.com/agency.htm

www.pozproductions.com/agtmainp.htm

For a complete updated list of URLs for this textbook, please see the accompanying CD.

Single-subject specialists also appear regularly on some talk shows and newscasts on topics such as gardening, cooking, exercise, consumerism, science, art, and health. These specialists sometimes perform solo on brief segments of one to three minutes; others work with station staff announcers who serve as hosts. During televised parades (Macy's Thanksgiving Day Parade, the Rose Parade), announcing teams identify participants, explain float construction, and provide color.

Employment as an Announcer

Approximately 85,000 men and women are employed as announcers. Of these, around 16,000 work as news reporters, anchors, analysts, and commentators. Most are full-time employees of radio and television stations, cable operations, and broadcast networks. Others are full- or part-time freelance announcers, some of whom perform as DJs under contract. Freelance announcers also include narrators for documentaries and instructional recordings or serve as both on- and off-camera voice-over performers of commercials.[1]

Cable television provides such nonbroadcast programing as the Discovery Channel, Comedy Central, Cable News Network (CNN), Entertainment and Sports Programming Network (ESPN and ESPN2), American Movie Classics (AMC), Lifetime, Nickelodeon, Arts and Entertainment (A&E), Sundance Channel, Independent Film Channel, Turner Classic Movies, Black Entertainment Television, MTV, and "shopping channels." So-called premium channels—channels for which subscribers pay fees beyond the basic rate for cable service—include Home Box Office (HBO), Showtime, and Starz, some of which have several channels.

Available on cable in many areas are channels devoted to narrowly focused interests, including golf, tennis, gardening, gymnastics, health, war movies and documentaries, Western movies and television dramas, detective dramas, love stories, cooking shows, game shows, specialized music channels, and daytime serials.

Figure 1-2
Consumer reporter Michael Finney hosts a daily feature, "Seven on Your Side," a service that acts on behalf of viewers who believe they've been treated unfairly by a business or governmental agency. Michael's path to his present major market position began as a television reporter in Pocatello, Idaho, followed by reporting and anchoring in Idaho Falls, Idaho; Bakersfield, California; San Diego, California; and finally at KGO-TV in San Francisco. *Courtesy of Michael Finney and KGO-TV.*

---

[1] These figures are far from reliable. The U.S. Bureau of Labor Statistics is usually several years behind in its reporting and, even then, does not break down its figures by announcing categories, such as DJs, news reporters and anchors, voice-over actors, narrators, and so forth. It also isn't possible, from its reports, to determine how many announcers are performing on satellite radio, community radio, podcasting, and so on.

Community radio stations and Internet radio operations offer informational and entertainment programs hosted by announcers. While most program hosts and DJs staffing these services are volunteers, they offer great opportunities for experience and for communicating with appreciative listeners.

While much cable programming is recycled material—movies, syndicated television packages, classic sports events, and television miniseries—as channels continue to proliferate, there's likely to be an increased demand for on-camera and voice-over announcers.

A growing number of men and women work in **industrials,** also called **corporate media.** Audio and video presentations are made to train employees, introduce new products, provide information to distant branches, and communicate in-house. The term **industrial media** is a loose one because it applies to media used by hospitals, government agencies, schools, prisons, and the military, as well as businesses. Few such media departments can afford the services of a full-time announcer, so if this work appeals to you, you should prepare for media writing and producing as well as announcing. (Chapter 13, "Starting Your Announcing Career," provides specific information on job seeking.)

Local television stations provide multiprogram service, but aside from newscasts and interview or talk shows, they employ few announcers. But many local television stations *do* produce commercials. Even the smallest community with a commercial television station may offer some work for announcers. If this field interests you, call a station's sales or promotion department for specific information about how it hires announcers.

Education and Training

Because announcers perform not only on broadcast stations and cable but also over the Internet, on recorded commercials, as mobile DJs, and as narrators for documentaries, they must be knowledgeable in a number of areas. Assuming that you're majoring in "electronic communication" (or the term used at your school), you should consider enrolling in one or more minor programs in such content areas as history, political science, urban studies, literature, sociology, economics, acting, or geography. Career-oriented courses of study also should be considered, including journalism, sports history, and meteorology.

Informational media reach millions of people with messages of critical importance, and there's little room for narrowly educated announcers. For one thing, the influence—for good or bad—of radio and television performers is immense and mustn't be underestimated. Announcers who don't grow with the times will be inadequate in the twenty-first century.

Television program hosts, DJs, interviewers, announcers covering sports and special events, and talk-show personalities use written material only occasionally; most of the time they're on their own. Radio and television field reporters covering breaking stories as they unfold never work from scripts; they ad-lib their reports

Student Voices

Terrestrial Radio versus Satellite Radio by Krystal MacKnight

ALL ABOUT ME: I recently received my B.A. in Radio and Television Production at San Francisco State University, and I have my Music Recording Industry Certificate. I love to work in front of and behind the camera. Making music and movies is my passion.

ALL ABOUT TERRESTRIAL VERSUS SATELLITE RADIO: Satellite radio began as a free service received only on car radios. Later, paid subscriptions for services such as XM and Sirius also brought signals to home and office. These stations offer niche programming that includes music, weather, news, and sports. Commercial free and sent over the Internet, satellite radio can be received with clear signals nearly anywhere on the planet. Unfortunately for announcers, most music channels don't use DJs.

Terrestrial radio (land based) has always been free to listeners, but its many commercials, while giving employment to announcers, is considered annoying to those who want advertising-free music. However, these stations are vital during times of community emergencies because, being local, the announcer knows exactly what audience she or he is reaching. Again, though, there are problems: Radio signals aren't always the best, frequent commercials lose listeners, and FCC regulations can be annoying to management.

. . . AND HOW DOES THIS AFFECT ANNOUNCING? Satellite radio is to terrestrial radio what cable is to public-access television. In satellite radio, there are more programs, variety, and specialty shows. Terrestrial radio is still strong and will never completely fade out, but it seems to be losing the popularity contest.

I personally do not have satellite radio, but I do listen to a lot of terrestrial radio. In the future I hope to see a collaboration between the two radio formats.

from hastily scribbled notes that are limited to basic information. The opportunity to frame your personal thoughts in words of your own choosing carries with it the responsibility to have much information at hand to share with your audience.

Checklist Courses to Build Your Career

Basic Preparation for Announcing

Take courses that focus on the following subjects:
- Interpretation
- Articulation
- Phonation
- Phonetic transcription
- Microphone use
- Camera presence
- Ad-libbing
- Script reading
- Adapting one's personality to the broadcast media
- Foreign language pronunciation
- Control-room operations
- Video production and editing
- Writing for radio and television

Specialized Courses to Prepare You for Specific Duties
- Broadcast journalism—courses in journalism, international relations, political science, economics, history, and geography
- Broadcast sales and advertising—courses in business, marketing, accounting, sales techniques, sales promotion, and audience research
- Sports, including play-by-play announcing—courses in the history of sports, sports officiating, and sociology of sport
- Weather reporting—courses in meteorology, weather analysis, weather forecasting, and geography

Courses to Further Your General Education
- Social, ethical, aesthetic, and historical perspectives on electronic communication
- The arts—music, theater, literature, or painting and sculpture

- Social and behavioral sciences—psychology, sociology, urban studies, and ethnic studies
- Quantitative reasoning—essentially math and computation
- Critical thinking—skills crucial to clear and constructive thought
- Media law and regulation
- Writing, writing, writing

Coursework Considerations

Your career goals should determine your choice of courses outside your major, but be aware of the expectations of future employers. Nearly all look for well-educated people who possess specific basic skills: good writing ability, outstanding proficiency in spoken communication, computational skills (basic math), and critical thinking. They also look for people who are hardworking, self-motivated, and pleasant to be around.

Within Your Major. Control-room operations should include practice with **audio consoles** and associated recording and playback devices. Even though operation of consoles is easily learned, and most announcers no longer actually operate them (as they once did), it's important to be prepared in as many areas as possible because it's impossible to know in advance what turns your career may take. You should also take courses in video production and editing because many television stations expect reporters to record and edit their news stories. Anchors and reporters must learn to write news copy. Many stations in medium to small markets expect announcers to write commercial copy and station promotional pieces as well.

Beyond Your Major. In studying to be a broadcast announcer, you obviously should pursue subjects that prepare you for your first announcing job, but you also should select *courses that qualify you for one or more specializations beyond straight announcing*. Plan your coursework to obtain a broad background in the liberal arts and sciences. If you're serious about an announcing career, your education must have breadth, so maintain a positive attitude about required general education courses—even if they seem unrelated to your career goals, they will add to a storehouse of knowledge that you'll find yourself visiting many times over the years. You probably won't be able to study all areas mentioned in the Checklist on page 11, but you should at least discuss them with an adviser.

Expand your ability to pronounce names and words in French, German, Italian, and Spanish. Whether you become a specialist in news, sports, voice-overs, or interviewing, your ability to pronounce names and words in languages other than English will be of great importance.

Sound Bytes

The accompanying CD for this textbook provides extensive information on rules of pronunciation for French, German, Spanish, and Italian, with a less extensive discussion of Chinese pronunciation.

Figure 1-3

General assignment reporter Carolyn Tyler has earned many awards, including citations from the National Association of Black Journalists, the Black Media Coalition, and American Women in Radio and Television. Carolyn received her bachelor's degree in broadcasting from the University of Wyoming. Prior to her current employment, Carolyn worked as a reporter in Minneapolis and Philadelphia. *Courtesy of Carolyn Tyler and KGO-TV.*

Many general education courses, including English composition, are required for a liberal arts degree. You should go beyond minimum English requirements by choosing from such offerings as expository writing, essay writing, creative writing, and dramatic writing. But, as you work to improve your skills in writing traditional English, be aware that there's another writing challenge that is unlikely to be met by English instructors: *learning to write for the ear and the eye.*

While it must be obvious that, unlike stories written for newspapers and magazines, radio scripts are written to be *heard,* and television scripts to be *seen and heard.* It's important to remember always that your scripts will never be seen or read by your audience. Scripts are blueprints to be turned into sights and sounds by interpreters. To write well for the electronic media, you need to cultivate the ability to conceive and then encode your visions into words and sentences. So a different kind of writing from that used for print is demanded.

For television, you must use words that enhance and clarify what's shown on the screen. For radio, you should practice putting together words that create pictures in the minds of listeners. Clear writing for the electronic media is a necessity, not because your audience is simpleminded but because sentences received by our ears are processed differently from those received by our eyes. Take advantage of every opportunity to write scripts and then experience them when they're turned into productions. Aside from scriptwriting classes, look for opportunities to write for production classes and community-access cable outlets.

Computers are central to video editing systems, character generators, word processors, graphics systems, scheduling and billing systems, and data-retrieval systems. Most DJs work with an audio console and a computer to record intros and back-announcements of music played. They work air shifts and from time to time go live, but much of their work is stored on disks to be inserted into the running schedule of the station for play during holidays, weekends, or days off.

Computers are used in newsrooms in the writing and editing of news copy. Familiarity with information systems is highly desirable, and the ability to type well is mandatory.

Evaluate these suggestions in light of your own aptitudes, interests, and career plans. College counselors can help you determine the appropriateness of the courses available to you. The important point is that only you can apply your growing knowledge to your announcing practice.

Most community colleges require sixty semester hours for an associate in arts or science degree. Four-year colleges or universities require about 125 semester hours for a bachelor's degree. Whether you're enrolled in a two- or four-year program, it's unlikely you'll have available more than six semester hours of performance courses. You should, therefore, look for performance opportunities wherever they present themselves—on a campus radio station, in television directing and producing classes, or on a community nonprofit radio station. Remember, though, that you'll spend most of your broadcasting class hours in nonperformance courses, all of which are important to your development as a well-rounded broadcaster.

Figure 1-4
Classical music announcer Al Covaia reads a list of music events in the area within his station's reach. While there are relatively few openings in radio for classical music announcers, for those who love both this music and radio, this is a position worth pursuing. *Photo courtesy of Al Covaia.*

Clearly, announcing encompasses a wide range of activities. Most modern liberal arts colleges and their broadcasting departments are well equipped to help you begin the process of becoming a competent and versatile communicator—which is what you must become if you're to manage challenges such as these:

- You're a staff announcer and must read news headlines containing the place names *Qatar, Zimbabwe, Eritrea, Peshawar, Bosnia-Herzegovina, Santa Rosa de Copán, São Paulo,* and *Leicester.*

- You're a commercial announcer, and the copy for a pharmaceutical company demands that you correctly pronounce *isoflavones, ipratropium bromide, gingivitis, fungicide,* and *ketoconazole.*

- You're a play analyst on a sports broadcast, and you need to ad-lib knowledgeably about game strategies and give examples from the past of incidents relating to the game in progress.

- You're the play-by-play announcer for a semipro baseball team, and you must pronounce such "American" names as Buchignani, Gutierrez, Yturri, Sockolow, Watanabe, Engebrect, and MacLeod.

- You've been assigned to interview a winner of the Nobel Prize in astrophysics, and you must obtain basic information about the field as well as biographical data on the winner—and do so under extreme time limitations.

- You're narrating a documentary and must analyze the intent and content of the program to determine the mood, rhythm, structure, and interrelationship of sound, picture, and script.

- You're a DJ, and you're on duty when word is received of the unexpected death of a great American (a politician, an entertainer, or a scientist). Until the news department can take over, you must ad-lib appropriately.

It's obvious that no one type of course will completely educate you as an announcer.

In addition to academic studies, you can benefit from becoming a member of one or more organizations open to students. Through such organizations, you may attend meetings and conventions and receive news and information over the Internet. You will also make connections that may someday pay off. Join broadcast-related organizations such as College Students in Broadcasting, American Women in Radio and Television, the Association for Women in Communication (AWC), the International Radio and Television Society–Alpha Epsilon Rho, and the National Black Media Coalition. Students with a broadcast journalism emphasis may become members of the Radio-Television Journalism division of the Association for Education in Journalism and Mass Communication. Membership in the student category of the Radio and Television News Directors Association (RTNDA) is also available to you.

Figure 1-5

Reporter Thuy Vu interviews a protester representing restaurant employees who lost their jobs when ownership of the restaurant changed. Thuy was born in Saigon and left Vietnam with her family when it fell to the Vietcong. She says, "I think my experience as an immigrant actually gives me more insight as a reporter. When I cover stories about immigrants or disenfranchised communities, I have a fuller understanding of the issues because I have been in their shoes." Thuy received her bachelor's degree, with honors, in rhetoric from the University of California, Berkeley. *Courtesy of Thuy Vu and KTVU, Oakland, California.*

The Announcer's Responsibility

Before committing yourself to a career as an announcer, you should recognize that, along with the undeniable privileges and rewards that come to people working in this field, there are several areas of responsibility as well. First is the obligation all performers owe their audiences: to be informative, objective, fair, accurate, and entertaining. Announcers who are sloppy, unprepared, given to poor usage, or just plain boring usually get what they deserve—two weeks' notice.

There are, as you undoubtedly know, announcers who work hard and possess talent but who at the same time pollute the public air, chiefly on radio and television talk and interview shows. A number of radio and television performers are willing to say almost anything, however outrageous or hurtful to others, to attract

Sound Bytes

For information about joining these organizations, use these URLs:

American Women in Radio and Television:
www.awrt.org

Association for Women in Communication, Inc.:
www.womcom.org/

International Radio and Television Society–Alpha Epsilon Rho: www.onu.edu/org/nbs/

Radio and Television News Directors Association: www.rtnda.org/

National Black Media Coalition:
www.nbmc.org/index.html

Society of Professional Journalists:
www.spj.org/

The National Association of Hispanic Journalists:
www.nahj.org/

National Association of Black Journalists Online:
www.nabj.org/

Society of Environmental Journalists:
www.sej.org/

For a complete updated list of URLs for this textbook, please see the accompanying CD.

Sound Bytes

Use the Internet to find and print copies of codes that pertain to announcers, such as the Radio and Television News Directors Association (RTNDA):

www.rtnda.org/ethics/coe.shtml

and the Statement of Principles of the American Society of Newspaper Editors (ASNE):

www.asne.org/kiosk/archive/principl.htm

For a complete, updated list of URLs for this textbook, see the accompanying CD.

and hold an audience. In our free society such announcers are protected by the First Amendment to the Constitution; the only protection the audience has resides in the integrity of each announcer. Most departments of broadcasting offer courses in ethics and social responsibility. Grounding in this subject, together with serious consideration of the effects of mass communication, should be understood as vitally important to your development as a responsible public communicator.

Social responsibility goes beyond the normal obligation of performer to audience. Nearly all announcers, whether they realize it or not, have influence because of their visibility and prestige. Years ago, Paul F. Lazarsfeld and Robert K. Merton perceived and described what they called the **status-conferral function** of the mass media. In essence, they said the general public attaches prestige to people who appear in the mass media and that the average person is more readily influenced by prestigious people than by equals. The public's reasoning is circular: "If you really matter, you will be at the focus of attention, and if you are at the focus of mass attention, then you must really matter." A newscaster, then, is not simply an efficient conveyer of information; as a radio or television star, he or she is trusted and believed as a qualified authority. Even an entertainment show announcer or a DJ has automatic, though sometimes unwarranted, authority. As an announcer for any of the electronic media, you should be aware of your status and measure up to it.

Announcers must demonstrate a sense of social commitment. Be aware of opportunities you may have to either enlighten or confuse the public. As a nation we've been slow to perceive and attack the serious problems of urban deterioration, increasing crime, environmental pollution, racial inequities, world hunger, poverty, homelessness, AIDS, the rise of antidemocratic action groups, and increased drug use. If you're committed to using the mass media to help build a better society, you're already socially responsible and potentially important as the kind of communicator demanded by our times.

Another area of responsibility for announcers is that of emergency notification. When floods, hurricanes, earthquakes, tornadoes, and other disasters occur, broadcast announcers are in a position to save lives through early warnings and post-disaster information. The U.S. government has established the **Emergency Alert System (EAS)** to replace the Emergency Broadcast System (EBS). The alert system requires broadcast licensees to

Figure 1-6

DJ Dave Sholin moved directly from graduation to music director of a popular station close to a major market. Within a year, he had taken that station to number one. Dave credits his major in broadcasting and his DJ work on the campus radio station—which reached only dorms and student residences—with laying the basis for an extremely successful career. After several years in other phases of the music industry, Dave returned as DJ in 2007 to one of his first stations, KFRC. *Photo courtesy Dave Sholin and KFRC.*[2]

disseminate disaster information. It's imperative that all announcers study the disaster manual (found at all stations) and be prepared to act swiftly and appropriately in emergencies.

---

[2] Leaving his first station for KFRC, a major market station, Dave Sholin guided the station to earn *Billboard* magazine's "Major Market Top 40 Station of the Year" for an unprecedented seven years in a row. Sholin was promoted to national music director, where he oversaw the play lists of all RKO's music stations. Sholin later moved to the record industry, where he served as vice president of promotion for both Island Records and Capitol Records, vice president of Musicbiz.com, as well as senior director of adult promotion for the EMI Music Collective and director of adult formats for Caroline/Astralwerks Records. *The lesson: Even a campus station that reaches but a few hundred students offers an environment where motivated students can fuse knowledge of communication theory, audiences, performance skills, music (or news, writing, or whatever) into a synthesis that leads to success.*

SPOTLIGHT

Broadcast Ethics and the Announcer's Responsibility

Beyond textbook theory, ethics includes a broad range of decisions you'll have to make on your job. Here are some hypothetical situations in which you could find yourself as a radio or television announcer:

- You're a music director on a radio station where you select all songs to be played on the air. A friend offers you $1,000 to play a song he's produced. Because you think the music is quite good, you accept the money and schedule the record at least once during each of the daily air shifts. You justify your action on the grounds that you would have programmed the piece without the gift of money.
- You're a television reporter, and you've been told by a reliable witness that some children at the scene of a disturbance threw rocks at a police car before you arrived. You pay the children $5 each to throw rocks again while you record the action. Your position is that you recorded an event that actually occurred, and you brought back to the station some high-impact footage for the nightly news.
- You're a talk-show host on an early evening radio show. Your guest is an outspoken advocate of free speech on radio, arguing that there should be no language restrictions whatever. During your interview, you use a number of words that are generally considered indecent to determine whether your guest is sincere in her (to you) extremist position. You maintain that only by saying the words on the air can you test her conviction.
- Your morning drive-time partner takes a two-week vacation. To stir up a little audience interest, you announce that he's been kidnapped. For most of the two-week period, you broadcast regular "flashes" on the status of the "event." Audience ratings skyrocket as

you report on phony ransom notes, police chases, and so on. You feel that your reputation as an on-air jokester justifies this hoax.
- As the business reporter for a talk-radio station, you decide to mention with favor a company in which you own stock. The interest you generate causes listeners to invest in the company, and the value of its stock rises. You feel justified in the favorable comments you made, because you didn't receive payment from the company in return.
- As a television reporter, you're given some highly sensitive information about the misdeeds of an important local politician. You report the details as accurately as you can, but to protect the person who gave you the information, you invent a fictitious informant.

What all of these scenarios have in common is that each violates a law, a regulation, or a provision of a professional code of ethics. As an announcer, your words reach and influence vast numbers of people; because of the potential for wrongdoing, your freedoms to speak and act are restricted. Freedom of speech, as guaranteed by the First Amendment to the Constitution, doesn't always apply to those using the public airwaves. Areas of restriction are obscenity, fraud, defamation (making libelous statements), plagiarism, inciting insurrection, and invasion of privacy.

Generally speaking, laws regarding obscenity, indecency, and profanity are governed by the U.S. Criminal Code. *Obscenity* may be defined as something "offensive to accepted standards of decency or modesty." *Indecency* is defined as that which is "offensive to public moral values." *Profanity* is defined as "abusive, vulgar, or irreverent language."

Payola and **drugola** refer to the acceptance of money, drugs, or other inducements in return for playing specific recordings on the air. **Plugola** refers to the favorable mention of a product, company, or service in which the announcer has a financial interest. The Federal Communications Commission (FCC) prohibits the acceptance of any sort of bribe in return for favors.

Figure 1-7

Talk-show host Ronn Owens is highly respected for his breadth of knowledge and his evenhanded treatment of studio guests and call-in listeners. With a format that explores everything from politics to popular culture, Owens conducts his program as an electronic town meeting. He tackles sensitive issues but avoids sensationalism. His top-rated weekday morning program draws nearly half a million listeners each week. Ronn is up before most of his listeners, at 4:00 a.m., to prepare for the show and spends several hours after a show getting ready for the next day. You can access his brief biographical section at www.kgoam810.com/. *Courtesy of Ronn Owens and KGO Newstalk Radio.*

The *Code of Broadcast News Ethics of the Radio and Television News Directors Association* specifically labels as irresponsible and unethical such practices as staging news events, misrepresenting the source of a news story, sensationalizing the news, and invading the privacy of those with whom the news deals.

The radio and television codes of the National Association of Broadcasters were invalidated by a 1980s' court decision, but many broadcasters continue to use the ethics portions of those codes as models for professional and ethical behavior. Among the provisions still widely honored are those prohibiting the broadcasting of any matter that is deemed fraudulent and the provision that requires clear identification of sponsored or paid-for material.

Most libelous statements aren't *criminally illegal;* most are civil offenses, in which the person offended can sue another person—such as an announcer—and in which the government acts as arbiter. Laws regarding libel vary from state to state, but in no state is an announcer given total freedom to make accusations against others.

As an announcer, you must be thoroughly aware of the realities of broadcast law and ethics. Only by having in-depth knowledge of the applicable laws and codes can you routinely avoid violating them in your behavior or words.

PRACTICE

➤ Practicing with Equipment

The regular use of audio and video recorders can be of immense help in your development as a broadcast performer. After hearing and seeing yourself perform over a period of several weeks, you should begin to note and correct annoying mannerisms, faulty speech habits, and voice deficiencies that displease you. Ask others to comment on your performances because you may fail to detect some of your shortcomings. As you make adjustments and improve, you'll gain confidence; this, in turn, should guarantee further improvement.

You can also work on speech improvement without equipment of any kind. You speak with others every day; without sounding affected, practice speaking clearly in ordinary conversations. Many college students tend to slur words as they speak. Make note of the number of times each day someone asks you to repeat what you've just said, often by uttering a monosyllabic, "Huh?" Frequent requests of this kind tell you that you're not speaking clearly enough for broadcast work.

For improvement of nonverbal communication skills, you can practice in front of a mirror. Note the degree—too pronounced, just right, or too weak—of your facial expressions and head movements. Watch for physical mannerisms that may be annoying or that interfere with clear communication. Through practice you can improve your performance abilities significantly, even without the use of recording equipment.

Closely related to performance ability is **ear training**. It's difficult for anyone who doesn't hear well to speak well. Develop a critical ear as you listen to television and radio performers. Listen for vowel deviations, mispronunciations, poor interpretation, and other qualities of spoken English that may interfere with good communication. Listen, as well, for those who articulate clearly, who have a pleasant voice quality, and who are effective in communicating thoughts and ideas. Decide who impresses you as an outstanding user of spoken language. Identify speakers who make you pay attention, as well as those who cause you to tune out. Try to determine the positive and negative characteristics and qualities of speakers and apply what you learn to your work. (Speech diagnosis, speech problems, and suggestions for improvement are covered in Chapter 3, "Voice Analysis and Improvement," and Chapter 4, "Pronunciation and Articulation.")

Chapter 2

The Announcer as Communicator

For centuries performing artists have created an illusion: that of making their skills seem natural and easily acquired. Musicians, for example, undergo years of study, daily practice, and performances in small venues before reaching large crowds and significant financial rewards. As they perform, however, it's important that audiences think only of their skill and not of their early struggles, disappointments, and hard work.

This is true of actors, dancers, singers, storytellers—and announcers.

Successful announcers share both the hard work and early struggles of other performers. Nearly all of today's topflight announcers went through lengthy learning processes and apprenticeships that culminated in outstanding abilities to communicate. Announcers must be skilled in several kinds of performance: ad-libbing, ad-libbing from notes, impromptu speaking, script reading from **cold copy** (material not seen until the very moment of delivery), and script reading with preparation.

Ad-lib announcers may have sketchy notes but no script, so they have little time to think through what they're going to say. News anchors often see much of their copy for the first time when it appears on a prompter; at the other extreme are documentary narrators and readers of recorded commercials. Hours—and sometimes days—are required for them to deliver the performances demanded by a producer.

You should practice all these modes of performance until you're comfortable with each. As you progress, be sure to avoid trying to "sound like an announcer." As you work to perfect your abilities, make sure you aren't abandoning your own personality. Good announcing isn't *imitation*—it's *communication*. Top announcers retain their individuality as they concentrate on conveying their messages. True communication as an announcer begins when (1) you learn *who you are,* (2) *reflect yourself in your delivery,* and (3) *realize that you are speaking to individuals, not to a crowd.* As you work to improve your voice quality, develop appropriate articulation and pronunciation, and expand your vocabulary, you should also develop two other aspects of successful oral communication: *reflecting your personality* and *conveying to your audience the ideas and feelings inherent in the words you speak.*

This chapter discusses the communication process and offers detailed advice on interpreting copy, as well as suggestions for ad-lib announcing.

Principles of Effective Communication

Copy begins not as a *script* but as *ideas* in the mind of a writer. Having conceived the idea, the writer next casts it into words (and, in television, pictures). Conceiving compelling messages; selecting fresh, meaningful words; and arranging them effectively are all components in the art of broadcast writing. Communicating the writer's words effectively is the art of announcing.

As a professional announcer, you're expected to make scripted messages more effective than they would be if communicated only in writing. Beyond accurate reading and pronunciation, you can convey emotions appropriate to your copy—enthusiasm, seriousness, or humor—and so provide meaning for your listeners. You can clarify a message's meaning by stressing the relative importance of its various parts. In short, you can present the material in its most persuasive and readily understandable form.

Announcers who work under close supervision of producers or directors, as when recording commercials or documentary narration, are generally among those who perform most effectively. Ad-lib performers, including talk-show hosts and those doing sports play-by-play, nearly always communicate well because they've arrived where they are through years of practice in small markets.

Too many announcers merely read the words before them and consider themselves successful if they don't stumble over them. A word is a symbol of an idea. If the idea isn't clear to the announcer, or if it isn't expressed compellingly, the chances are that the idea won't be effectively delivered to an audience. Announcers are paid to be effective, so they must develop oral reading skills that are more than just adequate.

Make a point to listen attentively to announcers of all specializations; study their deliveries and decide which are true communicators. You'll likely discover that you listen closely to those who communicate well and mentally tune out those who don't. Most of us pay attention to announcers who help us receive and assimilate ideas.

Radio announcers who believe that they can express feelings and emotions by using only their voices may attempt to project vitality without using gestures. As an announcer, you should speak as though your listener were sitting nearby, and this means using your face, hands, and body just as you do in ordinary conversation. Integrating all of the tools of communication—verbal and nonverbal—will help you clarify and intensify your message, even for radio listeners who can't see you. Appropriate gesturing for radio and television demands honest motivation and harmony with the importance and mood of the ideas expressed. Energy is easy to simulate, but unless you're genuinely motivated by the content and purpose of a message, energy usually comes across as phony. Good communication occurs when the listener or viewer receives an undistorted and meaningful impression of the ideas of the writer with appropriate verbal and nonverbal emphasis given to each part of the message.

Student Voices

Podcasting by Abby Roetheli

ALL ABOUT ME: I am a graduate student at Southern Illinois University Edwardsville, pursuing an M.S. in mass communications. I enjoy reading and writing—particularly nonfiction—and I also like traveling, films, discovering local restaurants, and spending time with friends, family, and my dog, Fran.

ALL ABOUT PODCASTS: Podcasts are digital media files distributed through the Internet for playback on portable media and personal computers. The word <u>podcast</u> is a marriage of Apple's portable music player, iPod, and the term <u>broadcast</u>—<u>podcast</u>. A number of media are available for podcast—music videos, television and radio programs, as well as other educational materials. Podcasts are unique in that they can be syndicated—allowing users to receive updated episodes instantly. Users may "subscribe" to particular podcasts by enlisting the help of an aggregator (often referred to as a "podcatcher"), which is an application that can search and automatically update a user's collection.

Podcasters—those who author or host the podcast—create and release information quite quickly through this format. Alternatively, because the information has been recorded, users may watch or listen to the material when they want.

. . . AND HOW DOES THIS AFFECT ANNOUNCING? Because of the accessibility, anyone who can afford the equipment can attempt the format. This makes the Internet an arena overwhelmed with many source outlets—I think it is often difficult for serious podcasters to be heard. Nonetheless, podcasts are a great way for amateurs to express themselves and to gain experience in an innovative way!

Interpreting Copy

When you give voice to words written by others, you're an *interpretive artist;* you're the link between writer and audience. No matter how beautiful your voice may be and how rapidly or accurately you read copy, you're truly not a good announcer unless you communicate ideas and values as they were conceived by a writer.

News anchors are the most challenged script readers because they must read their stories with limited preparation; only copy written by them will be completely familiar as they go on the air. As a news anchor, most of your stories will be written by news writers—or taken from a wire service—and you'll barely have time to scan them to make note of topics and the general mood of each piece. Your own preshow preparation will keep you busy until airtime, so you'll be only superficially acquainted with the stories you're to read, and you'll have no knowledge at all of new or revised stories that come to you during the broadcast. To become skilled at interpreting cold copy you must develop the ability to rapidly analyze scripts, and this ability will come only if you engage in methodical practice as a student.

Stanley T. Donner, late professor emeritus of the University of Texas at Austin, prepared an excellent approach to analyzing copy. He suggests that you work on the points in the Checklist "Analyzing Broadcast Copy" when approaching a new script. If you use this checklist for serious analysis of many different types of copy, you should develop the ability to size up a new script almost unconsciously. Donner's advice is generally applicable only to those who have the luxury of adequate time to prepare in advance of performance. His suggestions imply much

Checklist   *Analyzing Broadcast Copy*

1. Read the copy as often as necessary to get the general meaning. If the message is brief and written clearly, perhaps one reading is enough. For a longer or more complex script, you may need to read it two or more times to ferret out its meaning.
2. Determine the objective of the message. State the specific purpose of the copy in one brief sentence.
3. Identify the general mood of the copy. Most short messages have one overriding mood. Longer scripts frequently have shifts in mood.
4. After determining the general mood, locate any shifts in mood.
5. Determine the copy's structure and its parts. Find and mark the beginning and end of each part.
6. Analyze punctuation to see what help punctuation provides in understanding the copy.
7. Note any words you don't fully understand or can't pronounce. It's good practice to underline, for later research, all words that are unclear or new to you.
8. Read the copy aloud.
9. Think about how you can convey interest in the copy's subject matter.
10. Visualize your listener. Establish a mental rapport and imagine you're actually talking to that person.
11. Decide if there's anything you should know about the origin and background of the copy.
12. Decide if characterization is needed.

more than might seem obvious at the first reading, so they're offered here with appropriate elaboration.

Identifying the General Meaning

Before concentrating on pronunciation or timing, determine the script's overall meaning and purpose. Form an impression of the entire piece by silently reading through it at least twice—more, if necessary—before undertaking any of the more detailed work of preparation. Make sure you know the pronunciation of all names and words in the script; develop a means of checking on these and convert difficult words into some form of easily read phonetics.

Stating the Specific Purpose

Stating the specific purpose is the most important point in Donner's checklist. Just as it's pointless to begin a trip without deciding where you're going, it's foolish to begin to interpret copy without first determining its goal. Sentences can be read in different ways depending on their context or purpose. Raising questions about the purpose of the copy will help you determine the most appropriate delivery.

Here's a recent example of an announcer failing to communicate the writer's intent. In reading "Most of us want to succeed, not just get by," the announcer stressed *want*. The writer, however, wanted to contrast two outlooks on life— *succeeding* and *getting by*. The sentence, when performed, was read "Most of us *want* to succeed, not just get by," rather than "Most of us want to *succeed*, not just *get by*." This may seem a small point, but announcers risk their careers by such carelessness.

Identifying the General Mood

After determining the purpose of the copy, identify the copy's mood, because this will influence your *attitude* as you read it. The number of words in the copy limits your control of mood, especially with commercials. Many commercials, particularly those written for clients who want to send a fast-paced, high-energy message, may require you to read at your top rate of speed, and this will lock you automatically into the mood desired by the sponsor.

The commercial in Chapter 3, page 71, for Dairyland Longhorn Cheese uses only seventy-eight words for a thirty-second spot. You should be able to "milk" this commercial (pun intended) as you gently evoke warm feelings about the product, nostalgia for the "good old days," and, if successful, hunger for Longhorn Cheese.

Because the mood of a piece of copy determines your attitude, it's helpful to attach an adjective to your script. Attitudes may be described as *ironic, jocular, serious, somber, urgent, sad, light, gloomy,* and *sarcastic.* Read the following items aloud, communicating the indicated attitude of each. The mood of each item, except the tornado reports, is to be conveyed with only a hint of the emotion mentioned.

URGENT

(Chicago) The National Weather Service has issued tornado warnings for the entire upper Midwest. Small-craft warnings have been raised for Lake Michigan, and boat owners are urged to secure their craft against the expected heavy weather.

SOMEWHAT ANGRY

(Miami) A civilian pilot has reported sighting two more oil slicks off the coast of Florida near Fort Lauderdale and Palm Beach. Cleanup crews are still at work on a massive oil slick that spread one week ago.

SLIGHT NOTE OF VICTORY—WINNING ONE FOR THE PEOPLE

(Washington) The Federal Election Commission has voted to halt secret congressional "slush funds," a practice in which lawmakers use private donations to pay personal and office expenses.

VERY URGENT

(Minnesota) I've just been handed a bulletin. A tornado has been spotted about twenty miles from Duluth. There are no additional details at this time, but we'll keep you informed as more reports are received.

STRAIGHTFORWARD

(Washington) The government said yesterday that people are taking better care of themselves now than ever before, and that the problem now is to find ways to care for the large number of people who live longer as a result. Our nation's success in keeping people healthy and helping them to live longer is placing great stress on the nation's health care resources.

LIGHT, SLIGHTLY HUMOROUS

(Montpelier, Vermont) It took eighteen days, but searchers have finally tranquilized one of the baby elephants lost in the woods. The manager of the Carson and Barnes Circus says the elephant will be tied to a tree in an effort to lure the other lost baby elephant out of the woods.

Figure 2-1
News announcers should check their scripts prior to airtime to become aware of the nature of each story, as well as to make sure there are no problems of pronunciation. Bessie Moses, the radio announcer shown here, must do more than analyze the news: She must also translate it into the Inupiaq Eskimo language. *Courtesy of Bessie Moses and KICY Radio, Nome, Alaska.*

Determining Changes in Mood

Scripts may contain several moods, even if the dominant mood remains constant. Commercial copy often calls for a change from concern to joy as the announcer first describes a common problem and then tells how Product *X* can solve it. Spot changes in mood as you analyze copy and mark them on your script.

In a lengthy television documentary or a thirty- or sixty-minute radio or television newscast, changes of mood come more often and should be reflected in your delivery. As you monitor newscasts, look for such changes and note how speakers reflect the shifting moods. Effectively varying mood adds much to the flow, unity, and overall meaning of a presentation. There are techniques to help smooth your change in mood from one item to another. As you end one news story and are about to begin the next, find transitional words or phrases to shift mood: *meanwhile, locally, in other news*, or *on a lighter note* are examples of this.

Many newscasts begin with brief headlines that call for abrupt changes in mood. Read these headlines and determine the mood of each:

Here is the latest news: More than eight inches of rain have fallen on eastern Iowa in the last twenty-four hours, and there are reports of widespread damage and some deaths.

> An all-male jury has acquitted a Chicago woman who claimed she killed her husband in self-defense after ten years of abuse.
>
> A 14-year-old Milwaukee boy has been awarded the city's heroism medal for rescuing an infant from a swimming pool.
>
> And, there's joy at the zoo tonight because of the birth of a litter of ligers— or is it tigons? Anyway, the father is a lion, and the mother's a tiger.

The range of emotions in these stories requires rapid changes of mood—a challenge facing anchors daily.

Determining Parts and Structure

Almost any example of well-written copy shows clearly defined parts. On the most basic level, copy may be broken down into a beginning, middle, and end. The beginning is customarily used to gain attention. The middle, or body, contains most of the information. The end summarizes the most important points.

In most copy these three parts may be subdivided further. Commercial copy that attempts to offer rational reasons for purchasing a particular product frequently employs an organization or outline such as this example:

1. Capture the listener's or viewer's attention.
2. Offer a concrete reason for further interest and attention.
3. Explain why the particular product or service is superior.
4. Mention or imply a price lower than the listener has been led to expect.
5. Repeat some of the selling points.
6. Repeat the name and email address or phone number of the commercial's sponsor.

Many commercials are successful in gaining audience attention but fail to follow through with logical or otherwise persuasive information. As an announcer, you can persuade only when you're given the words to do so. Be prepared to make wildly exaggerated claims or other nonpersuasive comments if that's what your script calls for.

The following is an example of a commercial written according to a logical organization. The commercial isn't particularly creative, but it represents a type of commercial that's heard often on radio. Notice how it conforms to the six-part outline. (Note: **SFX** is short for "sound effects.")

AGENCY:	Andria Advertising, Inc.
CLIENT:	Mertel's Coffee Mills
LENGTH:	60 seconds

ANNCR: Are you a coffee lover? Most Americans are. Would you like to enter the world of gourmet coffees? Mertel's can help.

SFX: SOUND OF COFFEE BEING POURED INTO CUP

ANNCR: Gourmet coffee begins with whole beans, carefully selected, freshly roasted.

SFX: SOUND OF COFFEE BEANS BEING GROUND

ANNCR: Gourmet coffee is ground at home, just before brewing. Choose your coffee according to your taste and time of day. A rich but mild Mocha Java for breakfast. A hearty French roast for that midday pickup. A nutty Arabian with dinner. And a Colombian decaf before bed. Sounds inviting? You bet. Sounds expensive? Not so. Mertel's Coffee Mills feature forty types of coffee beans from around the world, and some are only pennies more per pound than canned coffees. And there's always a weekly special. This week, it's Celebes Kalossi, at just $8.99 a pound! Remember—if you want gourmet coffee, begin with whole beans, then grind them just before brewing. So, come to Mertel's Coffee Mills and move into the world of gourmet coffee! We're located at the Eastside Mall, and on Fifth Street in downtown Dickinson. Mertel's Coffee Mills.

In contrast to the coffee commercial, this spot for a boutique store is funny and informative and should be delivered in a casual, almost pixielike but convincing style.

CLIENT:	Peaches & Cream
SUBJECT:	Undergarments
LENGTH:	60 seconds
ANNCR:	As a public service, Peaches & Cream is now selling undergarments. There's hardly anyplace you can buy cheap, neat, unders. Well, we stock lots of them. Because the more unders you have, the less often you have to go to the laundromat. In addition, we carry soft bras—in case you have to go to dinner with your in-laws. And underwire bras in a number of outrageous colors. Plus camisoles, which can be quite useful—and teddies, which are not. A teddy is something like a lace camisole, with little legs on it. Fancy ladies used to wear them in the '20s. One lady bought one from us and said it was just the thing she'd like to be caught in if a burglar ever broke into her house. Teddies are eight dollars, and everything else is considerably less. And just remember that fancy underwear can be very good for your morale. So, if you'd like to feel a little improper—or just stay out of the laundromat— visit Peaches & Cream. There's a Peaches & Cream in Sausalito and in Mill Valley. Peaches & Cream.

Outstanding commercials are both subtle and complex. Special consideration is given to the analysis of superior commercials in Chapter 7, "Commercials and Public-Service Announcements."

Analyzing Punctuation Marks Used in Scripts

Punctuation is helpful to announcers because it shows the author's intentions regarding mood and meaning. However, while you should pay attention to the punctuation in your copy, you needn't be a slave to it. Copy is punctuated by a writer who has no way of knowing you and therefore can't possibly write to your speech personality. When you perform, you need to make the copy your own—true

Sound Bytes

The Internet is a source of information on usage and grammar, including specific rules for punctuation. With a search engine, type in "dictionary," and you'll find many choices, including foreign language dictionaries.

For a complete, updated list of URLs for this text-book, please see the accompanying CD.

to your particular personality, as long as you don't misinterpret its intention. Repunctuate when appropriate.[1]

Punctuation marks, like diacritical marks used to indicate pronunciation, are so small and differ so subtly they may cause difficulties for an announcer—especially when there's little time to study a script. Announcers working with written material need near-perfect eyesight, and some wear reading glasses during their air shifts or recording sessions even though they don't wear reading glasses at other times. Whenever possible, review your copy prior to airtime and, if you find it helpful or necessary, add to and enlarge punctuation marks. (Some suggestions for the use of emphatic punctuation marks are found on page 36.)

You most likely have a good grasp of punctuation, so the review that follows discusses only a few punctuation marks and then only as they relate to writing and interpreting broadcast copy.

The Period

In written copy, abbreviations such as FBI and AFL-CIO appear without periods. Ms. and Mr. may appear with or without periods. An acronym such as SCSCI (pronounced "scuzzy") should have no periods. If there's doubt about the pronunciation of an acronym, a script should include a phonetic transcription in parentheses.

The Comma

The comma usually marks a slight pause in broadcast speech, which gives you an opportunity to breathe. Good writing for oral delivery uses commas with precision and frequency. You may find it appropriate to use many commas when writing broadcast copy, and fewer when writing papers and essays for nonbroadcast instructors, such as English composition teachers, who tend to favor long, complex sentences with a minimum of commas.

The Question Mark

In written English, the question mark appears at the end of a sentence that asks a question. Because the question mark comes at the end, you may find it helpful to adopt the Spanish practice of adding an upside-down question mark (¿) at the beginning. This way, as you begin to read the sentence, you'll know it's an interrogative. ¿Do you think this will help you?

---

[1] In a recording session, you'll most likely adjust punctuation marks according to the interpretation requested by the director.

Quotation Marks

Quotation marks are used in broadcast copy for two different purposes, to indicate that words between the marks are a word-for-word quotation and to substitute for *italics*. The first use of quotation marks is found extensively in news copy:

. . . he said an anonymous male caller told him to "get out of the case or else."

In reading this sentence, you can indicate the presence of a quotation by the inflection of your voice, or you can add words of your own to make it clear that it's a direct quotation:

. . . he said an anonymous male caller told him to, and this is a quotation [or "and I quote"], "get out of the case or else."

Don't say "unquote" at the end of a quotation, because you can't cancel a quotation you've just given.

Parentheses

Parenthetical remarks—remarks that are important but not necessary for the sentence to make sense—are used occasionally in radio and television copy, but the same result is more often achieved with dashes, as shown in this sentence. Parentheses are used in radio and television copy to set apart instructions to the audio operator, to indicate music cues, and to contain instructions or interpretations for announcers or performers:

```
(SFX: OFFICE SOUNDS)
(MUSIC UP AND UNDER)
(SLIGHT PAUSE)
(MOVE TO SOFA)
```

Parenthetical remarks sometimes are added to newspaper copy, usually for purposes of clarification, as in this example:

Mayor Bacic said that he called the widow to demand that she "return my (love) letters immediately."

Reading this sentence in a newspaper it can be seen that "(love)" was added by a reporter or editor. If the same copy were used on the air and the announcer did not indicate that "(love)" had been added by an editor or writer, the mayor's statement would be misrepresented.

Ellipses

An ellipsis, a sequence of three dots (. . .), indicates an omission of words within a sentence or between sentences. Ellipses are used rarely in broadcast copy but may be used more often in newspaper copy, as in the following example:

> Senator Meyer stated yesterday, "I do not care what the opposition may think, I . . . want only what is best for my country."

In this example, the dots of ellipsis have been used to indicate that one or several words have been omitted from the original quotation. There's no way to indicate the omission on the air, so quotations with omissions should be used with care to avoid misinformation.

Newswriters often use ellipses to mark the ends of sentences and to substitute for commas, dashes, semicolons, and colons. Here's an example:

> The mayor was late to his swearing-in ceremony today. . . . He told those who had gathered for the ceremony . . . some 200 supporters . . . that he had been held up in traffic.

Figure 2-2

Anchor/reporter Ben McLintock reviews news stories and writes lead-ins to packages prepared by station reporters. He also writes and records voice-over narration for stories covered and recorded by station videographers.
Courtesy of Ben McLintock and KFSM-TV, Fort Smith/Fayetteville, Arkansas.

This practice is regrettable but so widespread that you can expect to be asked at some time to work from copy so punctuated. Should you become a newswriter, you may be expected to write copy in this style. Obviously, such punctuation is workable. The problem is that ellipses can't indicate the shades of meaning conveyed by the six other more specific punctuation marks.

Marking Copy

Because punctuation marks are quite small, when time permits, enlarge punctuation marks that can more readily be seen. While far from standard, the following are a few that are often used:

- A slanted line (/), called a *virgule,* is placed between words to approximate the comma.
- Two virgules (//) are placed between sentences or between words to indicate a longer pause.
- Words to be stressed are <u>underlined</u>. Some announcers mark copy with a colored highlighter to indicate words, phrases, and sentences to be stressed. A highlighter, however, is useful only when working with printed scripts—as when recording voice tracks for commercials or documentaries. Highlighting can't be used when reading from a prompter or a computer screen.
- Question marks and exclamation marks are enlarged: **? !**
- An upside-down question mark (¿) is placed at the beginning of any sentence that is a question.
- An upside-down exclamation point (¡) is placed at the beginning of any exclamatory sentence.
- Crescendo (ᴧ) and decrescendo (ᵛ) marks are placed in any passage that is to receive an increase or a decrease in stress.

For practice, select several scripts from Appendix A and, as you study them for interpretation, use the marks to indicate pauses, words to stress, and so forth.

Verifying Meaning and Pronunciation

It's obvious that, when interpreting copy, you must understand the meanings of the words used. Most copy makes use of familiar words, so it's not often that you need to question the meaning or pronunciation of words in your script. However, some scripts are written for narrow target audiences, and unfamiliar words may cause problems in interpretation or pronunciation. You should cultivate the habit of looking up all unfamiliar words in an authoritative dictionary. Develop a healthy skepticism about your own vocabulary; through years of silent reading you've probably learned to settle for approximate pronunciation and meanings of many words. As a quick test, how many of these words can you define and use correctly?

voilà (French)	yahoo
impassible	rhetoric
noisome	capricious
ordnance	catholic (uncapitalized)

Check the definitions of these words in any standard dictionary. Some of them are seen and heard frequently, whereas others only sound or look familiar.

Correct pronunciation is as important as accurate understanding. You should be skeptical about your ability to pronounce all words in a script correctly. Check your pronunciation of each word in Table 2.1 against the correct pronunciation, which is shown there with three different systems of phonetic transcription.

In addition to using and pronouncing words correctly, you must understand allusions in your copy. An **allusion** is an indirect but pointed or meaningful reference. Writers sometimes use phrases from the Bible, mythology, Shakespeare, and other sources from the past. Explanations of the phrases that follow can be found in dictionaries, encyclopedias, and collections of well-known myths. These allusions aren't common, but any one of them could appear in your copy. If you don't know their origins, search them out. (All may be found in *The American Heritage Dictionary*, or on the Internet.)

He was considered a *quisling*.	She was a true *Jezebel*.
She was given to *malapropisms*.	. . . as false as *Iago*.
He added his *John Hancock*.	. . . as vain as *Narcissus*.
He suffered as painfully as *Job*.	. . . as rich as *Croesus*.

TABLE 2.1 Correct Pronunciation of Some Tricky Words

Word	IPA	Diacritics	Wire-Service System
drought	[draut]	/drout/	(DROWHT)
forehead	['fɔrɪd]	/fôr′ ĭd/	(FOR-ihd)
toward	[tɔrd]	/tôrd/	(TAWRD)
diphtheria	[dif′θiriə]	/dĭf-thîr-ē-ə/	(diff-THIR-ee-uh)
accessories	[æk′ses ə riz]	/ăk-sĕs′-ə-rēz/	(ak-SESS-uh-reez)
quay	[ki]	/kē/	(KEE)
pestle	[pɛs əl]	/pĕs′-əl/	(PESS-uhl)
worsted	['wʊstid]	/wŏŏs′tĭd/	(WUHS-tid)

You can't expect to be familiar with all allusions in every piece of copy you receive. During your career you may read copy created by hundreds of writers, each drawing on a separate fund of knowledge. You can, however, cultivate the habit of tracking down allusions not familiar to you. Self-discipline is required, because it's easy to convince yourself that the context will make an allusion clear to your audience even if you don't understand it.

Reading Aloud

Because you'll perform *aloud,* you should practice *reading aloud.* There are two very sound reasons for doing so. First, when you speak, you move your articulators and exercise your vocal mechanism. This not only enhances your articulation abilities, but also strengthens the muscles that make speech possible. Many announcers speak for hours at a time—performing sports play-by-play, covering ongoing events such as parades and auto races, and working as talk-show hosts—and vocal preparation for such demanding assignments is essential. Your speech mechanism gets no workout at all when you read silently!

Second, good broadcast copy often makes poor silent reading. Short, incomplete, or ungrammatical sentences are often found in perfectly acceptable radio and television scripts. Consider the following example:

ANNCR: Been extra tired lately? You know. Sorta logy and dull? Tired and weary—maybe a little cranky, too? Common enough, this time of year. The season when colds are going around. And when you have to be careful to get the nutrition your body needs. Vitamin deficiency can be the cause of that "down-and-out" feeling. And Supertabs, the multiple vitamin, can be the answer. . . .

This is quite different from copy written to advertise the same product in a newspaper. Giving this copy the conversational quality it needs requires skill that can be developed only by practicing aloud.

Reading Ahead

Reading a long script aloud can be difficult. When you're on live, you can't afford to make even the minor errors a silent reader may make, such as skipping over words or sentences, passing over difficult material or unfamiliar words, and resting your eyes when they become tired. If you're asked to read a lengthy script, you'll need to read for extended periods of time, read everything before you, read it accurately and with appropriate expression—and do all this with little opportunity to rest your eyes. As your eyes tire, you're more and more likely to make mistakes.

One way of giving your eyes the rest they need is by reading ahead. Reading ahead means that your eyes are several words ahead of your voice as you read the copy. In this sentence, when your voice is at about *this point,* your eyes should be about *here.* When your eyes have reached the end of the sentence, you should be able to briefly glance away from your script while you finish speaking the words. Practice this technique, and you should be able to read even lengthy scripts without excessive eyestrain. But, as you practice, make certain you don't fall into the irritating habit of many announcers: using a monotonous, decelerating speech pattern at the end of every sentence. Unless you guard against it, you may be unconsciously relaxing your interpretation as you rest your eyes.

Conveying Interest in Your Material

Whatever the purpose or nature of the copy to be read, you must show interest in it to communicate it effectively. Most of the time, you'll have a genuine interest in the subject, as when delivering news or narrating a documentary. At other times— for example, when reading a commercial for a product you don't use or perhaps

Figure 2-3
News anchors Cheryl Jennings and Dan Noyes prepare for a return from a commercial break. They read their news copy into robotic cameras and are cued to the cameras by the only other person in the studio, the floor director. *Courtesy of Cheryl Jennings, Dan Noyes, and KGO-TV.*

even dislike—it may be difficult to feel genuine interest. As a professional, you can't afford to show disinterest in or disrespect for the copy you're paid to read. Try to put your biases aside. You're an intermediary between people who provide information and those who receive it. You act as a magnifying glass: It's your job to enhance perceptions with the least possible distortion. Of course, if you're asked to perform a commercial for a product you know to be shoddy or misrepresented, then your conscience should take over.

Even when working with good copy for reputable advertisers, it's impossible to develop a belief in every product. At many stations, announcers work shifts in a small control room, recording and editing copy for many products and services. Here are two suggestions that may help you:

1. When you must read a number of commercials and find it impossible to develop honest enthusiasm for all of them, your best option is to read each with as much effectiveness and interpretive skill as possible.

2. When you're in the enviable position of being the exclusive spokesperson for a product or have had a long personal relationship with a sponsor, you should gain firsthand knowledge of the product, and this should make it easy to communicate your honest belief in it.

Assuming that your announcing copy deserves genuine interest, how can you reflect it in your interpretation? Honest enthusiasm is seldom noisy or obtrusive. It shows itself in inner vitality and quiet conviction. As a commercial announcer, you won't be dealing with life-or-death matters, and you'll be speaking, in effect, to individuals or small groups of people who are only a few feet away. In a sense you're their guest. *Your conviction is revealed through a steady focus on your listeners and by your earnestness and personality.*

Figure 2-4
Before moving to the news set, anchor Dennis Richmond reviews stories that he will introduce (and perhaps comment on) during the 10 o'clock news. He writes lead-ins and, as he reviews copy written by station newswriters or by a news service, he rewrites as necessary to maintain his style of verbal expression. *Courtesy of Dennis Richmond and KTVU.*

SPOTLIGHT

Learning to Sound Local
by Dan O'Day

As a transplanted DJ, new to an unfamiliar market, one of your most urgent requirements is to learn about your new community as quickly as possible. Listeners will "turn off" in short order if you mispronounce local place names or call such diverse things as activities or foods by names not used by locals. To learn how to "sound local," leave the station and enlist the aid of others—friends, landlords, strangers, shopkeepers, taxi drivers—to get answers to basic questions about your new hometown. Don't accept one person's answer as correct, though; look for a consensus. Here are some particularly important areas to research.

Lingo

In the North, people "go to the movies." In the Deep South, folks "go to the show." Similarly, New Englanders have a "cookout," while Westerners have a "barbecue." What words will brand you as an outsider if you pronounce them the "wrong" way? For instance, do locals pronounce the word *route* as *root* or *rowt*? Pay special attention to people or places that outsiders are known to mangle. South Florida has a town named Riviera Beach. Obviously the first word is pronounced riv-ee-air-uh, right? Not if you're a local. Only a tourist enunciates all four syllables. Locals say *Rivera*—as in the name of muralist Diego Rivera.

What local cultural quirks affect the language? I was raised in a big city, but my first radio job was in rural Virginia. When I read a live spot for farm equipment, I pronounced *Deere*—as in *John Deere—Deerie*. It wasn't difficult for the average listener to detect I was a foreigner. Make a list of twenty difficult-to-pronounce names of streets, parks, or prominent citizens.

Government

Does your community have a mayor, city manager, or both? Who really runs things? Is there a city council or a board of supervisors? Are these officials elected in general or district elections? How long are the terms of office?

Find out which politicians have been on the scene forever. Ask how long the mayor has been in office. Talk to people about current political controversies. What's the best-known political scandal of the past ten years? What about the police department? Does the police chief get along with the mayor? What was the last big police department controversy?

Education

Find out what the hottest issue is in the public school system. Learn which schools are considered the best academically and which the worst. How do the schools compare with schools in other regions of the country? Which schools are the best in sports?

Sports

Speaking of sports, what are the local high school dynasties, rivalries, mascots, and so on? Who are the leading coaches?

Connecticut has duckpin bowling. Florida has jai-alai. What sports are played in your region but unknown to many others?

Food Facts

In Philadelphia, you order a "hoagie." To get the same thing in New York, you ask for a "hero." In some places it's a "submarine," and in others, a "grinder."

Local dishes may sound odd to out-of-towners but may be sources of pride to the community. What are they? And what about the bread served in local restaurants? San Francisco's big on sourdough; Los Angeles restaurants often serve multigrain. And don't think these little details are unimportant.

Are people very health conscious—or do they think a bran muffin is some sort of Danish? What are the most common ethnic restaurants? What are the most expensive, romantic, or famous restaurants? Which restaurants are known for their bad food?

Heroes

There are bound to be local heroes. Find out who they are; you'd better not make fun of them. Who are the high school, college, and professional sports legends? What celebrities were born or raised in the community?

Working World

What are the top ten industries or biggest employers? Which companies are popular or unpopular? What's the local unemployment rate—and how does it compare to the rest of the region? What is the starting salary of a policeman? Of a teacher?

Getting Around

Some places have subways; some have buses; some have both. What's the mass transit system, how much does it cost, and who uses it? What is its reputation for safety, cleanliness, comfort, reliability, and convenience?

What cars dominate the streets and highways? Toyotas and Nissans are ubiquitous in Southern California but are rare—and sometimes reviled—in Michigan. What models are the most popular—subcompacts, luxury sedans, station wagons, SUVs with four-wheel drive? Do people have cell phones or CB radios?

What are the most dangerous intersections? Where will you be stuck the longest at a red light? Which freeways (or sections of freeways) are most congested at what times?

Neighborhoods

What are the names of various ethnic neighborhoods? Where are they located? Is there a gay section? What's the most expensive area? Which neighborhoods are the most crime ridden?

Lifestyles

What are the favorite weekend activities? Where are the hot spots for singles? Where do teens, yuppies, seniors, and other groups hang out? Where is the local lovers' lane? When do people eat dinner—5:30 p.m., 9:00 p.m.? Or do they eat "dinner" at noon and "supper" in the evening?

One local newspaper is probably read more than the others. Certain movies do better than others. And the community is bound to have particular political and social leanings. Find out what they are. Are there any seemingly mundane subjects that can lead to controversy? What are the worst bugs or pests? What do the locals think of their drinking water? Is there one tragedy in the community's history you should never joke about?

Finally, discover the local tourist attractions and what people think of them.

Talking to Your Listener

Several suggestions for communicating effectively with a listener have been mentioned, but one more point should be made. Most of this chapter has emphasized the *reading* of scripts. It might be better to consider your job that of *talking* scripts. Even though you work from a script, and your listeners know it, they appreciate it when you sound as though you're not reading to them. The best way to achieve a conversational style is to visualize the person to whom you're speaking and "talk" your message to him or her. Of course, some scripts lend themselves more readily to intimate delivery than others.

Professional announcer and voice-over instructor Samantha Paris suggests that when you're asked to interpret a piece of copy, you should ask yourself several questions:[2]

Who am I as I read this piece?

To whom am I talking?

To how many people am I talking?

How old is the person to whom I'm speaking?

Where am I as I speak?

See also the section entitled "Achieving a Conversational Style" in Chapter 5, "Audio Performance."

Employing Characterization: The Announcer as Actor

Scripts that feature dialogue, conversation between two or more people, nearly always require you to give an individual personality to the person you're portraying. For announcers, the most common opportunity for characterization is in commercials that tell their stories through dialogue. Many such commercials begin with an introduction by an announcer, followed by a brief dramatization. Here's an example:

CREATION AND PRODUCTION:	Chuck Blore & Don Richman
CLIENT:	Campbell Soup
LENGTH:	30 seconds
ANNCR:	You're eating chunky chicken soup with a fork?
JOHN:	Well, you've gotta spear the chicken to get it into your mouth. Look at that. Look at the size of that. You gotta use a spoon for the noodles.
ANNCR:	You got some noodles on your fork.

---

[2] *Tips from a Voice-Over Pro*, the spotlight for Chapter 7, "Commercials and Public-Service Announcements," includes many more valuable insights from Samantha Paris.

JOHN:	Yeah, but they slide through.
ANNCR:	Well, then you use the spoon, you use the fork.
JOHN:	That's right.
ANNCR:	Is chunky chicken a soup or a meal?
JOHN:	I leave that up to the experts, but I personally . . .
ANNCR:	(OVER LAUGH) Why'd you say that?
JOHN:	I know, but I mean, you know, I'm not a connoisseur in the food department, but I'd say it's a meal.
ANNCR:	But it's a soup.
JOHN:	It's a meal within a soup can. Let's put it that way.
ANNCR:	Campbell's Chunky Chicken . . . it's the soup that eats like a meal.

In this commercial, it's essential that the person playing John bring out the humor of his remarks, and this calls for characterization, the projection of a personality that reveals an individual who enjoys the banter initiated by the announcer. As performed, John was portrayed as a middle-aged man with a Brooklyn accent, but the spot could also be done as a completely different type: cowboy, southerner, Vermonter, an innocent but intense child, or even a person with a non-English accent. The point here is that there is no set way to play John, the only requirement being to give the announcer a believable person to play off.

Because so many commercials, for both radio and television, are in part or wholly dramatized, you should enroll in acting classes and participate in both stage and television plays. These activities will help you learn character interpretation. Some commercials call for a foreign accent or a regional dialect. However, before starting to practice copy with a dialect, accent, or character voice, determine the purpose of the copy, the mood of the copy, the person or persons to whom you're speaking, and so on.

Make sure, when you read copy that calls for a regional dialect or foreign accent, that you don't project an offensive stereotype. Some commercials have been taken off the air because they offended an ethnic group. In today's world of broadcasting, there's no room for messages that are demeaning to any segment of society.

You can't apply every one of the points discussed here each time you pick up a piece of copy. In time, however, you should develop a conditioned reflex that allows you to size up a script and interpret it effectively without relying on a checklist. In the meantime, the suggestions given here may help you spot your weaknesses and measure your progress.

PRACTICE

➤ Analyzing the Delivery of Professional Announcers

Make recordings of radio or television newscasts and talk shows and listen as often as necessary to analyze each of these factors:

> Voice quality of announcers
>
> Clear or sloppy articulation
>
> Clear voicing of key words or names
>
> Too much or too little vitality
>
> Absence or presence of predictable pitch patterns
>
> Ability to convey a point
>
> Ability to hold attention
>
> Ability to communicate appropriate emotions

The purpose of such analyses is not to provide you with models but rather to help you develop an ear for those qualities that make some announcers stand out from the crowd. When you admire the work of a particular announcer, chances are you're attracted, in part at least, by that performer's uniqueness; to become an outstanding performer yourself, you should work always to reflect our own speech personality. The more acute you become as a critical listener, the more likely you'll be to recognize your own assets and shortcomings. Work always for improved communication skills while developing a unique and attractive air personality.

PRACTICE

➤ Talking a Script

The following two scripts may be used for practice in talking scripts. The automobile script should be delivered in a conversational, "down-home" matter-of-fact manner. The Six Flags commercial is marvelous for practicing changes in rate of delivery, pitch, and volume, as well as for practicing conversational style. Both scripts are appropriate for male and female announcers; where appropriate, just change "guy" to "gal."

AGENCY:	Oberste Advertising
CLIENT:	Melikian's Auto Mart
LENGTH:	60 seconds
TITLE:	an easygoing kinda guy

ANNCR: Y'know, I'm an easygoing kinda guy. Just give me pizza, a burrito, chow mein—I'll get by just fine. No sushi, steak tartare, chardonnay—just plain American grub. Like I say, I'm easy to please.

The same goes for the car I drive. I don't need a satellite telling me how to get from here to there; I'm annoyed by a computerized voice telling me to fasten my seat belt; and I don't believe the name of a car model has anything to do with masculinity—"the Cheeta," the "Grizzly," the "Coyote." Hey, I'd drive a car named "Poodle" if it had what I wanted: good looks, a smooth ride, and jackrabbit starts. Zero to 60 in five seconds. That's my kinda car!

Of course, I want a car that's priced right, gets good mileage, and has a 100,000-mile warranty. So, when I saw that Melikian's was having a sale on _____, I headed right down to Auto Row and staked my claim on their economy model. No frills, no deluxe paint job, and no fancy upholstery.

Now, I just laugh when I pass those monster, bulked-up gas guzzling SUVs, parked next to a $75,000 import, or see a luxury car being towed by a very unluxurious tow truck!
Like I say . . . I'm just an easygoing kinda guy.

AGENCY:	McDonald & Little Advertising
CLIENT:	Six Flags
LENGTH:	60 seconds
TITLE:	It Starts Off Slowly

ANNCR: It starts off slowly at first, climbing upward at maybe two miles an hour. Then it hits the crest, picks up speed, and before you know it, it happens. The ground is gone. The world is a blur far below; look down if you dare. And don't think about the fact that you're moving at almost a mile a minute and headed straight down into a lake. Or that you're screaming and laughing at the same time. It's all in good fun. Here on the biggest, fastest, highest roller coaster in the world. The Great American Scream Machine. Just one of the many, many new experiences now at the new Six Flags Over Georgia. There's a whole lot of new to do this year at Six Flags. Things you'll never forget. Because good times here are not forgotten.

Ad-Lib Announcing

The term *ad lib* is short for the Latin *ad libitum,* meaning "performed with freedom; freely, spontaneously." In broadcasting, to ad-lib means to improvise and deliver with no preparation whatsoever. Related adjectives are *impromptu,* meaning speaking on the spur of the moment with no prior preparation, and *extemporaneous,* meaning prepared in advance but delivered without notes or a script.

Outstanding voice quality, articulation, and interpretation are important assets for all announcers, but they alone won't guarantee effective communication. When you're on your own without a script, only your ability as a compelling communicator will earn you listeners. Much of the broadcast day consists of unscripted shows. Disc jockeys, field reporters, telephone talk-show hosts, interviewers, game-show hosts, and panel moderators are among those who seldom see a script and who must conduct their programs spontaneously. Field reporters often work from notes, but they work with a complete script only when they return to the station to prepare a "package."

Ad-lib announcing can be practiced, but it probably can't be taught. The formula for success is easy to state but difficult to achieve: *Know what you're talking about, be interested in what you're saying, be eager to communicate with your listener, and project an attractive personality. In interviews, show a genuine interest in your subjects and their views.*

Announcers working without scripts can be more spontaneous than script readers; at the same time, they run a greater risk of boring their listeners. Scripts are usually tightly written, while ad-lib or impromptu announcers can wander from point to point or get totally lost. Scripts have specific objectives, but ad-lib announcers are free to ramble without a clear intent. Scripts are often polished

---

Checklist *Improving Ad-Lib Announcing Skills*

1. *Know what you're talking about, research specific topics: Read widely to be knowledgeable about a range of current topics.*
2. *Be interested in what you're saying: Keep the material fresh every time you report.*
3. *Be eager to communicate with your listeners: Your announcing must reach real people on the other end.*
4. *Develop an attractive personality: Be yourself and be genuinely interested in others.*

and tightened during recording sessions; impromptu comments of an announcer can't be taken back once they're spoken.

Despite all of these potential pitfalls, ad-lib, impromptu, and extemporaneous announcing are crafts that must be practiced and perfected by anyone who wants to become a professional announcer. Keeping this in mind, practice unscripted announcing at every opportunity, using an audio recorder for self-evaluation. The following tips should be helpful.

Know What You're Talking About

We expect sportscasters to have a thorough knowledge of sports, and DJs to know much about the music they play. But problems arise when an announcer has to speak on an unfamiliar topic. As a field reporter, for instance, after delivering a live report from the scene of a breaking story, you'll often be asked by an anchor for specific details, which can be very uncomfortable if you haven't done more than gather the most obvious facts.

As a field reporter, you may be asked to interview a person about whom you know little and about whose special achievement you know nothing at all. Suppose, for example, you're to interview a medical researcher about an important discovery. How would you prepare? Go online, where inquiries will quickly provide you with reams of information on almost any topic or famous person.

As a competent talk-show host, you won't rely entirely on computer data banks. You'll be a voracious reader of newspapers, newsmagazines, current fiction and nonfiction best sellers, and general-interest periodicals. At a large station you'll have the help of a research assistant who'll gather information about a particular guest or topic. (Chapter 8 discusses the role of radio and television talk-show hosts.)

Sound Bytes

Audition performances by professional announcers may be found on the Internet and played through your computer's speakers. For a variety of audition tapes made by professional voice-over announcers, go to these websites:

www.ozvoxaudio.com (Click on "Voice Over Talent," then on "Access some of the best voiceover talent!")

www.voiceprofessionals.com

Many performers have their own websites. Here are samples:

David Sobolov: www.sobolov.com/

Beau Weaver: www.spokenword.com/

Denny Delk: www.ddelk.com/

Fernando Casanova (in Spanish): www.fernandocasanova.com

For a complete, updated list of URLs for this textbook, please see the accompanying CD.

Be Interested in What You're Saying

If you listen carefully to radio or television announcers, notice that some seem to have little or no interest in what they're saying. Among those are weather, traffic, and business specialists who make frequent reports throughout the day. It's difficult to avoid falling into a routine delivery pattern because there is a sameness about the structure and elements of each report. The tendency, then, is to speak too rapidly and show little interest in what's being reported. However, while it's easy to understand that each brief report should be treated as though it's the *only* report, it isn't that simple to do so. Remembering that one's job is on the line should be a good incentive to make each report "special"!

Be Eager to Communicate with Your Listener

Only if you really want to communicate to others should you consider announcing in the first place. If you want to speak merely for and to yourself, buy an audio or video recorder and have fun "doing your own thing."

Develop an Attractive Personality

Very little advice can be offered on developing an attractive personality. Most people who are found attractive by others have learned to be truly themselves, are eager to show their interest in others, and have wide intellectual curiosity. Wit, wisdom, and charm are also characteristics of those with appeal. These qualities are greatly appreciated but hard to come by. Use a recorder as an aid in developing a unique air personality, one that reflects your most attractive qualities. Save your recordings and check them from time to time to measure progress.

PRACTICE

➤ Ad-Lib Announcing

The exercises that follow require an audio recorder. Most can be adapted to video recording.

Don't look at the topics that follow until you're fully prepared to begin each practice session. To prepare, get a stopwatch or a clock or watch with a sweep second hand—digital watches may be used, but those with hands give you a spatial view of time elapsed and seconds remaining. Find an isolated area that's free from distractions. Choose a number from one to twenty. Without looking at any other topics, read the item corresponding to the number you've chosen. Start your stopwatch. Give yourself exactly one minute to formulate your thoughts. When the minute is up, reset the stopwatch and start it and the recorder simultaneously. Begin your ad-lib performance and try to speak fluently on your topic for a predetermined time—one minute for your first few efforts and two minutes after you've gained experience. Decide on the length of your performance before looking at your topic. Eliminate the number of each topic when you use it so you'll have a fresh challenge each time you practice.

As you form your thoughts, try to think of (1) an appropriate opening, (2) material for the body of your remarks, and (3) a closing statement. Don't stop your commentary because of stumbles, hesitancies, or other problems. Don't put your recorder on pause while you collect your thoughts. This exercise is valueless unless you work your way through your ad-libs in "real time." To improve, you must gain firsthand knowledge of your shortcomings. The only way to gather this knowledge is to follow these instructions to the letter, regardless of initial failures. Keep all your recorded performances so you can review them.

Some of the ad-lib topics that follow suggest a humorous approach; others demand a more sober delivery. All topics are general, and you should be able to find something to say about each. These topics serve well for initial practice, but eventually you must graduate to more current and realistic topics. As a broadcast announcer you'll be asked to speak on current events as reflected in newscasts and newspapers. To truly test your ad-libbing abilities with important topics, make a list of the week's headlines. A typical week will yield topics as diverse as Third World indebtedness, hunger in some parts of the planet, labor negotiations in your community or area, breakthroughs in medicine, important Supreme Court decisions, newly proposed legislation on various issues, election results and their implications, speedups or slowdowns of the economy, and news on the greenhouse effect. List each topic on a separate slip of paper and follow the same instructions for ad-libbing, but don't limit yourself to arbitrary time constraints.

1. Give reasons for agreeing or disagreeing with this proposal: "On graduating from high school, all students should be required to serve for one year in the Peace Corps or perform some type of community service."
2. Discuss the most influential book you've ever read.
3. Describe your memories of some important holiday during your childhood.
4. Name the most important college course you've taken and give reasons for your choice.
5. Describe your most influential relative.
6. Describe your most embarrassing experience.
7. If you could change one law, what would it be, how would you change it, and why?
8. Describe your first memories of school.
9. What do you hope to be doing in ten years?
10. Describe your most memorable vacation.
11. Tell about your most memorable pet.
12. Attack or defend this statement: "Final examinations should be abolished in favor of several quizzes and a term paper."
13. What turns you on?
14. What turns you off?
15. Tell about your recurring nightmares.
16. How should our government deal with terrorists?
17. What should the government do to be more effective in combating illegal drugs?
18. Tell how you feel about graffiti on buses and public buildings. If you disapprove, describe what you think should be done.
19. Describe the characteristics or qualities of a broadcast announcer whose work you admire.
20. What are your strengths and weaknesses as a person?

Chapter 3

Voice Analysis and Improvement

Ways of Communicating with Others

We communicate with others in many ways: by written messages, body movements, and spoken words. At times, we send messages through silence, as with a stare, smile, frown, or quizzical look. Each works well to make known our ideas, feelings, advice, and other thoughts, but most often we reach and affect others *through our voice,* the most important instrument of communication we possess.

As you prepare for an announcing career, you should make an assessment of your speaking voice. Record several readings and listen to them on playback, noting anything you find displeasing or less than acceptable. Few of us reach adulthood with voices that are developed to their full potential. The sound—the tonal quality, the resonance, the "music"—of an announcer's voice requires training and practice. This text offers many suggestions for analyzing voice quality and pinpointing what needs work. It offers diagnostic tests, exercises, and scripts that will improve your voice quality. Carefully analyze your speaking voice to identify what you'd like to improve, then develop an exercise plan you'll use daily to bring about change.

How We Speak

Speech is created in a three-step process:

1. Air from the lungs is pushed up by a membrane called the **diaphragm** (see #1 in Figure 3-1).
2. As air moves through the windpipe (**larynx**, #2), sounds (including vowels and **unvoiced sounds**) are created. When the **vocal folds** (#3) are tensed, they vibrate to produce the voiced speech sounds, including all vowel sounds; such nonvowels as *r, l, j* (as in *just*); and the nasals: *m, n,* and *ng* (as in *sing*).

   Sounds are also created by air alone as it passes through areas restricted by the positioning of tongue and lips. When the vocal folds are relaxed, articulators help form voiceless sounds, including hissing for words with *s,* and *sh,* and popping sounds, as with *p* and *t.* (For a detailed discussion of voiced and unvoiced sounds, see Chapter 4.)
3. Sound waves are broken up into speech sounds by the **articulators: lips** (#4), **tongue** (#5), **teeth** (#6), **jaw** (#7), **alveolus** (gum ridge) (#8), **hard palate** (#9), **soft palate** (velum) (#10), and **uvula** (the small tag of tissue that hangs from the rear of the soft palate, not seen in the diagram.)

You learned to speak as a child, not by analyzing speech sounds, but by imitating grown-ups. Because speaking came easily to most of us, you may be surprised to learn that human speech is extremely complex. Examine the opening words of a novelty song from the early days of rock-and-roll. The lines read, "Splish splash,

Figure 3-1
Diagram of the throat and chest.

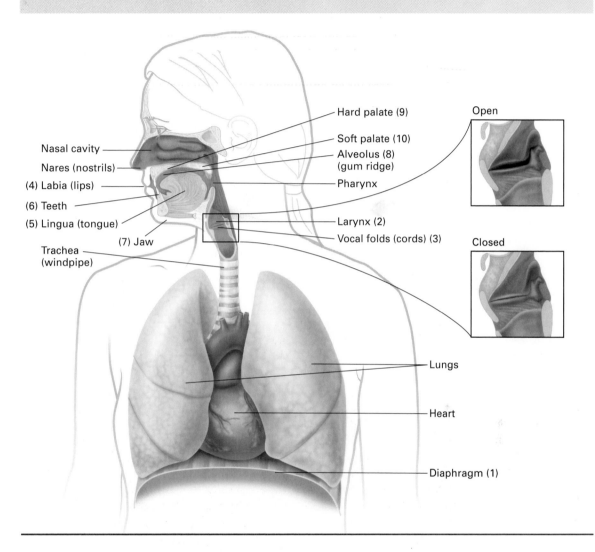

Hard palate (9)

Soft palate (10)

Alveolus (8)
(gum ridge)

Pharynx

Nasal cavity

Nares (nostrils)

(4) Labia (lips)

(6) Teeth

(5) Lingua (tongue)

(7) Jaw

Larynx (2)

Vocal folds (cords) (3)

Trachea
(windpipe)

Open

Closed

Lungs

Heart

Diaphragm (1)

I was taking a bath." As simple as this may seem, the seven words include several different speech sounds, some voiced and others voiceless.

Converting these sounds from letters on a page to human speech, the first sound is unvoiced *s,* a stream of air passing through a restricted space between the tongue and the teeth. *S* is quickly followed by the unvoiced puff of air made by *p.* (We now have the *sp* sound.) The first voiced sound, *l* follows (we now have *spl*) and, after that, the vowel *ih* sound (*splih*). The final sound in this word is the unvoiced *sh*. So *splish*, while a one-syllable word, is actually a combination of three unvoiced and two voiced sounds. *Splash* is the same, except that the vowel sound *ah* replaces the *ih* sound. The final words, "I was taking a bath," are made up of nine voiced sounds, including the semivowel *ng,* and five unvoiced sounds. It's amazing that such a complex combination of sounds can be uttered so easily!

So, what's the relevance of this to you? Even if your speaking voice needs no improvement (is that possible?), this information will help you to better understand and respect the instrument that's basic to your success as an announcer. More important, if your speaking voice is less than perfect, your ability to analyze it will give you information you need for working on, and overcoming, problems of articulation and phonation.

Aside from working to improve your voice, you should take measures to protect and strengthen it. Yelling until hoarse at sports events is one way of "losing" or seriously impairing your voice. Smoking, in addition to affecting voice quality, will decrease your lung capacity, and this will negatively affect your breathing. At worst, smoking can cause a permanently hoarse voice, a rasping cough, and, eventually, emphysema or lung cancer. If you have a smoking habit, yet want to succeed as a professional announcer, you should seriously reassess your priorities.

Figure 3-2
Radio talk-show host Michael Krasny gears his weekday two-hour programs to an audience interested in current events, developments in international affairs, scientific discoveries, and similar topics. Because his discussions with guests are intellectual by nature, he believes that his soft-spoken, conversational style of speech not only reflects his personality but also is conducive to discussions that are long on information and rational discourse. *Courtesy of Michael Krasny and KQED-FM.*

Speech Personality

Your speech personality is the way you sound, what makes you instantly recognizable when you speak to a friend on the phone. Speech personality is made up of seven variables: (1) **pitch,** including pitch range and inflection patterns; (2) **volume,** or degree of loudness; (3) **tempo,** or rate of delivery; (4) **vitality,** or energy; (5) **voice quality,** including resonance, timbre, and tone; (6) **pronunciation;** and (7) **articulation,** sometimes referred to as diction or enunciation (the movement of speech organs to make speech sounds). The first six of these variables shape the overall sound of your voice.

In addition to vocal sounds, you have a distinctive manner of articulating—the way you break up both phonated tones (voiced consonants, diphthongs, and vowels) and unphonated sounds (the unvoiced consonants discussed in Chapter 4) into words and phrases. Pronunciation and articulation are closely linked and are examined in detail in Chapter 4. This chapter focuses on pitch, volume, tempo, vitality, and voice quality.

You can isolate these speech qualities and characteristics and work on each separately for speech improvement. Using appropriate exercises, you can concentrate on your pitch, for example, without at the same time working on volume or tempo. Eventually, however, your efforts must come together if your speech is to avoid affectation and to blend successfully into the aural representation of the personality you want to project.

Analyzing Your Speech

The reading that follows, "William and His Friends," is designed to help evaluate your speaking voice. Every speech sound of American English appears in initial, medial, and final positions, unless a sound isn't used in one of those positions. The exercise is intended to meet four objectives: (1) to require you to manufacture all speech sounds to help detect possible speech problems, (2) to use the more difficult sounds several times, (3) to detect any problems of slurring words, and (4) to make the reading as brief as possible. The passage may seem nonsensical, but you should read it as though it makes a great deal of sense. Try to use your regular patterns of inflection and stress and your normal rate of delivery; only by doing so can voice or articulation problems be detected. It's highly recommended that you record your reading so that, after detecting specific problems, you can work on them and use your initial recording to measure progress.

Diagnostic Reading

WILLIAM AND HIS FRIENDS

This is the story of a little boy named William. He lived in a small town called Marshville. Friends he had galore, if one may judge by the vast numbers of children who visited his abode (*uh-BODE*). Every day after school through the pathway leading to his house, the little boys and girls trudged along, singing as though in church. Out into the yard they came, a vision of juvenile (*JOOV-uh-nuhl*) happiness. But, joyous though they were, they served only to work little William up into a lather. For, although he assuaged (*uh-SWAYDGD*) his pain with comic books and the drinking of milk, William abhorred the daily routine. Even Zero, his dog, was aghast at the daily appearance of the running, singing, shuffling, open-mouthed fellows and girls. Beautiful though the sight may have been, William felt that they used the avenue leading to his abode as an awesome item of lush malfeasance (*mal-FEEZ-unce*). Their little oily voices only added fuel to the fire, for William hated music. "Oooo," he would say, "they mew like cats, baa like sheep, and moo like a cow. My nerves are raw." Then back into his menage (*may-NAZH*) the little joker would scamper, fast action earnestly being his desire.

After recording and listening to your performance on playback (preferably several times), make a list of concerns that need to be worked on, such as lack of, or too much, pitch variation, slurring or running together of words, poor use of microphone with resultant sound distortion, popping or hissing, and so forth. This list will form a basis for choosing, and then practicing with, drill material.

SPOTLIGHT

Improving Your Voice Personality

Your voice is the most important instrument of communication you possess. This is a strong statement, but it's by no means an exaggeration. Diagnostic exercises can help identify whatever problems you may have in voicing and articulating the words you use, and hours of practice can improve your speaking voice. However, there's another aspect to speech improvement, and that's the unlearning of bad attitudes toward oneself, as those attitudes were developed in childhood.

Barbara Lazear Ascher has done an excellent job of identifying a variety of attitudes that contribute to good and bad use of our vocal mechanism. Her essay is reprinted here through her generous permission and that of Self magazine.[1]

Voice Lessons

The right voice can persuade a desperate person not to jump. It can extract a raise from your reluctant boss. It can calm a cranky pet. A dog trainer once told me: "Always speak in a low,

[1] Barbara Lazear Ascher, *Self*, August 1995, p. 132.

quiet voice. You can yell and scream, and it'll never work, but the minute you speak softly, you've got his attention." Could it be that what works on pups also works on people?

The voice I'm talking about flows from gentleness—a firm, adult gentleness not to be confused with timidity. Our voice conveys who we are, according to New York City acting coach Elizabeth Parrish. The problem is that too often it still carries inflections of who we were. We all know those voices that survive childhood. The "don't-expect-too-much-of-me" voice. The whiny "life-is-unfair" voice. To change your tone and your future, says Parrish, "You have to break a barrier as to who you think you are—the barrier you grew up with."

Tune in to Your Tone

To convey gentleness and authority in an attractive, persuasive tone, we first have to hear ourselves. Voice specialist Arthur Joseph suggests you record and play back samples of your speech. What if you don't like what you hear? First, identify what you're conveying about yourself with your voice. Then, Joseph tells his students, "Choose your vocal persona." He has them write down how they think they're perceived and how they'd like to be perceived. "What you write becomes a mission statement."

Say Who You Want to Be

You can use your voice as a tool for change, says New York City psychotherapist David S. Wilson, Ph.D. He has discovered that if his patients speak about themselves positively and aloud, they become what they say. Do this positive "self-talk" as many times a day as possible, he says, and your own voice will begin to replace the formative voices of childhood that scolded you to "Be quiet!" or to "Speak up."

But first, according to Dr. Wilson, you need to hear your negative "self-talk," those self-defeating opinions about yourself, whether it's "I'm fat" or "I'm no good at languages." You must hear yourself speak the accusation aloud

because hearing it is how the thought originally got planted. Wilson points out that little children will say "I'm a bad girl (or boy)" because they hear their parents say it. "By the time you're in your teens their opinion has become your belief, a primal belief, so that even if you're a winner you think you're a loser," Wilson says. "People start saying, 'I'm no good at languages' or 'I'm no good at numbers,' and it becomes self-fulfilling."

Once you hear it, you can stop the negative self-talk and replace it with a positive statement that says what you want to be. Speak statements that contain no negatives. "I'm thin" rather than "I'm not fat," for example.

Repeat your positive statement aloud every chance you get, urges Wilson, and keep it simple. "I'm successful," for instance, or "I'm an adult in control." "If people stick with this," he says, "their self-image is changed—and the change begins with the first utterance."

Stand or Sit Tall

Physical tension and body position affect the sound of your voice, according to New York City veteran voice teacher Ralph Proodian. If your lower back is tight, then your chest tightens and that tension radiates into the larynx. Relax your shoulders and neck; when tense, they also raise the pitch. The free flow of breath that will bring the most beautiful resonance to your voice requires perfect posture.

Proodian recommends testing your posture by standing with your back to a wall with your heels almost against it, your shoulders touching it. Then, with your palm facing the wall, run your hands behind your lower back. If there is just enough space to slide your hand in and out, then your posture is speech perfect.

Take a Deep Breath

The vocal muscles are the only muscles that function through air pressure, according to Arthur Joseph. The velocity of air moving through the vocal folds creates vibration and pitch. "Inner conflict can stifle the airflow and prevent functioning," he says. When we're holding back feelings, we don't breathe properly, and our voice is thin, unpersuasive. We need to breathe freely to promote the richest cadence and melody in the sounds we make.

To breathe properly, Joseph reminds his students that breath is both emotional and physical. He instructs them to "allow a silent and loving breath" to move through the body before speaking. Then take another deep breath and send your voice out in an arc, as though it were a ski jumper.

Explore the Emotional Power of Sound

Vocal sounds, even more than words, have tremendous power to release emotions and bodily tension. Don Campbell, founder and senior adviser of the Institute for Music, Health and Education in Boulder, Colorado, recommends making long vowel sounds like *aaaah*, *eee*, and *ooooh* to "learn the depths of your own personal voice." To do this, sit comfortably in a chair, close your eyes, and begin with *aaah*. Make the sound as long and at as many different pitches as you like.

Experiment—let it sound like a yawn or a moan or a sigh. Go wherever your impulse leads you. Do this for three minutes and notice how you feel. Work your way through each vowel, noting how different sounds evoke different feelings, pitches, and rhythms. For most people, low slow sounds are soothing, while higher-pitched sounds (like *eee*) are energizing and lift the spirits. Like deep breathing, vocalizing can calm you down, which is crucial to a melodic speaking voice.

Hear the Music

"Listen to the French and Italians," suggests Dwight Owsley, a New York City cabaret singer with a voice you'd want to curl up with. "Notice how many different pitches their voices have.

Figure 3-3

Barbara Lazear Ascher is a noted essayist, novelist, poet, and lecturer. She's written and read essays for National Public Radio's *Morning Edition*. A lawyer-turned-journalist, she's most at home with essays because, she says, "I'm impatient," and short pieces enable you to "get to the point right away." Her article "Voice Lessons" is an example of a short piece loaded with useful information. *Courtesy of Barbara Lazear Ascher.*

Americans tend to be very limited in their range, so that their voices, by comparison, seem flat."

It's true about the French. One of the many reasons that we find French women beautiful is the sound of their voices. Listen for a moment to the lilt, to the upward inflection and then the dip to a deeper range. They are able to convey tenderness and aloofness through the melody of their basic speaking voices.

The music of the voice is aesthetic, it's character forming, and, according to Campbell, it can be good for your health. Campbell teaches that the sound of one's voice affects the body. Our voice, he says, is capable of harmonizing our inner and outer worlds—as the shamans and the singers of Gregorian chants know. Campbell tells the story of a French physician called in to treat a general malaise affecting monks in a Benedictine monastery. Following the reforms of Vatican II, the life of the monastery had changed radically. The physician determined that the problem was audiological—not physiological—and prescribed a return to the pre-Vatican II "diet

of Gregorian chant." The monks returned to their former practice of chanting eight or nine times a day for ten to twenty-five minutes, and the group was brought back into harmony with one another and their God. Their appetites returned and their fatigue vanished. "Within six months the monastery was intact," says Campbell.

The sound of their voices healed them.

Four Aspects of Your Speech

When describing the way a person speaks, we say the voice is of high or low *pitch;* the speaker's *volume* is loud or quiet; the speaker's *tempo* is fast or slow; the speaker shows energy, or *vitality*, or the lack of it; that the *voice quality* of the speaker is pleasing, grating, resonant, or "thin"; that words are, or are not, spoken according to established *pronunciation;* and that the speaker clearly enunciates or slurs words, which refers to *articulation.*

Pitch and Inflection

Medium- to low-pitched voices are generally more pleasant than high-pitched voices. An exception occurs when a voice is pushed so far down the pitch scale as to sound guttural, unnatural, or even grotesque. You should speak near a pitch level that's comfortable and easy to vary for emphasis or variety and that doesn't strain your voice. Whatever your pitch range, make sure you don't consistently speak at your lowest level, because good speech demands variety in pitch (inflection). If you always speak at your lowest level, you have no way of lowering your pitch for selected words.

Pitch in human speech is determined by the rate of vibration of the vocal folds, often referred to as the vocal cords; the faster they vibrate, the higher the pitch. The vocal folds of a mature woman generally vibrate about twice as fast as those of a mature man, so female voices are generally about an octave higher than male voices.

To make the best of your voice, find and develop your optimum pitch—the pitch at which you feel most comfortable and are able to produce your most pleasant sounds. Most of us sound best when we're speaking in the lower half of our available pitch range.

You can determine your **optimum pitch** in one of several ways. One effective system is based on the theory that your optimum pitch is that level at which the greatest amount of resonance is produced. **Resonance** is the amplification of vocal tones during speech as the result of vibrations of the chief resonators: the bones of the chest and face, the **trachea** (windpipe), the **larynx** (connecting the trachea and the pharynx and containing the vocal folds), the **pharynx** (between the mouth and the nasal passages), the mouth, the nose, and the sinuses and cheekbones. When you resonate, you can feel these vibrations most noticeably alongside your nose. Place your palms on your cheekbones and your fingers on the sides of your nose. Now read a series of short sentences, each at a different pitch level. You should be able to feel it when you hit your optimum pitch. And, by recording and playing back the test sentences, you'll hear, without the distraction of bone-conducted sound, what you sound like when you're at or very near your optimum pitch.

Another way to determine optimum pitch involves a piano. Sitting at the piano, sing the scale as low and as high as you comfortably can, playing the note that corresponds with each sound. If your singing voice covers two octaves, your optimum speaking voice should be at about the midpoint in the lower of the two octaves. In other words, optimum pitch is very close to a quarter of the way up from your lowest to your highest pitch. Having found the note that corresponds to your optimum pitch, start reading a prose passage. When you reach a vowel sound that can be prolonged, hold the tone and play the note that matches your optimum pitch. You can easily tell if you're consistently above, on, or below your optimum pitch level.

Your vocal folds are actually two muscles, and in a taut, contracted state, they vibrate at a more rapid rate than when they're relaxed. The faster they vibrate, the higher the pitch. Because of this, your pitch may become more pleasant sounding if you can relax your vocal folds. To relax your throat muscles, however, you must simultaneously relax the rest of your body. Because announcing is a performing art, and because performing usually causes tension, it's important that you learn to relax.[2] Professional announcers with several years of work experience behind them usually have no problem with nervousness. But students of announcing who perform before an instructor and fellow students or audition for that coveted first job can expect to be nervous.

Inflection is employed to avoid a monotone delivery by altering the pitch or tone of the voice. Repetitious inflection makes some voices singsong, while lack of inflection causes others to speak in a monotone. Good speech avoids the extremes and reaches a happy medium. Untrained speakers often fail to use variations in pitch sufficiently, and the result is a boring performance. On the other hand, some poorly advised speakers (who apparently were told at one time that they must avoid a monotone delivery) employ pitch patterns that regularly and repetitiously go up and down, without regard to the meaning of the words spoken. When practicing to increase pitch variety, avoid falling into predictable patterns in which you raise your pitch every so many words. Pitch should be altered to give emphasis to words that are important for understanding your message. Inflection should *always* be used to stress words that in print would be italicized or *underscored*, as indicated in *this* sentence by the use of *italics*.

---

[2] Mic fright is often the cause of tenseness. Suggestions for overcoming this common problem may be found early in Chapter 5, "Audio Performance."

You should be self-critical about the degree and style of your pitch variations. Listen intently to recordings of your speech. If you feel that improvement is needed, use the exercises at the end of this chapter. Always speak aloud, and record, replay, and note your progress.

Volume

Volume level is seldom a problem in broadcast speech, except for laypersons who don't know how to use microphones and reporters or sportscasters covering events that produce high levels of **ambient noise.** In a studio or control room, sensitive microphones pick up and amplify all but the weakest of voices. An audio console, properly operated, ensures that the correct volume of speech goes through the board and onto the transmitter. Always remember that your listener is very close to you, so speak in a normal voice, as you would in a face-to-face conversation.

Outside the studio environment, volume level can be a problem. The noise from a parade, political convention, or sports event may make it necessary to use a louder voice. Under these circumstances, you may achieve the best results by moving closer to the mic and actually reducing your volume level. On the other hand, if conveying the excitement of the event dictates an increased volume, back away from the mic and speak up. Your pitch may go up as you do so, but that might enhance the excitement of your report.

Most radio and television speech is at its best when it's delivered at a conversational level. Because this level remains relatively constant for all of us, there's an optimum distance from mouth to mic to achieve speech that's suited to the event. A weak voice, too distant from the microphone, will require an increase in the **gain** (volume level) of the console; this in turn will increase the volume of the ambient noise. Conversely, a strong voice too close to a microphone is likely to produce popping, excessive sibilance, or an unpleasant aspirate quality. **Sibilance** is the hissing sound when speaking words that include the letters *s, sh,* and sometimes *z.* **Popping** is a blast of air when the plosive sounds *p, b, t, d, k,* and *g* are spoken. To **aspirate** is to release a puff of breath, as when saying the word *unhitch.* Aspirate sounds, like sibilance, are part of our spoken language and are exaggerated by microphones. A windscreen or pop filter, as well as an audio device called a **de-esser,** will reduce popping and excessive sibilance, but any such device will also eliminate the higher frequencies.

Some television performers unconsciously attempt to project their voices to a camera positioned several feet distant, rather than to the mic that's only ten or twelve inches from their mouths; this habit raises both the volume level and the pitch. Use your medium: Electronic communication doesn't usually require high volume.

Establishing your optimum volume level and microphone placement (distance from the mouth) should be one of your first priorities as a student of announcing. Because microphones vary in sensitivity, pickup pattern, and tonal reproduction, it's important to experiment with each type of microphone you're likely to use.

Tempo

Your tempo, or rate of delivery, is determined by various factors: the number of words to be read in a specified time; the mood or nature of the occasion; and when dubbing **(looping),** to synchronize speech with pictures. In general, newscasts and hard-sell commercials are read quite rapidly, while documentary narration, announcements on some laid-back popular music stations, and institutional commercials are spoken more slowly. When ad-libbing, judge what speed is appropriate to the mood of the event and adjust your rate accordingly.

There's no single correct rate at which to speak or read. When you have no time limit, gear your speed to the mood of the occasion or of your script. But keep in mind that most of us speak too rapidly much of the time. Speed is often the enemy of clear articulation. If read at too rapid a rate, the sentence "So give to the college of your choice" becomes "So give tuhthukallage uvyer choice." There's an absolute limit to the reading speed you can achieve without sacrificing good articulation. Few of us are good judges of our own speech; this is doubly true when it comes to judging tempo. Aside from requesting help from others, the best way to learn to achieve your optimum speaking or reading rate is by frequent use of an audio recorder. Isolate the one problem of tempo and work on it until a good rate of speed becomes automatic. If you detect slurring in your speech, the discussion and exercises in Chapter 4 should help improve the clarity of your speech.

Aside from a good basic rate of delivery, you should also work for variety in speed. Speeding up for throwaway phrases and slowing down for emphatic words or phrases will help give more meaning to your message. Throwaway phrases include "member, FDIC," "substantial penalty for early withdrawal," and "your mileage may vary."

Vitality, Energy

Two speakers with nearly identical speech characteristics may sound quite differ-ent if they vary in *vitality,* or *energy.*[3] Though a sense of vitality is easily communi-cated through rapid speaking or an increase of volume, it isn't necessary to rush your delivery or speak loudly to convey vitality. Many speakers are able to com-municate feelings of energy or enthusiasm even when speaking slowly and softly; others may speak rapidly but use little energy and therefore come across as unen-thusiastic. Many DJs and some sports announcers speak at a fairly low volume level but attain a feeling of vitality by speaking very rapidly.

Working toward two objectives should help you project vitality: First, use a de-gree of energy that's appropriate to your personality; and, second, gear the degree of vitality to the mood or significance of the event you're describing. Above all, don't push yourself up to a level of vitality that's forced, unnatural to you, or inap-propriate for the occasion. Most announcers are at their best when they're being themselves. It may take years of study and practice to develop your latent speaking potential, but the effort will pay off.

---

[3] The terms *vitality, energy,* and *intensity* are used interchangeably in this discussion.

Many beginning students of announcing are more subdued (and therefore show less energy) in performing in-class assignments than they are in their normal, out-of-class speech exchanges with friends. When performing, your objective might well be to lift yourself up to your customary level of vitality when driving home a point in a spirited discussion. If, however, you're a low-key person, you may want to capitalize on your natural qualities as you project vitality through restrained urgency. Use a relatively low volume—speaking almost with a hushed voice—and a measured delivery. When doing this, stress key words by prolonging them, or by pausing slightly before and after them, and by using whatever other means you possess to indicate that you are "holding back" your emotions.

Here are two readings that ask for differing degrees of energy. The first radio commercial demands a great deal of vitality. You should read and record this with subdued volume but a high level of intensity because this is what the author had in mind. You next may want to try it with all the stops pulled out: using as much volume, energy, and vocal pyrotechnics as you can muster. Then try it several more times, varying different elements of speech production with each reading. First use a fast pace; then a slower pace. Try it with more inflection and then with a limited pitch range; finally, try it with reduced vitality and increased volume. Listening to and judging the results of each variation should help you gain an understanding of the ways your interpretation changes both the impressions conveyed to listeners and the way you feel about your performance.

The second reading asks for a more restrained delivery. It's whimsical and slow paced and is to be read in a tongue-in-cheek manner. After recording it in the style indicated, try it with every variation of mood, rate, volume level, pitch, and degree of energy you can evoke.

The first spot was created many years ago, before Eastern Airlines folded. It's revived here, even though it may sound dated, because it's an excellent illustration of a hard-hitting, staccato, and brash writing style that mirrors the brash qualities of the city it promotes.

AGENCY:	Young and Rubicam, Inc.
CLIENT:	Eastern Airlines
LENGTH:	60 seconds
MUSIC:	(UP-TEMPO FULL ORCHESTRA)
ANNCR:	For sheer brass, nothing can touch it. Houston. The big rich. Brash. Confident. A brawler. That just opened the finest opera house in the Southwest. That calls itself one of the world's fashion centers. And is. Houston. It's oil. Hard cash. Enchiladas. It's a fast quip. A millionaire who rode

before he could walk. The NASA Space Center. If ever
there was a frontier, Houston is it. If ever there was a
cosmopolitan city, call it Houston. But mostly, call it guts.

SFX: (SOUND OF JET TAKEOFF)

Houston . . . an Eastern address. Eastern Airlines has three nonstop
jets going there every business day—throughout the business day. A lot
of people want to get to Houston. We'd like to make it easier for every
one of them. We want everyone to fly.

A much different mood is asked for in the next commercial. It, too, requires energy, because without energy a reading can be boring. The energy asked for,
though, is that born of conviction; to be successful in the performance of an announcement such as this, you need to project restrained belief in the story you're
telling and the product you're selling.

AGENCY: Allen and Dorward

CLIENT: New Century Beverage Company

LENGTH: 60 seconds

ANNCR: Here is your one-minute gnu (NEW) training lesson for today. Gnu is spelled G-N-U. The first question most new
trainers ask is, "What's gnu?" The gnu is part ox, part ante-
lope, and part horse. This gives him a slight identity complex and makes him mean. He may charge, hook you with
his horns, throw you down, and stomp on you. That's when
you start the lesson. Remember, you can't teach an old gnu
new tricks. Give the command, "Pay attention." If he
hooks you and throws you and stomps you again . . . you
have his attention. So stop the lesson and pour yourself a
frosty, ice-cold Mug old-fashioned root beer. Mug root beer
is the ideal drink for gnu trainers and old gnu trainers. Mug
old-fashioned root beer. Regular or diet. You haven't tasted
root beer like this in years.

Voice Quality

Resonance versus Thinness

A good voice for the electronic media is one with *resonance*—an intensification of vocal tones during articulation as a result of vibrations of the vocal folds. A sensitive, top-quality microphone can enhance your natural resonance, but even the best equipment can work only with what you give it, and a voice that's thin or lacking in resonance can be significantly improved only by its owner.

The sound vibrations that originate with your vocal folds are weak and colorless. As described in the section on pitch, sound vibrations need resonators to strengthen and improve the quality of sound. The chief resonators are the bones of the chest and face, the windpipe (*trachea*), the *larynx*, the *pharynx*, the mouth, the nose, the cheekbones, and the sinuses.

In general, thinness of voice is caused by one or more of three factors: shallow, weak breathing; speaking at too high a pitch (usually the higher the pitch, the less the resonance); and inadequate use of the movable resonators (the pharynx, larynx, and tongue).

As with any other speech problem, the first step is diagnosing it. Do you have a thin voice? What causes it? What do you need to do about it? The following passage is provided for diagnostic purposes. Read it slowly, working for your most resonant quality. Record it, using a sensitive professional microphone and a high-quality recorder.

Figure 3-4
Vocal sounds are emitted through the vocal folds (cords), shown open and relaxed (upper right) and tensed and closed (lower right). Vocal folds are small bands of tissue that stretch across the larynx. When you begin to speak, larynx muscles pull on the vocal folds, narrowing the opening. Air emerging from the lungs vibrates against the tensed folds and forms the sounds you produce.

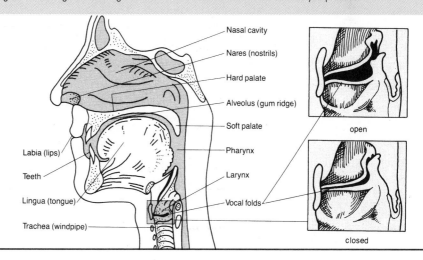

If possible, ask help from a person qualified to assess both voice quality and the apparent causes of thinness. If you're enrolled in an announcing course, your instructor should be your guide. Begin this reading approximately five feet from the microphone, speaking at a volume level appropriate to that distance. At each number, move forward about six inches, until you're reading the final sentence about eight inches from the mic. Lower your volume as you move in. On playback, determine whether distance and volume level significantly affect your resonance. Unless other negative qualities interfere (excessive sibilance, popping, nasality), this test should help you find and use your optimum microphone position to bring out resonance.

1. Johnny has an IQ of 170, but he can't read. The words are jumbled, upside down. Mirrored.

2. He has dyslexia. A learning disability that affects one out of every ten children.

3. Johnny goes to school and faces frustration, humiliation, and ridicule.

4. It's a tragedy because the techniques are there to help the dyslexic child. He can learn to read and write. And survive in school.

5. He can even go to college. If—and only if—dyslexia is diagnosed early. And dealt with.

6. Today, there are over a dozen centers in Massachusetts that can diagnose dyslexia—even among preschoolers.

7. To find out more, call 1-555-6880.

8. 1-555-6880.

9. One out of every ten kids has dyslexia.

10. And every one of them needs help.[4]

If yours is a thin, colorless voice, you should be able to increase resonance by following these suggestions:

- Practice deep breathing. Learn to breathe from the diaphragm, the large muscle that separates your chest from your stomach. Shallow breathing will result in a shallow or thin voice. While you speak or read, try to increase the force of air coming from your lungs.

---

[4] Courtesy of Ingalls Associates, Boston.

- Make sure you're moving your articulators. (Use the exercises in Chapter 4 to work on an exaggerated use of jaw, tongue, and lips.)
- Make sure there's no blockage of your nasal passages.
- Try to lower your pitch. (See suggestions given earlier in this chapter.)
- Read passages that emphasize vowel sounds (nineteenth-century American and British poetry are excellent for this). Prolong those sounds when they occur and try to keep your throat as open as possible. The suggested readings for this chapter list several standard speech-improvement books that include exercises. You will find suitable poems for practice on the Internet by entering "British Poetry, 19th century" on a search engine.
- Discover the best microphone for your voice and establish your optimum distance from it. (A ribbon mic will generally make your voice sound more resonant than will a dynamic mic.)

Breathing and Breathing Exercises

It's all but impossible to have a strong, resonant voice if you're given to poor posture and shallow breathing. Correct breathing requires you to maintain good posture; that your neck, shoulders, and face be relaxed; and that you breathe from the diaphragm. Good posture means sitting or standing with a straight spine and your shoulders drawn back. It's impossible to breathe properly when you're hunched over. Check your posture frequently throughout the day, every day. Become aware of when you're slumping. When speaking or reading aloud, first check your posture, then eliminate any tension that may be present in your neck, shoulders, or face. In time, you should become so conditioned that good posture will be natural.

In the glory days of radio, those who announced, acted, sang, related stories, read the news, told jokes, or did play-by-play coverage of sports typically stood as they performed. Standing reduces pressure on the upper torso and diaphragm and increases lung capacity. Even today, voice-over specialists stand as they rehearse and record commercials and documentary narrative. Many radio and television reporters stand as they make their on-screen reports and when delivering introductions, tags, and other bits of speech to be edited into "packages." Some sports announcers also stand as they describe football and other high-intensity games. Whenever possible and appropriate, stand as you perform announcing assignments; your voice quality and general effectiveness will be enhanced if you do so.

As described earlier, your diaphragm is a muscular membrane that separates your stomach from your chest cavity (lungs). Place your fingers just at the point where your upper abdomen meets your lowest ribs. When you breathe in, you should be able to feel outward movement as air fills the lungs. When you speak, try

Remedies for Keeping a Smooth Voice by Adrienne Sabo

ALL ABOUT ME: I am a senior at Youngstown State University, majoring in journalism with an emphasis in advertising and public relations. I am the editor-in-chief of <u>The Jambar</u>, the student newspaper at YSU, and a member of the Society for Collegiate Journalists, American Marketing Association, Sigma Alpha Lambda, and the 2007 Advertising Competition team. Outside of school I love traveling and going to Pittsburgh Pirates games.

ALL ABOUT TOPIC: Most radio announcers have their own tricks for curing a sore throat or eliminating nasty phlegm; whether avoiding milk or adding honey to their tea, the remedies are never ending. While the most important element in making your voice smoother is studying voice technique—irritation is caused by not using your voice properly—broadcasters also use specialized products to protect their voice. Announcers pick up specialty teas like Throat Coat, which is a blend of licorice root, wild cherry bark, fennel seed, cinnamon bark, orange peel, slippery elm bark, and althea root. When mixed in hot water, the tea releases a protective coating over the throat. Throat sprays like Throat Note are also useful to revive dry throat cords and heal overworked vocal cords, and Vitamin E and zinc spray can be beneficial for throat health. Remedies, fancy sprays, and teas aside, all broadcasters can protect their best asset by simply staying hydrated and getting plenty of sleep.

. . . AND HOW DOES THIS AFFECT ANNOUNCING? While each broadcaster has his or her own go-to products, studying vocal technique is key to keeping the voice strong. Home and herbal remedies can be quick fixes, but proper technique will protect the broadcaster's voice in the long term.

to "push" your voice all the way up from your diaphragm. You simply can't have a strong, resonant voice if you're manufacturing speech sounds mainly in your mouth. Speech sounds other than sibilants and plosives, are initiated by the vibration of the vocal folds. These sounds are then broken up into speech by the articulators. To produce a strong and healthy voice, the air stream that vibrates the vocal folds must be strong, which means that the stream should be forced up by the diaphragm.

To begin a regimen of breathing exercises, you need only to count aloud and see how many numbers you can say without effort. As you practice this exercise several times each day, you should soon find yourself able to count to thirty before beginning to run out of breath.

Other exercises to develop good breathing habits may be found in a number of texts on speech improvement, including suggested resources in Appendixes D and E.

Common Voice Problems

Nasality and Denasality

Nasality is caused by allowing air to exit through the nose, rather than the mouth, when sounding *m*, *n*, and *ng*. **Denasality** is caused by a blocked nasal passage and often is present when one is suffering from a cold. Pinch your nostrils and speak a sentence or two; you'll find that by preventing air from passing through your nose, you're producing a certain vocal quality—this is denasality. Now, without holding your nose, try to speak with a nasal tone. You'll find that the sound can be generated only when you force air up through the nasal passage—this is nasality.

Proper use of the nasal passage involves selectively closing off sound with the lips or the front or rear of the tongue, to force sound through the nasal cavity. If you say, in turn, *sim, sin,* and *sing*, holding on to the last sound of each word, you'll find that for *sim* your lips close off the *m* sound, for *sin* the front of your tongue against the upper gum ridge (alveolus) creates the *n* sound, and for *sing* the rear of your tongue against the soft palate (or velum) produces the *ng* sound. These three nasal sounds are properly produced only by the correct placement of your articulators and an unblocked nasal passage.

If you have a nasal voice quality, you should determine whether it's caused by not properly sending the *m*, *n*, and *ng* sounds up through your nose or if it's the result of sending nonnasal sounds through the nasal passage. The following sentence should help you determine this. Read it very slowly, pausing to prolong every vowel sound that can be held without change. Record and play back the results.

> Many men and women can do this in many differing manners.

All of the sustained *m, n,* and *ng* sounds should have resonance associated with them (as a matter of fact, unless these sounds are allowed to pass through the nose, they can barely be sustained). All nonnasal vowels should have no trace of nasality.

You can check for nasal resonance by placing the tips of your fingers lightly on either side of your nose. When holding a nasal consonant, you should feel a distinct vibration; when prolonging a nonnasal vowel, you should not. If you speak the word *women,* for example, the first prolonged vowel sound, *wiiiii,* should have only slight resonance. The *wiiiii* gives way to *wimmmmm,* and this should produce nasal vibration. The next vowel sound is *ihhhhhh,* which should be free from vibration. The final sound, *nnnnnnn,* should bring back the vibration. If you find that your nose doesn't produce vibrations on the nasal consonants, your problem is typical of the most common type of nasality. If, on the other hand, you find that you're nasalizing vowels that should not be nasalized, you have a less common and more difficult problem to work on.

If you're not nasalizing the nasal consonants *m, n,* and *ng,* your problem may be a physiological blockage, or you may simply be experiencing nasal congestion. In either case, there's no point in working on nasality exercises as long as the blockage exists. Do whatever is appropriate to end the blockage, even if it means a trip to an allergist or a nasopharyngologist. If you have no physiological problem or congestion and still lack resonance on the nasal consonants, the exercises on resonance at the end of this chapter should help. If your problem is nasalization of nonnasal vowels, these exercises should also help. Work to avoid any nasal resonance in nonnasal words, but don't try to eliminate it from words that legitimately call for nasality.

Huskiness

There *is* such a thing as a *pleasant husky* voice, one that suits a particular personality and is neither grating nor raspy; however, an *excessively* husky or hoarse voice usually indicates a medical problem. Laryngitis, smoker's throat, infected tonsils, or infected sinuses can cause a husky voice. You should see an appropriate medical specialist for any of these conditions because they're a handicap for any type of voice work.

To some extent, huskiness can arise as the result of excessive nervous tension. If yours is an unpleasantly husky voice, and if there's no medical explanation for it, you can improve your performance by drinking warm liquids such as tea or water and by using exercises designed to relieve tension. A section of Chapter 5, under the heading "Preparation," presents one such relaxation exercise. Vocal exercises will help you overcome excessive huskiness or hoarseness only if your problem is the result of misusing your speech organs.

Excessive Sibilance

Because the sibilant *s* is a common source of trouble to announcers, a diagnostic exercise is included here. Read the following passage into an audio recorder, play it back, and determine if you have excessive sibilance. If so, make extensive use of the exercises at the end of this chapter.

SIDESHOWS

How long has it been since you saw a first-rate sideshow? Some of us certainly should be sad over the disappearance of the classic circus sideshow, once a staple of civic celebrations—six or seven acts, set forth in circumstances that seemed awesome, or at least mysterious. Certainly, sideshows were sometimes scandalous, and sometimes in questionable taste, but they served to keep our curiosity in a steady state of astonishment.

PRACTICE

➤ Achieving a Low Pitch

There's nothing intrinsically better about a low-pitched voice than a high-pitched one; either extreme can be unpleasant to the ears. A very high-pitched voice can remind listeners of fingernails being scratched across a chalkboard; conversely, an excessively low-pitched voice can sound guttural, one step removed from grunting. Many producers of commercials and documentaries are convinced that low-pitched male voices carry with them a certain "authority," despite the fact that many outstanding performances are regularly accomplished by both women and men with mid-pitch range voices. Extremely low voices continue to be heard on voice-over introductions to news programs and televised feature films, on car commercials, and for products of any kind that have "macho" type men as their target.

Although you may not want to drive your pitch down into the cellar, you may feel that your voice would benefit from a slightly lowered pitch. Many of us, male and female alike, speak at a higher than desirable pitch. You can evaluate the appropriateness of your pitch by recording some of the exercises found in Chapter 4, "Pronunciation and Articulation." If an analysis of your voice makes you decide to lower your pitch level, the following commercial may be used to see just how much lower you want to (or are able to) go. Read and record this piece several times, listening between takes to judge each performance. If you already have a very low voice, make sure you don't creep along the bottom. Remember to work for variety in pitch (inflection). In addition to concentrating on pitch, try to read the commercial in exactly thirty seconds. If you read it in less time, you're probably not savoring the key selling words, and your speed may be interfering with the achievement of optimum pitch.

DAIRYLAND LONGHORN CHEESE

Mellow. Smooth and mellow. That's the way to describe Dairyland Long-horn Cheese. We use the finest Grade A milk from happy cows. Nothing but pure, natural ingredients. We take our time, letting the cheese age to the peak of perfect taste. We package Dairyland Longhorn in cheesecloth and wax, just like in the old days. And we speed it to your grocer, so that you get it at its flavorful best. Dairyland Longhorn Cheese. It's smooth and mellow.

PRACTICE

➤ Varying Your Pitch

Say these sentences, inflecting on the italicized word or words:

When did *you* get here?	When did you *get* here?
I *hope* you're right.	I hope you're *right*.
Which *one* is it?	Which one *is* it?
Which one is *it*?	*Which* one is it?
We *lost* the game!	*We* lost the game!
Don't say *that*.	Don't *say* that.
She found the key.	She *found* the key.
The *dog* ate the steak.	The dog ate the *steak*.

Inflect these words in isolation:

What?	Tremendous!
Certainly!	Ridiculous!
Maybe.	Surely.
Awful!	Life?
Sure!	How?
Try!	Stop.
Go!	Caught?

Note that the challenge is greatest with one-syllable words. The word *life*, for example, asked as a question, can accommodate both an upward and a downward inflection without becoming a two- or three-syllable word.

PRACTICE

➤ Varying Your Tempo

The following commercial provides good opportunities for employing shifts in reading speed.

SFX: SOUND OF GRIZZLY MOTORCYCLE IN DISTANCE, GRADUALLY APPROACHING

ANNCR: I can hear it in the distance. (PAUSE) Can you? (PAUSE) The *"grrr-ing"* of the Grizzly motorbike. (PAUSE) No, not a *"purring,"* a *"grrr-ing."* What's the difference? A *"purr"* comes from a contented cat—a *"grrr"* is made by a hefty Grizzly, looking for adventure. Cats are great, but they're usually gentle. The Grizzly is wild, but not unmanageable.

SFX: GRIZZLY VOLUME CONTINUES TO INCREASE

ANNCR: The Grizzly doesn't *"putt-putt,"* and it doesn't purr. It has a warm, furry sound, as befits a creature of the wild. (PAUSE) Here's the Grizzly, speaking for itself.

(PAUSE)

SFX: SOUND UP FULL, THEN BEGIN FADE

ANNCR: There it goes! (PAUSE) *"Grrr*-ing" its way to where it's going. Hear the *"grrr"*? You can own the *"grrr"*—if you don't want a pussycat and think you can tame a Grizzly. Check us out. (PAUSE) We're in the Yellow Pages. The Grizzly. (PAUSE) It's for people who want something on the wild side.

SFX: SOUND OF GRIZZLY TO CLOSE

 **PRACTICE**

➤ Excessive Sibilance

After determining that you make excessive hissing sounds when speaking the diagnostic reading on page 71, you should first find the cause. Before working to soften this sound, however, you should experiment with microphone placement and even the use of a windscreen or pop filter, for you may find that the problem is with the equipment or the way you're using it, rather than in your speech. If there's nothing wrong with the equipment try moving away from the mic, as well as speaking across, rather than into, the mic screen. If none of these actions solves the problem, read aloud and record the articulation exercises for *s* and *sh* sounds in Chapter 4, trying various ways of softening the sounds.

Chapter 4

Pronunciation and Articulation

After driving his motor home through forty states of the U.S. mainland, Nobel laureate John Steinbeck recorded these impressions in *Travels with Charley:*

One of my purposes [for making this trip] was to listen, to hear speech, accent, speech rhythms, overtones and emphasis. For speech is so much more than words and sentences. I did listen everywhere. It seemed to me that regional speech is in the process of disappearing, not gone but going. Forty years of radio and twenty years of television must have this impact. Communications must destroy localness, by a slow, inevitable process. . . . It is a rare house or building that is not rigged with spiky combers of the air. Radio and television speech becomes standardized, perhaps better English than we have ever used. Just as our bread, mixed and baked, packaged and sold without benefit of accident or human frailty, is uniformly good and uniformly tasteless, so will our speech become one speech.

These words, written in 1960, have not proved prophetic. People continue to speak with regional accents, despite the fact that, as John Steinbeck observed, an overwhelming percentage of broadcast announcers at both the local and national levels speak the "homogenized" English of broadcasting. *The American Heritage Dictionary* defines accent as "a characteristic pronunciation," so, in truth, everyone speaks with an accent.

There are many different but acceptable ways of pronouncing American English. Think of differences in the speech of a native-born Georgian, Texan, New Englander, New Yorker, Hoosier (Indianan), an Oregonian, and a person from Ontario Province.

The first section of this chapter investigates **pronunciation,** the way words are accented and inflected by a given speaker, and the second discusses a closely related topic, **articulation**—the breaking up of the sounds of speech into recognizable words. Pronunciation has to do with accent or dialect; articulation with the precision or lack of it in sounding words and syllables.

Variations in U.S. and Canadian Speech

Despite the richness represented by regional differences in pronunciation, most broadcast executives long favored what came to be called broadcast speech, or, more precisely, **Standard American Speech** or **Standard American Dialect.** Although these terms are roughly defined as the native speech of well-educated Americans and Canadians of the Midwest and Far West, many acceptable variations of English are spoken in this vast geographical area. These variations are reflected on nationwide radio, television, and cable by some news anchors and reporters, talk-show hosts, sports announcers, and stand-up comedians. Additionally, announcers doing cartoon voices and commercial voice-overs often employ accents or dialects. Announcers on stations that broadcast in every language from Korean to Spanish to Polish certainly do not employ Standard American Speech!

Standard American English is spoken by local announcers in every part of the United States, as well as by most television network announcers, which shows that most broadcast executives still cling to belief in a "correct" way of speaking. (See the Spotlight for this chapter, "The Debate over Standard American Speech," p. 84.)

Student Voices

Announcing in Other Languages by Jonathan Davis

ALL ABOUT ME: I am a television and radio broadcasting major at San Francisco State University. My passions are playing sports, fantasy sports on the Internet, art, and learning all I can about animals and nature. My goal is to be a sports broadcaster or have my own sports or nature show.

ALL ABOUT ANNOUNCING IN OTHER LANGUAGES: While many languages are spoken in America, with more than 28 million Spanish-speaking people in this country, Spanish is the second most popular language to English. This shift in the population has caused more stations to reach out to the growing market with Spanish-speaking announcers. One of many such shows is ESPN's Deportes, a 24-hour sports channel where the announcers speak Spanish and use many Hispanic-American colloquialisms.

. . . AND HOW DOES THIS AFFECT ANNOUNCING: In today's job market, speaking Spanish or being bilingual will give you an advantage in the workforce. You will have the option of working for a station that reaches out to viewers whose native tongue isn't English. In the Bay Area where I live, there are many Spanish radio and television stations. I plan to work on my Spanish to open job options after I graduate. I believe this is something that all students should think about, because it gives you the option of working for a Spanish television or radio station or even working for a station out of the country.

There are signs of change, most noticeably on cable, Internet radio, and independent radio stations, where it's possible in nearly every region of the United States and Canada to hear voices that are identifiably African-American, Latino, Southern, "country," New York–New Jersey, or New England. This trend may continue, but **voice tracking**—a practice in which a single announcer's voice is heard on dozens of radio stations across the United States—relies on the standard American model. Operators of radio station conglomerates regard this as the lingua franca of American speech because they own stations in all parts of the country.[1] Whether diversity in speech is reduced, sustained, or grows, your chances of succeeding in many types of announcing work may be improved if you speak with a so-called broadcast standard accent.

As a student of announcing, you should consider the question of pronunciation: If you don't speak standard broadcast speech, should you cultivate it? Because overall pronunciation is an important part of your speech personality, a decision to change it should not be made lightly. Keep this in mind as you consider modifying your mode of pronunciation: If you're truly an outstanding communicator with things of importance to say, the skill to say them clearly, and the ability

Figure 4-1
News anchor Rosie Allen prepares for her afternoon drive-time newscast. Born in Louisiana and reared in Denver, Colorado, Rosie speaks Standard American English. Her career has taken many turns, including vocalist for a band at age 18, three years in the U.S. Army, radio station news director, and head of public affairs. She's worked as a coanchor with Ed Baxter since 1984.
Courtesy of Rosie Allen and KGO-AM.

---

[1] For an extended examination of the consequences of the Telecommunications Act of 1996, see Chapter 11, "Music Announcing."

to project an engaging personality, your regional, international, or ethnic dialect, whatever it may be, is of reduced importance.

More important than accent, though, are several qualities found in the speech of most successful announcers. In no particular order, these qualities are *articulation,* the breaking up, of speech units into syllables in such a way as to be clearly understood and *speed,* or *rate of delivery,* which is directly related to articulation because no matter how clearly one may speak, excessive speed can make comments difficult to follow. Then, there's *inflection,* the basis of good *interpretation*—a monotone voice, which may be appropriate for a certain characterization, is usually boring. *Vitality,* or *energy,* unless it's "over the top," can gain and hold audience attention. Finally, *voice quality,* when pleasing to the ear, will help establish a critical ingredient of one's speech personality.

Figure 4-2

Christiane Amanpour is CNN's chief international correspondent based in London. Her pronunciation reflects her Iranian childhood, as well as the English learned from her British mother. Amanpour has reported from many news hotspots including Iraq, Afghanistan, Iran, Israel, Pakistan, Somalia, Rwanda, and the Balkans. She is seen here reporting from Jerusalem. The numerous awards she has won are listed on CNN's biographical sketch at www.cnn.com/CNN/anchors_reporters/amanpour. christiane.htm © Karen ZIV/Corbis Sygma.

Causes of Mispronunciation

Aside from regional deviations from Standard American, there are deviations that are not regional, but are related to the speech of individuals. One or more of the following problems can cause mispronunciations.

Sloppy Articulation

If you say *air* for *error* or *wih-yum* for *William,* you're mispronouncing because of a failure to use your articulators. Say the words *air* and *error* aloud. Note that *air* can be sounded by a simple opening of the mouth and a drawing back of the tongue; *error,* however, requires more effort—two distinct movements of the lips and two movements of the tongue. Other words often mispronounced because of sloppy articulation include *variable,* pronounced *VAR-uh-buhl* instead of the correct *VAR-ee-uh-buhl,* and *government* pronounced as *GUV-munt* instead of *GUV-ern-munt.* Articulation, which is related to pronunciation, is discussed later in this chapter.

Physical Impairment

Missing teeth, a fissure in the upper lip, a cleft palate, nasal blockage, or any degree of facial paralysis may make it impossible for a speaker to pronounce words clearly. If you have a correctable physical impairment that interferes with effective speech, such as missing teeth, you should consult an appropriate specialist.

Sound Bytes

The accompanying CD for this text includes a list of 300 words that are often mispronounced or that are uncommon but likely to turn up in broadcast copy. Examples are *bouclé* and *denier* from the world of fashion, and *sciatica* and *diverticulosis* from medicine. In addition, Appendix C includes an extensive discussion of American English usage.

Misreading

Mispronunciations may result from a simple mistake, such as reading *amendable* for *amenable, outrage* for *outage, meditation* for *mediation,* or *through* for *though.* If you consistently misread words, you may have a learning impairment (such as dyslexia and related challenges) or a problem with your vision; either condition calls for consultation with a specialist.

Affectation

Some Americans who employ Standard American English for nearly all their speech pick up a Briticism here and there, and this practice can be jarring to a listener. Saying *EYE-thuh* for *either* works well with New England or Southern speech, but usually sounds out of place when used by a Westerner or Midwesterner. Affectation can be worked on and eliminated, but this task requires a keen ear, and in some instances calls for the help of a qualified speech teacher.

Unfamiliarity with Correct Pronunciation

Most of us have a reading vocabulary that's far more extensive than our speaking vocabulary. From time to time, we err (correctly pronounced *er*, not *air*) when we attempt to use a word known to us only through our eyes. The word *coup* (pronounced *koo*), for example, might be pronounced *koop* by one who knew it only from the printed page. Those who grew up in homes in which American English was poorly pronounced, or who learned English as a second language, sometimes must work to overcome a limited vocabulary and unfamiliarity with correct pronunciation.

To be truly professional, you must develop an extensive vocabulary and cultivate clarity and consistency in pronunciation. There are many books that can help you build your vocabulary, but be sure you're not simply adding to your *reading* vocabulary.

Pronunciation

Speech Sounds of American English

In this discussion of the speech sounds of American and Canadian English, **wire-service phonetics** and **diacritics** are used to illustrate sounds. For the benefit of those who've learned—or are learning—the **International Phonetic Alphabet (IPA)**, those symbols are also given. Wire-service symbols are always enclosed in parentheses: (*puh-REN-thuh-seez*). Diacritical marks appear between virgules: /*vur ' gyoolz*/. IPA symbols are enclosed in brackets: ['bræksts].

A **virgule** is a slanted line used to separate words, as in "either/or." In marking copy it's sometimes used to indicate a pause. **Diacritical marks** are symbols added to a letter to indicate its pronunciation. For example, a straight line over the letter *a* as in *bāss* indicates that it rhymes with *face*. When referring to a fish, a tiny *u*-shaped mark over the *a* (*băss*) gives a pronunciation that rhymes with *class*.

Speech sounds may be classified as vowels, diphthongs, and consonants. You may have been taught that the English language has these vowels—*a, e, i, o, u,* and sometimes *y*. While this is true of *written* English, the statement is misleading. Our language actually requires us to manufacture twelve vowel sounds.

A **vowel** is defined as a pure phonated (sounded) tone that doesn't use the articulators and can be held indefinitely without changing. If you say aloud the vowel (AH)/ä/[a] as in *father*, you'll note that you can hold it as long as your breath lasts without substantial change in its sound. If you say the diphthong (OY)/oi/[ɔɪ] as in *toy*, you'll notice that it glides from (AW)/ô/[ɔ] to (IH)/ĭ/[ɪ] and that you can't hold its entire sound. You *can* hold the last part of this diphthong indefinitely, but only because it's actually the pure vowel (IH)/ĭ/[ɪ] as in *it*.

Now say aloud the consonant *p*. You'll notice that you can't do so unless you add some vowel sound, such as *o*. The *p* sound is merely exploded air and can't be prolonged. Other consonants, such as *n*, can be prolonged; but as soon as you stop using your articulators (in the case of *n*, the tip of the tongue has been placed on the gum ridge behind the upper front teeth), the sound turns into a vowel sound such as (UH)/ə/[ə]. Consonants, then, may or may not require phonation but always involve use of the articulators.

Vowels

The English language contains twelve vowel sounds, if we ignore the three or four sounds that lie between some of these twelve and occur rarely—and only region-ally—in American speech. Vowel sounds are usually classified according to the placement of the tongue in the mouth, the tongue being the only articulator that materially affects their production. The front vowels are produced through the vi-bration of the vocal folds in the throat and are articulated by the tongue and teeth near the front of the mouth. The back vowels are produced nearly the same way, but they're articulated by the tongue and the opening in the rear of the mouth.

These are the front vowels:

(EE)/ē/[i] as in *beet*
(IH)/ĭ/[ɪ]as in *bit*
(AY)/ā/[e]as in *bait*
(EH)/ĕ/[ɛ] as in *bet*
(AAH)/ă/[æ] as in *bat*

If you pronounce each of these sounds in turn, beginning at the top of the list and running to the bottom, you'll find your mouth opening wider as you move from one sound to the next. As your mouth opens, your tongue is lowered and becomes increasingly relaxed.

Here are the back vowels:

(AH)/ä/[ɑ] as in *bomb*
(AW)/ô/[ɔ] as in *bought*
(OH)/ō/[o] as in *boat*
(OOH)/o͞o/[ʊ] as in *book*
(OO)/o͞o/[u] as in *boot*

If you pronounce each of these vowel sounds in turn, you'll find your mouth closing more and more and the sound being controlled at a progressively forward position in your mouth.

There are two more vowel sounds that aren't classified as front or back: the (ER) sound, as in *her* (HER) and the (UH) sound, as in *fun* (FUHN). In the International Phonetic Alphabet, two symbols are used for the (ER) sound: one when the sound is stressed, as in *bird* [bɝd], and the other when the sound is unstressed, as in *bitter* [bɪtɚ].

The IPA also has two symbols for the (UH) sound: one when the sound is stressed, as in *sun* [sʌn], and the other when the sound is unstressed, as in *sofa* [sofə].

The twelve vowel sounds can be described according to the way each is manufactured. This is done in Table 4-1.

Vowel Deviations. In the section that follows, standard broadcast or Standard American Speech is the reference point for pronunciation. In other words, despite what was written earlier about the growing acceptance of regional and other variations in pronunciation, this section is written for those who want to practice standard broadcast speech. Pronouncing vowel sounds in ways that deviate from standard broadcast speech shouldn't necessarily be regarded as "substandard."

TABLE 4-1 How the Twelve Vowel Sounds Are Produced

Front Vowels	Back Vowels	ER and UH
(EE), as in *beet*, is formed by holding the mouth slightly open, placing the tip of the tongue on the back surface of the lower front teeth, and arching the tongue toward the front of the mouth so that the sides of the tongue are in contact with the molars.	(AH), as in *bomb*, is formed with the mouth quite open and the tongue lying flat and relaxed in the mouth.	(ER), as in *bird* and *bitter*, is formed by holding the tongue back in the mouth, with the tip poised somewhere about the midpoint between the hard palate and the floor of the mouth.
(IH), as in *bit*, is formed by placing the tip of the tongue on the back surface of the lower front teeth and lowering and relaxing the tongue slightly more than for (EE).	(AW), as in *bought*, is formed by holding the lips open (but not rounded) and raising the tongue slightly in the rear. The tip of the tongue lies low on the gum ridge under the lower front teeth.	(UH), as in *sun* and *sofa*, is formed by holding the mouth slightly open with the tongue quite relaxed and flat on the bottom of the mouth.
(AY), as in *bait*, is formed in much the same way as the (IH) sound, but the mouth is in a more open position and the tongue lies almost flat in the mouth.	(OH), as in *boat*, is made by rounding the lips and raising the tongue slightly in the rear of the mouth.	
(EH), as in *bet*, is formed with the mouth open still farther than for the (AY) sound but with the tongue in just about the same relative position.	(OOH), as in *book*, is formed in much the same way as (OO), except that the lips are more relaxed and slightly more open.	
(AAH), as in *bat*, is formed with the mouth quite open and the tongue lying flat on the bottom of the mouth. A certain tenseness in the jaws is noticeable.	(OO), as in *boot*, is formed by holding the front of the tongue in approximately the same position as for the (EE) sound and the rear of the tongue in a raised position. The lips are rounded and extended.	

SPOTLIGHT

The Debate over Standard American Speech

From the very beginning of radio broadcasting in the United States, attempts were made to require announcers to use standardized pronunciation. In 1929, less than a decade after the first radio broadcast, the American Academy of Arts and Letters began the yearly award of a gold medal to the radio announcer who best exemplified the kind of speech that the academy approved. In awarding the 1930 medal to Alwyn Bach of NBC, the academy commented, "We believe the radio announcer can not only aid the European immigrant to acquire a knowledge of good English, but he can influence the speech of isolated communities whose young people have no other means of comparing their own accent with the cultivated speech of those who have had the advantage of travel and education."[2]

In taking the position that one style of American English speech was superior to others, the academy was following a European model. England and France each had a great variety of dialects within their borders. But not all ways of speaking were considered "proper." Cockney, Midlands, and Cornish dialects in England and the speech of the people of Marseilles and Strasbourg in France were looked down on by those who spoke with "correct" pronunciation. Also, during the eighteenth and nineteenth centuries, many small European kingdoms, duchies, provinces, church-owned lands, and independent cities were consolidated into the nations of Germany and Italy. The boundaries of these nations coincided roughly with language groupings.

But the German spoken in Berlin was quite different from that spoken in Bavaria, and the Italian spoken in Sicily sounded "peculiar" to those in Genoa. Before long, "correct" or "official" ways of pronouncing these languages were established in these newly formed nations. From this action it was but a short step to social discrimination based on regional accent or dialect.

Many feel that the United States, the land of equal opportunity and upward mobility regardless of origins, had no reason to follow Europe's lead. Until the advent of radio broadcasting, there were two standards for correct American pronunciation. The first was *platform speech*, an overarticulated, oratorical manner of speaking, with a strong Oxford-British flavor. The second was speech used by "the enlightened members of the community." This phrase is significant, for it sanctions regional differences in pronunciation. Correct American speech could therefore vary—being that spoken by educated persons in New England, the South, the Midwest, or the West Coast, for example.

Regional differences in pronunciation have been tacitly accepted by linguists and those who compile dictionaries, but they were abandoned by broadcasters during the early years of radio broadcasting. Platform speech was precisely what the American Academy of Arts and Letters was promoting, as spelled out in its statement of criteria for good radio speech: "first, clear articulation; second, correct pronunciation; third, *freedom from disagreeable local accent;* fourth, pleasing tone color; fifth, evidence of cultivated taste."[3]

By the mid-1930s, objections to the stilted, quasi-British manner of speaking began to force change, which brought about a more natural and conversational style of speech. Despite this, the

---

[2] "Broadcast Announcing Styles of the 1920s," by Michael Biel, a paper presented at the convention of the Broadcast Education Association, March 16, 1974.

[3] Biel, "Broadcast Announcing of the 1920s," italics added.

Figure 4-3

Two young men from the streets of Times Square audition as vee-jays 3 an MTV promotional event. MTV programming, which began as music videos, has become a showcase for all sorts of music, pop culture, youth culture, fashion, and reality television shows, geared to adolescents and young adults. Every variation of American English speech may be heard on MTV.

objective of standardized *pronunciation* remained. Standard American Speech became the model for announcers all over the United States and English-speaking Canada.

Standard American is thought to be pleasant, easily understood, and more common than any other regional accent. Even though it's not the only style of American speech that's pleasant and effective, for years those with Southern, New England, Eastern, or Southwestern accents (as well as those with Asian, Latin American, or Middle Eastern accents) have been underrepresented on announcing staffs. A few exceptions may be noted: New England accents have long been accepted for announcing symphonic and operatic music; Southern and Eastern accents have been heard on many sportscasts; and nearly all regional accents have been accepted for news reporters, analysts, and commentators—though not news *anchors*. All regional accents are heard on commercials and talk shows. It may be that this trend will continue and even accelerate. Regional pride may some day bring the full richness of our language in all its variations to the American radio and television public.

Some people have grown up in environments where scores of words were spoken with vowel sounds that deviate from broadcast speech. Those who say (MELK) for *milk* or be-KUZ for *because* are voicing vowel deviations. Vowel deviations can be changed, but first they must be identified.

It's not uncommon for speakers of American English to distort one or more vowel sounds. This doesn't refer to those who speak with regional accents other than Standard American. It's not incorrect for an Easterner or a Southerner to say (FAH-thuh) for *father*, but it *is* substandard for speakers of American English anywhere to say (fer-GIT) for *forget* or (JIST) for *just*. This type of vowel deviation is the focus of the following discussion.

Five vowel deviations occur with some regularity among Americans in any part of the United States and Canada, and several others occur less frequently. It's not surprising that these deviations take place between vowel sounds that are next to one another in the place of production in the mouth.

Five Major Vowel Deviations. The following five chief vowel deviations are accompanied by readings to help you discover whether you have problems and to provide you with exercises to overcome them.

1. **(EH) for (AY)   /ĕ/for/ā/   [ɛ] for [e]**

   Those who distort the (AY)/ā/[e] sound, turning it into (EH)/ĕ/[ɛ], usually do so only when it's followed by an (UL) sound. This is because it's quite easy to sound the (AY) in a word such as *pay* but more difficult to sound it in the word *pail*. Say, in turn, *pail* and *pell*, and you'll see why some speakers slip into the easier of the two, thereby distorting the vowel sound of this and similar words. Read, record, and play back this diagnostic exercise to see if you're distorting the (AY) vowel sound:

   The pale graduate of Yale hailed the mail delivery daily. She failed to go sailing, for fear of gales and whales, but she availed herself of the tall tales told her by the mail deliverer. "I shot a quail out of season and was sent to jail," he wailed, "but a female friend put up bail, so they failed to nail me." The pale Yale graduate did not fail to hail the mail deliverer's tale.

   (In its most extreme form, some speakers read the first sentence as "The pell graduate of Yell helled the mell delivery dehly.")

2. **(AAH) for (EH)   /ă/for/ĕ/   [æ] for [ɛ]**

   Unlike the problem just described, this deviation tends to be of regional or ethnic origin and isn't caused because one manner of pronunciation is easier than another. Those from cities or areas where there's a sizable German-American or Scandinavian-American population are most prone to make this vowel distortion. (FANCE) for fence and (TAL-uh-fohn) for telephone are examples. Here's a diagnostic exercise for this sound:

> My friend, who is well but elderly, helped me mend my fence. I telephoned him to let him know when to get here, but he didn't answer the bell, so I guess he'd left. He's a mellow friend who never bellows, but he sometimes questions everything a fellow does. He took some lessons on television about fence mending, or else he wouldn't be able to help me mend my fence.

3. **(EH) for (AAH)**   /ĕ/for/ă/   [ɛ] for [æ]

Many Americans don't distinguish between the vowel sounds in the words *Mary* and *merry*, giving both the (EH)/ĕ/[ɛ] sound. Whereas (AAH)/ă/[æ] is seldom a source of trouble in the sounding of words such as *bat, champion,* and *sedan,* it often slips into (EH)/ĕ/[ɛ] in words in which it's more difficult to sound the (AAH), such as *shall.* Here's a diagnostic reading:

> Mary left the Caribbean to visit Paris. She carried her clothes in a caramel-colored carriage. Mary tarried at the narrow entrance of the barracks. There was a caricature of Mary that chilled her marrow. Mary said, "I shall never tarry in Paris again."

Note the difficulty of hitting the (AAH)/ă/[æ] sound when many words using this sound appear in rapid succession. Note, too, how the passage begins to sound "foreign" to our ears. The (AAH) sound will remain in American English speech, but there's no doubt that it's gradually disappearing from words in which its manufacture is difficult.

4. **(AH) for (AW)**   /ä/for/Ô/   [ɑ] for [ɔ]

Some speakers don't distinguish between these sounds, giving the same vowel sound to the words *bought* and *bomb.* Of the following readings, the first uses words for which the (AW) sound is appropriate, while the second mixes words using both sounds.

> We all talked about the day in the fall when Loretta sawed off the longest stalk. Our jaws dropped in awe of her raw courage. She caught the stalk in a bolt of gauze and waited for the dawn to prevent the loss of her awful haunted house of horror.

I saw them haul the bomb from the bottom of the waterfall. All around, I saw the awesome possibility of large-scale horror. Lost souls watched in a state of shock. The bomb slowly fought its way clear of the pond. Water dripped from the bottom of the bomb. I lost my fear, for I saw that the bomb was not awfully large.

5. **(IH) for (EE)**   /ĭ/for/ē/   [ɪ] for [i]

Sounding (EE) before an *l* calls for slightly more effort than sounding (IH) in the same construction. For this reason, some speakers habitually say (RIH-lee) for *really* and (FILL) for *feel*.

Sheila Fielding had a really strong feeling that something really bad would come of her deal to have the keel of her boat sealed. She wanted to shield the keel, so that peeling paint wouldn't be a really big deal. Sheila really hit the ceiling when she saw the bill. As Sheila reeled, she took the wheel and dragged the keel with the peeling paint across the pier and into the field where her feelings were really healed.

Several other vowel deviations are occasionally heard. Those whose speech includes these deviations (with some exceptions) tend to be quite consistent.

TABLE 4-2 Some Vowel Deviations

Vowel Sound	Word	Standard Pronunciation	Deviation
(AW) for (OOH)	*poor*	(POOHR) /po͞or/ [pʊr]	(PAWR) /pôr/ [pɔr]
/ô/ for /o͞o/	*your*	(YOOHR) /yo͞or/ [jʊr]	(YAWHR) /yôr/ [jɔr]
[ɔ] for [ʊ] as in	*sure*	(SHOOHR) /sho͞or/[ʃʊr]	(SHAWHR) /shôr/[ʃɔr]
book	*tourist*	(TOOHR-ist) /to͞o r'ĭst/	(TAWR-ist) /tôr'ĭst/
		[ˈtʊr,ɪst]	[ˈtɔr,ɪst]
	jury	(JOOHR-ee) /jo͞or'ē/	(JAWHR-ee) /jôr'ē/
		[ˈdʒʊr,i]	[ˈdʒɔr,i]
(ER) for (OOH)	*jury*	(JOOHR-ee) /jo͞or'ē/	(JER-ee) /jûr'ē/
/ûr/ for / o͞o /		[ˈdʒʊr,i]	[ˈdʒɝ,i]
[ɝ] for [ʊ] as in	*sure*	(SHOOHR) /sho͞or/ [ʃʊr]	(SHER) /shûr/ [ʃɝ]
book	*insurance*	(in-SHOOHR-uns)	(in-SHER-uns)
		/in-sho͞o r'əns/ [ɪnˈʃʊrəns]	/ ĭn-shûr'əns/ [ɪnˈʃɝəns]
	assure	(uh-SHOOHR) /ə-sho͞o r'/	(uh-SHER)
		[əˈʃʊr]	/ə-shûr/ [əˈʃɝ]

(IH) for (EH)	tender	(TEN-der) /tĕn′dər/	(TIN-der) /tĭn′dər/
/ĭ/ for /ĕ/		[ˈtɛndɚ]	[ˈtɪndɚ]
[ɪ] for [ɛ]	get	(GEHT) /gĕt/ [gɛt]	(GIT) /gĭt/ [gɪt]
	send	(SEND) /sĕnd/ [sɛnd]	(SIHND) /sĭnd/ [sɪnd]
	engine	(EN-juhn) /ĕn′jən/	(IN-juhn) /ĭn′jən/
		[ˈɛndʒən̩]	[ˈɪndʒən̩]
	friend	(FREHND) /frĕnd/ [frɛnd]	(FRIHND) /frĭnd/ [frɪnd]
(ER) for (UH),	familiar	(fuh-MIL-yer) /fə-mĭl′-yər/	(fer-MIL-yer) /fûr-mĭl′-yər/
(AW), or (IH)		[fəˈmɪljɚ]	[fˈɚmɪljɚ]
/ûr/ for /ə/, /ô/, or /ĭ/, or	forget	(fawr-GET) /fôr-gĕt′/	(fer-GET) /fûr-gĕt′/
/ĭ/ [ɚ] for [ə], [ɔ],		[fɔrˈgɛt]	[fəˈˈgɛt]
or [ɪ]			
	congregate	(KAHNG-grih-gayt)	(KAHNG-ger-gate)
		/käng′grĭ-gāt/	/käng′gûr-gāt/
		[ˈkaŋˌgrɪget]	[ˈkangɚget]
	garage	(guh-RAHZH)	(ger-AHZH)
		/gə-räzh′/ [gəˈraʒ]	/gûr-äzh′/ [gɚaʒ]
	lubricate	(LOO-brih-kayt)	(LOO-ber-kayt)
		/lōō′brĭ-kāt/	/loo′bûr-kāt/
		[ˈlubrɪket]	[ˈlubɚket]
(EH) for (IH)	milk	(MIHLK) /mĭlk/ [mɪlk]	(MEHLK) /mĕlk/ [mɛlk]
/ĕ/ for /ĭ/	since	(SINSS) /sĭns/ [sɪns]	(SENSE) /sĕns/ [sɛns]
[ɛ] for [ɪ]	fill	(FIHL) /fĭl/ [fɪl]	(FELL) /fĕl/ [fɛl]
	think	(THINGK) /thĭngk/	(THENGK) /thĕngk/
		[θiŋk]	[θɛnk]
	cent	(SENT) /sĕnt/ [sɛnt]	(SIHNT) /sĭnt/ [sɪnt]
(IH) for (EH)	men	(MEHN) /mĕn/ [mɛn]	(MIHN) /mĭn/ [mɪn]
/ĭ/ for /e/	helicopter	(HEL-ih-kop-ter)	(HIL-ih-kop-ter)
[ɪ] for [ɛ]		/hĕl′ĭ-kŏp′tər/ [ˈhɛlikɑptɚ]	/ˈhĭl′ĭ-kŏp′tər/ [ˈhɪlikɑptɚ]
	many	(MEHN-ee) /mĕn′ē/	(MIHN-ee) /mĭn′ē/
		[ˈmɛnˌi]	[ˈmɪnˌi]
(UH) for (IH)	it (as in *get it?*) becomes *uht* (as in *get uht?*)		
/ə/ for /ĭ/			
/ə/ for /ɪ/			
(UH) for (AW)	*because* becomes *be-KUZ*		
/ə/ for /ô/			
[ə] for [ɔ]			

Diphthongs

The **diphthong,** or **glide** as it's sometimes called, is a combination of two vowel sounds, spoken in rapid order with a glide from one to the other. Note that this word is pronounced (DIF-thongs). The diphthongs are represented as follows:

(Y)/î/[aɪ] as in *bite* (BYTE)/bīt/[baɪt]

(AU)/ou/[aʊ] as in *bout* (BAUT) /bout/ [baʊt]

(OY)/oi/[ɔi] as in *boy* (BOY) /boi / [bɔi]

(YU)/yōō/ [ju] as in *beauty* (BYU-tee) /byōō′tē / [bjut͵i]

The vowel sound (AY)/ā/[e], as you'll see by saying it aloud, is actually a glide; it definitely goes from (AY) to (IH). Because of this move from one sound to another, it's sometimes considered a diphthong and given the symbol [eɪ] in the IPA.

Diphthongs are a source of trouble to some speakers. Diphthong deviation tends to be regional and, though not necessarily substandard, is not compatible with Standard American Speech. If you have trouble with diphthongs, practice making each of the vowel sounds that form them and then speak the two sounds consecutively with increasing rapidity. These exercises will help only if you're producing the sounds of the diphthongs according to the standards of broadcast speech.

Read these sentences to practice the diphthong (EYE)/ ī / [aɪ]:

1. I like my bike.
2. Lie in the silo on your side.
3. Fine nights for sighing breezes.
4. Why try to lie in the blinding light?
5. Cy tried to fly his kite.
6. My fine wife likes to fly in my glider.
7. Try my pie—I like it fine.
8. Shy guys find they like to cry.
9. My sly friend likes to be wined and dined.
10. Like all fine and right-minded guys, Mr. Wright liked best to try to find the slightest excuse to lie about his life.

These sentences allow you to focus on the (AU)/ou/[aʊ] sound:

1. Flounce into my mouse's house.
2. Cows allow just about too much proudness about them.
3. Round and round went the loudly shouting lout.
4. A mouse is somewhat louder than a louse in a house.
5. A bounding hound went out on the bounding main.

6. Grouse are lousy bets when abounding results are found.
7. A cow and a mouse lived in a house.
8. The louder they proudly shouted, the more the crowd delighted in seeing them trounced.
9. They plowed the drought-stricken cow pasture.
10. Allow the grouse to shout louder and louder, and she'll just about drown out the proud cows.

Use the following sentences to practice the diphthong (OY)/oi/[ɔi]:

1. A toy needs oiling.
2. The soybeans are joyously coiling.
3. Floyd oiled the squeaky toy.
4. Goya painted Troy in oils.
5. His annoying voice was boiling mad.
6. The oyster exploited the joyous foil.
7. Roy and Lloyd soiled the toys.
8. Joy, like a spoiled boy, exploited her friends.
9. What kind of noise annoys an oyster? A noisy noise annoys an oyster.

Read these sentences for practice with the (YU)/yo͞o /[ju] sound:

1. I used to refuse to use abusive news.
2. The kitten mewed, but I refused to go.
3. The music was used to imbue us with enthusiasm.
4. The beautiful view used to confuse.
5. June was beautiful.
6. The newest pupil was wearing his suit.
7. The cute kitten mewed.
8. He eschewed responsibility for the news.
9. The few new musical numbers were confusing to the beautiful girl.
10. A few beautiful girls are using perfume.

Consonant Sounds

The English language contains twenty-five consonant sounds *(phonemes),* which are classified in a number of ways, the most basic of which is whether or not they're voiced.

If you say your ABCs it might seem as though the letters actually sound the way you pronounce them. But the letter *a* becomes *ay, aah,* or *aw,* when you use the *a* as the first sound in *April, apple,* and *awful.* In each of these words, the vocal folds are vibrated so they become **voiced consonants.** The sound *sh,* when used to ask for silence, has no accompanying phonation, so it's an **unvoiced consonant.**

A more detailed and more useful system, based on how the sound is formed, classifies the consonants in this way:

- **Plosives** begin with the air from the throat blocked off, and the sound is formed with a release of the air. The plosive consonants are *p, b, t, d, k,* and *g.*
- **Fricatives** are created by the friction generated when air moves through a restricted air passage. The fricative consonants are *f, v, th* (as in *thin*), *th* (as in *the*), *z, s, sh* (as in *shoe*), *zh* (as in *vision*), *y* (as in *yellow*), and *h* and *hw* (as in *when*).
- **Nasals** are resonated in the nasal cavity. The nasal consonants are *m, n,* and *ng* (as in *sing*).
- **Semivowels** are similar to the true vowels in their resonance patterns. The consonants *w, r,* and *l* are the semivowels.
- **Affricates** combine a plosive with a fricative. The consonants *ch* (as in *choose*) and *j* (as in *jump*) are the affricates.

Still another system classifies consonants according to their place of articulation:

- **Labial, or bilabial, consonants** *Labia* is Latin for "lip." The lips are primarily responsible for the labial consonants *p, b, m, w,* and, in a less obvious way, *hw.*
- **Labiodental consonants** The lower lip is in proximity to the upper teeth. The labiodental consonants are *f* and *v.*
- **Interdental, or linguadental, consonants** For these sounds the tongue (lingua) is between the upper and lower teeth. The interdental consonants are *th/ th/* [θ] (as in *thin*) and *th/ th/* [ð] (as in *then*)
- **Lingua-alveolar consonants** For these sounds the tip of the tongue is placed against the upper gum ridge (alveolus). The lingua-alveolar consonants are *n, t, d, s, z,* and *l.*
- **Linguapalatal consonants** For these sounds the tip of the tongue touches (or nearly touches) the hard palate just behind the gum ridge. The linguapalatal consonants are *y* (as in *yellow*), *r* (as in *rain*), *sh* (as in *shoe*), *zh* (as in *vision*), *ch* (as in *chew*), and *j* (as in *jump*).
- **Linguavelar consonants** For these sounds the rear of the tongue is raised against the soft palate (velum), and the tip of the tongue is lowered to the bottom of the mouth. The linguavelar consonants are *k, g,* and *ng* (as in *sing*).
- **Glottal consonant** The glottal consonant, *h,* is formed by the passage of air between the vocal folds without vibration of those folds.

Phonetic Transcription

As an announcer, you'll face unique and challenging problems in pronunciation. In reading news, commercial, and classical music copy, you'll frequently encounter words of foreign origin and be expected to read them fluently and correctly. As a newscaster, you'll be asked not only to pronounce foreign words and names with accuracy and authority but also to know when and how to Americanize many of them. Although British announcers are allowed to Anglicize freely, you'd be seen as odd or incompetent if you said *nice* (as in rice) for the French city of Nice (pronounced (nees) in the United States) or *lef-TEN-unt* for lieutenant, a word of French origin. Appendix B, "Phonetic Transcription," is devoted to helping you develop the ability to transcribe difficult words into phonetics. Wire-service phonetics, diacritics, and the International Phonetic Alphabet are discussed.

Microphones: Importance of Proper Usage

As discussed in Chapter 3, developing your speaking voice is a key step toward becoming a successful broadcast announcer. At the same time, misusing the instrument that picks up your voice and ultimately sends it to the ears of listeners can seriously undermine your best efforts. Microphone types and usage of each are the discussed in Chapter 5, "Audio Performance."

Articulation

Most articulation problems arise from speaking too rapidly or from improper placement or faulty use of the articulators (the jaw, the tongue, and the lips). Read aloud the brief selection that follows and see if you have difficulty sounding all of the syllables of each word.

THE DIAGNOSTIC CENTER

This is undeniably the most conscientiously designed diagnostic center imaginable. I recognize that, from an architectural standpoint, the building is magnificent. It also is strategically placed. At the same time, however, is it environmentally sound? Does it mirror our civilization's preoccupation with transcendental human competencies? Looking at the phenomenon from an unexpectedly malevolent point of view, we probably should ultimately find an alternative.

Many North American speakers have poor articulation, which may include slurring, mumbling, or omitting syllables and certain words. If you need help with this important aspect of oral delivery, you should work with the exercises in this chapter to improve the clarity of your speech. Analyzing your reading of "William and His Friends" (p.55) and "The Diagnostic Center" should help you pinpoint your specific difficulties. When you've identified your problems, perform the appropriate exercises daily for as long as necessary. The exercises will do you no good, of course, unless you read the material aloud, while making a conscious effort to form every syllable of every sentence. It's wise to exaggerate articulation at first, gradually moving toward normally articulated speech. Continuing to exaggerate your articulation, however, is nearly as bad as the problems that caused you to undertake remedial action.

Articulation Problems

Nine speech sounds usually cause slurred, unpleasant, or "fuzzy" speech and should be corrected by anyone who intends to become a professional announcer. Of the twenty-five consonant sounds in the English language, those that cause most articulation problems are discussed here, along with exercises to help you overcome any difficulties you may have with them.

T. The consonant *t* is an unvoiced lingua-alveolar plosive. The *t* sound is formed by the release of unvoiced air that's been temporarily blocked off by the pressure of the tip of the tongue (*lingua*) against the upper gum ridge (*alveolus*). Note that *t*, like all other plosives (*p, b, t, d, k,* and *g*) is best softened when speaking into a microphone.

The medial *t* is a problem for many American and Canadian speakers. In the West and Midwest, it's often turned into a *d*, as in saying (BAD-ul) for *battle* ['bæd for 'bætl]. In some parts of the Northeast, it's turned into a **glottal stop,** as in saying (BAH-ul) for *bottle* ['bɔʔ əl]. In some parts of Canada, Toronto becomes *tuh-RAHN-o*. To help determine whether you have a medial *t* problem, record and listen to this reading:

The metal kettle was a little more than half full. I settled for a little bit of the better stuff and waited while an Irish setter begged for a pitiful allotment of the fatter part of the kettle's contents. The setter left, disgusted and a little bitter over the matter of her lost battle for a better portion of the beetle stew.

For extra work with the medial *t* try saying the following with increasing speed: *beetle, bittle, bayttle, bettle, battle, bottle, bootle, berttle, buttle.*

Use the following sentences to practice the consonant *t:*

1. Tiny Tim tripped toward the towering Titan.
2. The tall Texan tried to tell the taxi driver twenty tall tales of Texas.
3. Attractive though Patty was, the battling fighters hesitated to attempt to please her.
4. The bottled beetles were getting fatter.
5. The fat cat sat in the fast-moving draft.
6. Herbert hit the slight brat with his short bat.

Th. The consonant *th* (as in *thin*) is an unvoiced interdental fricative. This sound is frequently a source of trouble, because microphones tend to amplify any slight whistle that may be present. In making this sound, place the tongue *up to*, but not *into*, the space between the upper and lower teeth, which are held about an eighth of an inch apart. Air passing over the top of the tongue and between its tip and the upper front teeth makes the *th* sound.

These sentences are for practicing the unvoiced *th* sound:

1. Think through thirty-three things.
2. Thoughts are thrifty when thinking through problems.
3. Cotton Mather lathed his bathhouse.
4. The pathway led to the wrathful heath.
5. The thought of the myth was cutting as a scythe.
6. Thirty-three thinking mythological monsters, wearing pith helmets, wrathfully thought that Theobald was through.

S. The consonant *s* is an unvoiced linguapalatal fricative. It's one of the most common sources of trouble for announcers. A slight misplacement of the articulators can cause a whistle, a thick fuzzy sound, or a lisp. There are two methods of producing *s*, neither of which seems clearly superior. In the first, the sides of the tongue are in contact with the upper teeth as far forward as the incisors. The tip of the tongue is held rather high in the mouth, and a fine stream of air is directed at the tips of the upper front teeth. The teeth, meanwhile, are held slightly apart. In the second method of making *s*, the tongue is fairly low in the mouth at the rear and at the tip and is raised just behind the tip to make near contact with the gum ridge. A fine stream of air is permitted to flow through this passage, down toward the front teeth, which are held slightly apart. Because most microphones tend to exaggerate any slight whistle or excessive sibilance, work for a softened *s*.

If you produce excessive sibilance, use these exercises:

1. Should Samson slink past the sly, singing Delilah?
2. Swimming seems to survive as a sport despite some strange circumstances.
3. Lessons on wrestling are absurd, asserted Tessie.
4. Assurances concerning some practices of misguided misogynists are extremely hysterical.
5. The glass case sits in the purse of the lass.
6. Past the last sign for Sixth Place, the bus lost its best chance to rest.

Sh. The consonant *sh* (as in *shoe*) is an unvoiced linguapalatal fricative. It's made by allowing unvoiced air to escape with friction from between the tip of the tongue and the gum ridge behind the upper front teeth. Although this sound isn't a common source of difficulty, you should guard against its becoming a thick, unpleasant sound. To form *sh*, make certain that air doesn't escape around the sides of the tongue; keep the central portion of the tongue fairly low in the mouth.

Exercises for sounding *sh* include:

1. Shortly after shearing a sheep, I shooed off a wolf.
2. The shapely Sharon shared her chateau with Charmaine.
3. Mashed potatoes and hashed cashews are flashy rations.
4. The lashing gale thrashed, lightning flashed, and the Hessian troops gnashed their teeth.
5. A flash flood mashed the cash into trash.
6. Fish wish that fishermen would wash their shoes.

N. The consonant *n* (as in *nothing*) is a voiced lingua-alveolar nasal. Unlike *m*, it can be sounded with the mouth open because the tongue, rather than the lips, blocks off the air and forces it through the nasal cavity. The sounding of *n* is responsible for much of the excessive nasality characteristic of many irritating voices. If you detect, or someone detects for you, a tendency to overnasalize such sounds, spend several sessions with an audio recorder learning how it feels to soften them.

You can use these sentences to practice the sounding of *n:*

1. Ned's nice neighbor knew nothing about Neil.
2. Now the new niece needed Nancy's needle.
3. Indigestion invariably incapacitated Manny after dinner.
4. Many wonderful and intricate incidentals indirectly antagonized Fanny.
5. Nine men were seen in the fine mountain cabin.
6. Susan won the clean garden award and soon ran to plan again.

Ng. The consonant *ng* (as in *sing*) is a voiced linguavelar nasal. It's formed much as the consonant *g,* but it lacks the plosive quality of that sound. One of the most common problems with *ng* involves turning this sound into *in* in words that end with *ing,* saying *runnin* or *losin* for *running* and *losing.* Each announcer must, of course, determine when and whether it's appropriate to do this. A newscaster will undoubtedly decide not to. Drive-time music and sports announcers, depending on their speech personality, may decide it's permissible.

A less common pronunciation problem involving this sound is the practice in some parts of the East of adding *g* in the middle of a word such as singing (*SING-ging*) [ˈsɪŋ gɪŋ].

Use these sentences to practice the *ng* sound:

1. The English singer lingered after the lengthy contest.
2. He mingled with winged, gaily singing songbirds.
3. The long, strong rope rang the gong.
4. Running and singing, the ringleader led his gang.
5. Among his long songs, Engelbert mingled some lilting things.
6. Along the winding stream, the swimming and fishing were finding many fans.

L. The consonant *l* (as in *willing*) is a voiced lingua-alveolar semivowel, formed by placing the tip of the tongue against the upper gum ridge and allowing phonated air to escape around the sides of the tongue. This sound causes little difficulty when it's in an initial or final position in a word, but it's frequently a source of trouble in a medial position. If you say aloud the word *William,* you'll notice that the tip of the tongue is placed low in the mouth for *Wi,* raised to the upper gum ridge for *ll,* and returned to the floor of the mouth for *iam.* Obviously, it's easier to speak this name without moving the tongue at all, but then it sounds like *wih-yum* (*WIH-yum*), and the *l* sound is completely lost. Unlike some English speech sounds that may be softened or dropped without loss of effectiveness, the lost medial *l* is definitely undesirable.

Here's a diagnostic reading for the medial *l:*

Millions of Italians filled the hilly section of Milan. The milling celebrants whirled all along the palisades, down by the roiling river. Lilting lullabies, trilled by Italian altos, thrilled millions as they willingly milled along the boulevard. "It's really thrilling," said William Miller, a celebrant from Schiller Valley. "I'm compelled to call this the most illustrious fellowship in all of Italy."

If you have difficulty with the medial *l,* practice with these exercises:

1. A million silly swallows filled their bills with squiggling worms.
2. Willy Wallace willingly wiggled William's million dollar bill.
3. Lilly and Milly met two willing fellows from the hills.
4. A little melon was willingly volunteered by Ellen and William.
5. Bill filled the lily pot with a million gallons of water.
6. The mill filled the foolish little children's order for willow leaves.
7. William wanted a million dollars, but he seldom was willing to stop his silly shilly-shallying and work.
8. Phillip really liked Italian children, although he seldom was willing to speak Italian.
9. Enrolling in college really was thrilling for William, even though a million pillow fights were in store for the silly fellow.
10. Billy Bellnap shilled for millions of collegians, while his colleagues collected alibis galore in the Alleghenies at Miller's celebration.

Hw. The consonant *hw* (as in *where*) is an unvoiced labial fricative. It's a combination of the two consonants *h* and *w* and is achieved by forming the lips for *w* but releasing the air that makes *h* first; then the *w* sound follows immediately, so the *h* sound is barely heard. Although the *hw* sound in words such as *when* is lost by most speakers, announcers should include it—at least until it drops out of our language altogether.

These sentences are useful for practicing the *hw* sound:

1. Mr. Wheeler waited at the wharf.
2. Wherever the whip-poor-will whistled, Whitby waited.
3. Why whisper when we don't know whether or not Mr. White's whelp is a whiz?
4. "Why not whet your knife?" whispered the white-bearded Whig.
5. Whitney whittled the white-headed whistle.
6. On Whitsun, Whittier was whipping Whitman on a whim.

R. The consonant *r* (as in *runner*) is a voiced linguapalatal semivowel. In some areas of the United States and in Canada and England, *r* is frequently softened or completely dropped. In Standard American, or broadcast speech, however, all *r*s are sounded, though they needn't and shouldn't be prolonged or formed too far back in the throat. A voice described as harsh is frequently one that overstresses *r* sounds. However, in attempting to soften your *r*s, be careful to avoid affectation: A pseudo-British accent is unbecoming to Americans and Canadians. Few speakers can successfully change only one speech sound. The slight softening of *r* should be only one part of a general softening of all harsh sounds in your speech.

Use these sentences to practice the consonant *r:*

1. Rather than run rapidly, Rupert relied on rhythm.
2. Robert rose to revive Reginald's rule of order.
3. Apparently a miracle occurred to Herman.
4. Large and cumbersome, the barge was a dirty hull.
5. Afraid of fire and sure of war, the rear admiral was far away.
6. The bore on the lower floor left his chair and went out the door.

Audio Performance

Audience Rapport: Radio

The term audience rapport refers to a bond between performers and listeners. Most successful radio announcers have a special quality that's communicated through their voices. We're affected by this when a news anchor or reporter conveys both authority and self-confidence, when a disc jockey projects the human being behind the voice, and when a talk-show host earns our trust by being open minded, a good listener, and ready with sensible opinions and advice.

Without ever mentioning the word *rapport*, Steve Walker, a popular Pennsylvania DJ, wrote these words that reveal his thoughts on "being yourself."

Guest Editorial: Being Yourself
Steve Walker

As I look at some of the stuff people have done on the air to be entertaining or a personality, most has nothing to do with them as people, and that's the weakness. You can make people laugh with a joke—anyone can tell a joke—but it's the *you*, the person who's on the radio, sharing the many facets of your life and comparing it constantly with the individual you talk to on the other end of the radio, who makes the distance between you and your listeners disappear.

You won't learn how to *be* a personality until you *have one*, and you won't be valuable to a radio station until you *are* a personality: sharing your life with your listeners, little bits at a time, endearing yourself to them by dropping little embarrassments so they can learn to love you because you're a human being.

If you're on the radio, and not just a voice doing liner cards selling the radio station and the music, but relating and comparing your life to your listener's life, you'll find that you're a *real person*, not just another voice. Doing this in small quantities over a period of time lets listeners know *you*, and that makes *you valuable*.[1]

In this brief statement, Steve does an excellent job of defining what rapport is about, as well as indicating how you might cultivate this quality. As you read the tips, suggestions, and guidelines throughout this text, never lose sight of the fact that to be successful you must project a personality that says to listeners, "I'm human, we share the same joys and sorrows, and I'm here to communicate with you."

Establishing and maintaining rapport on radio isn't limited to DJ work; you can achieve affinity with your listeners in any aspect of radio announcing.

All your preparation for radio announcing will culminate in performance, and it's your on-air qualities that determine your success as a performer. Before you're ready to go before an audience, you must develop several qualities and abilities: a good and pleasing voice; interpretative skills; excellent pronunciation of English,

---

[1] This guest editorial appeared in the web page "almostradio," a DJ prep service that ceased publication on the death of its founder, Cosmo Rose.

as well as of foreign words and names that may be in the news; competence in your area of specialization; and the ability to "sell," whether as a DJ, commercial announcer, or talk-show host.

Microphone Fright

It may seem odd to bring up the topic of "mic fright" near the outset of this chapter, but nervousness when speaking into a microphone is very common with those of limited experience, especially when the results are recorded and will be heard and judged by others on playback. A few beginners relish every opportunity to perform and love listening to their voices. Most of us, though, when we begin to engage in audio performance, have butterflies before and during a performance and don't like the sounds of the voice we hear on recorded playbacks. So we begin here because real progress toward your goal will be limited until you become comfortable with microphones.

The good news is that some tension not only is to be expected but can actually help your performance. Mic fright, as this phenomenon is traditionally called, results in the release of adrenaline into the bloodstream, which can make you more alert and more energetic. A little mic fright can be an asset to a performer because a performer who's keyed up generates more positive energy than one who's routinely working through a piece of copy in an unfeeling manner.

The bad news is that *excessive nervousness* can seriously impair a performance. Extreme mic fright can lead to any combination of these symptoms: physical tension, shallow breathing, constricted throat, dry mouth, and (at an extreme) upset stomach and shaking knees and hands. During performance, these conditions can cause your voice to go up in pitch or to break or can make you run out of breath in the middle of a sentence, lose concentration, read or speak at an excessive rate of speed, or adopt a subdued attitude. Mic fright can also result in a completely dry mouth. At its greatest extreme, mic fright can make you unable to communicate.

The vocal folds (usually called vocal cords), which are central to good vocal tones, tighten up during times of moderate to extreme nervousness. The tighter the folds, the less they vibrate, which results in a lessened resonance and a strident sound to the voice. Hot liquids can relax the vocal folds. Hot tea, bouillon, coffee, or even hot water can help you achieve a better speaking voice. (This advice remains true even after nervousness has been conquered.) Make certain that the beverage of your choice is not too hot, however, and avoid carbonated beverages and any beverage containing milk.

Generally speaking, mic fright is caused by one or more of these conditions: *inexperience, lack of preparation, lack of self-esteem, lack of mental preparation,* and *dislike of one's voice*. Taken one at a time, these observations may help take you on the path to self-confidence as an audio performer. Even if you've had considerable experience with on-mic performance, you may benefit from this discussion, if only by helping you understand—and perhaps help with—the struggles of others.

Inexperience

Nothing but time and regular performances will boost confidence and overcome inexperience. Performances needn't take place on the air or in a class session. You can perform written and ad-libbed or impromptu assignments in isolation and record them for playback and evaluation.[2] To speak ad-lib is to perform without a script but with some preparation; impromptu describes speaking without preparation or rehearsal. When a talk-show host opens an on-air session with unscripted comments about a news development, these comments are *ad-lib* speech: The host has read and thought about the item, and has most likely formed opinions about it, but has not committed these thoughts to paper. When an on-the-scene reporter, after delivering a report, speaks in answer to questions from an anchor, this is *impromptu* speaking, because the reporter has no idea of what will be asked. Both modes of unscripted performance require practice.

> ### Sound Bytes
>
> Appendix A has many scripts for practice. Additional scripts may be found on the Internet. Look up "Drew's Script-o-Rama", and http://www.geocities.com/tvtranscripts/ for scripts to polish your interpretative skills.
>
> Essays and commentaries are heard on some public radio stations, but their scripts are available only through purchase. However, excellent essay and commentary scripts are available from the *Newshour with Jim Lehrer* on PBS. While these are written for television, most of them are equally appropriate for radio delivery. The URL is: www.pbs.org/newshour/essays-dialogues.html.

Importance of Preparation

Unless you have the opportunity to report live from the field, or perform as a talk-show host, you can't experience the actual challenges these jobs demand. You can, however, simulate on-air ad-libbing without equipment of any kind. To gain confidence and develop a smooth delivery, begin by observing and describing aloud things you see during the day. Walk through your living quarters and describe what you see; when driving or riding a bus talk quietly about what you see along the way. Sharpen your ability to hold your friends' attention as you relate anecdotes or discuss matters of mutual interest.

You can, of course, practice *reading* scripts. Though time pressures frequently make it impossible for working announcers to rehearse, you're under no such restrictions. If you want to improve your performances, you must prepare thoroughly. Chapter 2, "The Announcer as Communicator," has exercises for evaluating, marking, and performing scripts.

The Failure Syndrome

Most of us are more afraid of failing—of making fools of ourselves—than we are of physical dangers. This fear must be overcome because you can progress only by daring to experiment, trying a variety of approaches in your announcing work.

---

[2] Despite the general belief that tape recorders are obsolete, for most students of audio performance they remain the least expensive, most widely available, and most easily cued and operated recorders.

To remain safely within a comfortable shell and perform in a safe, low-key manner is to sacrifice any chance of major improvement. If you're enrolled in a broadcast announcing class, keep in mind that you and your classmates are in the pressure cooker together. Mature students will applaud and encourage the efforts of others to improve.

You can make almost any performance better by speaking with conviction. That is, if you believe in your message and sincerely want to communicate it to others, your fear of failure may be pushed aside by your conviction. Professional announcers don't always have the luxury of believing in what they're paid to say, but as a student you're usually free to choose messages that are of interest or importance to you. Take advantage of this opportunity and choose your topics wisely.

As you perform, concentrate on your message. Forget about self and forget about the audience. Assume you're speaking to one or two people, individuals you respect and with whom you want to communicate. If you truly have a desire to get your message across, you can overcome your concern about failure.

Self-Esteem

Some of us simply feel we're not important enough to take up the time and attention of others. This is an incredibly debilitating attitude that has nothing to recommend it. Modesty may be a virtue, but self-effacement is not. You may not even be aware of such negative feelings, but if you habitually withhold your opinions or allow others to cut off your comments, you need to consider possible reasons why.

Each of us is a unique creation. You're the only person just like you who has ever lived. Because you're unique, you have something special to offer. If you respect yourself, you'll perform at an acceptable level; if you respect your listeners, you'll find something worthwhile to say to them; if you respect your subject matter, you'll find ways to get it across. *Self, listeners,* and *topic* are interrelated variables that must mesh if you're to communicate effectively. Successful communication will inevitably increase your self-confidence and boost your self-esteem. Enhanced self-esteem will bring about further improvement in performances. Better performances will raise self-esteem-and so on. Believing that what you have to say is worthy of the interest and time of others is the start of a new and healthier attitude toward yourself.

But let's face it: If you're presenting dull material in a spiritless manner, you can't expect the rapt attention of listeners. If you conduct a boring interview with a boring guest, there's no reason to try to tell yourself that what you're doing is important. This brings us back to conviction—the belief that what you have to offer is important and valid. *To raise your self-esteem, be certain that what you offer your listeners is worthy of their attention.*

Mental Preparation

During the minutes before a performance, remove yourself (physically if possible, but at least mentally) from the confusion of a typical production situation. Find a way to relax, to gather your thoughts, to concentrate on the upcoming performance. Think over what you're to say or read. Think about mood, about appropriate pace, about the importance of the message, about any potential problems of diction, pronunciation, and so on. Perform relaxation exercises. If possible, sit in a comfortable chair. Begin to relax physically—starting with your head, then your neck, and then your shoulders. After you've attempted to relax your entire body, imagine that the tension or stress is being discharged from the ends of your fingers. If you try, you can actually feel the tension leaving your body. At this point, think again about your assignment and keep your message and your objectives clearly in mind as you prepare to perform.

The Way You Sound

Students of announcing often dislike the way they sound on playbacks. This response isn't surprising, because we don't hear ourselves as others do. Most people don't believe that their voice sounds like what comes back to them from an audio recorder. The reason is simple: We hear ourselves speak through *both air and bone conduction.* Sound waves emanating from our mouths are what others hear; only the person speaking hears the physical vibrations that go through the bones of the head to the tympanic apparatus of the ear. The combination of sounds conducted through air and bone is what we think we sound like to others.

Figure 5-1

Carter B. Smith stands as he reads a commercial. Few radio commercials are performed live, but there's a special vitality and persuasiveness when copy is delivered in real time by a familiar and respected performer. *Courtesy Carter B. Smith.*

Only when we hear ourselves through air conduction alone, as from an audio player, do we truly hear ourselves as others hear us.

If you understand that an audio playback of your speaking voice surprises only yourself and that others accept your recorded sound just as they accept you as a person, you're well on your way toward overcoming mic fright.

Microphones: The Link between You and Your Listeners

The bridge between you and your listeners is made of several elements, but it begins with a microphone. You should become familiar with various types of microphones and their usage, and this discussion is an introduction to most mics in common use.

As already noted, sound waves are generated through the actions of your phonators and articulators. To communicate through the electronic media, speech sounds must be converted to another form of energy. Microphones transform sound waves into electric energy. This transformation of energy is called transduction. An understanding of the relationship between you and your mic is important to your development as an announcer.[3]

Classification of Microphones

Microphones are classified in two related ways, according to internal structure and pickup pattern. As an announcer, you won't have a say in the microphones you use, but you should recognize the types given to you to use each to its best advantage.

Internal Structure.
Ribbon, or Velocity, Microphones

The **ribbon, or velocity, microphone** contains a metallic ribbon, supported at the ends and passing between the poles of a permanent magnet. The ribbon moves when sound waves strike it, generating voltage that's immediately relayed to an audio console. Ribbon mics are extremely sensitive to all sounds within a great frequency range, flattering to the human voice, and unaffected by changes in air pressure, humidity, and temperature. In addition, they're not prone to picking up reflected sound.

When using a ribbon mic, it's best to stand or sit eight inches to one foot from it and speak directly into it. If you find you have voice reproduction problems at close range, including excessive sibilance and popping, speak at an angle across the mic's front screen. A *windscreen* or *pop filter*, as well as an audio device called a de-esser, will reduce popping and excessive sibilance.

[3] Lavaliere mics are important in broadcasting, but are used mainly in television productions. Play-by-play announcers seldom use desk mics, preferring instead headsets with attached mics. Lavaliere mics are discussed in Chapter 6.

Dynamic, or Pressure, Microphones

In the **dynamic,** or **pressure, microphone,** a lightweight molded diaphragm attached to a small wire coil is suspended in a magnetic field. Sound waves striking the diaphragm are relayed to the coil, and the movement of the coil within the magnetic field transforms physical energy into electrical impulses.

When using a dynamic mic, stand or sit six to ten inches away from and to one side of the front screen of the instrument. By talking slightly across the screened surface, you should project your voice quality at its best, especially if you speak at high volume or are given to excessive sibilance or popping.

Condenser, or Electrostatic, Microphones

Often found in professional recording studios and FM stations, the **condenser,** or **electrostatic, microphone** is similar to the pressure mic in that it has a diaphragm; but instead of a coiled wire, it features a fixed plate opposite the diaphragm. As sound waves strike and move the diaphragm, the voltage between the plates changes, thereby varying the sound signal.

If you're asked to work with a high-quality condenser mic, you should treat it as you would a dynamic mic. If you find that the extreme sensitivity of the condenser mic is creating sibilance or popping problems, try working farther away from it or speaking into it at an angle. One or both of these adjustments should correct the problem. Condenser mics require power for their operation. Condenser mics used away from a station are powered by batteries. If you experience problems with a condenser mic, first check to make sure that the battery is present, is properly inserted, and is not dead.

The Pressure Zone Microphone (PZM)

The PZM is a condenser mic designed to allow direct and reflected sound waves to enter the microphone at the same time. Other mics pick up both direct and reflected sound but with a slight lag between the two, the result of varying distance from sound source to mic. The PZM eliminates this lag and has very little sound distortion. One definite advantage of a PZM microphone is that it doesn't look like a mic, which can reduce nervousness on the part of inexperienced guests.

Pickup Patterns. The **pickup,** or **polar, pattern** of a microphone is the shape of the area around it in which it can accept sounds for transmission with maximum fidelity and optimal volume. **Fidelity** refers to the degree to which the electronically produced sound corresponds to the original sound—in other words, its faithfulness to the original.

Nearly all microphones pick up sounds from areas outside their ideal pattern, but the quality of those sounds isn't high. For best results, you as a speaker (sound source) should be positioned within the pickup pattern and should be generating enough volume so that the control knob can be kept at a minimal level. If you're **off mic** (out of the pattern) or if you speak too softly, the volume control will have to be turned up, causing the microphone to distort your voice as it transmits

Figure 5-2
Sports play-by-play announcer Vince Cotroneo receives instructions and cues from the show director and during breaks in the game, sends questions and messages back over a headset microphone. *Courtesy Vince Cotroneo and the Oakland A's.*

unwanted sounds from outside the pattern. Whether you use a stand, handheld, or control-room mic, you can't ignore the pickup pattern of the instrument. You must position yourself properly and adjust your voice level to optimize the sound.

Manufacturers classify microphones according to four pickup patterns:

1. **Unidirectional,** only one side of the microphone is live
2. **Bidirectional** (or figure eight), two sides of the mic are live
3. **Omnidirectional** (also called *nondirectional* or *spherical*), the mic is live in all directions
4. **Multidirectional** (**polydirectional,** or **switchable**), two or more patterns can be achieved by adjusting a control

Nearly all unidirectional microphones have pickup patterns that are **cardioid** (heart shaped). Cardioid patterns range from wide to narrow (or tight) to **hypercardioid** (or supercardioid). Hypercardioid mics are used chiefly as shotgun mics in television studios and are seldom used in radio. They have a narrow front angle of sound acceptance and pick up very little sound from the sides.

The PZM has a **hemispheric** pickup pattern, which means that, when the mic is placed on a flat surface such as a desk or table, the area of sound acceptance is one-half of a sphere, like the northern hemisphere of the globe.

Figure 5-3

Microphone polar patterns show how sounds are absorbed in different shapes, depending on what type of mic you use. Note that these pickup patterns are actually three-dimensional and that the shapes alter with the changing relationship between the instrument and voice.

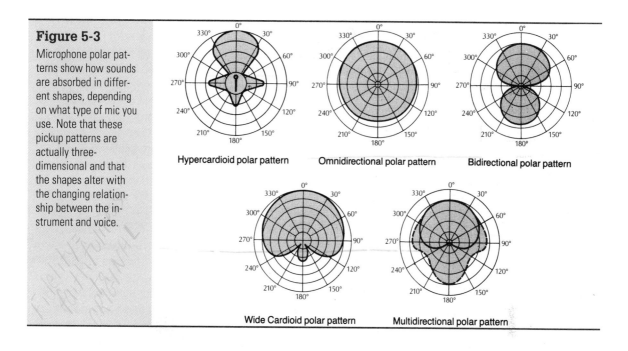

Hypercardioid polar pattern   Omnidirectional polar pattern   Bidirectional polar pattern

Wide Cardioid polar pattern   Multidirectional polar pattern

Descriptions and engineering diagrams (see Figure 5.3) of microphone pickup patterns are misleading because they can't show the three-dimensionality of the pattern, nor can they indicate that the pattern changes when the relationship between instrument and sound source changes. Because cardioid mics can be placed in every conceivable position with respect to the sound source, their pickup patterns vary in design and are especially difficult to understand from engineering diagrams. The cardioid pattern shown in two dimensions on engineering data sheets will differ significantly depending on whether the mic is handheld or mounted at a thirty-degree angle. The microphone data sheet shows whether a particular cardioid microphone has a narrow or a wide angle of front sound acceptance and designates the areas of rear acceptance and rejection. Only actual practice with cardioid mics will teach you how to position them.

As you study the pickup patterns of cardioid mics shown in Figure 5.3, assume that the microphone is exactly in the center of the circle in each instance. Also remember that the actual pattern is three-dimensional.

Microphone Consciousness

Microphones are marvelous instruments, but they can do their job only when they're used properly. Improper use sometimes results from inexperience or ignorance, but is more often due to a lack of microphone consciousness. To be mic conscious is to be always aware that the misuse of a microphone will result in a

flawed or failed performance. Typical examples of faulty microphone consciousness include these:

- Clapping your hands near an open mic
- Making unwanted noises near an open mic, such as drumming fingers on a table near a desk mic
- Moving from side to side away from a mounted mic
- Moving in and out in relation to a mounted mic
- Failing to move a handheld mic properly between you and a guest you're inter-viewing
- Positioning yourself and a guest improperly in relation to a desk mic
- Making sudden and extreme changes in the volume of your voice
- Failing to understand and properly relate to the pickup patterns of micro-phones
- Wearing jewelry, such as metal bracelets, that clanks when moved

During rehearsals and on the air, always assume that your microphone is open. Watch what you say. Always assume that profanity or backbiting comments about others will be heard by someone, possibly with devastating consequences. And beware of possible misuse of wireless mics! Because you most likely won't have an on–off switch, an engineer's lapse could have your voice reach the listening

Figure 5-4
News anchor Cheryl Jennings checks the placement of her lava-liere mic, while co-anchor Dan Noyes waits for a cue to open the newscast. *Courtesy of Cheryl Jennings, Dan Noyes, and KGO-TV.*

audience while you're on a break, and saying things that could cause you considerable embarrassment.

Taking a Level

When working with an audio engineer, you'll be asked to take a level before each performance, which allows the engineer to adjust the volume associated with your microphone. As a DJ or radio news anchor, you'll frequently do your own engineering, but as a talk-show host, or when performing voice-over commercials or narration, you'll usually work with an audio engineer who adjusts volume level as you speak. Because time can be wasted in taking voice levels and because getting faulty results will make the quality of the production suffer, it's necessary for you to understand this procedure. When taking a level, an engineer will tell you if you're off mic, if your volume is too loud or too soft, or if you're popping or creating excessive sibilance. Popping is an air blast when plosives are sounded; plosives are the consonants *p, b, t, d, k,* and *g.* Sibilance is the hissing sound made when the letter *s,* and sometimes *sh* or *z,* is sounded.

You can't sound your best if you're misusing your mic. An audio engineer can help you make the most effective use of your voice, but you must cooperate. When you're asked to take a level, it's essential that you read from your actual script (or, if ad-libbing, that you speak at exactly the same volume you'll use during the performance), that you position yourself in relation to the mic exactly as you will during the show, and that you continue reading or ad-libbing until the engineer is satisfied with the result.

In taking a level, follow this procedure:

1. As you sit or stand before a mic, remain silent. Unnecessary chatter is distracting.
2. Wait patiently and alertly for a signal to take a level; in a recording studio, the signal will probably be given orally by an engineer over an intercom. If you must depend on a visual signal, keep watching the engineer.
3. On receiving the signal, move into the exact position and posture you'll use during the performance and read or speak exactly as you will later.
4. When working with a script, read from that script, using all of the vitality, emotion, and other qualities you intend to use in actual performance. Don't hold back, thinking that it's wise to save yourself for "the real thing."
5. As you read or speak, remain alert for any hand signals given by the floor director or engineer, which might indicate "louder," "softer," or "move closer to (or away from) the mic."
6. As you make the suggested adjustments (if any), continue to speak until the signal is given that everything is satisfactory.

Hand Signals

Hand signals were developed in the early days of radio because soundproof glass partitions separated directors and engineers from performers. As radio turned more and more to recorded music, most DJs did their own engineering and therefore needed no signals. Today, most radio stations don't even have a control room adjacent to the announce booth or studio, and hand signals aren't needed.

Hand signals are still used in some radio applications. An announce booth director of live sports broadcasts—usually the audio engineer—uses a limited number of signals to cue sportscasters when going to or returning from commercial breaks. Popular morning drive-time disc jockeys, especially those working with sound effects and much "production," perform in an on-air studio/control-room complex and have engineering help. Radio talk-show hosts generally work with a producer/phone screener, separated by glass, who uses some hand signals.

Most of the signals that follow are standard throughout the industry, but be prepared for variations.

- The *attention signal*, a simple waving of the hand, usually precedes the standby signal.

- The *standby signal* is made by holding the hand slightly above the head, palm toward the announcer. The standby signal is given at any time when the announcer can't judge the precise moment at which to pick up a cue.

- The *cue signal* is made by rapidly lowering the hand from the standby position, with the index finger extended and pointing directly at the person being cued. The cue signal nearly always follows the standby signal; neither signal is normally given alone.
- *Increase volume* (speak up!) is made by holding one hand, palm up, and raising it.
- *Decrease volume* is made by holding one hand, palm down, and lowering it.

Performance Skills

Preparing for a Performance

Preparation for a performance is necessary for all but the most seasoned veterans, and proper preparation involves several considerations. After you've worked in the field for even a few years, announcing will be as natural as breathing. Until then, follow the suggestions in this section to prepare for smooth and confident performances.

Pirate Radio by Sitsofe N. Luh

ALL ABOUT ME: I am from Ghana in West Africa. I recently graduated from Southern Illinois University Edwardsville with an M.S. in mass communications. I am interested in news reporting, producing, and hosting my own TV show. I love reading, watching TV and movies, and listening to music.

ALL ABOUT PIRATE RADIO: Pirate radio operators are not professionals—they are technology-savvy people who purchase the right software and tap into the air waves to illegally share their thoughts and opinions with listeners. They don't pay for airtime, and they do their work in secret so that they don't get caught and shut down. While these operators have the money to run their own outfit, they consider themselves above the rules, standards, and ethics that govern the industry, and oftentimes they create shows that would never make it onto a traditional station. Listeners tend to like this about the stations, and they tune in to hear the nontraditional style of broadcasting.

. . . AND HOW DOES THIS AFFECT ANNOUNCING? Pirate radio is growing stronger and drawing increasing numbers of listeners away from traditional stations. While the shows are interesting, the more listeners tune in, the less they'll listen to professional stations, and that puts many announcers' jobs at risk. Pirate radio is also a bit degrading for those who go to school to train for such a career—the operators make it seem as though all you need is access, and suddenly you have the right to reach the masses.

Personally, I believe pirate radio operators are exercising their freedom of speech, which I support, but if they continue to do whatever they please it could lead to disorganization on the airwaves.

First, if you're working with a script, and if time permits, you should study and mark it. Underline words to be stressed. Write, in phonetics, the correct pronunciation of difficult words or names. Note any words that might be mistaken for others. For example, the following words are sometimes confused because of similar spellings:

though–through

county–country

uniformed–uninformed

united–untied

mediation–meditation

complaint–compliant

impudent–imprudent

outage–outrage

couch–cough

To eliminate the possibility of reading such words incorrectly, mark your copy. You might write *tho* and *thru* for the first pair of words and use hyphens for the others: *coun-ty, count-ry; uni-formed, un-in-formed; u-nited, un-tied;* and so on.

The final ten minutes before a performance are critical. Try to separate yourself from any distracting activities and concentrate on your upcoming performance. If you're excessively nervous, try to relax; if you're apathetic, try to psych yourself up to an appropriate degree of energy.

If your performance is to be ad-lib, go over its objectives and make determinations about how you'll structure your ideas within the allotted time. How much time will you give to your opening? How much will you give to your conclusion? How much time remains for the body of your presentation?

Finally, remind yourself that you're going to control any tendency you may have to speak too rapidly; that if you make an error, you'll correct it as naturally and unobtrusively as possible and continue; and that if you stumble, you'll move on, putting the error behind you (dwelling on it will divide your attention and make further stumbles almost inevitable). Above all, don't stop to ask if you may begin again, unless such a possibility has been agreed to in advance. Even if your performance will never actually leave the classroom or studio, always adopt the attitude that it's going out live over the airwaves.

Checklist   *Preparing to Perform*

1. *Study the script: Mark it for correct pronunciation.*
2. *Use the final ten minutes before your performance to separate yourself from all distractions; concentrate on calming your nerves and "psyching up" your energy level.*
3. *Remind yourself to speak slowly; and, if you should stumble, be prepared to continue in an unruffled manner with your broadcast.*

Achieving a Conversational Style

A conversational style is one that's natural to you, is appropriate to the intimacy of radio, and sounds as though you're talking, rather than reading from a script. Speaking naturally is one important element of building rapport. When listening to the radio, you may notice the speech of affected, stilted, and (perhaps) pretentious speakers who clearly enunciate every syllable of every word and who speak with repetitious changes in inflection; this is one extreme of spoken English. At the other extreme are those who mumble, barely move their lips, and whose energy (lack of it, really) is marked by a scarcely audible volume level.

Good conversational delivery is somewhere in between. It avoids overarticulation and slurring. It's marked by variety in pitch (inflection) and volume level, and it uses changes in pitch and volume to stress words that help convey meaning. Much of our daily conversation with friends is natural and effective because it's designed to communicate ideas, points of view, or convictions. We automatically find the simplest and best words to make a point, and we naturally stress key words to get our points across. Because we use it every day, conversational speech should be easy to apply when speaking for the electronic media. It usually is not a problem when speaking impromptu or ad-lib but can become a problem when working from a script. You can best achieve a conversational style by remembering a few simple principles.

First, don't hesitate to smile or laugh when it's appropriate. Don't be afraid to pause as you silently grope for an idea or a word, because pauses are perfectly natural. Fear of pausing can lead either to *ers* and *uhs* (**vocalized pauses**) or to spouting inanities as you try to fight your way back to where you left off.

Additionally, conversational quality can be lost by reading *ay* for the article *a*. Read this sentence, pronouncing the article as *ay*:

A good way for a person to make a fortune is to open a savings account in a bank.

Now read the sentence again, and instead of *ay*, substitute a sound somewhere between *uh* and *aah*. Work with a recorder to hear how you say this article in conversation with others. It's important, though, to not place stress on any of the *uh*s.

Note how stilted the sentence sounded the first time you read it and how much more natural and conversational it was when you used *uh* for the article *a*.[4]

---

[4] This general point does not take into consideration regional differences in pronunciation.

The word *the* is sometimes pronounced *thee* and sometimes *thuh*. The general rule is to say *thee* before a word beginning with a vowel sound and *thuh* before a word beginning with a consonant.

SCRIPT: The appetite is the best gauge of the health of the average person.

READ AS: *Thee* appetite is *thuh* best gauge of *thuh* health of *thee* average person.

Note, however, that when saying *thee*, soften the *ee* sound. At times this general rule is broken for purposes of emphasis, as in "It's *thee* best buy of the year!"

The conversational quality you already use when speaking with friends can be transferred to the reading of a script. Make recordings of impromptu discussions between you and one or more of your friends. Note on playbacks how you and others use variations in pitch, volume, and tempo to stress important points. Note how speakers use pauses and how energy increases and decreases according to the significance of the point being made. Record yourself reading a script. Compare your deliveries in unscripted and scripted speech. It may take some time to transfer your conversational quality to the reading of scripts, but it's essential if you're to achieve your optimal on-air conversational style.

Reading Telephone Numbers

When reading a telephone number that includes an area code, read it with a pause after each part, and, unless it's a well-recognized toll-free number, say "area code" before you give the code:

SCRIPT: Phone (332) 555-6666.

READ AS: Phone area code three-three-two / five-five-five / six-six-six-six.

When reading a telephone number that includes zeros, you should, in most instances, use the word *zero* and not *oh* or *aught*.

SCRIPT: Phone 555-0087.

READ AS: Phone five-five-five / zero-zero-eight-seven.

However, when you repeat a number, you can vary the way you say it:

SCRIPT: Phone 555-8200; that's 555-8200.

READ AS: Phone five-five-five / eight-two-zero-zero; that's five-five-five / eighty-two hundred.

Some sponsors have special numbers that must be read in a certain way. Part or all of the number may spell out a word, as in 555-SAVE. Often such numbers are given twice: once with the word(s), and then in the all-number version: five-five-five, seven-two-eight-three.

Toll-free telephone numbers should be read with the beginning given as "one-eight-hundred," "one-eight-seven-seven," or "one-eight-eight-eight." Increasingly, announcers are omitting both the phrase, "Call our toll-free number . . . ," as well as the first digit, "one."

Developing a Sense of Time

Announcers must develop a keen sense of time, for split-second timing is a part of most radio broadcasts. Most all-news stations follow a "clock," an hourly schedule of segments, such as local news, network news, commercial clusters, traffic reports, and so forth. Many music stations also have clocks that must be adhered to by on-air DJs. Accurate timing also is essential when recording commercials, station promos, and public-service announcements (PSAs). News anchors must work with precision so that there will be neither unwanted pauses nor overlaps when playing recorded actualities.

Other Tips for Improving Your Performance

First, there's no substitute for practice. Theoretical knowledge of broadcasting is important and will enhance your development, but without practice you'll never become truly professional. You don't need to confine your practice to class assignments. You can practice nearly anywhere, and you can practice without a single item of equipment. When reading newspapers, magazines, and books, isolate yourself from others and read at least some of the printed material aloud.

Second, if your budget permits, invest in a few basic items of equipment. Most practical is a good-quality, battery-operated audio recorder. It needn't be state of the art—you can find recorders to meet your needs on eBay or craigslist for less that $50. Look for a portable minidisc or cassette machine that will accept an external mic—internal mics in most consumer recorders are inadequate for your needs. With a recorder you can practice any type of announcing that appeals to you—news, interviewing, sports play-by-play, music announcing, or commercial delivery. You can also use it to record and play back exercises for improving your voice quality, pronunciation, and/or articulation.

Third, become honestly self-critical. As you listen to playbacks, imagine the voice you hear is that of another person. Listen for communicative values. Listen for voice quality, precise diction, and correct pronunciation. Experiment. Try various styles of delivery, levels of energy, and rates of delivery. You shouldn't try these things in imitation of another performer; rather you should experiment to find ways of bringing out the best that's in you.

When performing a newscast, commercial, or interview as a class exercise, don't do takeoffs unless the assignment calls for it. You may amuse yourself and others by doing a parody of your material, but it really affords you no useful practice unless, of course, you intend to make a career of doing spoofs and takeoffs. This warning doesn't rule out humorous commercials or humor-oriented interviews, as long as they're realistically related to your growth as an announcer.

Finally, save your recordings and review them from time to time to measure progress. When you compare performances made four or five months apart, your improvement will be both impressive and encouraging—if you've practiced!

Evaluating Your Performance

Critical self-evaluation is the mark of the true professional in any of the performing arts. Here *critical* doesn't mean *scornful*—it means careful, objective, and exact evaluation. Self-evaluation also requires the development of a mature attitude toward one's performance. A superior performance doesn't make you a superior person, any more than a wretched performance makes you a wretch. Learn to distinguish between yourself as a *person* and your *performance* on any given assignment. Growth and improvement depend on your ability to learn from your mistakes, rather than being disheartened by them.

PRACTICE

➤ Gauging Your Own Performance

Consult a daily news source (newspaper, radio, or television newscast) and write your own version of a local or national story. Prepare a script that will take two to two and one-half minutes to read. Read through your copy as you would if someone else had written it, marking for emphasis, pronunciation, and so on. Read it aloud several times. When you're ready, record your performance. Use the following audio checklist to evaluate all aspects of your performance.

Checklist *Evaluating Audio Performances*

1. Pitch
   Good   Too low   Too high

2. Pitch variety
   Good   Too little   Too much

3. Volume
   Good   Too weak   Too loud

4. Tempo
   Good   Too slow   Too fast

5. Tempo variety
   Good   Too little   Inappropriate variations

6. Vitality
   Good   Too little   Too much

7. Articulation
   Good   Underarticulated   Overarticulated

8. Voice quality
   Good   Nasal   Husky   Thin   Other

9. Sibilance
   Good   Excessive

10. Plosives
    Good   Popping

11. Use of microphone
    Good   Note any problems:
    _____
    _____
    _____

12. Note any mispronounced words: _____
    _____

13. Give performance an overall evaluation: _____
    _____
    _____

14. Note specific things on which to work: _____
    _____
    _____

SPOTLIGHT

Breaking into the Announcing Field

Denny Delk has loved radio as long as he can remember. His mother, when reading bedtime stories, used her voice to add sound effects. As early as age 4, he tried to emulate her. He started playing with a tape recorder when he was 13, varying sounds by speeding up and slowing down his recorded voice and trying out vocalized sound effects. Today, Delk does voice work for commercials, cartoons, and promos and narration for industrials and documentaries.

Delk enjoys voice work more than any other mode of performance. "Radio, as has been said many times, is the theater of the mind," he says. "You can do anything you want to do. You can be anyone you want to be. You can make the imagination of the listener work by the way you treat the microphone, by the things the producer does with you, by the way you react with people—you can't raise an eyebrow; you can't give a sidelong glance—you have to do those things with your voice. And it's fun to be able to play that way."

Originally from Oklahoma, Delk got his start at a small-town radio station. There was a sign on the door that read "dollar a holler," meaning that each commercial message broadcast on the station cost only one dollar. It was a small beginning, but he loved radio. He later moved on to other jobs in broadcasting, all of them related to communication with an audience—camera operator, television director, studio engineer, sound technician for a television station, newspaper reporter, concert promoter, disc jockey, and radio talk-show host—all before becoming a voice-over announcer.

An English major who performed in many stage plays during his college days, Delk has worked in theater everywhere he's lived. He does improvisational comedy with the National Theater of the Deranged. He calls this "lazy man's theater—no need to memorize." Delk is convinced that doing theater helps a voice-over actor become a more complete performer. He urges students to become involved in college or community theater. Even behind-the-scenes work can teach you what communicating with an audience is all about.

Delk offers advice to aspiring announcers:

- How do you market yourself? Your first challenge is to get agents and producers to listen to your audition presentation. Most likely, they're already working with a stable of regulars—outstanding voice-over people, with all types of personalities and ages—and you have to make them want to listen to your performance.

- The packaging of your presentation can create a strong impression. Delk prefers to use standard audio cassette tapes for most purposes. Like most voice-over performers, though, he creates both audiotapes and CDs. Cassettes have the advantage of being easy to edit, inexpensive to produce, and acceptable by agents and station managers. CDs are best for specific purposes, as explained by Delk: "Many of us tailor CDs for various markets (industrial, commercials, cartoons, CD-ROM games, promos, etc.). Some go so far as having one track for technical corporate programs and one for more 'sales-oriented' material, like at trade shows. There may be seven or eight segments to a demo, some as short as a minute or two (commercials) and as long as five or six minutes (industrials and books on tape). I can easily see that you'd wind up with as much as twenty minutes of material."

- Never include your photo for voice-over work. Your appearance has nothing to do with the job you're auditioning for. Casting agents and producers will expect you—or want you—to sound like you look. Don't give them a chance to say, "No, this person doesn't look right for the part." Force them to judge you only by the sound of your voice and your interpretive abilities, which are the only things that are relevant.

- On my audiotapes, I use three separate "packages": one each for straight announcing, cartoon and character voice work, and industrial narration. Creating separate portfolio packages allows you to tailor each one to a distinct style and market.

- After sending an audition presentation, follow with a card and a note that says, "Hope you had a chance to listen." Never call the person, who won't have the time, and you really won't have anything to say. If you ask what was thought about your presentation, you've put that person in an awkward and difficult position.

- Put on your demo as many different things as you can do well. Don't include any voices or attitudes that are marginal or questionable. If you can't determine on your own what things you do well, ask a qualified person, such as your instructor, for help.

- If you create a tape, rather than a CD, it must never be longer than three minutes; two and a half is better. For industrial work or other tapes of voice-over narration, you may do a longer demo and dub it to a CD, as noted earlier.

- You must have an attention-getter at the front. Use your best-sounding effort at the start. If you place it later, the agent may never hear it.

- Don't do complete spots—ten seconds is enough to establish any one thing.

- Show a variety of attitudes (better than accents): soft sell, snooty, seductive, downtrodden, and so on. Don't put them together in a haphazard or random order. Work for variety. Do a soft sell, followed by a hard sell—in other words, break up the pieces. This approach makes each segment more impressive than it would be if it stood alone or if it were surrounded by similar readings.

- Don't ask to have your recording returned. Audiotapes and CDs are inexpensive, and you want your work to be sitting on producers' shelves. If they have your performance at hand when the person they usually use is unavailable, perhaps they'll remember you and listen to it again—and then they may call you.

- Even if a producer likes your performance, you'll still have to audition for a job. Sometimes demos are better than people are, and they want to know if you're as good as your presentation.

- Finally, remember that you won't succeed without the help of many others—agents, writers, producers, directors, sound engineers, advertising agency personnel, secretaries, union officials, and so forth. The profession is a highly rewarding one in which cooperation is eventually as important as talent and in which people have feelings and very long memories.

Chapter 6

Video Performance

Chapter Outline

Audience Rapport, Television

Chapter 5 began with a discussion of rapport as applied to radio announcers; this chapter continues that discussion with a focus on television performers.

To be successful at the highest levels, you must develop a personal quality, an asset that can be examined, worked on, and improved, but can't be bought at any price—*the personality you project to your viewers*. And, aside from voice-overs, including narration, you can't achieve this solely with your voice!

Advertisers look for announcers—especially those who make direct presentations to the camera—who not only deliver messages effectively, but who project a "presence" that invites attention, while conveying believability of the messages they deliver. Sports play-by-play announcers, who are heard but almost never seen during games, have a unique problem; they must gain acceptance and build credibility using only their voices to bring viewers "into the game."

Those seen by their viewers, including the most respected and popular news anchors and reporters, radiate warmth, sincerity, and integrity. News directors and station managers have long recognized the importance of an elusive quality that makes one performer stand out from all others. Its nature has been investigated, and the results of one important study are cited here. Professor Rick Houlberg set out to find the reason why viewers preferred one newscaster over another; after analyzing the results, he had this comment:

> After all the preparation, clothing, hard work, and luck, something more is needed for the on-air broadcaster to be successful. We know what that something is although we haven't been able to fully describe or study it. This something makes us choose one television newscaster over another. . . . This something is a connection made between the on-air performer and the audience.[1]

In his research, Houlberg found that most respondents chose the television newscaster they watched because: "He or she made their problems seem easier"; "They would like to know more about the newscaster off the air"; "The newscaster is almost like their everyday friends"; and "He or she made them feel contented."

Of course, audience rapport is not everything. News anchors and reporters must also have significant professional qualities, including objectivity, reliability, honesty, and appropriate preparation as journalists, but making a positive connection with viewers is vital.

The messages here are clear: After achieving professional competency, and while maintaining the integrity that's expected of news personnel, television performers must project an attractive and friendly personality to the audience. *Attractive* in this sense doesn't refer to physical appearance. Houlberg found that

---

[1] This research was conducted by Rick Houlberg with respondents in Ohio. His complete report is in *Journal of Broadcasting*, Fall, 1984. Despite its age, the findings are not dated—later studies support his results.

neither physical appearance nor gender was significantly important to his respondents. Synonyms for attractive are *appealing, engaging,* and *charming.* A sensitive performer can use these qualities to build audience rapport—a relationship of mutual trust or emotional affinity. It's not likely that every student can be taught these qualities because they come from within. Being aware of them can, however, help you channel your inner feelings of respect for your audience, concern for people, and dedication to your profession into more effective communication. Audience rapport is a state of mind. It relies heavily on your integrity. It's a reflection of who you are and what you care about.

Microphone Consciousness for Video Performers

To be mic conscious is to be always aware that the misuse of a microphone will result in a flawed or failed performance. Several examples of faulty microphone consciousness may be found in Chapter 5, "Audio Performance"; most of these also apply to television performance.

Television makes much use of both wired and wireless lavaliere and clip-on mics, and it's important to recognize the limitations of this convenient and unobtrusive instrument. Lavaliere mics must be used carefully to prevent picking up unwanted noise. A script being thumbed or rattled three inches away from the lavaliere may sound as loud as a voice coming from a foot or more away. Clothing brushing against the surface of the mic will sound like a forest fire. Because the mic is so close to your mouth, you may produce a popping sound as you pronounce *p, t,* or *k* or excessive sibilance with *s* or *sh*. If so, you may benefit from having a windscreen placed over the face of the microphone.[2] Several manufacturers supply open-cell polyurethane foam windscreens that only slightly affect the frequency response while eliminating some of the highs.

Television performers should study the problems with microphone misuse listed in Chapter 5 and consider those that relate specifically to television performance. Here are some of the most common:

- Failing to clip on a lavaliere mic before beginning a performance
- Attaching a lavaliere mic improperly—too far away from the mouth or under clothing that muffles the sound
- Clapping near the lavaliere
- Walking away from the set after a performance without remembering to unclip the mic

---

[2] Popping and excessive sibilance are discussed in Chapter 3, "Voice Analysis and Improvement," and Chapter 4, "Pronunciation and Articulation."

When rehearsing and performing for television, always assume that your microphone is open and that the camera is on. Always assume that profanity and backbiting comments about others will be overheard by someone!

Camera Consciousness

Just as a microphone begins the process of sending your voice to listeners, a camera is the first element in the transmission of your physical image. Camera consciousness begins with an understanding of the needs and limitations of cameras and a recognition of the problems faced by camera operators and those controlling robotic cameras. The discussion that follows covers only those technical aspects that are relevant to you as a performer.

A television camera picks up reflected light in much the same way the human eye does. Like the eye, a digital camera has a lens, an iris (or diaphragm), and a surface on which images are focused. The retina in the eye is like the photosensitive surface in the camera's pickup chips. The lens focuses the picture, the iris opens or closes to control the amount of light entering the system, and the photosensitive surface converts the light patterns into electrical impulses.

Unlike the human eye, the television camera has a zoom feature that allows it to handle anything from a wide shot to an extreme close-up. To the human eye, a person standing ten feet away will always be on a medium shot, so to speak. Humans have the advantage of being able to rapidly move their heads approximately 180 degrees horizontally, focusing on one object at the start and on another at the end of the head movement without any sensation of blurring. A television camera can't do the same.

Keep these elementary facts about cameras in mind as you consider these aspects of television performance.

Hitting Marks

Hitting marks means moving to an exact spot in a studio or in the field marked by a piece of tape or chalk. During preparation for all but the most routine television productions, the director will "block" the movements of performers. **Blocking** is the term used in theater, film, and television for the planning of movements to be executed during the show. When a specific movement is called for, it's important to move exactly as required and to stop at the predetermined position. There are at least three reasons why precision in hitting marks is critical:

1. The amount of light entering a lens defines the depth of field—the extent of the area in front of the camera in which everything is in focus. (Objects closer or farther away will be blurred.) The greater the amount of light entering the lens, the smaller the iris opening and the greater the depth of field. Because zoom lenses have a great deal of glass through which the light must pass, because prompting

devices cut down further on light entering the lens system, and because studio lighting is kept to the lowest possible level for the comfort of performers, the iris is generally quite open, and this setting reduces depth of field considerably. To put it plainly, if you don't hit your marks, you'll likely be out of focus.

2. Another reason for hitting marks is that the camera operator, whether actually behind the camera or in a control room operating robots, is responsible for the composition of the picture. Where you should stand for the best composition will have been determined earlier, and you must follow through to enable the camera operator to do a professional job.

3. A third reason for being meticulous about hitting marks is that studios often feature area lighting, which means that not all parts of the set are illuminated equally. If you miss your mark, you may be literally "in the dark."

Robotic cameras require announcers to be even more careful in hitting marks, because these cameras move to preprogrammed positions, and their lenses are prefocused. Although an operator sitting in a control booth can change the position and focus of each robotic camera, that operator is responsible for the control of three or more cameras, and the complexities of this task make precision in hitting marks extremely important to the technical quality of the show.

On-Camera Movement

Standing. When standing on camera, stand still and avoid rocking from side to side. Weaving or rocking from one foot to the other can be distracting on a long shot and disastrous on a close-up. In a studio, a monitor is placed where you can see whether the camera has you on a wide, medium, or close-up shot, so you'll know if you're moving out of the picture. In the field, however, it's unlikely you'll have a monitor, so you'll have no way of knowing if you're moving out of the frame.

Practice standing with a minimum of movement. To reduce a tendency to rock, stand with your feet slightly apart with one foot turned out to form a 15- to 20-degree angle to the other foot; the turned foot should be four or five inches in front of the other. Standing in this manner should make it all but impossible to rock.

Sitting. You'll find it easier to avoid excessive random movement when seated, but remember that most movements appear exaggerated on television. If you're habitually moving your upper torso and head in rapid or wide-ranging motions, work to reduce such movements—without at the same time seriously lowering your natural energy level. Sideways movement can be very annoying, especially on close-ups, and movement toward and away from the camera can take you in and out of focus. You want to be animated, but restrict head, hands, and shoulder movement to that which would be appropriate in a living room discussion.

Telegraphing Movement. When rising or sitting down, or when moving from one part of the studio (or exterior location) to another, you must move somewhat more slowly than you ordinarily would, and you must telegraph your movement. To **telegraph a movement** is to begin it with a slow and slight motion followed by a pause before following through with the intended movement. Camera operators are trained to follow even fast-moving athletes, but you shouldn't test their skill unnecessarily. And operators of robotic cameras need even more careful preparatory movement. A little thoughtfulness on your part can guarantee that you won't cross them up.

Don't sit down or stand up on camera unless the movement was planned in advance or is signaled by the director. When the camera is on a head shot of a standing performer and the performer suddenly sits, the head drops right out of the picture. When the camera is on a bust shot (upper torso to top of head) of a seated performer who suddenly stands, the result is even worse; the viewer is treated to the infamous crotch shot. If you find you must stand when no such movement was planned, telegraphing is imperative—it will give the director time to zoom out to a wider and safer shot.

Cheating to the Camera. To **cheat to the camera** is to position yourself so as to create the impression that you're talking to another person (as in an interview) while still presenting a favorable appearance on screen. When a performer speaks to a guest or a cohost, viewers want to see the faces of both persons and to believe that the two are speaking to one another rather than to the audience. So, to avoid presenting only their profiles as they speak, interviewer and guest position themselves at about a 25-degree angle from one another—thereby opening up to the camera—while continuing to speak as though they were facing one another directly.

When standing or sitting near another person—as when conducting an interview—position yourself nearer the other person than you ordinarily would. We're all surrounded by an invisible area we consider our own personal space. When talking with others, we usually sit or stand at a comfortable distance. Television, however, is no respecter of this psychological space. The intimacy of television is

Figure 6-1
Kai Pederson shows what happens when he suddenly stands on camera without being cued to do so and without telegraphing his move. We are suddenly given not only an awkward shot but one that also is momentarily out of focus.

best exploited when both interviewer and guest can be seen in a medium shot. Sitting or standing too far from another performer forces the director to settle for close-ups of individuals or wide-angle "two-shots"(two people in the picture). In unrehearsed programs, the director wants to have an acceptable cover shot, a shot that can be used regardless of which person is speaking. The farther apart the performers, the smaller they'll appear on the television screen. So, if the only two-shot available is a long shot, the director is forced to settle for a view that makes viewers feel they're watching from a distance, and intimacy is lost.

Addressing the Camera. When directly addressing the camera (the viewer, actually), look straight into the lens and focus your gaze about a foot behind the glass; that's where your viewer is. When searching for a thought or a word, many of us tend to raise our eyes toward the ceiling as we pause for inspiration. This tendency is distracting and unflattering; if you have such a habit, work to overcome it.

Make certain you don't try to hold a smile on your face while waiting for the director to go to black, to another camera, to a recorded segment, or to a commercial. Try to make small and natural movements while you wait. Don't continue to stare at the camera unless you've been told to do so. If appropriate to the type of performance being given, look down at your script, pick up a pencil and make marks on your script, or, when sitting beside another person—an interviewee or a coanchor—start a conversation. Just remember that the mic may still be on. In Figure 6.2, Diana Hsu demonstrates the look that results when a director stays on a shot too long and the performer attempts to hold a smile. Television performers jokingly refer to this as the **egg-on-face look.**

In a studio production, you can expect to work with from two to four cameras: Three are standard. From time to time you'll change your attention from one camera to another on cue. Unless you're working with robotic cameras, the cuing sequence begins when the floor director points both hands to the **taking camera**

Figure 6-2
Diana Hsu, impatient to get out of the limelight, wears the egg-on-face look as she waits for the director to go to a commercial break.

(the camera that's on, indicated by an illuminated red light called a **tally light**). On a signal from the director through the intercom, the floor director rapidly moves one or both hands to point to the camera to which you're to turn. When you perform as a news anchor, you first notice the cue, glance down at your script, and then raise your head in the direction of the second camera.

When working with robotic cameras, you'll hear your cues through your earpiece.

Don't stare at the camera. Just as staring at a person with whom you're speaking can make that person uncomfortable, staring at the camera lens can have the same effect on viewers. As you speak (read), let your head make small, subtle movements. These should be natural movements motivated by the words you're speaking. Be careful to avoid a machinelike pattern, one in which you automatically nod your head to emphasize every syllable. Make your movements small, motivated by the mood and meaning of what you're saying, and natural to you and your personality.

When addressing the camera, it's important to communicate through pitch patterns (inflection), rate of delivery, and nonverbal movements that match the level of energy appropriate to both medium and message. If you exaggerate any of these factors beyond what's justified, you'll come across as an actor playing a role, as with an overly hyped-up news report, or near-frantic on-camera commercial delivery. Always remember that few news stories, and no commercials at all, are matters of life or death! Believable facial expressions and head, hand, and torso movements can add much to your communicative abilities.

Examine your appearance closely when viewing playbacks. In addition to watching for such obvious problems as poor posture, look at your mouth on a close-up. See if you've developed an unattractive and distracting habit of speaking out of the side of your mouth—speaking with one side of your mouth noticeably lower than the other. If so, practice straightening out your mouth while performing before a mirror; better still, practice while you record performances. A lifelong habit of speaking with a crooked mouth may be difficult to overcome, but correcting it will enhance your chances of having a successful career as a television announcer.

Holding Props

A **prop,** short for *property,* is an object that a performer holds or displays or to which he or she points. Typical props are goods used in demonstration commercials, the food and utensils used in cooking shows, and books displayed by talk-show hosts.

Hold books, products, or other props with a steady hand. Chances are the director will want an extreme close-up of the object, and even a slight movement can take it out of focus or off camera. Position the prop so that the taking camera has a good view of it. Glance at the floor monitor, and then position the prop correctly.

When pointing to an object or a portion of it, move your hand, with the index finger extended, slowly and evenly toward the spot to be highlighted. Hold that hand as steady as possible. Don't make quick motions here and there—the camera can't follow them. Always rely on a monitor to check both your positioning and your hand movements.

Figure 6-3

Floor director Amy Gill uses hand signals to alert anchor Mike Orme to an upcoming camera switch. This allows Mike to alter his eye contact by glancing down at his script and then up to Camera 6.

When holding any object that has a reflective surface, such as the dust cover of a book, check your monitor to make sure you're holding it at a correct angle. Studio lights reflected from any glossy object can totally wash out its details. If the object being held is reflecting light, tilt it forward or backward to correct the problem.

Additionally, few of us can speak fluently while using our hands to demonstrate. When demonstrating a product or a procedure on camera, don't feel compelled to keep up a nonstop narration. Constant chatter, especially when marred by hesitancy and repetitions, isn't good communication. Because television is a visual medium, action alone may sometimes work best. However, because commentary is sometimes helpful or even necessary, you should practice and perfect the skill of simultaneously speaking and demonstrating.

Holding Scripts

Scripts are used in live television primarily by news anchors, usually as a backup to a prompting device. If the prompter fails or the feed falls behind or rushes ahead of your delivery, you can refer to your script. At some stations, however, you won't have a prompter and must work entirely from handheld scripts. (Working with a prompter is discussed in a later section.)

When working with a script, hold it with both hands, above the desk and tilted toward you at a comfortable angle for reading. You should hold the script above desk level for three important reasons: (1) to reduce the degree of up-and-down motion of your head as you look down to the script and then up to the camera; (2) to more easily keep the script in front of you as you look from camera to camera, thereby eliminating diagonal head movements; and (3) to avoid bending your head down to read a script that's flat on the surface of the desk, which restricts the airflow and thereby impairs voice quality.

Using Peripheral Vision

A periphery is a boundary. If you look straight ahead, you'll find that the left and right boundaries of your vision extend in an arc of about 150 degrees. This is the range of your **peripheral vision,** and you should be able to pick up movements, such as hand signals, given to you within this area. Actually, on-air you'll need to use only about a 45-degree arc of your peripheral vision because floor directors will give you signals as near as possible to the camera you're addressing. When receiving signals, don't allow your head or even your eyes to turn toward the signaler. When working with robotic cameras, you'll receive signals over your **IFB (interruptible foldback),** a small earpiece.

Clothing and Makeup

When performing on television, plan your clothing carefully. If your station's system uses chroma-keying, you should avoid wearing any shade of the color used for the mattes (blue or green in most instances). **Chroma-keying** is a process that allows a picture from one camera to be keyed in to a portion of the picture from

Figure 6-4
It's important to use peripheral vision. Reporter Jacqueline Gonzalez shows what happens when a performer on a close-up tries to continue facing the camera while, with only her eyes, she glances away for a cue.

another camera. If blue is the color of the chroma-key backdrops (mattes) and you were to wear a blue shirt or blouse, the second picture would appear in the area of your blue clothing whenever a chroma-key matte was used.

Avoid, too, any article of clothing that has small checks or narrow stripes. Television cameras can't handle fine, high-contrast patterns, and a wavy, shimmering look, called the **moiré effect** (pronounced *mwah-RAY*), results. Also avoid black-and-white clothing. Pastel colors are best for nearly all broadcast purposes and are complimentary to people of all skin shades. Performers with extremely dark faces should wear clothing somewhat darker than that worn by people with light skin tones. The principle to follow is to avoid excessive contrast between your face and your clothing and to avoid clothing of the same shade and color as your skin.

Jewelry can cause video problems, as can sequins. Studio lights reflected directly into the camera lens cause **flaring**—light reflected from a highly polished object causing signal overload, which results in a flash on the television screen. This effect may be used to assert the glamour of a particular guest, but it's very distracting if created regularly by a program host.

If your vision needs correction, contact lenses will usually give you your best on-camera appearance. If you prefer to wear glasses, have the lenses treated with an antiglare coating. The frames you choose are an important aspect of your appearance, so look for frames that are flattering and suit your on-air personality. Generally speaking, frames should not be so unusual as to call attention to themselves. Metal eyeglass frames may cause flaring, so choose plastic frames.

Makeup for television performers is usually quite simple and quickly applied. Makeup can help reduce skin shine, eliminate "five o'clock shadow," improve skin color, and hide minor blemishes. It's seldom intended to drastically change the appearance of a television performer, because close-ups too clearly reveal attempts to change basic facial features. If your complexion is sallow, be careful to cover your entire face, neck, and ears with makeup, because the contrast between the near-white of uncovered skin and almost any color of makeup is noticeable. If your complexion is quite dark, you won't have the same problem of contrast, but you should experiment with a variety of shades of makeup, including eyeliner and, for women, blush and lipstick. Dark skin should be toned down to avoid unflattering highlights; find a pancake hue that works well with the bright lights and the technical requirements of television. Some men, even when freshly shaven, show a dark cast in the beard and mustache area. Although pancake makeup helps cover five-o'clock shadow, a special beard stick eliminates the problem in nearly all cases.

Always have powder or pancake makeup near you. Some sets are brightly lit, and the heat from lighting instruments may cause you to perspire. Check frequently to make sure you're not perspiring; if you are, apply powder when you're off camera.[3]

Cue Cards

Cue cards are used at most television stations for short announcements made by on-air performers; lists of items to be mentioned, such as the names and professions of program guests; or to supply some bit of information to the performer—a telephone number or a reminder to mention an upcoming segment of the show. For lengthy messages, nearly all television stations use electronic prompters.

Working with Prompters

Most **prompters** are entirely electronic; scripts are typed on a computer, stored, and transmitted to a display terminal. Older prompters combine mechanical and electronic components. With both systems, the image appears on a monitor attached to each television camera; a mirror reflects this image onto a sheet of glass mounted at a 45-degree angle in front of the camera lens. The performer sees the script while looking directly at the lens. The speed of the moving script is regulated to match the reading speed of the performer. **Hard copy**—a script printed on sheets of 8 ½-by-11-inch paper—is used by producers, directors, news anchors, and others. The script is written on a computer and duplicated in the number of copies required for production.

Prompters are used extensively on television newscasts. On talk, interview, game, variety, and other programs that are predominantly ad-libbed, prompters are used only for short messages that must be delivered verbatim (word for word) and, in some operations, to pass on information such as the nature of an upcoming program segment.

When delivering a television commercial or commentary, you'll seldom have a script in your hands or on a desk in front of you. Nearly all such performances are recorded and can be redone if the prompter malfunctions. During a live newscast, on the other hand, you must have a complete script to turn to in case the prompter ceases to work or gets out of phase with your reading.

---

[3] Herbert Zettl's *Television Production Handbook,* 10th edition, 2009, includes an extensive treatment of television makeup.

Figure 6-5

Jennifer Stanonis reads from a prompter as she delivers the news. In front of her are monitors showing the weather set and the prompter from which she reads the script.
Courtesy of Jennifer Stanonis and KCWY, Casper, Wyoming.

Instructions and Cues

Nearly all television performers work as members of teams and must develop harmonious relationships and efficient means of communicating; it's essential that you coordinate your efforts with those of others.

Television performers working with robotic cameras receive instructions and cues from directors over an IFB (interruptible foldback), a small speaker that fits in a performer's ear. In stations where cameras are manually operated, floor directors use both oral and visual means of communicating. Oral instructions are preferred whenever possible, as during a commercial break.

Television commercials, because they're nearly always rehearsed and recorded for broadcast, focus on matters of interpretation and timing, rather than on the fast changes that may arise during live broadcasts, as when sudden changes of plan, such as dropping a news story, arise. Regardless of the type of production and who issues the instructions, it's your responsibility to carry them out promptly and effectively.

Sound Bytes

Scripts of complete television dramas, both serious and comic, may be found on the Internet. One source, Drew's Script-o-Rama, may be found by typing its title into a search engine and following the instructions.

Commercial scripts may be found on The Television Transcript Project. Note: Most of these spots have the product name changed, so you may want to enter a real product name before printing. Most important, you must not use these spots for any on-air performance, because they are copyright protected. The URL is: www.geocities.com/tvtranscripts/.

Achieving Good Working Relationships

Several considerations are involved in developing good working relationships. For example, you may find yourself disagreeing with a director on interpretation of lines and want to express your point of view. Sounds reasonable, but there are acceptable and unacceptable ways of doing this. To openly and directly question a director's instructions is to defy established authority and challenge the director's competence. Needless to say, unless you're in such demand that you can get away with any degree of rudeness, you may soon be without a job! At the same time, as an announcer you're not expected to act like a mindless automaton. Ample opportunity exists to discuss your ideas and concepts with producers or directors, but you must choose the right time and adopt an appropriate and nonthreatening manner.

When rehearsing or doing a number of takes of a performance under the coaching of a producer or a director (for example, when recording the narrative for a television documentary or doing voice-over commercials), do your best to implement instructions. If your director welcomes it, you may discuss alternative ways to deliver lines, but always remember that the producer's word is final. One effective way to express your opinion is to say, "What if I tried it this way?" This approach is tactful and nonthreatening and will most likely be productive.

During rehearsals, avoid explaining why you did something this or that way or why you made a mistake. No one is interested, and alibis and explanations only delay the project. Always remain alert for cues and instructions. Sometimes you'll wait an eternity for a problem, usually a technical one, to be ironed out. This is no time for daydreaming and certainly no time to leave your position. When the problem is corrected, you'll be needed—at once.

Always treat every member of the production team with respect. No one is unimportant, and your success—and that of the production—depends on the degree of commitment and the quality of performance of every member.

Hand Signals

Hand signals were developed in the early days of radio for communication from directors to performers, separated by the control room's double-glass panes. Signals were also used in-studio to give cues when they were on the air. When television

Figure 6-6
Floor director Shahim Ali gives the "attention" signal, which nearly always is followed by the "standby" signal.

came along, it picked up those signals that were appropriate to it. Today, with most radio announcers working without directors or engineers and television moving to robotic cameras, hand signals are used less and less. However, until they disappear, you should learn the signals you're most likely to encounter in both media because, when they're needed, it's imperative that you know how to send and interpret them. Most of the signals that follow are standard throughout the industry, but be prepared for variations.

- The *attention signal,* a simple waving of the hand, usually precedes the standby signal. It's given by the television floor director, sometimes called the stage manager.

- The *standby signal* is made by holding the hand slightly above the head, palm toward the announcer. The standby signal is given at any time when the announcer can't judge the precise moment at which to pick up a cue.

- The *cue signal* is made by rapidly lowering the hand from the standby position, with the index finger extended and pointing directly at the person being cued. The cue signal nearly always follows the standby signal; neither signal is normally given alone. At some television stations, the cue signal is thrown toward the camera that is going on the air.

- The *attention, stand-by,* and *cue* signals are mainly used in television newscasts and talk shows. When given at the start of the show, or when returning from a commercial break or recorded package, the attention signal is given near the lens of the camera to be called up; after the standby signal is given, the cue is thrown and the announcer begins addressing the indicated camera.

- The *switch-camera signal* tells you to look from the taking camera to the camera to which you will be waved. The floor director will progress from the standby signal to the switch-camera signal by moving one or both hands from the first to the second camera. (See Figures 6.3a–6.3f.)

- The *break signal,* used chiefly on interview and talk programs, tells you to wrap up the present segment for a commercial break. The signal is made by holding the hands as though they were grasping a brick or a stick of wood and then making a breaking motion.

- The *introduce-report* signal consists of a thumbs-up sign given to a news anchor to indicate that a planned report from the field is ready to go on the air. The *drop-report signal* is a thumbs-down sign meaning that the report is not to be introduced. Reports may be dropped because of technical difficulties or because of time pressures.

It's natural to want to acknowledge that you've received and understood a hand signal. Experienced performers working with professional crews don't send back signals indicating "message received, will comply." At some television stations, however, and especially when new, unrehearsed, or unusually complex programs are being produced, performers are asked to acknowledge hand signals. In some instances this acknowledgment is conveyed by an unobtrusive hand or finger movement; in others it may involve a larger gesture. Follow the practice preferred by the director or producer of the show.

- The *cut signal* is made by drawing the index finger across the throat. This signals an emergency; on receiving it, stop speaking at once. After stopping your performance, wait for oral or visual signals before beginning again.

- The *slowdown,* or *stretch signal,* is given by a television floor director. It's made by pulling the hands apart, as though stretching a large rubber band. Because to slow down and to stretch mean somewhat different things, you must rely on the context in which the signal is given to know how to interpret it. When you're reading from a script, the signal means to slow the pace of your delivery; when you're ad-libbing, it means to stretch (in other words, to keep talking until a further signal is given).

- The *speed-up signal* is given by holding a hand before the body, index finger extended, and then rotating the hand. On receiving this signal, you should increase the pace of your delivery. The signal is imprecise; it doesn't tell you how rapidly you should speak, or for how long. Later directions or signals will give you this information. Be careful not to confuse this signal with a wrap-up sign.

- The *wrap-up signal* is made by holding both hands in front of the torso and then rotating them about eight inches apart so that first one hand and then the other is on top. On receiving this signal, you should bring the program or the segment to a close as soon as possible in a smooth and natural way.

As a program nears its conclusion or as a segment of a program nears a station break, it's important for you to know the exact number of minutes or seconds remaining. Time signals are no longer used in radio or recording studios but are very important in television. They are as follows:

- *Three-minute signal:* three fingers held up and waved slowly
- *Two-minute signal:* two fingers held up and waved slowly
- *One-minute signal:* the index finger held up and waved slowly
- *Thirty-second signal:* the right and left arms crossed, or the index finger of one hand crossed with the index finger of the other
- *Fifteen-second signal:* a clenched fist held upright and near the head
- *Ten-to-zero signal:* all fingers on both hands held up and then lowered one at a time as the seconds are counted down

Be prepared for local variations of these signals.

Performance Skills

Preparing for a Performance

On entering the television studio for a rehearsal or performance, make note of the placement of microphones and cameras. Note where you'll hold or place your script (if any). Check out the lighting and determine exactly where you'll stand or sit and how far you may be able to move in each direction without moving into shadows. If appropriate, consult the director or floor manager to make sure you know which camera will be called up to open the scene and ask about any critical or unusual camera shots.

If you're to hold or demonstrate an object, decide exactly where and how you'll hold it and to which camera you'll present it.

Finally, to repeat a caution from the chapter on audio performance, remind yourself to avoid speaking too rapidly and, if you make an error, to correct it as naturally and unobtrusively as possible and then continue. If you stumble, move on and put the error behind you—dwelling on it will divide your attention and make further stumbles almost inevitable. Above all, don't stop your performance and ask if you may begin again unless such a possibility has been agreed to in advance. Even if your performance will never actually leave the classroom or studio, always adopt the attitude that it's going out live over the airwaves.

Assuming you'll have a full production team in the studio, you'll receive signals from a floor manager or floor director. Among other signals, in a newscast or an interview-talk show, you'll often be given a countdown as you introduce recorded stories. The floor director will first hold up the correct number of fingers and then, on instructions from the director, lower the fingers one at a time. When the countdown is completed, the director has gone to the recorded insert.

At other times during a program, you may be given a hand signal meaning you have twenty or thirty seconds to wrap up, or that there are three minutes, then two minutes, then one minute left in the program or a segment of it. It's important that you develop a sense of how long these periods of time are. Smooth transitions and unhurried endings require accurate timing. To develop this sense, practice extensively with a stopwatch. Without looking at the watch, start it and then stop it when you think a given number of seconds have passed. At first, you'll typically think that a minute has passed when the actual elapsed time is closer to thirty or forty seconds. With practice, you should become quite accurate at estimating elapsed times. Then, practice speaking and reading lead-ins and program closings, pacing your words to match a predetermined number of seconds.

Other Tips for Improving Your Performance

Lacking a studio setting, you can practice television delivery with consumer equipment. A camcorder is the most useful way of practicing on-camera delivery; if you shop around, you should be able to buy a camera for $100 or less. A camera plus a tripod will, in most cases, give you the basics for television practice. Adequate audio may be a problem unless you acquire a more expensive camera—inexpensive cameras lack a **mic input** for an external mic.

There's no perfect substitute for performing before a camera with later playbacks for critical evaluations, so see if you can volunteer as talent on the projects of others. You may also obtain on-camera experience at a local cable station.

Evaluating Your Video Performances

As with audio performances, you should critically review your television performances to identify areas to work on and to assess improvements. The Checklist that follows covers physical aspects of television performance. You should also use the Checklist for audio performance found at the end of Chapter 5.

Checklist *Evaluating Television Performances*

1. *Eye contact*
   Good_____   Needs work_____
2. *Use of peripheral vision*
   Good_____   Needs work_____
3. *Posture*
   Good_____   Needs work_____
4. *Standing on camera*
   Steady_____   Rocking_____
5. *Moving on camera*
   Telegraphed movement?_____
   Moved smoothly?_____
   Sat correctly?_____

6. Were transitions smooth when switching cameras?_____

7. Were props held correctly for cameras?_____

8. Was pointing clear and even?_____

9. Was eye contact with camera maintained while using cue cards?_____

10. Were cues correctly responded to?_____

11. Was dress appropriate?_____

12. Facial animation

     Appropriate?_____   Too much?_____   Too little?_____

_____

_____

13. Note specific areas on which to work: _____

_____

_____

14. Note areas that showed improvement: _____

_____

_____

SPOTLIGHT

Feature Reporting as Storytelling

Television reporters engage in a great range of specializations; one of these is feature reporting. **Feature reporters** cover soft news events that engage audiences with stories that move, entertain, amuse, and/or illuminate. After receiving their assignment, they go to the scene of their story, almost always with a camera operator, a partner who makes important contributions to the completed package.

One outstanding feature reporter is Wayne Freedman. This chapter's Spotlight focuses on him; reveals how he regards himself and his work; follows him through a day in his life as a writer, producer, and performer; and includes his advice to those who want to excel in this demanding specialization.

"Most good stories boil down to five key elements . . . beginnings, middles, endings, main characters, and simple truths." With this sparse description, KGO-TV feature reporter Wayne Freedman summarizes his approach to the creation of stories that have earned him forty Emmys, nine awards from the Associated Press, six from the United Press, and nine from the Radio and Television News Directors Association.

Freedman considers himself, first, a writer and storyteller. He began his career as a photographer in Louisville, Kentucky, but switched to reporting because "it's the best way to tell stories." As to his record number of awards, he comments: "I guess it says I'm consistent.

"Above all, I think a newscast needs someone to remind viewers that, even with all the lunacy in this world, normal people still exist. I look for the untold story, and the person—a main character—and that person's simple truth." As a feature reporter, Wayne ignores the sensational story because his vision of reporting doesn't lend itself to hard, breaking news. Hard news is impersonal; a feature report should be the opposite.

A few of the hundreds of stories told by Wayne indicate what he looks for as a storyteller: an entertainer facing the closure of his nightclub; a child entrepreneur who operates a lemonade stand; a man who specializes in photographing cemetery art; and two women who worked for years, five feet apart, one inside and one outside separated by a window, who were strangers to one another. Simple stories. Simple truths.

Skill in revealing the inner person sets Freedman apart from most television reporters. He offers this advice: "You want to get ahead in television news? Then remember that, day to day, this is a business of little stories. Learn to do those well, and the big ones will fall into place because you've learned how to tap into concerns and values, not only of the people whose stories you tell, but also of those who are moved by them. Why do so many reporters make pieces so complicated? This should be an *emotional medium*. The path to the head runs through the gut." He adds, "You'll serve a piece better by staying out of the story's way."

Wayne believes that you shouldn't invent the story but instead try to discover it from the inside. You'll inevitably be *in* the story, but it's your responsibility to *tell* the story without *becoming* the story. "I want to be thought of as a good writer and storyteller. I know I'm different. I try to respect the viewers and let the person in the story be the star of that story. Many feature reporters spend too much time trying to feature themselves, writing the proverbial elephant. I think the most important difference would be that beneath the surface, even the most simple story contains layers and subtleties. A good feature story is often about something other than the main subject. If I do my job exceptionally well, viewers may not remember me, but they'll remember the story—not for minutes or days, but for years."

To illustrate this point, one of Wayne's stories on the 11:00 p.m. news was about a three-legged dog. The next day, a great number of calls came to the station from people offering help. For Wayne, the dog was the surface story; the more important story lay beneath this. "People pass others daily who need help, and turn away, yet they'll rush to the aid of an animal in distress." Wayne then raised the question, "Why do we animalize humans and humanize animals?" Again, a simple story, a simple truth—something for viewers to remember the following day and, perhaps, ponder; maybe even act on.

Asked if his intimate stories are tough sells to news directors, Freedman replies: "Generally, they trust that if I see a story, I'll deliver a story. Call it the 'inside strike' syndrome. I've hit enough round-trippers by now that they figure I know the zone. By my standard, a story that humanizes a person is often a good, solid triple; maybe even an inside-the-park job. Very good for a five-hour turn. And offbeat stories are a lot like baseball. Don't think. Trust your instincts, your reactions, and swing."

A Day in the Life . . .

Two factors are key to understanding the unique success of Wayne Freedman. The first is his thorough preparation for, and meticulous execution of, each story. It isn't unusual for him to spend nine hours on a report that runs under five minutes.

The second is his instinct for selecting people who lend themselves to being humanized through their stories. His objective is to give viewers a reason to care. He says, "I try to do that with everything."

The following sketch provides a glimpse of the effort that goes into his making of a feature report.

The Scene: The Newsroom of KGO-TV, an ABC Affiliate[4]

2:00 p.m. Wayne and James Sudweeks, Wayne's long time video editor, spend an hour and a half editing material shot a week earlier. A once-popular nightclub is closing after sixty-three years. The recordings were made in advance to be run on the night of the closing. The digital tape had been logged by Wayne, and the report is now edited into a package for the 6:00 p.m. news.

3:30 p.m. Sitting at his desk, Wayne prepares a brief script. It's to be his live introduction to the report, delivered by him from the sidewalk before the club, and run on the 6:00 p.m. newscast.

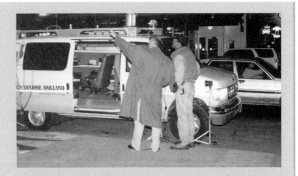

5:00 p.m. With an hour available before he's cut into the early news, Wayne and John go backstage to shoot scenes of the nightclub performers arriving, getting into their costumes, and applying their makeup. Brief comments from the performers on closing night are recorded.

6:00 p.m. All is set for the live introduction. One more rehearsal, and it's time for the stand-up.

4:00 p.m. Wayne goes to the nightclub, where camera operator John Griffen has parked the remote truck. John has set up lights and a tripod and has spent time looking for interesting backgrounds. After arriving, Wayne decides on the shot sequence and his on-camera movements and then rehearses his introduction. A field monitor is placed atop the remote truck, so later Wayne will be able to watch the 6:00 p.m. news. Audio levels are set.

6:15 p.m. The introduction is delivered, and the report is on the air. At the close of the package, Wayne tosses back to the station with "This is Wayne Freedman, reporting live." Wayne returns to the station and logs the recordings just made at the club for later editing.

7:30 p.m. Back at the club, hundreds of people are lined up at the ticket booth. Wayne interviews a few of them and then conducts a lengthy

---

[4] All photos courtesy of Wayne Freedman, John L. Griffen, James Sudweeks, and KGO-TV.

conversation with one of the nightclub performers he's chosen to carry the essence of the story. The conversation isn't recorded; its purpose is to cement a relationship with the performer, to develop two-way empathy before the on-camera interview. Wayne doesn't reveal the questions he'll ask later during the interview. He wants spontaneity. When he's satisfied that he's found the right person to carry the story, he interviews the person on camera.

8:30 p.m. Back at the station, Wayne writes a script that now ties together all of the recorded elements of the piece. He enters a small announce booth and records voice-over narration. Wayne then moves to an editing booth and works with video editor James Sudweeks to edit the entire piece into its final form. It's then duplicated and fed into a computer.

11:15 p.m. Back in front of the nightclub, Wayne introduces the recorded report and, when it ends, makes his closing comments live. He then tosses back to the news anchors. He and John Griffen strike and stow equipment, and both enter the van for the return to the station. Wayne's workday is over.

Freedman joined KGO in 1991 after moving from CBS News, where he traveled throughout America as a feature correspondent for CBS. In his twenty years of reporting, he's done general assignments, politics, and investigative reports. He began his television career in Louisville, Kentucky; took a reporting job in Dallas, Texas; and then moved to San Francisco's KRON in 1981. Wayne's syndicated program *California Offbeat* is heard on Britain's Channel Four. Respected for his lectures on the craft of television newswriting and reporting,

Wayne's taught at stations in most of the United States, in parts of Canada, and in Europe.

Becoming a television writer and performer came naturally to Wayne. He grew up in and around television. His father, Mike, pioneered the first live handheld camera for ABC in the late 1950s and 1960s as "the first guy to walk a football sideline, to go underwater, to walk a convention floor, live." Wayne's mother was a ballerina who, among other performances, danced the part of Laurie in the original cast of *Oklahoma*.

Wayne earned his bachelor's degree in political science from the University of California–Los Angeles and graduated from the University of Missouri with a master's degree in journalism.

Chapter 7

Commercials and Public-Service Announcements

Chapter Outline

In the Beginning . . .

Radio began its life in controversy, and commercialism was the core of the dispute. Because of radio's inherent power, it was immediately recognized as a unique phenomenon, a resource that could be used for the betterment—or the opposite—of the American public.

Unlike telegraph and telephone systems that were privately built and owned, radio broadcasters owned nothing but their transmitters, so laws protecting the ownership of physical property didn't apply. Because of the societal importance of the medium and its uniqueness, the government concluded that it had both the right and the obligation to control its output.

Early on, the question of who would pay the cost of creating programs arose. Some favored commercial sponsorship, while others offered solutions that would keep radio commercial free. David Sarnoff, vice-president of RCA, believed that companies making and selling radios should foot the bill; he later decided that government support, like that given to cultural institutions, was the answer. Just about every idea that would avoid commercialization was floated.

Herbert Hoover, then secretary of commerce, and later thirty-first president of the United States, called a conference in 1924 to examine possible uses of this new medium. In his address to the conference, he made these remarks:

> We may well be proud of this wonderful development, but in our self-congratulation let us not forget that the value of this great system does not lie primarily in its extent or even in its efficiency. Its worth depends on the use that is made of it. . . . For the first time in history we have available to us the ability to communicate simultaneously with millions of our fellow men, to furnish entertainment, instruction, widening vision of national problems, and national events. An obligation rests upon us to see that it is devoted to real service . . . for it is only by this that the mission of this latest blessing of science to humanity may be rightfully fulfilled.[1]

He later added,

> I believe that the quickest way to kill broadcasting would be to use it for direct advertising. The reader of the newspaper has an option whether he will read an ad or not, but if a speech by the president is to be used as the meat in a sandwich of two patent medicine advertisements there will be no radio left.

As we all know, a compromise was reached: Commercial interests eventually won their case, but the government insisted on controls against excessive abuse of their right to use the airwaves. Controls began under the Federal Radio Commission and were later transferred to the Federal Communications Commission

---

[1] Recommendations for Regulation of Radio, adopted by the Third National Radio Conference called by Herbert Hoover, Secretary of Commerce, October 6–10, 1924. Washington, D.C.; U.S. Government Printing Office, 1924.

(FCC). When television came along, it slid nicely into the same mixed arrangement of controlled commercialism.

Today advertising is the lifeblood of American commercial broadcasting. Advertising supports nearly 14,000 American radio and more than 2,000 television stations; it's also the major financial support for most cable channels other than those designated as "premium."[2] Commercial stations offer hundreds of hours of information and entertainment daily. Although commercials are often maligned, they sometimes are amusing, frequently provide useful information, help fuel our economy, and offer work for writers, producers, directors, audio engineers, sales personnel—and *announcers.*

Often, commercials surprise us with their creative use of new technologies. Some commercials are so creative and engaging that DVDs of television commercials are bought and enjoyed by thousands. Superbowl Sunday and the annual CLIO Award broadcasts are eagerly anticipated by huge television audiences.

Announcers as Actors

All announcers are *performers,* but not all are *actors.* Many talk-show hosts, sports play-by-play announcers, news anchors, and others deliver commercials, station promos, and public-service announcements as part of their jobs, but their scripts are unaccompanied by music or sound effects and read without "dramatization." Reading such unembellished scripts demands convincing use of the voice and effective interpretation, but not acting ability. In other words, there's neither a need nor an intention that the announcer project a "character."[3]

In contrast, some radio and nearly all television commercials require elaborate effects, synchronized in postproduction with sound effects, music, and voice-over messages. They're assigned to experienced voice-over actors, sometimes after several auditions; carefully rehearsed; and ready for distribution only when they've achieved maximum effectiveness.

Freelance announcers are employed for specific projects through their agents and are unaffiliated with stations or networks. Some devote themselves exclusively to the making of commercials and station promos, but most also work in documentary narration, dubbing of films, and other voice work that calls for their special acting talent. Freelance performers prefer to be called "voice actors," and this term provides an important insight into what makes for success in this highly competitive field.

Here's a commercial that calls for an interpretation showing several changes in a brief period of time: type and degree of emotion, varying rate of delivery, high and low volume, use of pitch (inflection) to highlight the most important points, and, most importantly, a really convincing performance.

---

[2] *Broadcasting & Cable Yearbook* is an accepted source for unbiased media information.

[3] Brief single-voice scripts may be found in Appendix A, "Scripts to Develop Performance Skills."

Goodby, Silverstein & Partners[4]
Adobe Photoshop Album
"Adam/Rev. 1": 60 ADBR-4606
:60 Radio
As produced—4/13/04

ANNCR: It's a common tragedy—photos trapped in computers because no one can get them out. These are their stories.

PHOTO: My name's Adam. I'm a photo stuck in Chad's computer—with a bunch of other camping photos he took last year. Early on he tried to e-mail me outta here. But my file size was too big. Can you try again, Chad? There's wild animals in here, and they're stalkin' me. You know how many times I've played dead? They're catchin' on. Unless I weave myself a coat outta tree bark, I'm gonna freeze. I just wanna get out.

ANNCR: Perhaps it's time to set your photos free with Adobe Photoshop Album. It's the all-in-one software for beginner photographers. So now you can fix, print, or share with the click of a button. Adobe Photoshop Album. Free your photos. Ten dollar instant rebate available at participating Best Buy, Staples, and CompUSA stores.

$49.99 MSRP. Prices may vary. Good until May 29, 2004. Void where prohibited. While supplies last.

Denny Delk, a well-known voice actor, believes that stage acting is extremely important for a voice-over actor to become a more complete performer. He's worked in theater everywhere he's lived and recommends that students become involved in college or community theater.[5] He advises students to enroll in drama classes as the best means of getting the acting experience needed to become a competent voice-over actor.

---

[4] © 2004 Adobe. All rights reserved.

[5] See the Chapter 5 Spotlight.

Stage and screen actors spend weeks studying their scripts. To be effective, they must "get inside the character"; in other words, they must identify with the person they're to portray and work to adapt their own personality to meet the author's vision of a fictitious being. Writers establish several features: gender, age, marital status, ethnicity (if relevant), disposition (outgoing, shy), style of speaking, and so forth. The art of the voice-over actor can be summed up in a few words: *to become so identified with an agent that all aspects of decision making, speech habits, speed of thought and manner of voicing ideas, likes and dislikes, and much, much more, combine to make that agent believable.*[6]

So, what's the relevance of this to you as a commercial voice actor whose "part" may begin and end in thirty or fewer seconds? To be truly effective in delivering commercial messages, you must learn to approximate in less than a day—at times, less than an hour—the process followed by actors who spend weeks developing their characterizations. This assumes, of course, that you receive your script prior to the recording session, which is not uncommon for voice-over artists hired through agents.

Many commercials fall back on *stereotypes* because their brevity invites this easy means of establishing the character of an agent within a few seconds. We recognize the frantic housewife, the wimp, the bullying boss, the tough guy, and many other types almost immediately—on radio through the sound and vocabulary of the speaker or on television by a combination of physical features and dialogue. This is unlikely to change, even though many of the most offensive stereotypes have been dropped from commercials. The challenge for a voice actor is to individualize agents whose very definition defies individuality. Read and reread the advice given by Samantha Paris, in the Spotlight for this chapter, because she provides questions to ask and answer before settling on your interpretation.

For more detailed help in analyzing scripts, you may turn to books devoted to voice-over performance, a few of which you'll find listed on the Internet. But, before ordering any of these, look for user comments. Some books, including a few written by experienced professionals, are shallow and devoted more to self-promotion than to useful information. These include those that simply offer "how-to" information, which has some value but will not help you dig deeper into the process of individualizing those you're hired to portray.

Analyzing Commercial Copy

When receiving a fresh script to interpret, begin with a careful analysis that begins by determining its specific objective. This, if the script is well composed, should be easy to decide. Examples of determining objectives are given in Chapter 2, under

---

[6] *Agent* is used to identify a figure in a play. The term *character* is often used, as in "I play this strange character," but it is more appropriate to say, "The agent I play exhibits strange characteristics."

the headings, "Identifying the General Meaning" and "Stating the Specific Purpose." That chapter also goes into some detail on other aspects of analyzing copy and should be reviewed from time to time. One aspect, structure, is revisited here.

Structure: The Rule of Three

Most outstanding commercials are both subtle and complex. Chapter 2 goes into detail about analyzing structure; this discussion adds one more consideration—the **rule of three.** This long-recognized principle says that the sharpness and punch of one's comments are diluted by going beyond three words or phrases in a given sequence. To demonstrate this rule, two commercials are analyzed, one for radio, the other for television.

This Schweppes commercial has a Monty Python quality, and you should enjoy it as an exercise in mock disdain. Be sure to avoid a Cockney dialect—it calls for your best BBC accent.

AGENCY:	Ammirati & Puris, Inc.
CLIENT:	Schweppes
LENGTH:	60 seconds
ANNCR:	(*British accent*) I have before me a bottle of Schweppes Bitter Lemon. The soft drink loved by half of England. We British love the way it looks: a fine, sophisticated mist, with morsels of crushed whole lemon. We love the way it sounds: (*bottle opens*) a particularly masterful rendering of Schweppes cheeky little bubbles. And we especially love the way it tastes: (*pours*) refreshingly brisk, cultivatedly crisp, and thoroughly Schweppervescent. It's no wonder that Bitter Lemon is adored by half of England. Now, what about the other half, you might ask? The half that doesn't adore Bitter Lemon? Well, let me assure you, they're all whining children, grubby little urchins whose opinion is completely and totally insignificant. They are youthful upstarts and, as such, absolutely incapable of appreciating anything as forthrightly crisp as Bitter Lemon. The

> frightfully grown-up soft drink from Schweppes.
> The Great British Bubbly.

The first 60 percent of this commercial is to be read in a precise, dignified, and restrained manner. Then, beginning with "Now, what about the other half," you must begin to build in emotion, intensity, volume, and rate of delivery. As you reach the end of the third-to-last sentence, begin decelerating on "as forthrightly crisp as Bitter Lemon." The last two sentences should see you returning to the dignified mood with which you began.

Note how this copy applies the rule of three. The first group is

1. "We British love the way it looks."
2. "We love the way it sounds."
3. "We especially love the way it tastes."

Near the middle is this sequence of three:

1. "refreshingly brisk"
2. "cultivatedly crisp"
3. "thoroughly Schweppervescent"

Then, finally, the children are

1. "whining children"
2. "grubby little urchins"
3. "youthful upstarts"

Dialogue on television commercials often follows the rule of three, but because the visual element usually overshadows the words to be spoken, the principle isn't as obvious as in radio scripts. The following television commercial for DuPont— one of the most moving commercials ever produced—does show use of the rule of three.[7] (Note: VO is the abbreviation for *voice-over.*)

---

[7] Bernice Kanner, in her book *The 100 Best TV Commercials . . . And Why They Worked,* selected this spot as one of her favorites and added this comment: "Demby, intended as a short-term corporate ID, became a corporate image spot and ran for two years. It attracted the attention and interest of key business prospects while changing people's perceptions about DuPont."

AGENCY: BBDO
SPONSOR: DuPont
TITLE: Seattle Foot

VIDEO	AUDIO
A young man limps to an urban schoolyard where a basketball game is in progress.	**ANNCR:** (*VO*) When Bill Demby was in Vietnam he used to dream of coming home and playing a little basketball with the guys. That dream all but died when he lost two legs to a Vietcong rocket.
Demby arrives at the schoolyard where friends greet him. As he sits on a bench to remove his sweatpants, the camera pans to a teammate glancing sideways at his legs: prosthetic limbs.	**ANNCR:** (*VO*) But then a group of researchers discovered that a remarkable plastic from Du-Pont could help make artificial limbs that were more resilient, more flexible, more like life itself.
Demby goes for a shot, falls, and softly groans. But he refuses help and pulls himself up as if he had legs of flesh and bone.	**ANNCR:** (*VO*) Thanks to these efforts, Bill Demby is back. And some say he hasn't lost his step. At DuPont, we make the things that make a difference.
	FRIEND: Hey Bill, you've been practicing.

SUPER: DuPont, better things for better living.

ANNCR: (*VO*) Better things for better living.

The first group of three is "more resilient, more flexible, more like life itself." The second group follows:

"Thanks to these efforts Bill Demby is back."

"And some say he hasn't lost his step."

"At DuPont, we make the things that make a difference."

And had DuPont retained the slogan it used for many years, the tag line would also have reflected the rule of three: "Better things, for better living, through chemistry." When analyzing copy, always look for structure as revealed by the parts.

Recording a Commercial in a Studio

Radio Spots

As a voice-over announcer, you're referred by your agent to an advertising agency. Unless the agency has its own studio, a commercial recording studio is rented, along with the services of an audio engineer. Usually your script will be faxed or emailed as an attachment, so you'll have time to study it. At the studio, a producer or sometimes the writer will discuss the spot in general terms—the overall mood, the characterization expected of you, and so forth. You'll have a few minutes to further study, analyze, and mark your copy. Be sure to bring pencils and erasers.

Despite the analyzing and marking you may have done before the recording session, be prepared to make changes during the ten, twenty, or more "takes" that are necessary before the producer is satisfied. A typical recording setup for a radio commercial requires from three to five persons: one or two announcers, an agency producer, an audio engineer, and, sometimes, the writer of the commercial. Music is recorded in advance and added by the engineer.

After each take, the producer or writer instructs you to change words, phrases or entire sentences to eliminate awkward phrases, to delete or alter sentences with too many sibilant sounds (i.e., "The Silver Store serves several cities in Sandberg County . . ."), to change the emphasis of words or phrases, and, most often, to add or delete words or short phrases to conform to time limits. The producer or writer may also offer suggestions for interpreting the copy. The producer will inform you

Figure 7-1

Voice-over performer Mary Ptak interprets a commercial script at a recording session. Mary received her A.A. degree from Santa Rosa Junior College. Mary says that she "enjoys every aspect of radio" and adds, "How many people can say they love their jobs?" *Courtesy of Mary Ptak and KZST, Santa Rosa.*

if you're going too fast or too slow, are mispronouncing a word, or are slurring or having some other articulation problem. The writer (if the writer isn't also the producer) will decide what words to change or cut. As the announcer, you're expected to follow all instructions without comment or argument.

Not all agency representatives are competent in coaching performers. Some will give you vague instructions such as "give me more," "make it bright and perky," or "try it another way." As a freelance voice-over performer, you'll work with many different producers. Some will give you clear and helpful directions; others will be vague or confusing. There may be times when you'd like to offer suggestions, and to do so is appropriate only if you're confident that the producer feels secure and is open to your ideas. Be very careful when attempting to offer suggestions; remember that even constructive advice from you may be unwelcome to some agency writers and producers.

Not all aspects of commercial recording are standardized, but you'll soon learn what's expected of you. In some instances, for example, if you stumble or slur a word, you're expected to pause, say "pickup," pause again, and begin reading from the beginning of the sentence in which you stumbled.[8] This practice makes it easy

---

[8] The term *pickup* is used in at least two other ways in voice-over work. A pickup session is a recording session in which specific lines, recorded during an earlier session, have been judged unusable and must be recorded again. *Pickup* also refers to picking up one's cue—in other words, speaking more closely on the heels of a line delivered by another performer.

for the audio engineer to edit the recording. In other operations you'll begin again at the very opening of the spot.

Television and Film Voice-Overs

A more complex studio setup is required for film and television voice-overs. Moving images are shown on a monitor or screen, and your challenge is to match your delivery to the actions being portrayed. **Dubbing** (short for *postproduction synchronous dubbing,* also referred to as looping) is used in two modes or applications. In the first and simplest, you're expected to pace your reading to match visuals in a commercial, such as a series of brief scenes in which an actor is seen in several settings, trying on different items of clothing.

A more difficult challenge is dubbing to a tape or film soundtrack to match the lip movements and emotions of an actor in a film or video recording. Aside from its applications in broadcasting, the most common use of looping in the United States is the dubbing of non-English-language films to English. Looping is also employed if a producer, after recording and editing a film, becomes dissatisfied with the voice or acting ability of a particular performer and hires a voice-over professional to dub in, and thereby replace, the words spoken by the original performer.[9]

Working with Commercials during an On-Air Shift

As an announcer on a music, news, or talk-radio station, you'll likely record some commercials before your regular on-air shift. This may occur just before going on the air or in a recording session, where you'll voice a week's worth of spots. You'll perform the spots in a small production studio where you'll engineer, deliver the lines of the commercials, mix your voice track over a music bed, and record the mixed spot on a hard disk.

During your on-air shift, these and other spots will be played at the times and in the order scheduled by your station's **traffic** or **continuity department.** At some stations, all commercials, jingles, station IDs, and promos are played automatically by programmed computers, and your only announcing responsibility as a DJ is to make interesting or humorous observations, back-announce music sweeps, and give brief weather reports and traffic information during drive times. As a talk-show host, you'll be cued by your producer when breaks are scheduled for news, traffic, weather, or commercial clusters.

---

[9] For extensive information about dubbing, enter the word into a search engine and click on Wikipedia. Note especially the report on "New Technology" that describes an application developed at New York University, known as Video Rewrite, which uses computer animation to match lip movements with a new voice track.

At less highly computerized stations, you'll follow a log (most likely appearing on a display screen) that indicates when you're to play the various program elements by activating a computerized workstation next to your audio console.

In a technologically less up-to-date station, you might have a printed **log** and a **copy book,** sometimes called a **continuity book.** The traffic department prepares seven such, one for each day of the week. Each book contains, in order of presentation, commercial copy for spots that are taped or are on mass-storage hard disks. You merely keep track of the sequential placement of the commercials by entering a mark on the program log as you punch up each commercial and send each out over the air at the times stipulated in the log. A turn of the page brings you to the next commercial.

If you work at a station that still works with both recorded and live commercials, the on-air procedures are more complex. The commercial copy of your entire shift has been logged by the traffic department, and you'll have a copy of that log. The log indicates the order of the commercials, whether a given commercial is recorded or is to be read live, and the time each commercial is to be broadcast. If your station has a tight format, the times will be precise; if the format is casual and relaxed, the times will be approximate.

Most radio production and announce booths are equipped with a mounted stopwatch or an electronic digital clock that can be programmed to show elapsed time or remaining time. When performing commercials, whether delivered live or recorded, time is important. Use a stopwatch or clock each time you practice. Time is what radio stations sell, and clients expect precisely what they pay for.

SPOTLIGHT

Tips from a Voice-Over Pro

When it comes to voice-over, Voicetrax founder Samantha Paris has done it all. Her credits include more than a thousand national and regional commercials, major roles in nearly 200 animated television cartoon shows, three CLIO Awards for outstanding commercial performance, and the National Gabriel Award for public-service announcements. Samantha Paris also narrates corporate-industrial and documentary films, provides character voices for CD-ROM and interactive games, teaches voice-over performance to students, and, on occasion, loops a voice for a theatrical feature film. All of this is in addition to founding and supervising Voicetrax San Francisco, a training academy and voice-casting service for those preparing for careers as voice-over performers.

From her studio in Sausalito, minutes away from San Francisco, Samantha spends her days doing the things she loves within this industry: performing, teaching, directing, and casting, through her company, Voicetrax San Francisco, Inc. Voicetrax opened at this location in 1991 and has grown to become the most comprehensive voice-over training academy in the country, offering nearly one hundred introductory lectures, workshops, and seminars throughout the year, seven days a week, with cutting-edge instruction from top San Francisco and Los Angeles producers, agents, and directors.

Now entering her thirtieth year in the industry, Samantha attributes her success to years of

Figure 7-2

Voice-over actress and teacher Samantha Paris demonstrates how to convey specific moods when interpreting commercial copy. Note that she uses nonverbal communication, even though her audience cannot see her.

hard work. Knowing from a young age that this was the profession she wanted to pursue, she began taking voice-over lessons at age 15 four evenings a week. While the rest of her high school peers were socializing after school, Samantha was immersed in her lessons, spending extra hours each week practicing. This early training has been invaluable and has carried her through many high-pressure situations: how to size up a piece of copy in seconds; how to make instant decisions about character and moods; and how to adapt her voice quality and personality for any situation. At age 17—two years after she began her training—she started auditioning for voice-over work as well as throwing her hat in the on-camera arena, auditioning for

television commercials, episodic television, and feature films.

Although she was quite successful in these mediums, there was one major obstacle overshadowing her—the pain of rejection. "For every job I landed, there were twenty that I didn't get. I was constantly focusing on those and feeling like I wasn't good enough." So at age 23 she decided to take a break and became a voice-over agent. After six months of directing other actors and promoting their voices, she realized there were many enormously talented actors out there and that she was one of them! Not landing a role didn't have anything to do with a lack of talent, it was just a matter of who they (the producer or client) would select. It was with that revelation that Paris returned to her acting career, focusing solely on voice-over, and became one of the nation's top voice-over artists. "There were lots and lots of tears back then," she says, "but you can't give up. If you want it badly enough, you've just got to believe that you're good, and you can't give up. . . . Sometimes it's painful, but you've just got to stay with it and keep the faith. When you're first studying, you can't be looking down the road, wondering, 'Well, how long is it going to take?' You have to love what you're doing, and just enjoy the journey."

The following are some suggestions she offers to help performers achieve their highest potential:

- Read, read, read aloud. Use anything from actual scripts to newspaper articles; or, if you're interested in character work for cartoons and CD-ROMs, start by putting voices to the comics in newspapers. Do not record and play back your performances on your own. Concentrate on your work and rely on qualified teachers and coaches to judge your taped performances. We all sound pretty bad to our own ears.
- Always have a clear picture of who you are, to whom you're talking, and where you are. Make sure that each listener feels that you're talking only to her or him.

- Choose an attitude before you choose a character. Characterization comes only after all other decisions as to purpose, place, mood, nature of listener, and so forth have been made. The decision about attitude must be precise: Motherly is not the same as caring; caring is not the same as neighborly; neighborly is not the same as friendly.
- It isn't nearly enough to decide that in your performance you will be, for example, a middle-aged mother. You have to go deeper than that. As a mother, how do you feel about the child you are addressing? Are you talking to one child or two? How old are the children? How old are you? What is the setting in which you speak to the children?
- When you're given a technical direction such as, "I want you to really punch that word," make sure that your attempt to carry out the instruction fits your attitude and character. Make it believable.
- Techniques eventually come into play. For example, emphasis can be accomplished by intonation, by pauses before and after the words of importance, by a break in delivery, or by a change in rhythm or volume. However, before you even think about such techniques, make sure to establish your attitude, your objectives, and your character.

Character Voices

Despite the exceptions noted in the Spotlight discussion in Chapter 4, Standard American has been the accepted manner of speaking by both men and women announcers since the beginning of radio broadcasting in the United States. However, broadcasters have also used foreign accents, regional dialects, and character voices in some dramas and in a great many commercials. If you have a good ear for speech sounds and find that you're able to perform competently while using a character voice, you may want to develop a number of dialect specializations, especially if you intend to become a freelance performer of commercials.

Many commercials, especially those produced for Saturday morning television shows, are done as cartoons with voice-overs. The types of voices used in cartoon spots include pretend animal voices (such as that of a mouse or rabbit), monsters, aliens from other planets, and superheroes and heroines, to name a few.

In addition to foreign accents and regional dialects, commercial copy—especially that written for radio—often asks for a specific type of speech personality, such as the nag, the wimp, or the bully. Some commercials call for a speaker who can speak at a very rapid rate or who has an unusual voice. Nonstandard styles of speech may be grouped by categories: (1) unusually rapid delivery, (2) unusually low or high pitch, (3) unusual voice quality, (4) unusual personality type, (5) stage English, (6) regional dialects, and (7) foreign accents. As Table 7-1 shows, some of these are performed only by men, some only by women, and some by either. These categories are, of course, stereotypes, but that's precisely why they're used—they quickly identify types of persons to an audience that's been conditioned to associate character traits with certain voice qualities.

If you find employment as a "character voice" actor, you may at times be asked to play someone in a disparaging, demeaning way. You must then judge whether this is harmless—as when playing a person who is just plain nasty—or is a hurtful depiction of a member of a particular ethnic group or of some other societal category. In Appendix A, you'll find several commercials that employ a foreign accent that are unlikely to be found offensive by anyone.

TABLE 7-1 Nonstandard Styles of Speech Used in Commercials

Category	Example
Rapid delivery	Pitch "artists," speaking at over 200 words a minute; can be loud ("used-car sales associates") or soft-spoken
Unusually low- or high-pitched voices	Gravel-voiced "he-man," often heard on commercials for "muscle" cars "In the cellar," as in many commercials for financial institutions Children's voices performed by adults
Unusual voice quality	Breathy, as in spots for perfumes. Whispered and breathy, as in some spots for luxury automobiles
Unusual personality type	The whiner, the wimp, the dumbbell, the crab, the nag, the bully
Stage English	Sinister, pretentious, authoritative, often used to convey a feeling of superior quality, as in spots for luxury cars
Regional dialects	Folksy-country, New England, New York, Southern, drawled Southern, Hoosier (Indianan), Western, harsh Midwestern, Texan
Foreign accents	German, French, Italian, Mexican, Greek, Russian, other Slavic, Chinese, Japanese, Southeast Asian, Filipino, English (both Cockney and Oxford), Scandinavian, Australian, Arabic, and "Transylvanian" (often associated with Dracula)

Public-Service Announcements by Damien Quinlan

ALL ABOUT ME: I recently graduated as a double major, Audio/Radio and TV/Video Production, from Plattsburgh State University. I enjoy playing outdoor sports—especially baseball, golf, and tennis—and hosting a weekly music/talk hybrid radio show. I work in a local network television affiliate as an audio board operator.

ALL ABOUT PUBLIC-SERVICE ANNOUNCEMENTS: Whether they're spots for the Red Cross, Mothers Against Drunk Driving, or the Peace Corps, public-service announcements are designed to get listeners' or viewers' attention, inform them, and call them to action. Grabbing attention through "shock" campaigns, such as the Partnership for a Drug-Free America's "This Is Your Brain on Drugs" spots or the antismoking announcements by The Truth, has been more popular as of late. But shock is not the only tactic used by PSA producers. A popular case of a campaign pulling at viewers' emotional heartstrings was the "Keep America Beautiful" announcements that closed with a Native American man shedding a single tear as he overlooked a ravaged American landscape. Not unlike paid ads, these campaigns capture an emotional appeal and tell you who to contact and how to enact change.

. . . AND HOW DOES THIS AFFECT ANNOUNCING? Since 1942, the Ad Council has produced some of the most popular PSA campaigns, including "A Mind Is a Terrible Thing to Waste," but anyone can produce a PSA. Whether they are community, education, health, or safety based, writing and producing public-service announcements are a great way to get something you created on the air (via your college radio or television station). If there is a cause you're passionate about, get in touch with the organization or group and try to make the world a better place while getting some nice hits on your résumé, too.

Radio Public-Service Announcements

The Federal Communications Act of 1934 established the Federal Communications Commission (FCC) and defined its areas of responsibility. One requirement was that station licensees broadcast "in the public interest, convenience, or necessity." For license renewal, stations were required to submit data listing the ways in which they met the public interest. One of the most convenient and inexpensive ways of showing community service was by broadcasting, free of charge, brief messages promoting worthwhile nonprofit enterprises. From that time on, commercial stations have provided free time for public-service announcements (PSAs)—until now.

Since the adoption of the revised Telecommunication Act of 1996, stations have been free to ignore public service altogether, including the airing of PSAs. Despite this deregulation, many radio stations continue to carry PSAs. Along with the tradition of community service on the part of broadcasters, many station managers know that the goodwill of community members is important to the success of the station. Even though PSAs are less pervasive and influential than in previous years, it's still important for those entering the field to know about their nature, the way they are created and broadcast, and how to work with them.

Most PSAs are brief announcements for local activities: bake sales, car washes, benefit concerts, and similar fund-raisers. On the governmental side, spots may be aired urging citizens to attend town council meetings or remind people to vote in an upcoming election. Other PSAs, running from ten to thirty seconds, are produced either by nonprofit organizations or by the Advertising Council.

At times, announcements of community interest are paid for by local merchants who believe their interests are served by supporting local causes. These are not truly PSAs, because PSAs are broadcast without charge; but, except for the mention of the sponsor, these read like PSAs. Such a sponsored announcement will be broadcast during any **daypart** the sponsor pays for because it's treated like a commercial. Here's an announcement paid for by a brake and tire service:

ANNCR:	Maxwell's Brake and Tire reminds you that, with the opening of the school year, it's extra important to keep alert on the road. Kids often forget all the safety rules that are taught by parents and teachers. Drive carefully and cautiously and be ready to stop in a hurry if you see a ball

> bounce into the street—a child may be right behind it. As adults, we need to do some thinking for children. This message is brought to you by Maxwell's Brake and Tire, Middlefield and Grand Streets, in Madison.

Although PSAs and commercials have much in common, PSAs usually are shorter, as with brief mentions on a community billboard feature. Locally produced PSAs seldom are augmented by elaborate production, such as music and sound effects. In addition, PSAs are most often broadcast during off hours—those times of the day that are least attractive to advertisers.

Other important differences lie in objectives and motivational devices used. Some commercials present rational arguments to sell a product or a service, but these are minority voices. Advertising on radio and television is both competitive and omnipresent, so most sponsors seem desperate to make their spots stand out from the rest. On radio, pounding percussion, loud repetitious musical backgrounds, and sound effects often are employed to *demand* our attention. Television spots often show montages of abnormal activities: autos flying through the air, people jumping over buildings, physical objects exploding or morphing into humans—in short, anything to grab attention. Some begin with a noisy opening, followed by the arousal of the emotion of fear, greed, or insecurity.

Public-service announcements sometimes employ such tactics. As we all know, any near-deafening sound will attract attention—it's easy to catch people's attention—but what comes after that is what's really important. Also, fear, greed, and insecurity are basic human emotions, and exploiting them requires little effort. With PSAs, however, campaigns for famine relief or "save the whales" should indeed attract interest and also must appeal to basic human emotions, but the producers of PSAs for such causes usually avoid emotional overkill.

At a large-market station, the PSAs you're to read are duplicated and placed in your copy book. You may read some PSAs during a broadcast, but more often you'll record them, along with commercials, as part of your production duties. In smaller markets, PSAs will come to you in a variety of ways. Where there's a staff member assigned to public affairs, PSAs may be typed on 3-by-5-inch index cards. At regular intervals you'll read two or three of the brief messages as a community calendar. The following is typical:

MISSION HOSPITAL OUT: 8 APR. 5

The Sunrise Unit of Mission Hospital will present the film *Chalk Talk* and a discussion on alcoholism on April 5th, 6:30 p.m., at the hospital. Info: 555-9333.

At times, you may have to ad-lib an announcement based on a fact sheet such as this:

Dixie School
1818 Morgan Drive
Outland, MI

Dear Friends:
I'd appreciate having this announcement read on your Community
Billboard:
Parental Stress Workshop
Wednesday, February 24
Dixie School, Room 23
- Child Care
- Refreshments
Thank you!
Katie Rose Decker

Here are some suggestions for practicing the delivery of radio commercials and PSAs:

- Practice reading aloud and recording ten-, twenty-, thirty-, and sixty-second commercials as well as ten-, twenty-, and thirty-second PSAs, always working with a stopwatch. Listen carefully to playbacks. Ask yourself: Does this voice please me? Does the delivery hold my attention? Does the meaning come through? Is the rate of delivery too fast or too slow? Is there variety in pitch, rate, and emphasis? And, most importantly, am I sold on the product or the cause?

- As you practice ad-libbing PSAs from brief fact sheets, try to convey the essential information in ten seconds.

- Produce and record a commercial that requires sound effects, music, and dramatization.

- Ask a radio station or advertising agency for copies of recorded commercials, complete with copies of the scripts, and practice with the commercials until your timing becomes razor sharp.

Appendix A includes several public-service announcements to provide you with opportunities for practice. Additional PSAs may be found on our accompanying CD.

Television Commercials

Most television commercials differ from those on radio in several ways. They're shorter, running from fifteen to thirty seconds; they use music and sound effects more often; and they're almost never performed live. Because television is a visual medium, most advertisers want to show their products or services, and as a result, the majority of television commercials feature voice-over narration. The face of a television commercial announcer seldom appears on the screen, unless that person is a famous actor, singer, or dancer. Even in commercials that show an announcer, the appearance is usually confined to a few moments of introduction at the beginning. There are, of course, exceptions. Here is a commercial that asks for nothing in the way of elaborate visual effects, is easily and economically produced, yet is very effective in reaching and holding the attention of its target audience. In performing this, you should continue stuffing wieners into your mouth until you can barely speak.

AGENCY: McNamara & Perez

CLIENT: Hertzel's Baby Snaks

WRITTEN BY: John McNamara

TIME: 60 Sec.

CAMERA SETUP:

CAM 1: *Medium shot anncr & product on table*

CAM 2: *CU of product*

CAM 3: MCU of anncr

CAM 1: Hey, (*your name*) here. And I'm gonna tell you a little somethin' about cocktail wieners. Specially, Hertzel's Baby Snaks. (*eat one*) They're delicious! And you can fix 'em in scads of ways. (*eat another one*)

CAM 2: Add 'em to a breakfast sandwich, simmer 'em in bbq sauce, or just eat 'em alone—you can do anything with 'em. (*eat another*)

CAM 3: Hertzel's Baby Snaks are the best thing to add to your party when you just have no clue what to serve. Everyone will love 'em (*eat another*), so it's easy to be the hit of the party.

> **CAM 1:**   So keep in mind, next time you throw a Superbowl party, have a few friends over, or if you just plain love small sausages, go to the store and grab yourself some Hertzel's Baby Snaks. (*eat another*)
>
> **ZOOM IN TO CU:**   Mmmhmmm. . . .

There are two types of television commercials that differ considerably from those described above, those on **shopping channels,** such as QVC, and program-length commercials, known as **infomercials.** Hosts on shopping channels make lengthy pitches for products shown to viewers and mix their sales presentations with interviews and information on the quantity of pictured items that remain. Hosts also engage in chatty conversations with viewers who call in to say hello or to praise some product they purchased previously. Shopping hosts may also interview jewelry or clothing designers who appear as guests.

Infomercials typically are half-hour sales pitches, with two or more announcers demonstrating such products as exercise machines, hair restorers, cooking equipment, fishing gear, and beauty aids. Studio audiences sometimes are included in these programs. Both shopping channel and infomercial announcers speak ad-lib and are expected to know a great deal about the products they promote.

Aside from these lengthy television commercial presentations, most commercials are brief and, almost without exception, are recorded. As a television commercial announcer for pitches of thirty seconds or fewer, you'll have time to

Figure 7-3
Program hosts on shopping channels must ad-lib for extended periods of time about the products offered. All hosts must be effective communicators, with personalities that communicate friendliness and believability. Each is a specialist in the type of products being advertised: jewelry, cosmetics, clothing, cooking utensils, electronics, and much more. The QVC channel ("Quality, Value, Convenience") is seen on cable and satellite twenty-four hours a day. *Courtesy of QVC.*

prepare and discuss interpretation with a copywriter or agency producer. Recording and rerecording will give you a margin of safety.

Television commercials reach the air by processes similar to those for radio. Advertising agencies provide some commercials, almost always on one or another digital medium. Some are produced by production companies and sent to stations over the Internet or by courier. Others are produced by a station's retail services unit and are played on that station and then dubbed and sent to other stations.

If you're an announcer specializing in television commercials, you'll most likely receive your assignments through a talent agency. You'll perform in one of these settings: a sound recording studio (for voice-over commercials), a television studio, a video or film studio, or in the field with a remote crew.

Many television commercials appear to be locally produced when they actually originate in major production centers and are offered to local merchants as cooperative commercials. A **cooperative commercial** is one for which a national advertiser pays the cost of production and then shares the expense of broadcast with a local merchant. The bulk of such commercials arrives at the local station or local production house, where a closing tag on behalf of the local merchant is added.

If you work as a radio or television announcer, you may pick up extra money by doing television commercials as a freelance performer. Network news anchors and reporters are barred by contract from advertising products, but most other television performers, including announcers on local stations, are free to **moonlight** (to work at a second job during one's spare time, often at night). Television commercial announcing at the national level pays well, but it's a difficult field to enter. Most performers for national spots live in or very near New York, Chicago, San Francisco, or the Hollywood area, and a small number of them dominate the field.

Locally produced television commercials offer employment to many performers, mostly in voice-over roles. Portable electronic production equipment, along with character generators, graphics generators, digital video effects (DVE) equipment, and chroma-keying, make it possible for even small local stations to create elaborate and effective commercials. Recordings can be made on location—at a carpet store, an auto parts dealer, or a grocery store, for example—and then, during postproduction, station personnel may add written information, draw images onto the screen, create and manipulate multi-images, or key two or more pictures onto the same screen. A typical locally produced television commercial may show an announcer at or near the beginning of the spot and then show images of products or services while the announcer continues with voice-over narration.

Voice-over narration for television commercials differs from radio delivery only in that the words must be timed to match the pictures being seen by the viewers. This coordination is achieved through one of three production routines:

1. The announcer reads the script, and in postproduction the pictures are timed to match the words.

2. The visual portion of the commercial is shown on a monitor (or a large screen), and the announcer's voice-over performance is recorded as words and pictures are synchronized.

3. During postproduction, the recorded performance is edited to match the pictures.

In most instances the announcer is long gone before the commercial is completed and perhaps may never see the finished product.

Some television commercials are produced in the field, with the announcer playing a visible role. Because there won't be a teleprompter in the field, announcers have to ad-lib from cue cards and make direct addresses to the camera. Increasingly, though, commercials in the field are performed with the use of an earpiece, or earprompter.[10]

Although on-camera commercial delivery is rare, it's worth practicing. Elsewhere in this book—particularly in the chapters on performance (Chapters 5 and 6), interviewing (Chapter 8), and television news (Chapter 10), many suggestions are offered for improving your on-camera performance. Nearly all of these suggestions apply to on-camera commercial announcing.

In addition, the Checklist presented in this section includes tips that apply to performing commercials in the classroom or studio.

Try to reflect your own personality when you deliver radio and television commercials. Some commercials call for a slow, relaxed delivery, and others for a hard-sell approach. While sponsors usually ask for a particular style of delivery, this doesn't mean you must transform yourself totally each time the style or mood of a commercial changes. If you don't maintain and project your own personality, you run the risk of sounding like an impersonator rather than a communicator.

Checklist *Making Effective Television Commercials*

1. When practicing on-camera performance, dress as you would if you'd been hired to deliver the commercial.
2. Understand and convey the impression the sponsor wants to create.
3. When handling props or pointing to signs or products, make your movements slow, deliberate, and economical.
4. If television equipment is available, try to simulate actual broadcast conditions.
5. Adhere scrupulously to the time limits of the commercial.

---

[10] A brief explanation of this appears in Chapter 10, "Television News."

6. When appropriate, look into the camera lens; but don't stare.
7. In on-camera performance, practice switching smoothly from one camera to another on cue.
8. Don't do a parody or a travesty of a commercial unless the assignment calls for it. Your ability to sell a product or a service can't be judged if you turn your performance into a lampoon.
9. Communicate!

PRACTICE

➤ Delivering Radio Commercials and PSAs

Appendix A offers several commercial and PSA scripts. These materials provide practice with most types of commercials and PSAs heard on radio today. Look for additional practice material and write some of your own.

PRACTICE

➤ Producing Your Own Commercial

Ask a local merchant—the owner of an independently owned small grocery store, restaurant, or gift shop, for example—to help you fulfill a class assignment. Make sure the merchant understands that you have nothing to sell. Be clear about who you are and what you're asking of the merchant. Use a note pad to record basic information about items the merchant wants to promote. Write scripts, record them on audio and videotape, and then return to obtain the merchant's feedback.

PRACTICE

> ## Delivering Television Commercials

Because television commercials usually involve elaborate visual effects, you may have difficulty finding opportunities for realistic practice. Appendix A includes many radio scripts and a few television scripts. Some of these practice commercials call for animation, video inserts, or properties that may not be available. There's no ideal way of working with such commercials, but they're included here because they represent a large number of current commercials, and it would be unrealistic to exclude them. You can adapt some of the radio scripts for television performance, but you'll generally be limited to straight, on-camera presentations.

The following exercises should help you achieve satisfactory results with a minimum of production support:

1. Practice on-camera delivery with some of the simple presentational commercials included in Appendix A. Use demonstration commercials and those incorporating studio cards or one or two video inserts instead of those that involve elaborate production. Work for exact timing as well as camera presence. Practice with an electronic prompter, if available, or with cue cards.

2. Prepare slides and adapt a thirty- or sixty-second radio commercial for voice-over presentation. Practice synchronizing your off-camera delivery with the visual images as they appear on the screen.

3. Record television commercials currently being broadcast. Write out a script of the spoken portions of each commercial. Then, with the sound turned off, run the recording and practice voice-over delivery.

4. Produce a commercial with one person on camera demonstrating a product or a process while you're off-camera delivering the voice-over narration.

Chapter 8

Interview
and
Talk Programs

Chapter Outline

Interviews as Conversations

> I don't know where I got obsessed with the idea that interviewing was simply asking questions. It's so much nicer when it's more of a dialogue; it's so much easier when you have that breakthrough, and you get into something that resembles actual speech as it would be spoken away from the lights and the camera. Suddenly all that pressure that you usually feel falls away, and you realize that all this is happening almost—sometimes exactly—as in real life. When that happens, I feel that I'm in it as an equal, rather than somebody who is standing aside.[1]

So said Dick Cavett, for years the most highly regarded talk-show host on television. With these words, he summed up almost all you need to know to be an outstanding interviewer: *Be yourself, engage in conversation with your guests, enjoy the discussion.*

The word *interview* comes from the French and means, roughly, "to see one another." From its beginnings, radio included interviews in its offerings, so the "seeing" is best interpreted as "seeing *inside* a person" because that's what characterizes the best interviews.

Interviews serve many program needs. Some are brief, such as ten- to twenty-second **actualities** or **sound bites** made by witnesses to a fire, airplane crash, or similar event for insertion into news broadcasts.[2] Techniques for news interviews are discussed in Chapter 9, "Radio News," and Chapter 10, "Television News." Longer interviews are heard on radio talk programs that may last from one to three hours.

Interviews, including discussions with guests, are the chief activity of talk and interview show hosts. This chapter is devoted to practices and techniques appropriate to in-studio television talk shows and radio call-in shows that may or may not include studio guests; it is applicable as well to interviews gathered and edited for insertion into documentaries.

Talk and Interview Shows Today

Radio talk shows, after remarkable growth, from 238 in 1986, to nearly 2,000 in the first years of the twenty-first century, shrank to fewer than 800 today;[3] during those years, thousands of locally produced television variety shows were canceled. During their peak years of popularity, local television shows included interviews with authors of best-selling books and performers appearing with traveling plays, musicals, and lectures, as well as hometown politicians, athletes, and other newsmakers. Syndicated programs whose costs were less than those of locally produced shows replaced most shows in both media. But there was a price

---

[1] Dick Cavett and Christopher Portfield, *Cavett*. New York: Harcourt Brace Jovanovich, 1974, pp. 291–292. For five years, 1969–1974, Cavett was host of the ABC late-night program. *The Dick Cavett Show.* Cavett also hosted television interview shows on CBS, PBS, and CNBC. Many of his most compelling interviews are available on DVDs.

[2] *Actuality* is the radio term for a brief statement from someone other than a station employee, while the same feature is called a *sound bite* for television.

[3] *Broadcasting & Cable Yearbook*, 2006. Exact numbers are unavailable.

to be paid as local programs vanished, not a cost to broadcasters, but to audiences all across America who lost access to local voices and issues.

There are essentially two types of talk shows that appear on television and radio. One is a one-way presentation to audiences and is represented on television by Conan O'Brien, Montel Williams, and *Politically Incorrect with Bill Maher*. On radio, many talk shows depend on listener response with questions and comments. Examples are *Car Talk* on NPR, *Computer Outlook,* and the *WebTalk Radio Show* on Internet radio.

Some talk shows are deliberately biased, provocative, or sensationalistic. The suggestions for interview and talk performance described in this chapter are not advice on how to go for the jugular or humiliate guests but rather on how to achieve compelling discussions.

Some interviews are essentially question-and-answer sessions, often with controversial guests. Many are single-subject interviews on topics, selected daily, such as gun control, health care, or airport security. Others are essentially conversations intended to bring out interesting, amusing, or instructional anecdotes or advice from famous guests. Each type of interview demands a special technique, and technique is determined by purpose.

Every brief interview should have at least one clearly defined objective, and it's important to determine that purpose before beginning an interview. Some interviews—especially those with outstanding storytellers—are meant to entertain and require a lighthearted approach. When you interview a gifted teller of anecdotes, be prepared to let the guest narrate humorous or otherwise entertaining stories with little interruption. In the Spotlight within this chapter, Professor Arthur S. Hough Jr. describes his first television interview with a famous movie star. He says that he soon realized that he had one job to do, *to listen and respond,* and adds: "Of course there is a lot more to interviewing than effective listening, but it still is at the top of the list of things to do well."

Establishing the purpose of an interview before starting it is one of the most important decisions you can make as a talk-show host. When interviewing a writer with a book to promote, your aim should be to explore in an engaging way the most interesting, amusing, controversial, or noteworthy parts of the book. Your audience may also receive enough information about the book to motivate its purchase, but that must not be your objective. It's important to keep the interview from becoming merely a puff piece for the author.

Interviews on serious social problems must be designed to provide useful information on critical issues and should be approached with a serious, but not somber, attitude.

While television interview programs make almost exclusive use of studio guests, radio relies on guests and telephone callers. Regardless of medium, the key to success is the program host's interviewing ability. The intimacy of talk shows makes them naturals for radio and television. Also, they present contemporary issues, are entertaining and informative, offer variety, and often directly involve listeners or viewers. Talk shows also are relatively inexpensive to produce; many guests receive no compensation for their appearances. Others receive transportation, lodging, and per diem pay for meals. Some are required by their performer's union to receive at least minimum scale.

Figure 8-1

The late Harry Caray is seen interviewing a Chicago Cubs player prior to game time. Caray called more than 8,000 games for the St. Louis Cardinals, the Oakland A's, the Chicago White Sox, and the Chicago Cubs. On learning of Caray's death in 1998, Hall of Fame sports announcer Jack Buck said: "There's going to be a loud silence." Stan Musial added: "We're going to miss old Harry. He was always the life of the party, the life of baseball." *Stephen Green Photography/ Courtesy of the Chicago Cubs.*

Jobs as talk-show hosts aren't numerous, but they are rewarding and challenging. You may or may not succeed in having your own talk show, but the skills you develop as you work toward that goal will be useful in a range of announcing specializations. Some of those skills can be practiced; others come with experience.

You can practice interviewing by asking friends, one at a time, to discuss a specific topic with you—music, sports, current events, or whatever seems appropriate. As you interview, keep a recorder going so you can do your own postmortem and thereby judge your performance. Such practice will help you prepare for talk-show hosting, but the true measure of your effectiveness will be how well you function on a live broadcast. Talk-show hosts are among the few announcers whose auditions coincide with their first air experience in that capacity.

Principles of Effective Interviewing

Avoiding Abstraction

One of the most critical aspects of interviewing that affects every interviewer's approach is what semanticist S. I. Hayakawa calls the **abstraction ladder.** This phrase refers to the fact that several terms are usually available for the same phenomenon, some precise and some general. Take, for example, *food, fruit, apple,* and *Granny Smith.* An apple is a type of fruit, and it's also a food, so all terms are accurate. The term *food* is a high-level abstraction; *fruit* is below it on the ladder; *apple* is quite specific; *Granny Smith* (a tart, green apple) is at the lowest rung on the ladder. Some interview guests consistently speak at a level that's high on the ladder; that is, they consistently use vague and general terms rather than precise ones. It's up to you as the interviewer to "pull" such guests down the ladder of abstraction when appropriate. For example, consider this exchange:

> **ANNCR:** And just what does the administration intend to do about the problems of the inner cities?
>
> **GUEST:** We're aware of the seriousness of the situation. We feel that a more productive utilization of human resources must come before we can expect to overcome problems of the infrastructure.

What this guest is saying in an abstract way may be quite simple, but the fuzzy choice of terms makes it vague. Translated, it means "we need to find jobs for people before we can hope to clean up and rebuild." The interviewer's challenge is to find a way to get this guest to express the thought in clear, specific language. One approach is to ask directly for clarification of terms:

> **ANNCR:** And just what do you mean by "the development of human resources"?

A later question would steer the guest toward an explanation of the phrase "the problems of the infrastructure."

Avoiding Bias

A second basic consideration for any interviewer is *bias*. When interviewing a person on a controversial or extremely important subject, one has a natural tendency to accept without question comments that one agrees with. This isn't a problem when the statement is a matter of common knowledge or of record, as in this example:

> **ANNCR:** How do today's students compare with students of twenty years ago?

> **GUEST:** Well, standardized test scores of college-bound seniors have fallen pretty regularly over the past two decades.

On the other hand, a guest may state opinions or theories:

> **ANNCR:** And how do you explain the drop?
>
> **GUEST:** Video games and shared Internet websites are the primary culprits.

As a *person* with many opinions of your own, you're free to agree or disagree with this statement. As a *responsible interviewer*, however, you have an obligation to ask further questions to bring out any facts that led your guest to the conclusion reached. Probing may reveal that the statement is based on hard fact or that it's simply an unsubstantiated "feeling." Whatever the answer, you've provided a service to your audience by nailing down the statement's truth—or lack of it. Regardless of whether you like or dislike the answer, you owe it to your listeners to question undocumented assertions. To put it simply: Never allow your personal beliefs to keep you from questioning unsubstantiated statements.

If you pay attention to broadcast interviews, you know that some highly rated hosts reject this notion, priding themselves in disagreeing with, and even shouting down, guests who hold positions contrary to theirs. This may be a way to attract an audience, but no amount of rationalizing it can make it ethically acceptable.

Tips for Conducting Successful Interviews

Ernie Kreilling, a syndicated television columnist, compiled a list of do's and don'ts that are especially helpful to radio or television talk-show interviewers. These suggestions provide an excellent framework for discussing interviewing and are therefore used as subheads in this section. Think about them and work them into your practice where appropriate. It's also helpful to refer to them after each interview. As you'll see, despite the value of these suggestions, they should not be seen as *rules.* Where appropriate, exceptions are given, and they are as important as the suggestions themselves.

The tips cover three general areas: *preparation for the interview, treatment of guests,* and *the interviewer's strategy and contributions.*

Preparing for the Interview

Carefully Research the Guest's Background, Accomplishments, Attitudes, Beliefs, and Positions. You'll generally know from one to several days in advance who your guest will be, so you'll have time to do some research. Your quickest and most productive source is the Internet. If your guest isn't a person of national prominence, however, you may find background information through local newspapers, libraries, or chambers of commerce. If your guest has been scheduled by a booking agent, you most likely will be provided with a press kit containing useful information.

> **Sound Bytes**
>
> Biographies of nearly anyone famous or in the news may be found on the Internet. Using your favorite search engine, enter the person's name, click, and you'll find more information than you could ever use!

Researching your guest's background is as important as all other factors combined. No amount of style, personality, smooth performance, or perfect timing can compensate for a lack of knowledge.

Be Sure the Topic to Be Discussed Is of Interest or Importance. Although a dull guest can make even the most exciting subject boring, an interview always benefits if the topic itself is truly interesting or important.

When practicing interviewing as a student, don't settle for the most readily obtainable guest. Interviews with parents, siblings, classmates, and others you know well are seldom of interest to anyone, the participants included. A special energy is generated when interviewing people who are strangers to you, and an even greater intensity develops when you interview people of real accomplishment. Exception: If a person in any of the categories listed above has something special to discuss, something you're sure would be interesting to your audience, break the rule, and go with it!

Where Appropriate, Limit the Number of Topics to Be Explored So They Can Be Discussed in Depth. Depending on the intended length of the interview, it's best to explore only as many topics as can be dealt with in some detail. The least interesting interviews are those that randomly jump from one topic to another.

Don't Submit Questions in Advance, Unless You'd Lose an Important Interview by Refusing to Do So. Hostile guests and some politicians may ask you to submit your questions in advance. This practice is a bad one, because spontaneity demands that guests not rehearse their answers. On the other hand, it *is* good practice to let a guest know the general areas to be covered. To help relax an inexperienced guest, you might even reveal your first question slightly in advance.

An exception: If you're going to ask a guest for his or her most interesting, funniest, or most unusual experience, advance notice will provide time for reflection. Most guests draw a blank when asked such a question abruptly, but a little advance notice may make the answer the highlight of the interview.

Write Out, or at Least Make Notes on, the Introduction and Conclusion. Writing out or outlining the beginning and ending of an interview will free you during airtime to focus on its body. Note, however, that unless you're able to deliver your opening and closing in a totally conversational manner, the shift from reading to ad-lib speaking will be very noticeable. In most instances the conclusion should include a summary of important or interesting information revealed during the interview.

Plan at Least a Few Questions to Get the Interview Started and to Fill Awkward Gaps. Few sights are more painful than those of an interviewer struggling to come up with a question. Plan ahead but be ready to drop questions if they prove unnecessary.

The Guest

Make Your Guest Feel at Home. Introduce your guests to studio and control-room personnel when it's convenient. Show guests the area where the interview will take place and give them an idea of what's going to happen. Such hospitality should help relax your guests and make them more cooperative. With seasoned guests (people used to being interviewed), you can plunge right into the interview. With inexperienced guests it helps to spend a few minutes explaining how you'll conduct the interview and what you expect of them.

Establish Your Guest's Credentials at the Start of the Interview. Your audience needs to know how and why your guest is qualified to speak on a particular subject. The significance of a partisan statement about heart transplants differs depending on whether it's made by a heart surgeon, a heart recipient, a representative of a health plan, or a politician. One opinion is not necessarily better or more newsworthy than another, but your audience must be aware of the credentials of the speaker to assess statements in a meaningful way.

At the same time, confine your introductory comments to the bare essentials and give your guest an opportunity to be heard early in the interview. You can add additional biographical details later.

Occasionally and Indirectly Reestablish the Guest's Name and Credentials. On television, guests are identified periodically with supers at the bottom of the screen. It's also customary to mention a guest's name when breaking for a commercial—"We'll be back with author Annie LaMott right after these messages." On radio, of course, reminders must be given orally, and, because listeners can't see the guest, frequent reintroductions are essential. *Always end your interview by once again identifying your guest.* Many people are likely to have tuned in during the interview and could anxiously be waiting to hear the name of the person who has so charmed or outraged them.

Remember That the Guest Is the Star. Rarely is the interviewer of more interest to the audience than the guest. A few witty and wise hosts compete with their guests and, when this leads to spirited exchanges of opinion, it can be both stimulating and informative. In general, however, dominating an interview is not only contrary to its purpose of drawing the guest out but is simply rude.

Remember That the Guest Is the Expert. At times, you'll be an authority on the subject under discussion and will be able to debate it with your guest, but in most cases your guest will be the expert.

Don't "Preinterview" a Guest. Your conversation will lose spontaneity if you and your guest discuss the upcoming interview in detail before going on the air. Confine your contact with your guest to a general ice-breaking conversation unless your judgment tells you that you must mention a critical or sensitive topic that may arise.

Avoid Entrapment. Many "trash" radio and television interviewers deliberately mislead guests by hiding from them a sensitive or sensational item that the guest would prefer to leave undiscussed, then springing the question during the on-air interview. The term **trash television** (or trash radio) has arisen to describe their efforts. Such interviewers put two important concepts in conflict: the belief in freedom of expression versus the concept of a person's right to privacy. The First Amendment guarantees the right of freedom of expression. No such constitutional guarantee of right to privacy exists for a person who agrees to appear on a talk show, so the integrity of the talk-show host is the only guarantee that a guest's privacy will be protected.

Conducting the Interview

Discuss the Subject with the Guest. On typical talk shows, hosts aim for a conversation instead of a mere question-and-answer session (**Q & A**). Successful talk-show hosts participate in the discussion, adding information, anecdotes, and insightful comments. Unlike reporters, they don't rapidly fire questions, hoping to obtain sound bites from newsmakers. Questions are essential to an interview, but if you simply move from one question to another without revealing your feelings about the answers, you run the risk of seeming indifferent to or unimpressed by what your guest is saying. Feel free to express honest reactions, including laughter when appropriate.

Try to Establish a Nonthreatening Atmosphere. Don't cross-examine or otherwise bully guests. Because they may be nervous, it's your responsibility to put them at ease, no matter how much you may dislike or disagree with them. If you show hostility, unfairness, or lack of common hospitality, both your guests and your audience will resent it.

Many talk-show hosts make it a practice to bully their guests or insult call-in listeners. They thrive on dissension. These hosts are willing to ask any question, however tasteless, and to make any statement, however outrageous. Remember that viewers or listeners don't see a talk-show host as an actor playing a role; to them your role is the real you. If you value your reputation, you'll treat guests with fairness and respect.

Some hosts invite guests whose opinions they dislike and then proceed to argue with them, even shouting them down when they sense that the guest is about to make a telling point. This makes for a loud and energetic exchange, but the guest is always at a disadvantage; the bullying host is in a safe environment, while the guest is in unfamiliar surroundings and is in a defensive position throughout the entire discussion.

Establish the Importance of the Topic. Noteworthy topics need no special buildup, but others may require a brief explanation. People are interested in almost anything that directly affects them, so your interview will increase in significance if you can establish its relevance to them. One simple way of doing this is to ask your guest early in the session why the issue is important.

During the Interview, Listen Attentively to the Guest's Replies and React with Appropriate Interest. Next to preparation, listening is the most important aspect of interviewing discussed in this section. Listen carefully and follow up important statements with appropriate questions. Also, don't feign interest. If your interest isn't genuine, you're either conducting a bad interview or not listening to your guest's responses.

Another reason for careful listening is to avoid the embarrassment of asking a question that's already been answered. The ultimate penalty for inattention to guests' remarks is to have them say on the air, "Why, I just answered that!"

In General, Base Questions on the Guest's Previous Statements. Don't hesitate to dispense with preplanned questions if more interesting ones arise naturally from the discussion. The following dialogue is an exaggerated example of failure to pick up on an answer that begs you to switch to a new topic:

ANNCR: Now, Mayor Lutz, your opponent has charged you with a conflict of interest in the city's purchase of the new park. What's your answer?

MAYOR: Well, it hasn't been revealed yet, but I have evidence that my opponent has been living outside the city for years and is therefore ineligible to serve even if elected!

ANNCR: The *News–Democrat* claims to have copies of the deeds of sale and is ready to ask for your resignation. Will you tell us your side of the story on the park purchase?

Clinging to a planned question when another important topic demands a follow-up may be caused by rigidity. In reviewing your recorded interviews, be alert for moments when you've sacrificed effectiveness because of a previously determined plan. Have a plan but don't be a slave to it.

In Particular, Follow up on Important Contradictions. Public figures, especially politicians, often make contradictory statements that can lead to good dialogue. If you've asked a specific question, which you see from the answer your guest is avoiding, or perhaps even addressing an *unasked* question, ask it again. You may find it appropriate to preface it by saying "that wasn't what I asked," but if your guest remains evasive, adopt another line of questioning—leaving it to your audience to recognize the evasion. Unless you repeat the question, your listeners may not realize that it was avoided.

Try to Build an Interview toward a High Point or Climax. Hold back an especially interesting or provocative question until near the end of the interview. Try to lead up to that question. However, don't spring an important question too late because it's unacceptable to abruptly cut off the answer to a significant question because you've run out of time. But, note the comments made earlier about avoiding entrapment.

Avoid Referring to Conversations Held before Airtime. Ideally, you'll have an opportunity to chat with your guest before airtime. This conversation helps you determine areas of questioning, the general mood you want to establish, and other matters of importance. At the same time, an audience will feel excluded by a question such as, "Well, Pat. I'm sure the folks would find interesting that new hobby you were telling me about just before we went on the air." Listeners or viewers want to feel that they are taking part in the interview, not as if most of it has already taken place.

Seek out a Guest's Deep Convictions. Don't settle for mentally rehearsed platitudes and clichés. Probing usually means you must reveal something of yourself. Your guest isn't likely to open up unless you do.

Don't Interrupt with Meaningless Comments. "I see," "Uh huh," "Oh, yes," and "That's very interesting" add nothing to an interview and actually detract from what your guest is saying. Another reason for not peppering an interview with these meaningless interjections is that they quickly become predictable and annoying.

Some interviews are intended for editing (usually for newscasts or documentaries), and your words will be edited out and replaced with narration. If your voice can be heard uttering meaningless "I sees," it may be impossible to eliminate them in the editing. All announcers should cure themselves of the habit of using such vocal reinforcement when they interview. Practice giving *nonverbal* indications that you're paying attention but realize that smiles, frowns, and other expressions of approval or disapproval are inappropriate because you shouldn't indicate to your guest that you support or are opposed to what is being said.

At the same time, because a good interview frequently is a conversation, don't be afraid to make meaningful responses that are appropriate to the interchange, such as, "I can't believe you didn't know about your nomination."

You'll know in advance if your interview will be edited, so you'll know when interjections are acceptable and times when they're not. The nature of the interview determines the extent to which you should speak up.

Point out and Emphasize Important Answers. But don't parrot responses. Here's an acceptable example of how a significant answer is given emphasis:

ANNCR: Senator, if you were offered your party's nomination, would you accept it?

SENATOR: I've given much thought to that possibility, and my present inclination is to accept such a call, provided it's a mandate from the rank and file as well as the party leaders.

ANNCR: Senator, you've just said—for the first time, I believe—that you're willing to run for the presidency. That sounds firm and unconditional. Am I right in drawing that conclusion?

Paraphrasing the senator's answer emphasizes its importance; giving the senator a chance to confirm or deny it will nail it down. On the other hand, avoid the meaningless repetition of answers, as in the following:

ANNCR: You've been married five times. If you had your life to live over, would you try to stick with one of your wives?

MILLAR: No, I wouldn't do anything differently.

ANNCR: You wouldn't do anything differently. Well, which of your five partners did you love the most?

MILLAR: I loved every one of them.

ANNCR: You loved every one of them. Does that include spouse number three, with whom you lived for only two days?

Don't Patronize Your Guest. Avoid phrases such as, "I'm sure our viewers would like to know" and "Do you mind if I ask?" A few guests may be reluctant or hostile, but most have come to be interviewed and need no coddling.

Keep Cool. Interviewing is your specialization, and you should feel at ease. Your guest may be a stranger to the interviewing situation and may be awed by the equipment, a bit afraid of you, and worried about saying something wrong. If you fail to remain calm or are distracted, you'll only rattle your guest further.

Keep Control of the Interview. Experienced guests, particularly politicians, can take over and use an interview for their own purposes. Keep the questions coming so that guests don't have time to digress from the subject or the opportunity to indulge in speechmaking.

Make Logical, Smooth Transitions to New Topics. Here's a bad example of making a transition—one actually made by a novice talk-show host:

> **ANNCR:** You said a few moments ago that your most memorable experience was the time you nearly drowned. Tell us, are you into any other sports besides swimming?

Always Be Ready with Your Next Question, but Don't Allow It to Distract You from the Comments Your Guest Is Making. Be prepared to alter your plan on the basis of an unexpected answer, but don't be caught with no question at all in mind. The problem of thinking ahead to the next question without tuning out the present is solved only with practice and experience.

Don't Ask More Than One Question at a Time. It's poor practice to combine questions into a multipart form, as in this example:

> **ANNCR:** Where did you get your inspiration for "Moonlight on the Ohio," and is it true that "Love Song" was inspired by your first wife?

There's a good chance that you'll end up with muddled answers to multiple questions.

Make Questions Brief and to the Point, but Don't Be Rude or Brusque. Don't be afraid to ask more detailed questions when the circumstances warrant, but avoid rambling questions such as this:

> **ANNCR:** Pat, I remember when you won the Academy Award for *Broken Hearts*—that was '99, I believe—and at that time you said you wanted to give up motion picture directing and do something on the Broadway stage. That's when you got involved in directing a modern-dress version of *The Wizard of Oz,* and I guess they'll never let you forget that disaster. Well, looking back, is there any one moment you consider the turning point in your career? Any moment when you should have done something other than what you did?
>
> **PAT:** *Z-z-z-z-z-z. . . .*

Don't Ask Questions That Invite Yes or No Answers. Try instead to draw your guest into an amplified response. The key point here is that your interview will flow better and bring interesting answers if you concentrate on asking "why," "what," and "how" questions rather than "are you," "did you," or "can you" questions.

Here are three examples, the first bad, the other two productive of useful answers:

> **ANNCR:** Are you working on a book now?
>
> **AUTHOR:** Yes.
>
> **ANNCR:** What are you working on now?
>
> **AUTHOR:** I'm still looking at possibilities. I'm curious about . . . .
>
> **ANNCR:** How do you decide on a topic for a book?
>
> **AUTHOR:** I don't think "decide" is the right word—it's more like, "what topic has discovered *me?*"

Even if the author weren't writing at the time, it would be impossible to respond to the last two questions with a simple *yes* or *no*. If your guest does answer *yes* or *no* and the point is of significance, ask for an explanation of the response.

Ask Questions a Layperson Would Ask. Don't be afraid to ask some questions that are fundamental. Many of your listeners may need basic information on the topic.

Go a Step Further and Ask Interesting Questions Most Laypersons Wouldn't Think of. Outstanding interviewers bring out information that the audience wants but doesn't know it wants.

Avoid Obvious Questions. For example, don't ask a famous football player, "You were a football player, weren't you?"

Avoid Predictable Questions. Word some of your questions from a point of view that's opposite to that of your guest. Fresh and unexpected questions are necessary in two common circumstances: when the guest is someone who regularly appears on interview shows and whose opinions are, therefore, widely known, and when the topic has been so thoroughly chewed over by experts and amateurs alike that the audience can anticipate the questions that are likely to be asked. Because your primary task is to give your audience interesting and useful information, try to break away from the known and the obvious.

Don't Answer the Question as You Ask It. For example, what could the senator say in response to the following question except, "That's right"?

> **ANNCR:** Senator, you voted against the treaty. Just what were your feelings about it? Your statement to the news media indicated that you felt we were giving up more than we were gaining.

Don't Feel Compelled to Jump in with a Question the Second a Guest Stops Talking. Some interviewers feel that any dead air is unacceptable. One popular talk-show host was notorious for interrupting guests in the middle of amusing anecdotes, fearing even a moment of silence. Because good interviews are usually *conversations,* pauses are appropriate. Silence, together with an expectant expression, will often encourage a guest to continue in more detail.

A memorable example of a pause more eloquent and moving than spoken words came in the televised court hearing of a boxing champion accused of "throwing" a fight. After the momentous question was asked, at least eight seconds elapsed as the boxer gulped, drew a deep breath, began to answer, paused, blinked several times, and then—in a voice choked with emotion—quietly answered, "Yes sir, I did." It may be unlikely that such a dramatic exchange will occur again, but the principle remains valid: Always be aware of when you, as the interviewer, should just remain silent!

The panic that may set in when you can't come up with a question can make a bad situation even worse; fright can cause you to think about the *problem,* rather than allowing your mind to search for a logical question or comment to continue the interview. When appropriate, ask your guest to elaborate on the statement just made. Ask if there's anything she or he wants to comment on that hasn't been covered in the interview. However, the best protection for avoiding such a tense moment is to be a very careful listener. Going blank usually is the result of inattention to what your guest is saying.

Don't Hesitate to Interrupt if Your Guest Uses Jargon Not in Common Usage. The term *jargon* has several negative connotations, but it also has a neutral meaning: "the specialized or technical language of a trade, profession, or fellowship." When guests use jargon, you may need to ask for clarification so the audience won't be confused.

ANNCR: And what did you find?

GUEST: There wasn't a single PFD in the boat.

ANNCR: PFD? I'm not sure what that is.

GUEST: A personal flotation device.

ANNCR: What I'd call a life jacket?

GUEST: Yes.

Another example:

GUEST: He showed negative life signs.

ANNCR: You mean he was dead?

GUEST: Correct.

During an interview, you'll often find it necessary to make quick decisions about asking for clarification of jargon or in-group terminology. When interviewing a nurse, you may hear "ICU," and you decide almost at once that most of your listeners will know that, especially in a hospital context, this means "intensive care unit." On the other hand, if the nurse speaks of "NIC units," you most likely will decide to ask at once what this term means ("newborn intensive care").

Interviewers and reporters on the *NewsHour with Jim Lehrer* are excellent judges of the occasional need to ask a guest to clarify an obscure term or phrase.

On Television, Check Your Notes Openly, Not Furtively. There's no reason to try to hide your notes. Their use doesn't in any way detract from a good discussion. Notes can be on a clipboard or small file cards.

On Television, Be Aware of Your Posture and Your Facial Expressions. Don't slump and always be aware that your facial expressions are visible to your viewers. Grimaces, frowns, nervous mannerisms, and the like are seldom appropriate for interview hosts.

Before Ending an Interview—Especially if You've Run out of Questions—Ask the Guest Whether He or She Has Anything to Add. Aside from its obvious value when you're unable to come up with another question, this practice gives your guest one last chance to express something interesting or important that didn't come out earlier in the show.

Avoid Ending an Interview with "Well, I See Our Time Is Up." Of course your audience knows you're ending the interview because time is up! However, there are less hackneyed ways of indicating this: "I've been speaking with . . ." or, "I've enjoyed our conversation . . . ." The problem with "I see our time is up" is that it's a cliché that merely states the obvious.

At the Conclusion of the Interview, Thank the Guest Warmly but Briefly. Don't be effusive. Move on quickly to your concluding comments. *And don't forget to tell your audience with whom you've been speaking!*

Checklist *Becoming a Skilled Interviewer*

Preparing for the Interview

1. Carefully research your guest's background, accomplishments, attitudes, beliefs, and positions.
2. Be sure the topic to be discussed is of interest or importance.
3. Where appropriate, limit the number of topics to be explored so that they can be discussed in depth.
4. Don't submit questions in advance, unless you'd lose an important interview by refusing to do so.
5. Write out, or at least make notes on, the introduction and conclusion.
6. Plan at least a few questions to get the interview started and to fill awkward gaps.

The Guest

7. Make your guest feel at home.
8. Establish your guest's credentials at the start of the interview.
9. Occasionally and indirectly reestablish your guest's name and credentials.
10. Remember that your guest is the star.
11. Remember that your guest is the expert.
12. Don't "preinterview" your guest. Spontaneity is lost if you conduct an in-depth prebroadcast interview.

Conducting the Interview

13. Avoid entrapment.
14. Discuss the subject with your guest. Don't make your interview a mere Q & A session.
15. Try to establish a nonthreatening atmosphere.
16. Early in the interview, establish the importance of the topic.
17. During the interview, listen attentively to your guest's replies and react with appropriate interest.
18. In general, base questions on your guest's previous statements.
19. In particular, follow up on important contradictions.
20. Try to build an interview toward a high point or climax.
21. Avoid referring to conversations held before airtime.
22. Seek out your guest's deep convictions.
23. Be tenacious.
24. Don't interrupt with meaningless comments.
25. Point out and emphasize important answers.
26. Don't patronize your guest and don't be obsequious.
27. Keep cool.
28. Keep control of the interview.
29. Make logical, smooth transitions to new subjects.
30. Always be ready with your next question but don't allow it to distract you from the comments your guest is making.
31. Don't ask more than one question at a time.
32. Make questions brief and to the point but don't be rude or brusque.
33. Avoid questions that invite yes or no answers.
34. Ask questions that a layperson would ask.
35. Go a step further and ask interesting questions most laypersons wouldn't think of.

36. Avoid obvious questions.
37. Don't ask predictable questions.
38. Don't answer the question as you ask it.
39. Don't feel compelled to jump in with a question the moment your guest stops talking.
40. Question jargon unless its use is so widespread that you're sure the audience will understand it.
41. On television, check your notes openly, not furtively.
42. On television, be aware of your posture and your facial expressions.
43. Before ending an interview—especially if you've run out of questions—ask your guest whether he or she has anything to add.
44. Don't end an interview with "Well, I see our time is up." If you need to let both guest and listeners know that the program is ending, find a less hackneyed way of saying so.
45. At the conclusion of the interview thank your guest warmly but briefly.

SPOTLIGHT

The Art of Interviewing
by Arthur S. Hough Jr.

I was a young "floating intern" at San Francisco's educational television station, KQED, when out of the blue one day, a producer came to me and said, "Robert Taylor, the actor, is showing up unexpectedly today. Could you be ready to interview him by two o'clock?"

"Of course," I said, although I'd never conducted an on-air interview in my life. I raced to the library to study up on Robert Taylor, and to my horror found that most of his off-screen life was either completely dull or hotly controversial.

Taylor appeared at two o'clock, huge, handsome, and completely poised. I still had not found a way to conduct the interview, so, as our mics were being clipped on, I said in complete frustration, "Mr. Taylor, I've never done this before, and I'm at a loss as to how to approach you." He gave me the most welcome smile I've ever known and said in his deep voice, "Arthur, don't worry about a thing. I'll carry it."

I can't remember how I got him started, probably with some dumb question like, "What has it been like all these years, to be a Hollywood star and celebrity?" And off he went, like a finely tuned machine. I realized that I really had one job to do, to listen and respond. We had a great interview. We talked and laughed, and I made it through to the end just by being there, listening, following, listening, following.

Of course there is a lot more to interviewing than effective listening, but it still is at the top of the list of things to do well. Personal, in-depth interviewing is an art, badly done by most interviewers, mainly because they cannot let go enough to truly listen to their guests. The ace television interviewer, Ted Koppel, has said about himself, "I listen. Most people don't. Something comes along—and whoosh!—it goes right past them."

The considerations that I believe make a brilliant on-the-air interview are steeped in listening:

How do you prepare to listen?

How do you open up your guest to get something worth listening to?

How do you participate and still listen; how do you follow and lead?

How do you make listening an obvious part of your physical style?

How do you get out of it when the time is up?

Interviewing on the air takes everything you've already learned about listening and puts it on a professional, expert level. Like skiing, it is fast, exhilarating, full of unexpected soft spots and high lumps, and a constant test of your most delicate balance and skill.

You can learn the principles in minutes, but it may take years to incorporate them into your own personal style. Here are some quick starting rules.

Preparation

Conduct whatever research you can on your guest but don't conspire with him or her in a preinterview discussion. Preinterviewing kills spontaneity.

Accumulate questions ahead of time to give yourself some feeling for the structure you want to follow; write down key phrases on cards but know that in a really sparkling interview, your prepared questions will fade in importance. Don't be rigid. Follow the flow; be flexible.

Introduction

Introduce quickly and let the guest speak up early. More introductory material can be woven in later. This is especially true on radio, where the audience has no contact at all with your guest until they hear his or her voice.

Ask your guest to explain whatever you think the audience might not understand, special vocabulary, abbreviations, and "in-talk" as in, "When you speak of Jen, do you mean Jennifer Thomas?"

Avoid trivia, or hackneyed questions, such as, "How did you feel when you knew you'd lost the game?"

Participation

Be entirely quiet when the guest is speaking. Do not accompany him or her with little grunts like "Uh-huh," "I see," "Okay." Talk-along interruptions intrude on the audio of the interview and kill crispness.

Keep control but do not dominate. This is a delicate skill. Learn to interrupt but not to intrude. When you must, be sure you break into the guest's stream at phrase endings and breath points. Slip in between thoughts and snip him or her off without intruding. Don't wiggle into the conversation—break in with a strong (but not harsh) voice.

To stop a long monologue, listen closely, pick up the guest's point and grab it. That is, feed back his or her point, and then, without pause, move the guest on, as in, "You had a narrow escape there, but how did you finally find the treasure?"

Break the guest's "tape." Many guests are obviously well prepared on some topics; they've been interviewed before and have developed an inner tape that they play for you. You must get the guest to think rather than recite; break in with the pertinent but unexpected question, such as, "It must have taken some courage to do that; were you frightened?"

Do not kill a good guest run just because you have an agenda. If what you're getting is interesting, let it roll. The audience will hate you for spoiling an interesting chain of thought.

Figure 8-2

Dr. Arthur S. Hough Jr. is an author and professor emeritus of broadcast communication arts at San Francisco State University. He has years of on-air interviewing experience and has taught interviewing technique in a variety of performance courses. *Courtesy of Arthur S. Hough Jr.*

Show evident interest, not perfunctory, distracted, or obsequious attention. Keep eye contact with your guest, but don't just stare.

Participate in the interview, the content, and the feelings. Don't stand off with the objectivity of a scientist with a microscope. Every comment you make should not simply be another question. Feedback that leads to a further or deeper thought is good. Injecting your own opinion or experience is fine so long as it adds to the guest's contribution and does not compete with it. Don't hog the time.

Get rapport—an easy, even, equal relationship with the guest. Make your contribution friendly, not an interrogation, but don't fall into a style of exaggerated awe. Psychologically join your guest, unless your special purpose is to keep perspective.

Avoid these clichés:

So . . . (in introducing your next remark or question)

Right! . . . (to indicate you understand)

That's very interesting.

Thanks for joining us.

Nice to have you with us.

We'd like to thank you . . .

. . . needs no introduction

Listening

Feelings follow facts. Feed back *content* and then go for the *feelings beneath that content.* State, as feedback, what feelings you think you are hearing, as in, "It irritates you that people don't understand your position on this."

Follow subtle clues. Listen for the throwaway phrase, the thing not said or said hurriedly, the inconsistencies, the unusual or out-of-place adjective, as in, "You said 'unfortunate' accident. Do you think it could have been avoided?"

Ending

When your time is up, just say so and stop. The time limit is a real and acceptable factor, nothing to be embarrassed about.

End clean: no fuss, no cliché, no speech.

Radio Talk-Show Hosts

More than 700 radio stations in the United States describe themselves as talk stations. Nearly 1,300 stations are classified as news/talk. At some stations, talk and call-in programs are broadcast twenty-four hours a day with program hosts often performing in four-hour shifts. In contrast, other stations have one talk or call-in show a day, and this may be devoted to sports talk, pet care, or computer troubleshooting.

As an announcer for a radio talk program, you need two major related skills: to conduct interesting and informative interviews (or conversations) with studio guests and, if your show includes phone calls, to converse engagingly with the full spectrum of strangers who call in. You'll also read and respond to queries or statements sent in as e-mail or by fax.

Preparing for the Shift

At a typical talk-radio station, you may expect to work a two- to four-hour air shift, five or six days a week. If you work on weekends or the **graveyard shift** (from midnight on), longer hours may be assigned. Most stations, however, choose to limit talk-show announcers to a maximum of four hours, which is about as long as anyone can be expected to remain sharp, energetic, articulate, and patient. These may seem short working hours, but talk-show hosts spend many additional hours a day preparing for their airtime.

As a talk-show announcer, you'll likely work with a producer, a **phone screener,** and (at most stations) an engineer. The program director, or other designated administrator, suggests guests, may instruct you to schedule a certain guest, and evaluates your work frequently.

The producer assists in scheduling guests, handles correspondence, and acts as traffic director for arriving and departing guests. The phone screener handles all incoming calls during your air shift, cuts off obvious cranks or other undesirables, and lines up calls in order of their calling or according to station policy.

The engineer plays recorded commercials and station logos, cuts in the network for news summaries or breaking news events, and operates the time-delay system. At smaller-market stations, one person may perform the tasks of producing, screening, and audio board operation.

Your first task in preparing for a shift is to develop at least three or four timely, universally interesting, or controversial topics for discussion. Whether or not you have guests, you must open your program with talk that will stimulate listeners' interest and motivate them to call in to offer their opinions. Of course, you won't reveal all of your prepared topics at the outset of your program; you'll begin with the most logical one and save the others to be used if the first topic bombs. In nearly every instance, your first topic will be of current importance.

To be timely and interesting on the air, you must be widely read and knowledgeable about an extremely broad range of topics. There's an absolute limit to the number of times you can get away with saying, "Never heard of it." Unless you're hired specifically to do a sports or other specialized talk show, you must be a *generalist*. You can expect to find yourself discussing such diverse topics as local politics, conservation, and the details of a new and important book at any given moment. To do this effectively, you read several newspapers and magazines regularly and keep abreast of television, movies, books (both fiction and nonfiction), and other important media.

A typical talk-show host reads two local newspapers daily, as well as the *New York Times,* the *Wall Street Journal, USA Today,* and the *Christian Science Monitor.* Weekend reading might include the *New York Times* and the *Los Angeles Times,* as well as two local newspapers, and weekly reading will include *Newsweek, Time, The New Yorker,* and other magazines that keep you current on developments in technology, space exploration, medicine, economics, politics, and other areas of current importance. As program host, you may also read (mostly by skimming) three to five books a week.

Some talk shows are dominated by hosts who talk through their entire shifts without relying on in-studio guests or telephone callers; some hold forth for long periods but accept a few calls or e-mails when they feel their program is dragging. However, while studio guests aren't required, most radio talk shows feature guests to attract an audience—many newspapers list daytime programs, naming the scheduled guest for each. Guests add variety to programs and stimulate listener/viewer interest and involvement. And there's an economic factor that makes guests welcome: Even the most famous and sought-after guests seldom are paid for appearances on talk shows, so they represent a cost-effective source of program material.

Most guests agree to appear on a program because they see it as an opportunity to promote a book, a film, or a cause. There's nothing inherently wrong in such a trade-off, if both parties understand the conditions and as long as the announcer stays in control of the show. Well-known guests are usually on a circuit of appearances on both radio and television talk programs in a number of markets. Such guests know or soon learn they'll be welcome only as long as they help their hosts deliver engaging programs. If you take time to explain to your guests the nature of your show, the kinds of listeners you're attempting to reach (your **audience demographics**), and any station policies that may be relevant, you should have little trouble gaining their full cooperation.

When you schedule guests, you'll be required to inform your station several days in advance. This will give the promotion department time to publicize appearances, generally by sending notice of scheduled guests to local newspapers and by writing promotion copy to be read by other talk-show announcers at your station during their shifts.

Stations maintain a log to keep control over the appearance of guests. They want to avoid overexposing guests as well as repetitiveness in the type of guest or subject covered. A **debriefing log** contains postbroadcast comments, an evaluation of a guest's performance that usually consists of answers to these questions:

What topics did the guest actually cover?

Did the material covered match the preshow expectations?

How well did the guest perform?

How much interest did the guest generate, as measured by phone calls?

Performing as a Radio Talk-Show Announcer

You sit in a small studio immediately adjacent to a control room that houses the engineer and phone screener. You don't use a telephone for your conversations with callers; their voices are amplified so you hear them over a special speaker. You speak directly into an ordinary mic. A soundproof separation of studio and control room is absolutely necessary because of a time delay used as a precaution against the broadcasting of profanity or slander. Because your voice and those of your guests go out over the air approximately seven seconds after the words have been spoken, it's imperative not to be distracted by these sounds coming back to your ears.

The studio will likely have a special telephone console that handles several incoming lines from which you can select callers by punching the appropriate button on the phone base. Calls are fed to the phone base by the screener after sifting the calls to eliminate cranks and drunks, and at some stations to turn away those who don't fit the most desirable "demographic" which, regretfully, generally means people above a certain age or of a particular ethnicity.

A light that illuminates a push button indicates that you have a caller on a particular line. The lines are identified by geographical location and, at most stations, a video display terminal shows the name and hometown of the next person on the line.

You give out the call-in phone number and, from time to time, an e-mail address and fax number.

At the start of your shift, you ad-lib your introduction along predetermined lines. You state the opening topic for discussion and include identification of yourself, the station, the length of your program segment, and the guests (if any) who'll appear later.

Figure 8-3

Sports director Gary Radnich hosts a daily call-in show. Gary lists these qualities as requisite for success as a sports talk-show host: a passion for sports; a broad, up-to-date knowledge of the field; high energy (but not forced); respect for callers' opinions; ability to listen; and a sense of humor.
Courtesy of Gary Radnich and KNBR.

Stations have many policies for talk-show performance; these aren't standardized, but they do tend to be similar. Most ask talk-show hosts not to talk at the start of the program for more than a certain number of minutes before taking a phone call. A related policy insists that you never talk for more than a certain number of minutes during your segment without taking a call, even when you have a fascinating in-studio guest. Your station may ask for more and shorter calls, and if you ask, "More and shorter than what?" the answer may be, "More than you're taking and shorter than you're allowing." The aim of talk radio is maximum listener involvement.

Talk stations **cluster** their commercial announcements. Unlike a popular-music station, where program segments (songs) last three minutes or less, talk shows can't tolerate constant interruptions. A **commercial cluster** may consist of three or more commercials. It's mandatory that you, as the organizer and director of your own show, not get so carried away by ongoing discussions that you forget to deliver the commercial clusters at specified times. Because sponsors pay for the programming, all commercials must be read or played, and they should be spaced properly to avoid piling up toward the end of your shift. All radio announcers work with a log, called the **program log** by people in programming and as the **billing log** by the sales department. It's your responsibility to initial all commercial and public-service announcements as they're broadcast. The Federal Communications Commission (FCC) no longer requires program logs, but most stations continue to maintain them.

Legal and Ethical Concerns

Despite partial deregulation of radio by the FCC, broadcasters continue to be legally responsible for what they send over the airwaves. Many stations give talk-show hosts detailed instructions on their legal and ethical responsibilities.

Payola and plugola are illegal practices. *Payola* refers to the undisclosed payment of something of value to a station employee for the on-air promotion of goods, services, or events. *Plugola* is the promotion by a station of an item or event in which the station or one of its employees has an undisclosed financial interest. Plugola is not illegal if the management of the station is aware of the arrangement and if appropriate sponsorship information is announced. When FCC rules on payola or plugola are violated, fines or even the loss of a station's license could be the outcome.

Challenges and Responsibilities

One of your challenges as a radio talk-show announcer is to motivate many new or infrequent callers. To guarantee fresh call-in talent, you repeat the phone numbers often on the air and tell your listeners from time to time which lines are open. Even if only a few listeners respond to your invitations, don't beg people to phone in. If the telephone lines are dead and can't be revived by your best efforts, you may conclude that one of the following problems exists: (1) your comments are so fascinating that listeners don't want to interrupt, (2) you're so dull and uninspiring that no one is motivated to call, or (3) the transmitter has shorted out.

Occasionally callers may use profane language, mention the names of people other than public figures in a derogatory way, or make defamatory statements. Because your station's license may be at stake in such cases, you must develop quick reflexes with the panic button, which takes the offending comment off the air and replaces it with a beeping sound or a prerecorded warning about such utterances. At most stations, the phone screener/producer does the axing of such calls, but you must be quick to take action if necessary. It's far better to overreact in questionable situations than to let a caller's comments go beyond the point of safety. You can always apologize if your finger was too quick on the button, but there's little you can do constructively once things have gone past the point of no return. You will, of course, be extensively briefed on do's and don'ts.

One of your responsibilities may be to call your audience's attention to other segments of your station's broadcast day. In some cases you'll promote the news, music, contests, sports, or special features. In other instances you'll have to speak favorably of people who have comparable shows on your station—that is, people who might in some ways be considered your competition. Unless there's some station-endorsed mock feud between talk-show announcers, you'll be expected to do a conscientious job of fairly promoting your coworkers.

Television Talk Programs

Unlike radio talk shows, many of which continue to originate with local stations, television now relies almost entirely on nationally syndicated talk programs. Talk shows are available nearly every hour during weekdays, and most are broadcast live, although recorded segments are sometimes inserted. Network programs are early-morning (*Good Morning America*) and late-night offerings (*The Late Show with David Letterman*); most talk shows on unaffiliated television stations are broadcast in midmorning or during the afternoon. Some are network or cable offerings, others are syndicated talk programs sent by satellite, and as many as sixteen are available in one extended metropolitan area during an eight-hour period.[4]

Because it's impossible for anyone to view all of these shows, competition is fierce. And, while competition in many fields results in better products or services, in daytime television it usually brings out extreme sensationalism. Topics on one randomly sampled day are typical: *sex addicts, burdening breasts, interview with a star about her recent breast implants, lesbian lovers, cheating husbands, a man*

---

[4] As of 2008, a few of the most popular national talk shows included: *Dr. Phil, The Oprah Winfrey show, Larry King Live, The Late Show with David Letterman, The View* (with various hosts), *The Daily Show with Jon Stewart, Montel, Inside the Actors Studio,* and *The Tonight Show with Jay Leno.*

MTV and VJs by Ashley Tate

ALL ABOUT ME: I am a senior at Youngstown State University, where I'm a journalism major with a minor in economics. I enjoy reading magazines, writing, spending time with my family and friends, and attending church. I am involved in the Society for Collegiate Journalists, Alpha Kappa Mu National Honor Society, and our student newspaper, The Jambar.

ALL ABOUT MTV AND VJS: MTV (Music Television) is an American-based cable network that started as an airway for music videos but now has an array of syndicated and reality shows that complement its original purpose. MTV was established in 1981 in New York, and since then it has changed the music industry in many ways, including the creation of VJs (video jockeys). MTV got the VJ idea by studying a woman who developed film to go along with DJ music in the nightclub Hurrah in New York. VJs are not just on-air personalities who introduce videos; they are journalists who interview the hottest and most controversial celebrities, and they bring a sense of news reporting to a music channel. While they're quite similar to traditional announcers, VJs must emit a different style than other show hosts—showing off their top-notch social skills and vibrant personalities.

. . . AND HOW DOES THIS AFFECT ANNOUNCING? MTV VJs are important because they reach out to young people in a way that is fairly different than traditional announcers. I think VJs are role models to young people because even though their jobs may look fun and interesting, they still put a lot of work ethic and effort into bringing the audience diverse and interesting entertainment. VJs understand what viewers want, especially the younger demographic, and they know how to provide information in a way that captures and maintains a viewer's attention.

tells his girlfriend he is gay, a man tells his wife that he slept with her best friend on the eve of their wedding, unbelievable car crashes caught on tape, and *gay cross-dressing.* It's ironic that the discussions of breast implants came during the month of October—National Breast Cancer Awareness Month.

Despite excesses, there's room on television for discussions and interviews on topics that actually relate to ideas, values, concerns, and even issues and problems that have an impact on our daily lives. The discussion that follows centers around the hosting of such talk and interview programs.

Hosting Television Talk Shows

Nearly every aspect of talk-show hosting covered in the discussion of radio talk shows applies equally to television.

As a television talk-show announcer, you'll face constant demands on your abilities to ad-lib, cover quickly for slip-ups, concentrate in the face of multiple distractions, and help produce a smooth show without scripts or rehearsals.

Types of Talk Shows

Network and nationally syndicated talk shows are produced by large staffs. Guests are booked well in advance, and transportation and lodging are arranged. Staff members thoroughly research each guest's background and provide the program host with copious notes. Other staff members obtain photos or recorded material that will add to the show's effectiveness. The result is a fast-paced, smoothly produced program with enough variety to retain and please the viewers.

Most locally produced television talk shows are put together by small staffs with limited budgets. Small-market stations provide little support for the host. You'll likely spend the first several years of your career as a talk-show host at a station with limited resources. Many stations lack a floor crew and instead have two cameras locked in fixed positions, with a director sitting at the switcher, cutting from one camera to another as appropriate. Working at such a station will allow you to learn every aspect of talk-show performance and production and prepare you for a move to a station in a larger market. Medium-market stations offer more support but still work with somewhat limited resources. Program quality need not suffer because of modest support, but interview programs require great effort and adaptability from all members of the team.

● PRACTICE

➤ Interviewing for Radio News

These suggestions are offered to help you practice some of the varied assignments given to radio journalists:

1. Cover news conferences with a portable audio recorder. Record the entire conference and then record interviews with appropriate persons—including the spokesperson, if possible—as well as those who favor and those who oppose the speaker's position. Edit the statements to create actualities and wraps with the recorded material. Follow the procedures described in Chapter 9, "Radio News," for writing and recording lead-ins, lead-outs, and connecting commentary.

2. Conduct a range of interviews that demonstrate different types appropriate for radio newscasts: actualities about a specific hard-news incident, position statements of politicians, vox pop interviews, and features interviews, with, for example, a zookeeper about the birth of a rare animal or a city bus driver about the advantages and disadvantages of that vocation.

● PRACTICE

➤ Interviewing

Interviews serve a variety of purposes. The exercises that follow relate to interviews on talk-show programs and person-in-the-street features, sometimes called **vox pops.** The practice section at the end of this chapter suggests interviews for news packages and documentaries.

Before beginning any interview, decide on the interview's purpose; this will help you focus on the best approach (guarded or open, light or somber), the approximate length of the interview, and whether you should stay with one topic or go into two or more areas of discussion. Generally speaking, multiple-topic interviews are appropriate when your guest is a celebrity who can talk on several subjects; single-topic interviews are proper when your guest is a specialist in some area such as pediatrics, investments, or gardening. Vox pop interviews are by necessity single-topic interviews, as are interviews designed for later use in a documentary.

Like most other exercises in this book, those that follow are designed for the simplest possible production, using only a portable audio or video recorder. Any of these exercises can be adapted to full-studio television production:

1. For a multiple-topic interview, select a person you consider unusually interesting. Make sure to do some research about your guest so you have at least a general idea of what can be discovered and discussed. Notes on areas to be

explored are almost a necessity for this type of interview. Plan to interview without stopping your recorder for at least ten or, preferably, twenty minutes.

2. For a single-topic interview, choose a specialist whose field is of great interest to you and interview this person at length without significantly changing the subject. A list of possible questions should help you stay the course.

3. Choose a topic and conduct vox pop interviews. Here are a few suggested questions:

   - What's the most useless gadget on the market?
   - What can be done to reduce commuter traffic?
   - What's the worst advice you've ever received?
   - What would you do if you won the lottery?
   - Describe your dream job.

   You can also obtain samples of public opinion by asking more serious questions, such as probing people's feelings about an item in the news. Editing the responses and organizing them into packages, with appropriate opening and closing remarks, will complete this exercise.

4. Occasionally it's effective to conduct an interview for which all or most of the questions have been written out in advance. For example, you may want to pin down a guest by asking a string of precisely worded questions, such as these:

   - Why did you vote against the treaty?
   - Last May, in your Tulsa speech, didn't you say that you favored the treaty?
   - On May 20, the *Tulsa Record* printed this quote: "I fully support the administration, and therefore I support the proposed treaty." Do you still maintain that you never expressed support for the treaty?
   - Here's a quote from the *Dallas Advance,* dated May 30: "Senator James stated that, while he had some minor reservations about the treaty, he would support it when it came to a vote." Did the *Advance* also misquote you?

Select an interviewee and a topic that lend themselves to a scripted approach and practice this unusual, but sometimes highly effective, interview technique.

Chapter 9

Radio News

Chapter Outline

News, Essential for Democracy

Thomas Jefferson, third president of the United States, believed the continued freedom of our nation required two things, an educated and enlightened citizenry and a free press to investigate and report on government activities. In a letter to the Marquis de Lafayette, he stated, "Where the press is free, and every man able to read, all is safe."[1]

Since its beginnings in the 1920s, radio has been a source of news for nearly all Americans across a vast continent. Those who enter broadcasting as journalists should understand that they assume a serious responsibility. Pertinent information, honestly reported and devoid of "spin," remains the strong safeguard of a functioning democracy.

Radio News Today

News on radio ranges from twenty-four-hour coverage on all-news stations to stations that provide no news at all. Many stations have neither news directors nor reporters and announce news advisories only in emergencies. At some talk and music stations, news reports are provided by a national news service such as Associated Press Radio or CNN Audio. Local National Public Radio (NPR) stations carry many information and discussion programs and usually provide hourly news summaries near the beginning of these programs. NPR and independent stations may also carry Public Radio International (PRI), which is partnered with BBC World Service and whose newscasts give listeners a world perspective on current events. Some NPR stations carry an audio feed of the nightly PBS television broadcast with Jim Lehrer.

Stations that identify themselves as "news/talk," generally intersperse talk shows with news "headlines" at regular periods throughout the day and five-minute newscasts that, with two or more commercial interruptions, actually provide about three minutes or less of news.

At other stations, reports from a wire service are taken directly from a computer terminal, printed, and read without being edited. Announcing at such **rip-and-read operations** requires considerable skill in sight-reading but no journalism skills.

Nearly every broadcast market now has or can receive stations that carry news, but because of the lifting of restrictions on station ownership, hundreds of stations are now owned by large chains.[2] Although these stations may be believed by their listeners to be "local," in reality most of their reports are sent to them as packaged news from a central news department. At such stations, small staffs generate only

---

[1] Thomas Jefferson to Lafayette, 1823.

[2] See comments on the consequences of the Telecommunications Act of 1996 in Chapters 7 and 11.

a portion of their local news, with many stories being supplied by **stringers,** reporters who are paid only for stories chosen by a station's news department.

Most all-news stations offer more than news. Typical features are stock market and business reports; sports, traffic, and weather; and a community billboard. Some stations also feature special interest programs: cooking programs featuring local chefs, gardening specialists, or call-for-action consumer complaint programs. Some special-interest programs are performed by station news personnel; other programs rely on outside specialists, with a station announcer serving as host.

As you read the following discussion of performance and production aspects of radio news, keep in mind that only larger stations have the resources to provide the support described.

Anchoring Radio News

As a radio news anchor, you'll prepare some of the copy you read. There are advantages to this. First, as you write copy, you can contact sources to gather more details or to learn the correct pronunciation of any names or words that might otherwise cause trouble during delivery. Second, investigating stories and writing your own copy will help you develop into a journalist rather than a mere reader of news scripts.

In preparing a news script, you'll work with an editor who decides what stories are to be broadcast and the order of their delivery. You'll be guided by a log listing

Figure 9-1
News & Public Affairs Director Debbie Abrams reads hourly news briefs. She received her B.A. degree in English (UCLA) and her M.A. in broadcast journalism at California State University, Northridge. Debbie began her radio career at her on-campus radio station while studying for her master's degree.
Courtesy of Debbie Abrams and KZST, Santa Rosa.

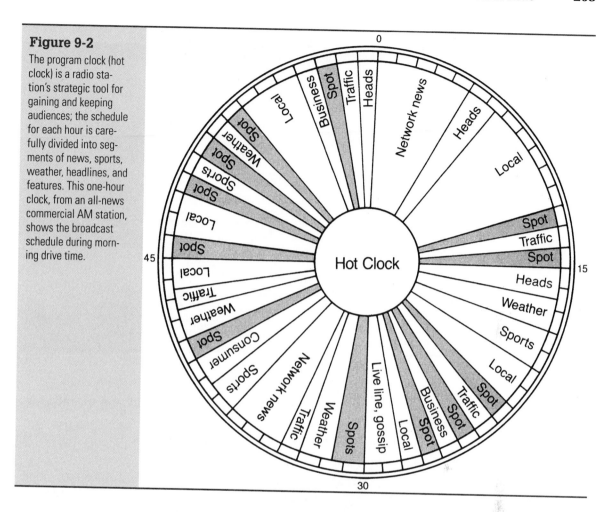

Figure 9-2

The program clock (hot clock) is a radio station's strategic tool for gaining and keeping audiences; the schedule for each hour is carefully divided into segments of news, sports, weather, headlines, and features. This one-hour clock, from an all-news commercial AM station, shows the broadcast schedule during morning drive time.

the sequence of components making up the newscast. Most news-oriented stations follow a cyclical format—called a **clock** or **newswheel**—that's repeated on an hourly basis. Some news clocks divide a drive-time hour into forty or more segments. A sample clock, or newswheel, is shown in Figure 9.2. A typical format begins or ends each hour with five minutes of network news, provides national and world news headlines at or near the half-hour, and has features, sports, weather, traffic, stock market reports, and local headlines at regularly established intervals. Commercials are also scheduled at stipulated times.

News Sources

When preparing copy for a news shift, you may expect to work with news from several sources. Some stories will be generated by station reporters; others will come from news providers. Here are resources typically available to radio news personnel:

TABLE 9-1 Terms Used on a Newswheel

Term	Meaning
Net news	Network news
Heads	News headlines
Local	Local news stories
Spot	Commercial
Traffic	Traffic reports
Sports	Sports briefs from station's sports reporter
Weather	Weather report from station's meteorologist
Business	Business report from station's business reporter
Live line, gossip, etc.	Special features done by news anchors, just for fun
National	National news reported by local anchors
Consumer/medical	A consumer report from station's consumer reporter or a medical report by a doctor or other medical specialist

- Audio reports, both live and recorded, from station, field, and special-assignment reporters
- Associated Press (AP) and Reuters newswires
- Associated Press Radio Network news feeds
- A city wire service, which may be independently owned and operated or supervised by a major news service
- Interviews or news reports received by telephone

The Associated Press (AP) services for radio stations are far too extensive to be listed here and will change as technology makes available more choices and delivery systems, but this overview will give you a general idea of services offered as of 2008.

The Associated Press sends news stories from computer to computer to member stations. News directors have available "custom categories," a menu of features such as state news, national news, international news, farm news, and more, so a station can receive only those stories that fit its needs. News stories in selected categories are printed directly on paper or stored in a station's computer and printed after a decision has been made whether to use them. An all-news station, a rock station, and a country music station can choose news stories appropriate to each station's format. AP also sends audio cuts of actualities, voicers, natural sound, wraps, and on-the-scene reports that may be selected and inserted into local newscasts.

The AP also provides audio reports, including:

- Three-minute top-of-the-hour newscasts, with an optional breakaway at :02 to allow stations to sell the third minute
- Sixty-second bottom-of-the-hour newscasts at :31, to fit with stations' traffic and weather reports
- Live special reports when major stories break, scheduled up to four times an hour and expanded for crisis coverage

AP NewsPower sends copy, written in broadcast style and ready to air, featuring state and national news as well as sports, business, entertainment, and weather. AP NewsPower allows station newswriters to call up a story paragraph by paragraph on their computers. At the push of a button, the paragraph from the news service moves to the top or bottom of the video display terminal, permitting the operator to paraphrase or to add a local angle by typing the story on the unoccupied portion of the screen. The push of another button directs the computer to print the rewritten story. At some radio stations, on-air newscasters read their scripts directly from a video display terminal. For editing at a radio station, AP NewsPower includes an integrated pronunciation lookup and insertion, as well as a thesaurus lookup and replacement.

When using stories from the wire services, you have three options:

1. Read the story as you find it.
2. Leave the story unaltered but add a lead-in of your own.
3. Edit the story to shorten it, sharpen it, or give it a local angle.

Whatever you decide, the story must be entered in the running sequence of the newscast. At some stations you'll make a copy for the files and insert the original in a loose-leaf book from which you'll work during your shift.

Sound Bytes

The Associated Press lists all its services to broadcast stations on
www.apbroadcast.com/

Many radio stations that feature news ask reporters to work the **beat check** (also called the **phone beat** or the **phone check**) as part of their shift. This consists of making phone calls to agencies and persons who are most likely to provide news items regularly. A typical beat list includes phone numbers and names of contacts for all nearby police, sheriff, disaster, fire, and weather departments; federal agencies such as the Federal Bureau of Investigation; the Secret Service; the Bureau of Alcohol, Tobacco, Firearms and Explosives; the civil defense headquarters and the National Guard; local and nearby jails and prisons; all local hospitals; all nearby airport control towers; and specialized agencies important to listeners in your community (for example, the farm bureau and earthquake stations).

When you work the beat check, plan to call each listed agency at the same time each day. Try to establish a personal relationship with the contact there. Discover how each contact prefers to work with you—whether you're allowed to record the conversation or are permitted only to paraphrase statements. If it fits the news report, give credit to the people who supply your station with news items; most people are pleased to hear their names on the air. At the same time, you must respect requests for anonymity.

Preparing for a Shift

When preparing for a news shift that will keep you on the air for two to four hours, you'll typically write, rewrite, and assemble about two hours' worth of material, including live copy, recorded reports, features, and commercials. While you're performing, a newswriter will be writing and assembling material for the remaining hours of your shift.

The checklist prepared by the news director or producer will include stories to be featured, the order in which you should give them, and the sounds with which you'll work. **Sounds** are different from **sounders,** which are short musical **IDs** or **logos** that identify a particular feature such as a traffic or sports report. Sounds come in several forms:

- An actuality is a brief statement made by someone other than station personnel, such as a newsmaker or eyewitness. It's recorded in the field on a battery-operated recorder or at the station by way of a cell phone. At many radio stations, the television term *sound bite* has replaced *actuality.*
- In a **wrap,** or wraparound, a reporter records an opening that leads into an actuality, followed by the reporter's closing comments. The conclusion may be a brief summary, followed by a tag line such as "Bill Hillman, KZZZ News."
- A **voicer** is a report from a field reporter, usually sent to the station by a cell phone, short-wave radio, or a conventional phone.
- A **scener** is a report on a breaking event. It's usually broadcast live but may also be recorded for inclusion in a later broadcast.
- **Raw sound** refers to what may be called "news noise"—protesters chanting or funeral music without reporter commentary.

Actualities and wraps need **lead-ins** and **lead-outs,** sometimes called **intros** and **outros.** As you prepare for your shift, you listen to the sounds with which you'll work and write introductions and ending statements. In preparing lead-ins and lead-outs, follow established practice at your station. Practices vary from station to station, but most follow a general pattern.

First, you'll make decisions about editing the actualities, voicers, and wraps with which you'll work, as well as any recorded sceners to be repeated after their earlier live presentation. As you listen to each cut, you'll make decisions about the various segments you'd like to use. Some of these will have been edited by a field reporter, a newswriter, or another newscaster, so you may add them to your on-air material without alteration.

Because there are fewer station personnel to help you prepare or update material during off-peak hours, as in the middle of the night or the weekend, you'll most likely rely on recorded stories prepared by others. Most recordings used in newscasts are edited electronically. The excerpts you intend to use must be dubbed to a storage medium. One actuality or recorded telephone interview often provides several sounds for a newscast. On your script you'll indicate the words that close each segment of the report so that the announcer who uses them will know the **out cues.**

You'll also write a log that lists the general nature of each actuality, the running time of each, and its out cues, or end cues. Figure 9-3 shows one example of current practice in logging actualities. The log shows that the editor (who was also the reporter) was able to obtain three brief actualities from one recorded telephone conversation with a forest ranger. The general nature of each actuality is listed under SUBJECT, and the end cues allow the anchor to pick up immediately when the cut ends. When the precise end cue is also spoken earlier in the actuality, the person preparing the log writes "double out" in the END CUE column to indicate that fact. For example, if the phrase "as of now" had been used by the ranger twice in the first actuality, "double out" would have warned the newscaster against picking up the cue prematurely.

In preparing for a newscast, you must have a fairly accurate idea of the number of lines or pages you'll read in the allotted time.

Figure 9-3
An actuality log prepared by a reporter.

RADIO NEWS ACTUALITY LOG   EDITOR: HEWITT

STORY AND REPORTER: Forest Fire, Hewitt

CART #	SUBJECT	TIME	END CUE
N-35	Mt. Sakea forest ranger James Cleary—fire has burned more than 3,000 acres	:16	"as of now."
N-99	No evidence as to cause. Arson not ruled out. Man seen leaving area at high speed in green sports car.	:11	"in a green sports car."
N-83	Should have it surrounded by tonight, and contained by midday tomorrow— depending on the weather.	:15	"a lot of tired firefighters will be able to go home."

To project the amount of time it will take to read copy, count the number of lines on a typical page of copy and time yourself as you read aloud at your most comfortable and effective speed. If you read at about 180 words a minute, you'll read the following numbers of lines in the given time:

15 seconds = 4 lines

30 seconds = 8 lines

45 seconds = 12 lines

60 seconds = 16 lines

If a page of copy has thirty-two lines, for example, you'll read a page in about two minutes. With such information you can easily project the number of lines of copy needed for a newscast of a specific length.

Of course, a time chart is useful only for developing a sense of the relation between space (the physical copy) and time (the newscast). Experienced reporters have so developed this sense that they can prepare newscasts without conscious thought of lines per minute or of their reading speed. As you work with a time chart, remember that actualities, commercials, and sounds—as well as your desire to vary your pace of reading to match the moods of the stories—will complicate your timing.

Writing News

As a radio journalist, you'll be expected to write well and rapidly. To help you develop your writing skills, Chet Casselman, a highly experienced news director

Checklist *Writing Effective News Copy*

1. Write for the ear rather than the eye.
2. Avoid confusing words and statements.
3. Avoid excessive redundancy.
4. Use the present tense and the active voice.
5. Avoid initials.
6. Don't give addresses.
7. Use official job titles.
8. Proofread for badly cast sentences.
9. Avoid using we to refer to yourself.
10. Don't refer to a suspect's past criminal record.

and former national president of the Radio-Television News Directors Association, offers the following guidelines. They are, for the most part, equally applicable to writing news for television.

Write for the Ear Rather Than the Eye. Your listeners don't see the script; they only hear it. Sentences should be relatively short, the vocabulary should be geared to a heterogeneous audience, and potentially confusing statistics should be simplified. Some specific rules:

- Say it the simple way. Eliminate unnecessary ages, middle initials, addresses, occupations, unfamiliar or obscure names, precise or involved numbers, incidental information, and anything else that slows down or clutters up the story.

- Convert precise or involved numbers to a simplified form. For example, change 1,572 to "almost sixteen hundred," 2.6 million to "slightly more than two and a half million," and 35.7 percent to "nearly 36 percent." Unless a number is an essential part of the story, it should be dropped.

- Express names of famous people and their relatives carefully to avoid confusion. For instance, "The wife of famous architect Sydney Nolan is dead; Mary Nolan died today in Chicago of heart failure" is much clearer than "Mary Nolan, 67, wife of famous architect Sydney Nolan, died today in Chicago."

- Avoid indiscriminate use of personal pronouns. Repeat the names of the persons in the story rather than using *he, she,* or *they* whenever there's the slightest chance that the reference may be misunderstood.

- Report that a person pleads "innocent" rather than "not guilty." The latter may be too easily misunderstood as its opposite.

- Avoid the words *latter, former,* and *respectively,* which are acceptable in print but shouldn't be used on the air because listeners have no way of referring to the original comment.

- Avoid hackneyed expressions common to newscasts but seldom heard in everyday conversation. Say *run* instead of *flee, looking for* instead of *seeking,* and *killed* or *murdered* instead of *slain.*

- Change direct quotations from first person to third person whenever the change will help listeners understand. It's clearer to say, "The mayor says she's going to get to the bottom of the matter" than to say, "The mayor says, and these are her words, 'I'm going to get to the bottom of the matter,' end of quote."

- Always use contractions, unless the two words are needed for emphasis.

Avoid Confusing Words and Statements. The following lead-in to a news story is seriously misleading: "We have good news tonight for veterans and their families. A House committee has approved a 5 percent cost-of-living increase." People unfamiliar with the legislative process might assume the money was as good as in the bank; in reality, the increase needs to be approved by a majority vote of the House, then by the Senate, and finally needs the signature of the president to take effect.

Confusion can also arise from using *homonyms*, words pronounced the same as others with different meanings. For example, when there was an outbreak of the deadly Ebola virus in Africa, radio listeners must have been puzzled when they heard ". . . ninety people were killed by Ebola virus" and thought they heard ". . . ninety people were killed by a bowl of iris." (Say this aloud, and you'll hear the cause of confusion.)

Avoid Redundancy. Repeating important facts is advisable, but too frequent repetition is dull. For example, a newscaster might say, "Senator Muncey has called the recent hike in the prime lending rate outrageous," and then go to an actuality in which we hear the senator say, "The latest hike in the prime lending rate is, in my opinion, outrageous." Work always for lead-ins that promote interest but don't duplicate the story that follows.

Use the Present Tense and the Active Voice. Because the electronic media can report events as they happen, the *present tense* is appropriate; it automatically gives news an air of immediacy. But you must be honest when using present tense, because there are times when the present tense won't work. Unless the event is happening as you cover the story, it would be misleading to say, "The hurricane is causing mass evacuations," when that action occurred and ended in the past. The *active voice* uses verbs that give sentences power. Instead of writing, "The passenger ship was rammed by a submarine in Hampton Roads," write, "A submarine rammed a passenger ship in Hampton Roads."

Avoid Initials. Use initials only when they're so well known that no mis-understanding is possible. A few standard abbreviations are readily identifiable; examples are FBI, U.S., YMCA, and CIA. Most abbreviations, not as well known, should be replaced with the correct title, for example, "The Michigan Teacher's Association," followed later in the story by an appropriate phrase such as "the teachers' association," and *not* by "the MTA."

Don't Give Addresses in News Copy. You may give addresses if they're famous or essential to the story. Ten Downing Street, the home of the British prime minister, is a safe address to broadcast. The address of a murder suspect or an assault victim is not.

Be Careful to Use Official Job Titles. Use *firefighters, police officers,* and *mail carriers,* rather than *firemen, policemen,* and *mailmen.*

Be Wary of Badly Cast Sentences. This example from a wire-service bulletin shows the peril of careless writing:

> Detectives found two and a half pounds of Asian and Mexican heroin in a large woman's handbag when the car was stopped in South Central Los Angeles.

Listeners probably missed the next two news items while trying to decide whether the heroin was found in the handbag of a large woman or in a woman's large handbag.

When Referring to Yourself, Use *I* Not *We*. Such use of *we* is inaccurate and pretentious. No one person can be "we," although monarchs and high church officials have traditionally used *we* this way.

Using Soundtrack Pro for Radio News Packages
by Marchelle Smalls

ALL ABOUT ME: I am a senior communications major at Pennsylvania State University: Altoona Campus. Originally from Philadelphia, I love editing in video, computer graphics, and photography. I also have a deep passion for all aspects of theater, writing poetry, and teaching.

ALL ABOUT SOUNDTRACK PRO: Soundtrack Pro is a multitrack audio editing program that allows users to create soundtracks and sound effects and do audio mixing by putting separate tracks together. It is included in the Final Cut Pro suite and can be used interchangeably with the other software within the program. Soundtrack Pro allows announcers to hear what better sound quality is and gives them the opportunity to create it. With this program announcers are given control of voice equalization, actualities, and much more.

. . . AND HOW DOES THIS AFFECT ANNOUNCING? Soundtrack Pro has such an inviting platform that even those who aren't tech-savvy can pick it up. Because the program is easy to use, many announcers are taking advantage of it and putting together clearer, crisper news packages. I love using Soundtrack Pro for class and for fun. It allows me to expand my creative abilities. Since I have become comfortable with the software, I have been able to embrace the world of announcing and reporting. I practice speech personality, analyze my voice and actualities, and use all the other tools. I plan on using Soundtrack Pro to create more complicated music scores and reporting packages and maybe do a special spoken word poetry segment for my school's newly developed radio station.

Don't Refer to a Suspect's Past Criminal Record. Unless it's known to be true and is an important aspect of a present case, a suspect's past criminal record should not be mentioned. In most instances, a suspect's criminal record should be reported only after the suspect has been formally charged. Also, don't refer to any history of mental illness or treatment unless the information is essential to the story and has been checked for accuracy. Not only may reporting such information be defamatory, it may also prejudice the public against the person accused of a crime but not charged, tried, and convicted.

Avoid the Misuse of *Allegedly*. Perhaps the most overused word in broadcast news reports is *allegedly*. It's impossible for a person to steal, kill, or lie in an alleged way. "Twenty people were allegedly killed or injured by the crazed gunman" makes no grammatical sense. Although many reporters and news directors believe that the use of *allegedly* protects the station from charges of libel, this is not true. You aren't protected when using the term unless the story includes the name or title of the person doing the "alleging." It's safe to say, "Police Captain Truitner alleged that the man threatened to kill his hostage." When you state the name or title of a person who is qualified to make an allegation (such as a police captain), you can omit the qualifying term *alleged* altogether.

The only sound reason for using any of the derivatives of allegation is to help preserve the notion that all people are innocent until proven guilty. There are, however, correct and incorrect ways of using these words. Here are three misuses noticed recently:

1. "The bullet allegedly fired at the president. . . ." This is ludicrous. The reporter can't possibly question the fact that a gun was fired and a bullet whizzed past the president, when viewers can see the incident on their television screen.

2. "Jones will stand trial for alleged auto theft." The notion of a trial carries with it the allegation, by a district attorney, of guilt. Therefore, *alleged* is unnecessary in this sentence.

3. "The experts have examined the alleged bullets used in the assassination." There are many kinds of bullets, but no one has ever examined an *alleged* one.

When considering the use of any term of *allegation*, ask yourself these questions: (1) Is the word necessary to qualify the statement? (2) Am I using it correctly? Clearly, *allegedly* and *alleged* are unnecessary in the three examples given. Is it possible or useful to say who is doing the alleging? "Meyer is alleged by his wife to have set fire to the store" is longer and more cumbersome than "Meyer, the alleged arsonist," but it contains more useful information and is fairer to Meyer than the shorter version. The indication that Meyer's wife did the alleging also removes the possibility of your being sued for libel! However, is the term *is alleged* the best way of saying this? Instead, say, "Meyer's wife claims that . . . ." The following are some correct and incorrect uses of these terms:

Correct	*Incorrect*
"The principal alleged that the striking teachers destroyed their attendance records."	"The striking teachers allegedly destroyed their attendance records."
"Benson is alleged by the State Department to be an undercover agent."	"Benson is allegedly an undercover agent for a foreign power."
"Chang is reported to be set to buy the hockey team at the end of the season."	"Chang allegedly is set to buy the hockey team at the end of the season."

Note that this last statement is wrong in two ways: First, it isn't possible to buy anything in an alleged manner; second, terms of allegation are to be used for instances in which there's possible wrongdoing.

Allegedly is a poor reporter's cop-out. This word fails to tell us who is doing the alleging. If you don't know who's doing the alleging, it's your responsibility to find out and to include that information in your report.

Checking Your Newswriting Style

A simple way to check the clarity of your broadcast newswriting was developed by Irving Fang, who calls his system the easy listening formula (ELF).[3] It's applied by counting, in each sentence, every syllable above one per word. For example, the sentence "The quick brown fox jumped over the lazy dog" has an ELF score of 2 : 1 for the second syllable in *over* and 1 for the second syllable in *lazy.* To find the total ELF score for a script, compute the ELF scores of all the sentences and average them.

Fang's investigation of a wide variety of broadcast news scripts showed that the ELF scores of the most highly rated newswriters average below 12. If your news scripts score consistently above that figure, you may not be writing well for aural comprehension. Fang points out, however, that no mechanical system of measuring language is infallible. Common sense must be applied at all times in using his formula, because "it is easy to devise a confusing sentence with a low ELF score, just as it is easy to devise a simple sentence with a high ELF score. . . . What the easy listening formula shows is tendency and trend."

---

[3] Irving E. Fang, *Television News, Radio News*, revised 4th ed. (St. Paul: Rada Press, 1985), pp. 42–43.

Delivering the News

When you've written and rewritten the copy you'll use during your air shift and when the sounds are assembled and logged, you're ready to go on the air. As you sit in the on-air studio, you'll likely have before you the following items:

- The **running log,** sometimes called a **run sheet,** which follows the established format of your station and indicates the times at which you'll give headlines, features, time checks, commercials, and other newscast elements or the times at which they'll be played. The log may be on sheets of paper, on a computer screen, or both.
- The continuity book, which contains notations of recorded commercials you'll play.
- Your **news script,** which will be on loose sheets or on a video display screen.
- An **elapsed-time clock,** which you can start and stop to help you time the commercials you'll read.
- **Switches,** or **buttons,** that allow you to open and close your announce mic, to open and close the intercom or talk-back mic, and to open a mic in the newsroom for feeding out a news bulletin.
- Equipment for playing actualities, commercials, station IDs, jingles, and such.
- One or more lights to send you information while you're on the air. (For example, a red light might indicate that the newsroom has a bulletin to be read; a yellow light might tell you that the station's traffic reporter has a traffic alert.)

The on-air studio may be equipped with a comfortable chair without armrests (they'd restrict movement) and castered legs to enable you to scoot in and out or from side to side. The chair may be designed to promote good posture, but no chair alone can make anyone sit up straight. The quality of your voice is directly affected by your posture; remember to sit comfortably, but try to keep your spine as straight as possible. A slumping person can't breathe correctly, and weakened abdominal muscles and diaphragm can't push air from your lungs through your phonators and articulators with sufficient strength.

Position yourself so you can easily reach the script, the continuity book, and the controls of both the elapsed-time clock and your mic. You'll be checking off commercials, PSAs (public-service announcements), and other program elements as they occur, so make sure you're in a position to reach the running log with your pencil. Unless you have an unusual voice or speech personality, you should position yourself six to ten inches from the mic. If you experience problems with excessive sibilance or popping, or if your voice sounds thin or strident, work with a station engineer to find a better way of using your mic.

When you're on the air with the news, you're the anchor. At times you may be joined in the booth by a feature reporter, a field reporter who's returned from the scene of a news event, or a coanchor (a second newscaster who'll alternate with you in the reading of news stories).

Most news announcers read copy at 175 to 200 words a minute. This speed is considered fast enough to give the appropriate degree of importance to the material yet slow enough to be understood easily. At a station that carries only infrequent and very brief reports, you may be asked to read at a much faster rate. The overall sound of the station will determine reading speed. To prepare for all eventualities, you should practice reading news in at least four different ways:

1. Practice reading the news slowly and casually, as preferred by many low-key stations.
2. Read the news at the rate you feel brings out the best in your voice, interpretive abilities, and personality.
3. Practice at a rate of approximately 200 words a minute. This is the rate that may be expected of you.
4. Practice reading at your absolute maximum rate, with the realization that you're reading too fast if you stumble, slur words, have trouble maintaining controlled breathing, force your voice into stridency, or lose significant comprehensibility.

As you read, be prepared for mistakes you may make from misreading or stumbling over words, introducing the wrong recorded message, or cuing prematurely. Some argue that mistakes should be covered up rather than acknowledged, but the best practice is to acknowledge mistakes as frankly but as unobtrusively as possible. Here's an example of a weak cover-up:

ANNCR: . . . and they'll have your car ready in a half-hour, or an hour and a half, whichever comes sooner.

The script said "in an hour and a half." The cover-up is improper because it gives false information. Here's another example:

ANNCR: The press secretary delayed and relayed the president's statement on the meeting.

Here the cover-up is so obvious that it would have been far better to have said, "The press secretary delayed—sorry, relayed—the president's . . . ."

When giving cues to a coanchor, stop talking after throwing the cue. If you ramble on, you'll talk over your partner's opening words. No well-run station will tolerate such sloppiness. In throwing cues, don't think it amateurish to make your gestures big, clean, and precise. The best professionals never lapse into practices that can damage the program or their own performance.

You may be handling a great deal of paper during your air shift, so develop skill in shifting papers without allowing the sound of rattling paper to be picked up by your mic. You'll need to lift script pages from the pile in front of you, move them to one side, and turn script pages in the continuity book. No materials should be stapled together, so there should be no need to turn over pages while on the air.

There will be many times during a normal shift when you'll have an opportunity to talk directly with your producer, coanchor, or sports, traffic, or weather reporter. Use these opportunities for questions or comments but keep such voice contacts to a minimum. It's important that you not lose track of what your audience is hearing at such times. Check details that might prevent errors. Tell the producer that you're going to shorten or dump a story because you're running late. If in doubt, ask what the next sound is to be. But be aware at all times of what's going out over the air. More than one anchor has followed a tragic actuality with an inappropriate wisecrack. Also, there's the possibility that the wrong package has been played. If you aren't listening, you can't possibly correct the mistake.

Be prepared to make constructive use of the minutes you have during your shift when you're not actually on the air. During breaks of thirty to sixty seconds, bring your logging up to date; check out the next few sounds you'll introduce or cue; and see whether you're running ahead of, behind, or right on schedule. During longer breaks, you may have to write intros to actualities or voicers that were received and edited while you were on the air.

Three- or four-hour shifts aren't uncommon at stations that feature news. It takes a healthy speech mechanism to continue to perform well day after day. You'll

Figure 9-4
During morning commutes, 5:30 to 7:00 a.m. each weekday, Stan Burford reports from a helicopter to inform television viewers of traffic conditions. During afternoon drive time, he works in a radio newsroom with a bank of audio monitors to keep drivers informed of traffic problems and alternate routes they may take.
Courtesy of Stan Burford, KGO-TV and KGO NewsTalk Radio.

very quickly become aware of any misuse of your vocal apparatus because you'll suffer from hoarseness, sore throat, or similar disorders. Always have such symptoms checked by a doctor.

Long before you apply for a position as a news anchor, you should practice performing as you'll be expected to perform on the job. Practicing means not only learning to work with all the elements of a contemporary newscast but also reading the news for extended periods. Such practice can't ordinarily be accomplished in a classroom, so you're encouraged to look for opportunities to perform wherever they present themselves. College radio stations offer realistic challenges to students preparing for careers as radio news personnel.

The Radio Field Reporter

Field reporters are responsible for (1) live coverage of events as they occur; (2) recorded actualities, voicers, and wraps; and (3) occasional research for, and production of, **minidocs,** brief documentaries presented as a series, usually over several days. Radio field reporters are sometimes called *general-assignment reporters, correspondents,* or *special-assignment reporters.* Their work is similar to that of their television counterparts, with obvious variations because of differences in electronic technology.

Live Reporting

When reporting live, it's your responsibility to create a word picture of a scene, including sights, sounds, smells, tension in the air, and factual details—for example, the extent of a blaze, the names of the victims, or the value of stolen goods. When reporting live, you'll use your cell phone to indicate when you're ready to give your report, and you'll hear your cue to start as the program line is fed to you. Even when you're describing events as they occur (a live scener), as opposed to reporting at the conclusion of an event, you may work from notes that you scribbled as you gathered information.

As you give a live report, keep these suggestions in mind:

- Don't report rumors, unless they're essential to the story—and then report them only as rumors.
- Don't make unsubstantiated guesses as to facts, such as numbers of people injured or the value of a gutted building.
- Control your emotions but remember that a bit of genuine excitement in your voice will convey the significance of the event.
- Don't identify yourself at the start of the report; the anchor will already have given your name. Identify yourself at the close of the story, following the policy set by your station.

- In the event of physical danger—a police siege or a confrontation between rival groups or street gangs—don't become so absorbed in your story that you endanger yourself or your station's equipment.

- Be prepared to discuss the event with the anchor after you've given your report. This means doing sufficient investigation prior to going on the air so that you can answer questions.

Voicers, Actualities, Sceners, and Wraps

Most of your work as a field reporter won't be broadcast live, but as **packages,** which consist of wraps, voicers, and edited sceners. When recording in the field, you'll likely use a digital recorder. When making packages at the station, you'll dub directly from the recorder to a computer equipped with an editing program, such as Adobe Audition. This program allows you to listen to your report as you watch a visual image of the audio. You may then make your edits to select, assemble, and condense the report to conform to time limitations. Eventually, you may send your report to a mass storage disk. These will be the sounds introduced by news anchors during their shifts.

Field voicers usually are transmitted to the station by cell phone. After making notes, you call the newsroom of your station and notify a reporter or producer that you're ready to file a report. The person taking your call will prepare to activate a storage medium and will place an index finger on the start button. You give a brief countdown—"three, two, one"—and start your report. The person taking the call presses the start button just after you say "one." If all goes well, the recording and your report begin at the same time. Voicers made at the station are produced in essentially the same way, although you'll typically perform all of the work without assistance.

When reporting live from the field, your voice is put directly on the air. The process becomes more complicated when you're sending a report that includes one or more actualities that you've recorded previously. You'll have to speak into the mouthpiece of your cell phone, press the start button on your minidisk digital recorder (or tape cart), quickly move the telephone's mouthpiece down to the speaker of your recorder to send the bulk of your report, and then move the cell phone up to your mouth to make your closing comments and tag.

A wrap is phoned in essentially the same way as a voicer except for this difference: When all elements are connected, your recorded report is cued and you give the countdown and begin your introduction to the actuality live. When you finish, you hit the play key, and the story rolls. When the actuality is completed, you stop your recorder and give your closing tag live.

In making voicers at the station, you'll write a script. In this case the log will simply indicate "script attached," the duration of the voicer in seconds, and the end cue, which is nearly always your name followed by the call letters of your station.

In making wraps at the station, you begin by making and recording telephone calls. If there's a news story of an impending strike, for example, your phone calls may be to the union leader, the speaker for the company or agency being threatened, and a labor negotiator. From the telephone interviews you should be able to make several usable wraps—edited, timed, and ready to be logged.

SPOTLIGHT

Philosophies of Radio and Television Journalism

As a journalist working for a television, radio, or cable news station (such as CNN), you'll make important decisions daily. The way you report stories will influence attitudes and actions of your listeners and viewers. Because of this, it's essential that you develop a working philosophy of broadcast journalism. When an important story breaks, it's far too late for you to start making decisions about your responsibilities, values, and philosophy of broadcast journalism.

In a democracy there are only two theories of the press worthy of consideration. The first, the **libertarian theory,** is based on the belief that, except for defamation, obscenity, or wartime sedition, there should be no censorship or suppression of news whatsoever. The second theory, which Wilbur Schramm named the **social responsibility theory,** maintains that journalists must exercise judgment as to whether a particular story should be covered or ignored and, if covered, how it should be covered.

The libertarian theory of the press grew out of democratic movements in England near the end of the seventeenth century and received renewed momentum a hundred years later through the writings and speeches of Thomas Paine, Thomas Jefferson, and other American revolutionaries. Essentially, the libertarian theory was a response to centuries of suppression and censorship by church and state. Jefferson, whose beliefs about the importance of a free press are found at the outset of this chapter, made this concise statement in 1816: If a nation expects to be ignorant and free, in a state of civilization, it expects what never was and never will be." The implications of this statement are clear: Allow full and free publication of all shades of opinion and all items of information. The basic assumption of the libertarians was (and is) that a free people in full possession of the facts will act responsibly.

The social responsibility theory was a response to what many saw as shortcomings in the idealistic libertarian theory. In practice, the public simply wasn't receiving all of the facts necessary to make responsible decisions. In the wake of the civil disorders of the late 1960s, a presidential commission called attention to what was seen as the failure of the press to adequately inform the public: "Disorders are only one aspect of the dilemmas and difficulties of race relations in America. In defining, explaining, and reporting this broader, more complex, and ultimately far more fundamental subject, the communications media, ironically, have failed to communicate."

A libertarian approach to riot coverage was unacceptable to the commission for several reasons: Reported facts may have been exceptional rather than typical; disclosing some facts may have caused even more serious incidents; and, although the reported fact indeed may have happened, it may have occurred only because the news media were encouraging certain actions by their very presence. The social responsibility theory of the press asks that journalists report not only the facts but also the truth behind the facts.

The concerns expressed regarding a libertarian approach to journalism are understandable when one thinks of serious news events such as riots, wars, or insurrections. The social responsibility theory demands that journalists apply their best judgment and weigh their conduct on a daily basis without regard to the nature or scope of the story being covered. Both the libertarian and the social responsibility theories of news coverage ask that reporters be responsible journalists; all reporters should start with good intentions, but a well-meant beginning is not enough. Only a solid education in broadcast and journalistic law, ethics, and investigative reporting can lead to success as a responsible broadcast journalist.

Preparing Feature Reports: Minidocs

Radio stations that emphasize news sometimes vary their programming by broadcasting feature reports or short documentaries. These may be a series of three- or four-minute programs, broadcast as three or as many as seven individual segments, each focusing on a different aspect of a topic. Feature reports deal with people, problems, events, or anything else that's of general interest but lacks the hard-news character that demands coverage on a regular newscast. Breaking news stories do, however frequently inspire feature reports, but features differ from news stories in that they provide much more detail, offer greater perspective, and often express a point of view.

Preparing a series of feature reports begins with the selection of a topic. An editor may assign a topic to you, but as feature reporter you're expected to come up with promising ideas of your own. It's obvious that your overriding responsibility is to report on issues of general interest. That's the easy part. The more difficult task is finding ways to make your reports appealing. As a reporter on radio, one of your first considerations should be sounds. Ask yourself what kinds of sounds, both spoken and natural environmental sounds, can be used to take advantage of your medium. No report can be considered a success unless it captures and holds the attention of your listeners. A succession of statements by public officials isn't likely to be dramatic or even interesting, but official position statements interspersed with more dramatic actualities, sound effects, and narration can deliver a series that first grabs audience attention and then satisfies audience curiosity through a fast-paced, varied, and aurally stimulating presentation.

Once you've chosen or been assigned a topic, your job will include researching the subject, identifying and interviewing people you hope will contribute the information you need, editing and organizing recorded materials, writing connective and interpretive narration, voicing the narration, and producing the final mixed versions of the program segments. The steps in conceiving and creating a series are illustrated in the following example.

Researching the Topic

Your research might begin before a topic has been chosen. Surveys are conducted regularly in major metropolitan areas to assess what local issues are of the greatest concern, so your starting point will be to obtain and evaluate possible issues for your series.

The survey shows that the top five concerns in your area are traffic congestion, the homeless, urban sprawl, potholes in city streets, and parking. In a discussion with the news director, it's decided that all of the concerns except one relate to issues that are well understood by the public; the one that needs more information about causes and cures is *homelessness*.

Having made this choice, your research plan becomes the essential base for the success of the series. Developing a personal system for doing research can save hours, reduce the possibility of mistakes, and result in a superior product. You most likely will want to begin your research with an online search engine, such as Yahoo! or Google. When you ask a search engine for articles on *homelessness,* the number you find is staggering, so you'll need to narrow it down by city or state, age, socioeconomic group, or some other criterion. As an example of the wealth of information available, entering the key word "homelessness" on Google gives you references to *10 million* articles and reports!

To reduce the number of hits, enter the name of your specific city—and you'll find more than 2 million documents! It's time now to use some reasonable assumptions for the quest. You've read that some—perhaps many—of the homeless are mentally disturbed or are addicted to drugs. To go down the abstraction ladder, you combine the key words "homelessness," "mental illness," "drugs," and the name of your city of concern.[4] By adding more specifics to the request you've focused down to a manageable number of documents. By adding more key words, you eventually select a number of useful articles and activate a printer to produce hard copy. With a few hours of searching, you've gathered many basic facts and representative opinions about homelessness.

Outlining the Series

After reading several articles and assembling significant statistics, you're ready to make some decisions about the series. After deciding that five or six segments should be allotted to the project, you begin by assuming that the first episode will be devoted to presenting the issue in such persuasive terms that listeners will both understand its importance and will want to learn more about this strange phenomenon; the final segment will summarize and offer solutions. These are the easy decisions; what will come between will be the meat of the series, and it's important to keep your mind open because you can't predict what will turn up in your interviews.

A story can be organized in several ways: in *chronological order;* in *order of importance;* or in *a logical sequence*—a step-by-step process of taking listeners from unfamiliarity to awareness. It can also be sequenced to move an audience from relative indifference to emotional involvement. Because your series will progress from describing the problem to proposing ways of addressing it, and because you want people to be moved to action, a logical order is most appropriate. You tentatively outline the segments that will satisfy your goals.

- Segment 1—Basic facts about homelessness and statistics. To make listeners aware that the problem of homelessness is large and growing, you include many sound bites of homeless people, citizens who are angry about people sleeping in parks or doorways, and some who are genuinely concerned for the safety and welfare of homeless people. You also "tease" a number of questions that you'll address in later broadcasts.

---

[4] See the discussion of the abstraction ladder in Chapter 8.

- Segment 2—What a homeless person goes through. This segment is made up of edited comments by several homeless people, recorded in a park, under a viaduct, or at any other site where the homeless live in isolation or where groups congregate.
- Segment 3—A police view of the homeless. This segment features the edited comments of police officers as well as police officials. It discusses the problems of sanitation and aggressive panhandling that are caused by some who are homeless.
- Segment 4—Attitudes of neighbors, tourists, and businesspersons. This segment shows a range of attitudes held by people who are not themselves homeless but who nonetheless are affected by homelessness.
- Segment 5—Causes of homelessness. This segment includes comments from social workers, psychiatrists, and other authorities on the subject.
- Segment 6—What society should do to help the homeless. This last segment consists of suggestions offered by several of the people interviewed for the series.

This sequence may be changed after you've thought through the comments made by those whose voices will be the most persuasive element of your series.

Recording Interviews

Having chosen your topic, researched it, and outlined the structure of your reports, you've pretty much determined its eventual value and effectiveness; what follows is devoted to the *mechanics* of carrying out your vision. While good interviewing techniques and the application of professional technical skills are important in all programs, your initial concept, plus a structure that first attracts, then retains, audience interest, will determine its usefulness and significance.

Because all of your interviews will be in the field, you'll need a high-quality, lightweight, battery-operated audio recorder. You'll also need a professional external microphone and headphones.

Before making dates for interviews, speak with the people you've selected tentatively for the program. Tell them that you want ideas and information but don't invite them to be interviewed until you're satisfied that they're articulate, knowledgeable, and cooperative. You may find you must look further for your talent.

Of course, you won't be able to phone homeless people to screen them or set up appointments, so there's no reason to delay recording them. Find them, obtain their permission, start your recorder, and begin asking questions. After you've completed your interviews, have permission forms signed—you may never be able to find them after you've completed the production. Be prepared to play back the interview you've just conducted if requested. Some interviewees may ask to hear the recording before they'll sign the permission form!

Before each recording session, prepare a list of questions. Be as thorough as possible in your preparation; the audio quality of your program will suffer if you have to record the same person on two or more occasions or in different locations. Ambient noise and acoustics should be as consistent as possible within each program segment.

Tips on interviewing are given in Chapter 8. The Checklist on the next page and comments add some suggestions that are applicable to recording material for feature reports.

Test your equipment before beginning the interview, no matter how experienced you are. Even professionals sometimes complete interviews only to discover that their batteries were weak, the machine was not recording, the volume level was too high or too low, or the absence of a windscreen on the mic resulted in excessive wind blast. Try to test your equipment under the exact conditions and in the precise location of the interview. After completing your recording, spot-check to make sure your equipment worked properly.

Take time to explain recording and editing procedures to the interviewee. It's important for your guest to know that all of your comments and questions will be removed and replaced by narration recorded in the studio. This means that the interviewee should make direct, complete statements that are not preceded by references to the questions. Here are two responses to the same question, one useful and another that will cause a problem in editing:

ANNCR: What do you feel should be done to combat homelessness in America?

RESPONSE 1:   To make a dent in homelessness, we need to find out just who the homeless are and how they became homeless.

RESPONSE 2:   I don't really have the answers. Maybe we need to know more about them and why they're without homes.

Both statements say approximately the same thing, but it's obvious that the first answer will be easier to edit, will provide more precise information than the second answer, and will allow a smoother flow from narration to statement. You can't expect every person you interview to overcome a lifetime of conversational habit, but you can expect reasonable cooperation.

Assuming you're recording in an office or other room, before beginning the interview ask the interviewee to remain silent and then start recording. Record about thirty seconds of **ambient sounds.** This precaution provides you with a sample of the background sounds that may be used for insertion at any point where you've made an edit and want an undetectable pause. All rooms other than those designed for scientific tests have ambient noise, and no two rooms are acoustically alike. Inserting the ambient sound from another interview would be noticeable to any attentive listener. Ambient sound is rarely needed, but when you do need it you'll be grateful for having developed the habit of recording it before every interview.

It's also good practice to allow the recorder to run for a few seconds after your guest has stopped speaking. Later, when you're editing and writing your script, you may want to do a fade-out at the end of one or another of your guest's comments. If you've abruptly stopped the recorder immediately at the conclusion of your guest's remarks, there's no way to do a fade.

When recording in the field—as for the homeless series—record every sound you might conceivably want to use later as you edit and write narration. If you realize you need a particular sound after you've returned to the station, it's probably too late to return to the field to record what you missed because timelines are so tight. Therefore, when interviewing a person living in an automobile, for example, record the sound of a car door slamming. Record the sound of a dog barking, if that's an appropriate (and genuine) sound relating to a pet-owning homeless person. Record traffic sounds and the sounds of buses, streetcars, and trains if they'll add a touch of honest reality. Record the songs of birds and of wind whistling through trees if those sounds are actually present in the environment about which you're reporting. Radio, being an aural medium, benefits greatly from the ambiance of an environment established through its sounds. At the same time, never resort to the use of faked sound effects in a piece that's offered as reality.

As you interview, avoid giving your guest vocal reinforcement, such as "uh-huh" or "I see." These will be a bother to edit out when you assemble the program. Non-verbal support—for example, a nod of the head—is sufficient to encourage a guest to continue, although you should avoid expressions or gestures that indicate that you agree or disagree with your guest's comments.

Checklist *Recording Interviews Successfully*

1. Test your equipment before beginning an interview.
2. Explain your recording and editing procedures to the interviewee.
3. When you're ready to begin, ask the guest to remain silent and then start recording.
4. Avoid giving vocal reinforcements such as "uh-huhs" during the guest's remarks.
5. Keep the recorder running.
6. Limit your recording sessions to a reasonable length.
7. Keep your station's format restrictions in mind.
8. If there is ambient noise, keep the mic close to the interviewee's mouth.

During the interview, try to keep the recorder running. Don't hesitate to stop it, however, if the session's going badly. The reason for an uninterrupted take is that most people are more alert and energized when they feel that what they're saying will be heard later on the air. Constant stopping and starting saps energy and reduces concentration.

Keep your recording sessions to a reasonable length. A ninety-minute interview to be edited as part of a three-minute program segment could cost you hours of production time. Therefore, work for interviews that are long enough to supply you with the material you need but not so long as to saddle you with hours of editing.

As you interview, keep the format of your station's feature reports in mind. If, for example, your station prefers to use both your questions and your guest's answers as recorded in the field, your interviewing technique should reflect that fact. You won't have to ask guests to answer your questions in the form of self-contained statements.

Train yourself to detect slurred speech patterns. Some people run words together so habitually and consistently that it's impossible to edit their comments effectively. If you aren't alert to this potential problem, it'll be too late to do much about it when sitting at an editing station. When your ears tell you that you're working with someone who slurs, do your best to slow the person down. If this attempt fails, ask the guest to repeat single phrases and sentences that seem to be the most important contributions you'll use later in your report.

When recording at any location that has a high level of ambient sound (machinery, traffic, crowds), hold your mic close to your guest's mouth. As mentioned earlier, authentic background sounds can enhance the realism of your report, but they mustn't be so loud as to drown out your guest's remarks. If you'll later edit out your questions, don't move the mic back and forth between you and your guest. If, on the other hand, you're to retain even some of your questions or comments, then you must develop skill in moving the mic. To avoid mic-handling noise, wrap the cord around your wrist. Mic-handling noises are especially troublesome because they can be heard only on playback or by monitoring during the interview, a practice seldom engaged in by people working solo.

It's essential that you follow station policy in having those interviewed sign release or permission forms. This requirement may not be a problem when interviewing a public official or other person who can be contacted later for the signing, but anyone who doesn't have a permanent address—such as a homeless person— must sign a form before you leave the site of the interview.

After completing each interview, make notes that later will help you in editing— for example, name of guest, topics covered, comments of special importance, and so on.

Next, you'll do a rough edit. You'll audition each recording and dub statements that seem likely for inclusion in your final version to another recorder or to a storage disk. If you have access to state-of-the-art equipment, your work can be done entirely on a computer and an editing system, such as Adobe Audition. To review your recorded material, you may plug your recorder directly into the computer or, if you prefer, insert the memory disk into the computer.

If time permits, make a typescript of each roughly edited interview on a word processor for easy cutting and pasting. The written word is far easier to identify, retrieve, manipulate, and edit than are words on a recording. When writing the narrative script, you'll find it easier to develop a smooth flow with precise lead-ins when working in print. Making a typescript may actually save time.

Having completed the script, do the fine editing of the rough dub. Editing allows you to remove any unwanted pauses, *ers* and *uhs*, or even single words. It also allows you to take a portion of an answer from one part of the interview and join it to an answer from another part of the interview. A word of caution: *It's critical that such editing preserve the sense of your guest's comments and never be used for any purpose other than clarifying your guest's position and making your report as factually honest as it can be.*

When editing, you may find that some statements that looked good in the written script don't come out well in sound. Be prepared to go back to the roughly edited version to look for substitute statements or to rewrite your script to make the narrative sound better or clearer.

Finally, record your narration. You'll sit in an announce booth or a small production room and do a real-time recording, alternatively feeding your voice and the edited actualities to a recorder. It's also possible to record your narration without the edited inserts and to mix the entire report later.

PRACTICE

➤ Reading News Copy Cold

As indicated in Chapter 2, you or your instructor can obtain printouts of up-to-the-minute news copy through the Internet.

Among many others, the Associated Press, Reuters, Pan Africa News Agency (PANA), Agence France Presse, and Voice of America offer current headlines, complete news scripts, and features. These can be selected and printed for practice in newsreading. Note: Some news providers restrict their service to those who subscribe to the service on a contractual basis.

PRACTICE

➤ Rewriting News Copy

Because most news copy on the Internet is written in newspaper style, you can use it to practice rewriting for a better news sound. Convert newspaper copy to shorter, crisper sentences; round out numbers (change "3.89 million shares" to "nearly 4 million"); and look for homonyms that may cause misunderstanding. Follow the suggestions noted earlier in this chapter for writing news for aural comprehension.

Chapter 10

Television News

Chapter Outline

News Media Today

Throughout much of its existence, America received most of the news that formed public opinion from newspapers. By the 1980s, television had become the primary source of local, national, and international news, but just a few years later, Internet websites began competing with television as the most influential source of news and information. One thing is certain about the future: Changes in news dissemination and retrieval beyond our imagination will occur during your years as a broadcast journalist.

The lesson of this is obvious: Prepare for media currently appropriate for your services but continue to study developing media, making sure that your competencies will be readily transferable to whatever media take over. In short, this means that your present goal should not be merely to obtain a *job* but rather to acquire the requisites of newsgathering, evaluating, and reporting, competencies that aren't limited to a single medium. Those who lose their jobs when television no longer dominates the news will be those unable to transfer their abilities to another medium.

News on Television

Television news varies from brief voice-over slide bulletins to the twenty-four-hour coverage of Cable News Network (CNN) and MSNBC. Many television stations in large markets produce two or three news programs daily, some thirty minutes in length, others an hour. News is typically broadcast at noon, at the dinner hour, and at ten or eleven at night, with a few stations adding an early morning newscast.

In small markets, newscasts may be mounted by a dozen or so employees, while in metropolitan areas network-affiliated stations operate with one hundred or more employees. Television news programs are planned by news directors and assignment editors and are put together by reporters, newswriters, remote crews, mobile van operators, operators of special-effects generators and computer graphics systems, video editors, and anchors. Production personnel may include a floor crew of five or more in the studio, and a producer, director, video engineer, audio operator, prompter operator, and other specialists in the control room, and master control. At highly automated stations, floor crews have been replaced by robotic cameras, and control rooms see only a director and producer.

Requirements for News Reporters and Anchors

All successful announcers have many qualities in common: compelling personalities, articulate speech, an ear for language, a keen sense of humor, and an ability to adapt quickly to changing circumstances. Television news announcers must have all these capabilities and more! The qualities sought by news directors are

Figure 10-1

A control center, known as "The Desk," is a prominently placed, high-energy site found in television newsrooms the world over. An editor is stationed there to assign reporters, camera operators, and newswriters to every detail of the day's effort. A record is maintained that follows the progress of each story from the time it's chosen, to when and whom it's assigned, and when it's delivered. The Desk is essential for the coordination of television news personnel and resources. *Courtesy KTVU, Oakland, California.*

stated in position vacancy notices placed by stations on the Internet. Here is a condensed overview of attributes considered by most broadcast executives to be essential to employment in television news:

Competencies and Personal Qualities

Skill in interviewing

Ability to construct coherent and compelling stories through scripts and video editing

Effectiveness in developing and maintaining reliable news sources

Capacity to retain objectivity in reporting the news

Effectiveness in public appearances

Ability to create for viewers a feeling of involvement, sincerity, professionalism, authority, knowledge, enthusiasm, and friendliness

Ability to pronounce names and words in major languages and knowledge of a phonetic system to encode words from any language

Education and Experience

Bachelor's degree (B.A.) from an accredited four-year institution, with a major in journalism

Additional course work in television, including courses and workshops in broadcast journalism

Good English writing skills

This chapter on television news doesn't stand alone. Additional competencies for those preparing for careers in broadcast news are described in detail in other chapters. To augment what's covered in this chapter, see suggestions for on-camera performance in Chapter 6, "Video Performance"; principles of effective newswriting in Chapter 9, "Radio News"; and comments on audience rapport that open Chapter 5, "Audio Performance," and Chapter 6, "Video Performance." The Spotlight in Chapter 6, "Feature Reporting as Storytelling," is a realistic overview of what's required to function as a features reporter. Exercises in ad-lib performance may be found at the end of Chapter 2, "The Announcer as Communicator."

Technology and Its Challenges

Technological advances have, in the past few years, necessitated more changes in performance requirements of reporters and anchors than in any comparable period in television's history. These changes can and will be described here, but many stations—especially some in smaller markets—have been slow to adopt the new technology; at the same time, the technology in use at well-funded stations may be obsolete by the time you read this chapter. So, the dilemma is this: How do you prepare for this field when you won't know until you enter it what skills and knowledge will be required? The best compromise is to study and practice with both the old and the new, but with an emphasis always not on machines but on your integrity and communicative abilities; remember, you bear the responsibility of providing useful and accurate news to the public.

Television Reporters

Journalists who work away from the station are called **field reporters, general-assignment reporters,** or just plain **reporters.** Reporters stationed some distance away are called **correspondents.** As a special-assignment reporter, you might cover a regular beat such as crime, politics, or a particular section of an extended metropolitan area. Tom Vacar, whose feature report on pet adoptions is examined later in this chapter, has two assignments, consumer editor and investigative reporter. Stations that can't afford such specialists on a regular basis often place field reporters on special assignment.

As a field or general-assignment reporter, you'll receive your daily schedule from an **assignment editor (The Desk).** Some assignments will be to cover **hard news**—serious accidents or crimes, fires, explosions, chemical spills, tornadoes, and other unanticipated events. Other assignments will be concerned with **soft news**—meetings, briefings, hearings, news conferences, and so on. News departments maintain a **future file,** consisting of thirty-one folders (for the days of the month), each containing information about scheduled soft-news events. As notices of planned events reach the station, they're scanned and filed by topic and date on a computer. Each day the assignment editor searches the file for news stories and schedules reporters and camera operators to cover the most promising ones. Scheduled coverage of soft news is often dropped at the last minute in favor of late-breaking hard news.

As a field reporter, you'll usually report live by way of microwave or satellite transmission, and you'll report events as they happen or afterwards as a summary of the occurrence; either way, live reporting precludes scriptwriting and reshooting. Your ability to ad-lib an unfolding news event in an accurate, effective manner is an essential key to success in live reporting.

You'll also record reports in the field on a camera's digital hard drive—or on tape if your station continues to use that medium. When recording a story, even though deadlines are always tight, you'll have time to plan your coverage, engage in on-site investigation, think through and write your opening and closing stand-ups, and record a second or third take if the first effort falls apart. A **stand-up** is a statement by a reporter directly into the camera lens (in other words, addressed to the viewers). It may come at any point in a recorded story, but it nearly always closes the story.

Recorded and live field reports on television are often longer than stories prepared for radio. Because television is much more expensive and time consuming and involves greater technical complexities, you'll be expected to cover only one or two stories a day. You must not assume that your field reports will dominate a

Figure 10-2
Special assignment reporter Mike Sugerman both chooses and is assigned the stories he produces. He works with a photog partner, and together on location they decide what to shoot. Mike writes his packages out in the field in the newsvan, watching the interviews and the other video, and the photog edits it. The completed package is sent back to the station by microwave. When it's time for the news, Mike usually goes live in the field, beamed back via microwave. Since 1980, Mike has won over 100 major local, state, and national awards, including thirteen Emmys, eight national Edward R. Murrow awards, a George Foster Peabody award, and two National Headliner awards. *Courtesy of Mike Sugerman and KPIX.*

newscast; most packages run between thirty and ninety seconds. Creating even a sixty-second report may take several hours, both in the field and at your station. You'll use part of the time investigating the story, lining up witnesses or others you want to interview, conducting interviews, making notes for stand-ups, and recording them. More time is consumed after you return to the station because, in many news operations, reporters edit their recorded material, write voice-over narration, record the narration, and assemble a complete package (a report that needs only a lead-in by a news anchor).

Preparing a Package

As a reporter, you'll follow certain steps in making a news package. The assignment editor will give you your assignment on a daily basis. If you report each day in the newsroom, you'll receive it there; if you live some distance away and cover that area as your beat, you'll get your assignment over the phone or by e-mail. Depending on the kind of news that's breaking, you'll be given either a hard- or a soft-news story to cover and, perhaps, be asked for ideas.

At many stations, you'll complete your package in the field. A remote truck, outfitted with editing equipment and a transmitter, makes it possible to do every step of the process, including dubbing, editing, writing a script on a laptop, recording your voice-over commentary, mixing the elements, and eventually transmitting the package to your station. Some field reporters, especially those who cover an area some distance away, seldom visit their stations.

Whether you complete your package in the field or at your station, after receiving your assignment, you'll go on location with an electronic news-gathering (ENG) operator, now often referred to as a **camtech** for "camera technician" and, at some stations, "shooter" or "photog." At many stations, you'll cover news stories without assistance and find yourself operating the camera.

You may travel in a station wagon with little equipment; a van equipped for viewing and editing your footage on the way back to the station; a truck equipped to send recorded, but unfinished, reports to the station via microwave transmission; or a truck with all the equipment needed to complete your package and an uplink transmitter that bounces it off a satellite to a receiver at your station.

When you arrive at the scene of the story, you undertake appropriate research to learn what's happened, who's involved, what's going on at the moment, and why the event is happening. In other words, you pursue answers to the traditional *who, what, when, where, why,* and *how* of journalism. While you investigate, your camtech records whatever may be essential or potentially useful in telling the story, including general scenes of action: for example, the overall wreckage of a multiple-car accident, waters spilling through gaps in a levee, or picketers marching and chanting. Seasoned camera operators know what to look for and will be engaged in shooting everything that might be useful when edited, even though they'll always be alert to your requests for particular shots.

As you gather information, you take notes. At this stage you haven't decided on how you'll structure the report, so you write down almost anything that seems likely to become a part of your story. As the story begins to take shape in your mind, you ask the camtech to record this or that person or object, most particularly your interviews with eyewitnesses or spokespersons whose edited comments may become sound bites, the television equivalent of radio actualities. After all notes have been written and all visual material recorded, you perform your stand-ups. You may begin your report by addressing the camera with an introduction, and you may also record one or more on-camera comments to be edited into the completed package. You then do an on-camera summary, closing with the phrase that identifies you and your station.

Before leaving the scene of your report, you may ask the camera operator to record material to be used as cutaway shots, or **cutaways.** Cutaways are a form of insurance used to avoid jump cuts. When editing an interview, you may want to delete some comments the speaker made while in front of the camera. The insertion of a brief shot of you apparently listening to the speaker will camouflage this kind of cut and keep viewers from noticing any change in positions—a jump—of the speaker between comments.

To prepare for the possible need of cutaways, you ask the ENG operator to record you *after* the interview as you look past the camera lens. If possible, do your cutaways while the person you've interviewed is still present. Also remember that because a cutaway is not an actual, real-time shot of you listening to the speaker, it's *imperative* that your reactions be as true to the spirit of the interview as possible. A popular motion picture of 1988, *Broadcast News*, made contrived cutaway shots the focus of its condemnation of unethical journalistic practices.

Back at the station—if you've not already done so on the drive back—you sit at an editing console in or near the newsroom to view the recorded material, make editing decisions, and write a script that you then record in an announce booth equipped with a microphone and an equalizer. You'll have worked with a station engineer to learn how to adjust the **equalizer** so your voice will sound as close as possible to the way it sounded when you recorded in the field. In writing a script,

Figure 10-3
Conditions are sometimes rough for field reporters. Think of those covering devastating hurricanes, earthquakes, or floods. Even when reporting from nearby locations during inclement weather, a reporter can experience teeth-chattering and hand-numbing problems. *Courtesy of Jennifer Stanonis and KCWY, Casper, Wyoming.*

you use a conventional format and certain abbreviations. Many of the abbreviations (and their meaning) used in television scripts are listed in Table 10-1.

Your final step is to mix recorded shots that tell the story, general shots of the scene, sound bites, stand-ups, and your voice-over audio narration into the package.

Other abbreviations and terms with which you should be familiar are **character generators (CGs),** which provide computer-generated written information, as in sports contests to show names of players and to give statistics, and in news broadcasts to add written information to augment pictures. **Bumpers** are snippets of stills or moving images used to "bump" a story from one scene to another.

TABLE 10-1 Abbreviations Used in Television Scripts

Abbreviation	Meaning
TS	Tight shot
CU	Close-up
MCU	Medium close-up
ECU or XCU	Extreme close-up
MS	Medium shot
WS or LS	Wide shot or long shot
ELS or XLS	Extreme long shot
OS	Over-the-shoulder shot (usually over the reporter's shoulder and showing the person being interviewed face-on)
RS	Reverse shot (reporter listening to person being interviewed)
TWO-SHOT	A shot with two people in the frame
PAN	Camera moves right to left, or left to right
TILT	Camera moves up or down
SOT	Sound on tape
SLO-MO	Slow motion
VO	Voice-over
CUT	A brief recorded scene, an actuality, a voicer, or a wrap
IN	Indicates the words that open a sound bite
OUT	Indicates the words that end a sound bite
SLUG	The slug line, a brief title given to a news story for identification purposes
TRT	Total running time

Figure 10-4

Anchor Jennifer Stanonis begins a story on a recent agreement that ended a dispute over condominium lease arrangements. The box offers a condensed statement, similar to a newspaper headline. *Courtesy Jennifer Stanonis and KCWY, Casper, Wyoming.*

Box graphics are pictures, with or without words, that appear in a rectangular box over the shoulder of a news anchor or reporter. A **wipe** occurs when one picture gradually replaces another.

At some stations, after completing your package in the newsroom, you'll return to the scene of the story to make a live intro to the package. Arriving about a half-hour before airtime, you and the camera operator set up in an appropriate area and later, on cue, you deliver the introduction. At the end of the package, you go live to engage in a brief question-and-answer session with the anchor. On completion, you sign off: "This is _____, reporting live from _____."

When you report without a camtech, you go to the scene of a story, conduct your investigation, and record sound bites, including interviews. Before leaving the scene, you place the camera on a tripod, start the recorder, walk to a position in front of the camera lens, and perform your stand-up. You may edit your takes in the truck—assuming you're not also the driver!—or when you return to the station, where you write the script and edit and assemble your package.

Reporting Live from the Field

To succeed as a reporter covering stories as they happen, you must have a solid background in journalism, have knowledge of many subjects, be able to control your emotions, and ad-lib fluently and informatively. Even if your major is broadcasting, studying journalism in college will prepare you to size up a story quickly, make judgments about its potential news value, identify the most noteworthy points about the event, and organize that information so that it's readily understandable to viewers. When covering slow-breaking stories (in fact, whenever time permits), your background in journalism will enable you to engage in investigative, or depth, reporting. Knowing how and where to look for hidden information is essential for depth reporting. Finally, journalism courses will familiarize you with laws regarding libel, contempt, constitutional guarantees, access to public records, the invasion of privacy, and copyrights. Of course, all reporters should be competent journalists, but those who report the news live must be especially well prepared. If you make a defamatory statement on a live broadcast, there's simply no way to undo it.

Reporters also need extensive knowledge of many subjects, and this is especially true for those who report live. You need a broad education in the arts and sciences and should consider yourself a lifelong student. The reading of selected new books, several newsmagazines, and two or more daily papers should be routine for you as you prepare to work as a reporter.

It's common practice for anchors to follow a live report with a Q & A (question-and-answer) session with the reporter. The stories you report may vary from a demonstration at a nuclear power plant to the verdict in a case of extreme local interest. A good Q & A session requires you to speak knowledgeably about the general subject area of the story you're reporting and, as with the jury verdict, your familiarity with the case is mandatory. Blank looks, incorrect information, and the response "I don't know" are unacceptable.

Studying media performance and participating in broadcast journalism workshops will help you develop the confidence and poise required to go live and script free before television audiences. Confidence that comes with a solid educational background makes it easier for you to concentrate under pressure—and sometimes in the midst of confusion—and to speak smoothly, coherently, and in an organized manner. Sometimes you'll address the camera amid high levels of ambient noise; you may be distracted by onlookers; you may even be in a position of danger. You'll work with notes, rather than a script. You won't have a monitor to show what's being seen by the television audience, though you will hear the words of the director and anchor on an earpiece, an interruptible foldback (IFB). So a solid education is essential to success when reporting developing stories live.

When you communicate with the anchor by way of satellite, you may need to anticipate a delay of about one and one-half seconds between the time the anchor speaks and the time you hear the anchor's voice. It's necessary to pick up cues as rapidly as possible to make this delay less noticeable. You can also expect to hear your own voice coming back to your ear one and one-half seconds after you've spoken. Engineers can minus out your voice so that the anchor and the viewers hear it but you don't, but when this technical adjustment isn't made, you must give your report smoothly despite the distraction of hearing your words on delay.

The News Anchor

Performance abilities are as important for a news anchor as journalistic knowledge. News directors look for anchors who are physically appealing (which doesn't necessarily mean young or good looking in the conventional sense), have pleasing voices, are skilled in interpreting copy, can work well with a prompting device, and can ad-lib smoothly and intelligently. In addition to on-camera performance ability, most successful news anchors have a background in field reporting. To continue the point made at the end of the preceding section, after hearing a report from the field, it's imperative that the questions you ask of the field reporter be appropriate, sensitive to the nature of the story, framed to bring forth answers that add significantly to the report, and are clear to both reporter and audience.

The chapters that discuss interviewing, voice and diction, and principles of communication provide suggestions and exercises that will help you perform well as an anchor. Some of the discussion of radio news in Chapter 9, especially the section on newswriting, applies to the work of television anchors. Chapter 6 provides details of working with scripts and prompters, addressing cameras, and moving, standing, sitting, and holding props on camera. The following section concentrates on aspects of preparation and performance that are unique to television news anchors.

Working Conditions and Responsibilities

Working conditions vary from station to station, but at a typical medium-market or large-market television station your news anchor job may involve

- Writing or rewriting 10 to 25 percent of the copy you read on the air
- Writing teases and tosses
- Covering some stories in the field
- Preparing occasional feature reports
- Working with a coanchor, as well as sports and weather reporters
- Preparing and delivering one or two newscasts daily, five days a week
- Meeting daily with newsroom management to discuss and help decide on the stories to be covered and the order in which they'll be presented to viewers

At some stations you might work three weekdays as a field reporter, and Saturday and Sunday as a news anchor.

As an anchor, you work with materials from a variety of sources: live and recorded field reports, stories written by newswriters, wire-service agency copy, recorded reports from a parent network or a cooperating station in a nearby market, and reports from CNN's NEWSOURCE, Fox, or Reuters. Final decisions on the content of newscasts rest with the news director (or the news producer), but you're involved in nearly every step in preparing for a broadcast. You were hired partly because of your journalistic judgment, so you need to keep abreast of developing stories. You check with reporters as they leave on assignment and as they return; you scan wire reports and newspapers; you confer at regular intervals with your producer; and you view recorded reports, both to determine their usability and to write lead-ins for those selected.

Your performance requires you to know the technological possibilities and demands of your medium, to write well and rapidly, to cope with confusion and last-minute changes, to work well with all members of the production staff, and to possess your own performance style. A few stations may permit anchors to merely show up in time to look over the news script, apply makeup and contact lenses, and spend the next thirty to sixty minutes playing the part of a broadcast journalist, but you shouldn't settle for such make-believe: There's little satisfaction or professional pride in doing so.

In general, your preparation is similar to that of a radio news anchor. You write lead-ins for packages, voice-over narration, and straight news stories that have no accompanying video, and you make notes for teases. A **tease** comes just before a commercial break and is designed to hold viewer interest by headlining a news item to be delivered after the break. Teases must be planned but are seldom written out. Be sure to review any news item or feature you tease; viewers are resentful of teases that keep them watching yet don't live up to advance billing. Viewers also resent teases if they believe that the information itself should have been given instead. Who wouldn't object to hearing, "And you'd better be on the lookout for an escaped lion—details when we come back."

A **toss** is a brief introduction to the weather or sports reporter, consumer affairs consultant, or other member of the news team. Tosses are indicated on the script but are delivered ad lib. You toss the program to someone else by turning to that person and making a smooth and quick transition to the next segment.

In writing your share of the news script, you begin with the standard opening used by your station on all newscasts: for example, "These are the top stories this hour." The opening is followed by headlines of the major stories of the day. As you write your copy, you may decide that you need graphics. Anchors sometimes are responsible for suggesting when a graphic aid is appropriate.

News scripts are typed in capital letters only. Scripts that go to production personnel use the left side of the script for video information and the right side for audio information. The video column is seldom marked by anyone other than the director, who indicates the shots to be taken. However, scripts on studio prompters—those read on-air by anchors—don't use the two-column format.

Using a Prompter

When you go on the air for a thirty- or sixty-minute newscast, you'll have a complete script, but expect it to be revised during the broadcast. Runners, most likely interns from a local college, will bring new copy to you, the camera director, the news producer, and the prompter operator.

Instructions to toss to a reporter in the field or in the newsroom will be given to you by a director or producer over an IFB, also called an **earprompter.** Unless you work with robotic cameras, you'll also receive instructions passed to you by the *floor manager* (sometimes called the *floor director* or *stage manager*) during commercial breaks, reports from the field, or recorded stories.

Skill in sight-reading is extremely important because you won't be able to study the entire news script or stories written and delivered after the start of the newscast. You may have a chance to skim the new copy for names of people, places, or things you may have trouble pronouncing, but there's no guarantee that anyone in the studio or control room will be able to help you with the pronunciation. For this reason, you should establish an understanding with newswriters, assignment editors, and associate producers that unusual words or names will be phoneticized on the copy that goes to you and the prompter. An example of how your script may read follows:

> The East African nation of Djibouti (*jee-BOOT-ee*) has been hit by a severe plague of locusts.

In this instance, the newswriter took the phoneticized spelling from the pronouncer included in the wire-service copy and inserted it in the script. **Pronouncer** is the term used by news services for the phonetic transcriptions of words and names that accompany wire-service stories. Another example required the newswriter to research the pronunciation of medical terms:

> (Washington) A dietary supplement that may cause a fatal blood disorder has been removed from sale by its manufacturer. L-Tryptophan (*el-TRIP-toe-fan*) has been linked to the potentially fatal blood disease eosinophilia (*EE-uh-sin-uh-FEEL-yuh*). A national consumer organization praised the manufacturer's decision and called the halt in sales, quote: "a prudent and cautious course of action."

If you type your own script, make certain that each sentence is indented four or five spaces. In the event the prompter fails, this will help you quickly spot the part of the story you're reading.

Never hyphenate a word at the end of a typewritten line in a script. You must be able to see entire words without having to shift your eyes back to the beginning of a new line for the conclusion of a word. If, for example, a line ended with *con-*, you'd have no way of knowing whether the rest of the word was *-tingent, -tinuous,* or *-vict.*

When working with a prompter, the camera usually will be ten to fifteen feet in front of you. Eye movement as you scan the projected script will be less noticeable at that distance. Glance down at your script frequently. This habit not only eliminates the staring look but keeps you in touch with the ongoing script—a necessity in case the prompter fails.

Earpieces, or earprompters, are also used to feed *spoken* words (as opposed to *written* words fed by teleprompters) to reporters in the field. This method is used when you're to give a report that must be delivered verbatim. The earpiece, usually wireless, fits in your ear, the one you use for phone calls, and on cue, you repeat your comments, staying a second or two behind the words you're hearing.

SPOTLIGHT

Special Assignment Reporting: A Feature Report

Many television stations employ specialists who report on stories in their areas of interest and special competency. These reporters generally decide—with the approval of the assignment editor—the stories they cover. They also are given more air time to tell their stories in more detail than that given to hard news. One special assignment area is **consumer affairs,** and nowhere is this charge more effectively handled than at KTVU, Oakland, by consumer affairs reporter Tom Vacar.

Vacar's credentials include a law degree and a stint with "Nader's Raiders." In the late 1960s, activist Ralph Nader organized a citizen activist group that investigated corporate and governmental wrongdoing. The press nicknamed these activists "Nader's Raiders." Their work helped bring progress and reform in many areas—including safer cars, cleaner air and water, worker rights, and insurance reforms.

Tom Vacar takes a broad view of his investigative charge: "As long as a law, a practice, or a condition negatively affects the public, I consider it a problem for consumers." During his years with KTVU, he has done more than a dozen stories—he's lost count—on pets: traveling with pets, an aid program for feral cats, marmosets as pets (not a good idea), bunnies for Easter (another bad idea), dangerous dogs as pets, and dog day-care centers.

One of his most moving reports was designed to promote pet adoptions and increase financial support for animal shelters. The report was initiated by notes from the assignment editor. The notes gave basic information, provided an overview of the agency's activities, and offered suggestions for contacts and potential interviewees.

The procedures followed in producing this package were roughly the same as those described in the previous section on "Producing a Package," so only the script and a few visuals are reproduced here. "Pet Adoptions"—a complete package—was introduced by news anchor Dennis Richmond and given the lead-in by reporter Tom Vacar. The package ran exactly four minutes and sixteen seconds. Note that Tom Vacar does not appear in this piece. He added his narration in postproduction. In the script, his comments are shown in CAPITAL LETTERS; words spoken by those who are part of the story are in upper- and lowercase. The script as shown here does not include time code numbers or other details of production and editing.

Figure 10-5

Consumer editor Tom Vacar reviews elements of a report on pet adoptions, making notes for use by a news editor who will assemble the desired shots in sequence so that Tom can add his voice-over narration. *Courtesy of Tom Vacar and KTVU.*

DENNIS RICHMOND (BUST SHOT, TO CAMERA): We often speak of the homeless in our society, and when we do we usually mean people. But there's another homeless problem—homeless animals. Tonight on Segment 2, Tom Vacar joins us with a story of two women who have dedicated themselves to finding families for pets that otherwise might have to be destroyed.

TOM VACAR (BUST SHOT, TO CAMERA): Two rescuers out of a small army all over the Bay Area. In this case, the homeless have four legs, and they show up at the Oakland SPCA for any number of reasons—some abandoned, some just misplaced—all in need of a home. Often, the only chance they have depends on the hard work of their SPCA saviors.

TAKE PACKAGE: PET ADOPTIONS

VACAR: SEVEN A-M . . .

MARY ATKINS AND TERESA MORALES . . . ON THEIR DAILY MISSION TO SAVE LIVES.

FOUR TIMES A WEEK . . . THE OAKLAND S-P-C-A REACHES OUT TO EASTBAY COMMU-NITIES IN AN ATTEMPT TO ADOPT OUT AS MANY CATS, KITTENS, PUPPIES, AND DOGS AS POSSIBLE.

IF NOT, THESE POTENTIAL PETS WILL BE AMONG TEN MILLION SUCH HOMELESS AND UNWANTED ANIMALS PUT TO DEATH IN THE U.S. EVERY YEAR.

ON THIS DAY . . . THEY PACK UP FIVE KITTENS AND TWO PUPPIES . . . CHOSEN AT RANDOM, FOR A TRIP TO EL CERRITO PLAZA.

EVERY TUESDAY THERE'S A WELL-ATTENDED FARMER'S MARKET HERE . . . A FOUR-HOUR CHANCE TO SHOW THE ANIMALS TO POTENTIAL ADOPTIVE FAMILIES.

<NAT SOUND>

He's soft . . . isn't he?

<NAT SOUND>

Mom, can we get this dog?

<NAT SOUND>

(girl and puppy play)

VACAR: THERE'S A SPECIAL COMMUNICATION BETWEEN CHILDREN AND BABY ANIMALS . . . A COMMUNICATION MARY AND TERESA HAVE LONG OBSERVED AND KNOW WELL.

Mary Atkins/SPCA Caretaker: They both have essentially the same type of needs. They need tender loving care . . . they need a good home . . . they need human contact. Puppies need to be around people daily . . . like little babies.

VACAR: BUT THE S-P-C-A HAS TO MAKE SURE THE FAMILIES AND THE ANIMALS ARE COMPATIBLE.

THE ADOPTION FEE IS FIFTY DOLLARS . . . FOR AN ANIMAL IN EXCELLENT HEALTH . . . WITH ALL ITS SHOTS . . . AND NEUTERED TO PREVENT UNWANTED REPRODUCTION.

<NAT SOUND>

The puppies are Lab mixes. They're both boys, and they are both fixed.

VACAR: WHY DO THEY DO IT? IT'S CERTAINLY NOT A HIGH-PAYING JOB.

Mary Atkins/SPCA Caretaker: Because I feel the animals need me . . . or need somebody like myself. It's very important to me that I can take care of the animals the way that I feel that they need it . . . and it gives me great satisfaction that I can do that.

VACAR: THESE FREQUENT FIELD TRIPS ALSO ENCOURAGE MANY PEOPLE, WHO MAY NOT SEE THE EXACT PET THEY WANT HERE . . . TO TAKE A DRIVE OVER TO THE S-P-C-A ITSELF.

Teresa Morales/SPCA Supervisor: So, since we go out . . . there's a lot of people who see us here . . . and they go to the SPCA to see us . . . so that we adopt out a lot of animals like that.

Mary Atkins/SPCA Supervisor: And we tell them to go to the SPCA and fill out an application to be put on the wish list for a specific breed.

Anne Hanson/Kitten Adopter: You see it . . . you're more aware of it . . . whereas if it's just in a building down the freeway like they are . . . it's a long way out of foot traffic.

VACAR: ANNE HANSON FOUND EXACTLY WHAT SHE WANTED HERE TODAY . . . TIMES THREE.

Anne Hanson/Kitten Adopter: When we lost one of our last cats . . . it was very, very sad . . . we still miss her . . . that's why we thought we'd bring some new life into the house with the kittens . . . because they do get to be a part of the family.

Anne Hanson/Kitten Adopter: We originally had three . . . and we wanted to get three young cats that would grow up together and be together.

VACAR: SHE SAYS ANIMAL ADOPTIONS FROM SHELTERS ARE AN ACT OF MERCY.

Anne Hanson/Kitten Adopter: Well, we don't want to buy cats out of the paper or pedigree cats . . . we'd rather save them.

VACAR: SHE SAVED THREE . . . AND CREATED A NEW FAMILY IN THE PROCESS. AND SO . . . MARY AND TERESA HAVE WON A VICTORY TODAY.

Mary Atkins/SPCA Caretaker: And it gives me great satisfaction to know I'm doing a good job.

VACAR: BUT . . . AS THE FARMER'S MARKET CLOSES DOWN AT ABOUT ONE P-M . . . THE PUPPIES AND TWO KITTENS . . . ARE NOT SO LUCKY AND HAVE TO GO BACK TO THE SHELTER . . . TO AWAIT THE MIRACLE OF A FAMILY AND LIFE.

Mary Atkins/SPCA Caretaker: It hurts me . . . it hurts me a lot to know they can't be placed in homes . . . and I can only do so much to get them a home.

VACAR: MIDAFTERNOON . . . BACK AT THE SHELTER . . . THE ADOPTED KITTENS TAKE THEIR PLACE ALONGSIDE DOZENS OF OTHERS WHO NEED HOMES JUST AS MUCH.

THE PUPPIES TAKE THEIR PLACE IN ONE OF SEVERAL ROOMS FULL OF OTHER PUP-PIES AND DOGS NEVER BORN TO BE CONFINED IN CAGES.

BUT LATE IN THE DAY . . . A MIRACLE DOES HAPPEN . . . IN THE FORM OF A YOUNG COUPLE BUILDING A NEW FAMILY . . . A FAMILY THAT WILL INCLUDE A PET.

<NAT SOUND>

Hi . . . You're a nice boy.

VACAR: IN THE THROB OF A LITTLE GIRL'S HEART . . . ONE OF THE PUPS GETS THE CHANCE FOR A LOVING FUTURE.

THE END OF THE DAY . . . HIS PLAYMATE AND BROTHER . . . WILL WAIT ALONE.

FOUR DAYS A WEEK, THE OAKLAND S-P-C-A GOES OUT ON THESE LIFE-SAVING MISSIONS. IF THEY HAD MORE MONEY . . . THEY COULD HAVE EVEN MORE VANS AND DO EVEN MORE MISSIONS. WHAT THEY NEED MOST OF ALL ARE MORE PEOPLE TO ADOPT THE ANIMALS.

<NAT SOUND—DOG BARKS>

<NAT SOUND—CAT MEOWS>

I'M CONSUMER EDITOR TOM VACAR FOR THE TEN O'CLOCK NEWS.

When the package ends, we return to the news set, where Tom Vacar makes this offer:

VACAR: Now the sad fact is, there's no corner of the Bay Area that doesn't suffer from this problem. To that end, we've created this brochure. It's called "Adopt a Pal—Save a Life." It lists every animal shelter and humane society in the Bay Area, including Oakland's SPCA. For a free copy, just send a stamped, self-addressed business-size envelope to: Pets, Channel Two News, P.O. Box 22222, Oakland, 94623

(This is shown as a graphic as he speaks and repeats the information)
It explains what you can do to help find homes for so many unwanted animals.

On a two-shot, Tom Vacar and Anchor Dennis Richmond comment on the story:

RICHMOND: Tom, how successful are they when they take the pets out to farmer's markets? Do they get people to come back to the shelter and actually adopt out as we saw here?

VACAR: If they're really lucky, they can adopt out all the animals they have with them. Usually they adopt about half, maybe less than that. But what does happen is a lot of people then end up going back to the various shelters and looking at all the animals, and very often there they do get an animal adopted.

RICHMOND: And hopefully because of your story we'll get even more people doing that.

VACAR: Indeed.

Weather Reporting

In the Beginning . . .

Weather reporting, like everything else on television, has undergone rapid and revolutionary change through the years. In television's infancy, newscasts featured a few minutes of weather reporting at or near the end of evening news broadcasts. Reports were made up of wire-service copy and sketchy maps from wire services.

Not only was weather coverage scanty and, by today's standards, primitive, but the means of reporting the weather matched the crudeness of weather data-gathering. In the first edition of *Television and Radio Announcing* (1959) the most advanced means of presenting the weather required a sheet of transparent Plexiglas.

A large sheet of Plexiglas is mounted much the same as the slate in a moveable blackboard. An outline map of the United States is painted upon its surface and may be seen from either side of the board. The *backward view* of the map is faced toward the television camera. . . . The weather reporter stands behind the board and writes the weather data on the map with a felt pen. But the map and the reporter's marks are backward for the television camera. The trick is that *the scan on the camera is reversed!* This makes the map and the writing correct for the audience and gives the impression that the reporter is writing backward!

In most markets, weather was reported by news anchors with a limited knowledge of weather forecasting. In time, especially in markets where weather can have serious consequences—agricultural areas and regions subject to tornadoes or hurricanes, for example—station reporters were designated to study weather reporting, often by taking one or more introductory classes in meteorology for nonscience majors. Along with male reporters, a new category of station personnel, "weather girls," arose, with performers chosen, not for their meteorological qualifications, but for their attractive personalities and the ability to deliver weather information in a pleasant and articulate manner. To be fair, even early on there were qualified men and women interpreting the weather, but they were greatly outnumbered by those with limited knowledge who "acted" the role.

Because the battle for viewers has always been with us, it's no surprise that the next move was to "weather buffoons," whose goal was to entertain with both jokes and comic pantomimic movement. One of the most successful was Willard Scott on the *Today* show.

And Then . . .

After several years of token weather reporting, television viewers and broadcast executives began to take weather reporting seriously. Because meteorologists made long-term, short-term, and local-area forecasts, this information became valuable to the general public to the degree to which it was accurate and timely. Over time, viewers came to expect and appreciate information, not only forecasts, but also air-pollution data and the study of trends in the Earth's climate such as global warming, droughts, and ozone depletion.

Weather Reporting Today

Weather in most markets is now reported by specialists who've been educated in meteorology and who regularly obtain and interpret detailed information from the National Weather Service. The importance of timely and accurate weather forecasting demands a specialist with knowledge of such topics as atmospheric physics and thermodynamics, dynamic and synoptic meteorology, uses of computers in meteorology, and weather analysis and forecasting. Qualified weather forecasters are awarded the Seal of the American Meteorological Society.

Bill Martin, chief meteorologist for KTVU, represents those currently reporting on television networks and most major stations. Martin comments on the changes in weather reporting that have occurred since the first weather satellites were placed in service:

> Reporting the weather has changed dramatically in the past ten years, and my focus is on good information. People are much more aware of their environment now, and although they do want to know whether they should plan a trip to the mountains this weekend, they also want to know about environmental concerns.
>
> People live in places now where they are much more affected by the weather, and they want the best information they can get on matters that are important to their lives.

As airtime permits, Bill Martin regularly goes beyond the bare facts of weather predicting to explain the causes of meteorological phenomena, subtly and gradually educating his audience.

In preparing daily reports and forecasts, Martin gathers data from weather satellites, weather radars, sensors, and observers throughout the world. Sophisticated atmospheric monitoring equipment transmits data as frequently as every few minutes. Doppler radar detects airflow patterns in violent storm systems—

Figure 10-12
Chief meteorologist Bill Martin arrives at his work station at 3:00 on weekday afternoons to prepare for his on-air presentations on the 6 and 10 p.m. newscasts. After graduating from San Francisco State University, Martin served an internship at the local NBC affiliate and then took a job as a meteorologist at a small-market station in nearby Santa Rosa, California. When KTVU launched a nationwide search for a weeknight weather person, Martin was the station's first choice. *Courtesy of Bill Martin and KTVU, Oakland.*

allowing him to predict tornadoes and other hazardous winds and to monitor the storm's direction and intensity. Combined radar and satellite observations allow him to predict flash floods.

Preparing and Delivering Weather Reports

After determining weather patterns from the complex information sent by the U.S. National Weather Service, Martin creates graphics showing weather fronts, storms, high and low temperatures throughout the immediate area, national weather conditions of unusual significance, and similar information. Satellite photos that show movement of storm fronts and high- and low-pressure ridges are received directly from the National Weather Service's satellite and are fed into the computer for retrieval during broadcasts.

Nearly all television stations use chroma-keyed maps and satellite photos for weather information. At KTVU, Bill Martin stands before a large screen, a medium shade of green, and points out noteworthy features of the day's weather. The screen is blank to him, but he sees where to point by watching a monitor that carries his picture and the weather map, which has been keyed in electronically. Computer-generated weather maps, which were selected and stored in the station's computer, occupy all areas other than that of the reporter.

Notes on Weather Reporting

As a weather reporter, you may be asked to do special features. If a given area experiences a snowstorm of unusual proportions or at a time of year when it's not expected, or if there's prolonged rain or a drought, you may be asked to do street interviews to assess public opinion. In doing so, you should follow essentially the same techniques as for any other interviews of randomly chosen passersby. The tone of your interviews should match the nature of the weather event: If a light snow has fallen in an area where snow is a once-in-a-decade event, a light mood might be appropriate. If, on the other hand, the event is about a destructive flood or tornado, a light approach would be in poor taste.

Be Creative. Too many television weather reporters stick to regular patterns, giving the data in an established order: making daily changes in predicted temperatures throughout their area, giving snow or rainfall figures, and so forth. True, most are under strict time limitations, so it's difficult to break the pattern, but if you offer your news director ideas that aren't established, you might find an open mind.

For instance, when reporting national weather, remember that most people don't much care about the weather elsewhere other than where they may be traveling, where they have family or friends, or where they've come from. Unless a weather report from 2,000 miles away is unusual, as with tornadoes, floods, or hurricanes, it's seen by most as not being news at all. However, although people in

Georgia may care nothing about the weather in Kansas, they do care about the price of wheat and pork; and, while New Englanders may feel that the weather in Florida doesn't affect them, they'll care when they learn that a winter freeze will send the price of citrus and other produce soaring. Therefore, whenever appropriate, *tie weather reports to something people care about.* In other words, when reporting the weather from distant places, try to increase interest by interpreting its significance.

It's obvious that weather is newsworthy when it's violent; however, slow-developing conditions brought on by weather—such as a two-year drought—also must be reported, and such nearly imperceptible events can't be adequately covered by a mere recitation of statistics. To best serve your public, you must go beyond the kind of weather news traditionally offered by wire services. In a drought, for example, you could periodically record interviews with experts on several drought-related problems. Ask the farm bureau about the effects on farming. Ask a representative of the Audubon Society about the effects of the drought on birds in your area. Ask a fish and wildlife expert about the prospects for survival of fish and wild mammals. Get drought information from professional gardeners and share plant-saving tips with your listeners. In short, as a weather reporter, you should use your imagination and constantly ask yourself these questions: *Why should viewers be interested in today's weather report? What am I telling them that will be of use?* Always work creatively to make your weather reports useful to your audience.

Gaining Experience

If you're interested in exploring a career as a television station meteorologist, the best starting point is to serve as an intern. To be considered, though, you must meet certain criteria, as set forth in this announcement:

INTERNSHIPS

Meteorology/Weather Center

Two internships available per semester.

Students will gain hands-on experience in operational meteorology.

Students must be enrolled in a meteorology program at an accredited school. Hours are flexible, with possible weekend schedules available.

Most of us don't think in terms of apprenticeships, but for centuries they've been the entree into a chosen profession.

PRACTICE

➤ Research: Comparing Local and National Newscasts

Record both a local and a national newscast—that of an independent station and that of a major network or CNN. Study the performances and list the ways local television news differs from national coverage. Omit obvious differences such as "national newscasts feature reports from all over the world." Look instead for differences in length of stories, use of visuals and computer-generated graphics, and inclusion of specialized reporters who focus on the environment, business, weather, sports, and entertainment.

Chapter 11

Music Announcing

Chapter Outline

Music Radio Today

As with everything, there's good news and bad news. To get started, the bad news is cited first; however, keep reading, because better news, and predictions that the good old days of music radio may eventually return, follows.

From the early '50s, disc jockeys were the rulers of radio. This changed almost overnight following the enactment of the Telecommunications Act of 1996, which abandoned stringent ownership rules that had been in place since 1934. Within a few years, twenty companies owned nearly 3,000 stations. The largest, Clear Channel, owns around 1,200 and dominates music radio in many markets, including eight stations each in Louisville, Kentucky; Memphis, Tennessee; Huntington, West Virginia; Cincinnati, Ohio; and Phoenix, Arizona.[1]

Monopolization of radio stations has led to standardized play lists, automation, and voice tracking. A DJ, sitting at an audio console in one of the conglomerate's locations, prerecords entire radio air shifts, including song and artist identifications, liners, tags, announcements, and calls from listeners. Music is added later. These voice-tracked programs are sent to stations in all areas of the country, where they're broadcast with the illusion that they are both live and local. Of course, they are neither.

Depressing? Read on . . . .

An Upturn for Music Radio?

While it's impossible to read the future, there are signs that a return to music radio's localism and vitality could eventually occur. In 2006 and 2007, the Federal Communications Commission (FCC) held a series of "Public Hearings on Media Ownership," with a focus on station consolidation. And the commissioners got an earful.

Speakers included representatives of the *Screen Actor's Guild* (SAG), the *Writer's Guild of America* (WGA), the *American Federation of Television and Radio Artists* (AFTRA), and the *Recording Artists' Coalition* (RAC).

Mike Mills of the Recording Artists' Coalition stated that consolidation has all but destroyed localism in radio. In past years, local stations met the music tastes of their geographic surroundings—jazz, country, rock, Tejano, Texas swing, bluegrass, and so on. He asked, "Where are the local radio outlets for these styles of music in an era of nationalized play lists?"

John Connolly of AFTRA noted that opportunities for airplay were severely reduced if not destroyed for recording artists by homogenization of radio formats and fewer stations with local content. Eric Boehlert, a senior writer at *Salon*, amplified Connolly's comments:

---

[1] These statistics were true as of late 2007, but music station ownership is extremely unstable.

Through a process known as "cyber-jocking," Clear Channel has eliminated hundreds, if not thousands, of DJ positions (and saved tens of millions in salary) by simply having one company jock send out his or her show to dozens of sister stations. Thanks to clever digital editing, the shows often sound local.

There's no question but that the FCC listened to these angry complaints; during and after the hearings, several commission members promised to review decisions that made uncontrolled monopolization of radio possible. The FCC listened, but will it take remedial action? We'll know in time.

Aside from possible government action, a listener's revolt is under way that, if continued, could force changes by station owners. Angry protests from all parts of the country have come from individuals and organized groups frustrated over several issues: the loss of one or more favorite DJs; the disappearance of their preferred music format; and the lack of significant differences in the play lists of the three to eight music stations dominating their markets. If corporate stations begin to lose audience, they could be forced to become more competitive, and this could bring about a return to something closer to the music stations that existed in the past.

Finally, some conglomerates have had second thoughts about their empires. In 2007, Clear Channel announced its intention to sell its radio and television holdings, and in a separate statement said that it would first sell off 448 radio stations. Is it possible that Clear Channel's decision to unload its radio holdings grew from concerns over the growth of *satellite radio companies?* Or did it anticipate actions by the FCC that would loosen its grip on the nation's airwaves? The return of 448 stations to local ownership, added to the many stations throughout the country that remain independent, could trigger the rejuvenation of music radio. We can only watch and wait.

The DJ's Job

The term *disc jockey* came about years ago because announcers of hit music recordings selected, cued, and spun vinyl records; in other words, they "jockeyed" them. Today, music announcers work with CDs or hard drives and, although records no longer are played, popular music announcers remain known to most of their fans as *DJs.*

In addition to introducing or back-announcing musical selections, the work of DJs involves engaging in pleasant chatter, delivering or playing commercials, promoting contests, and—most important of all—establishing a bond with listeners. During morning drive times at many stations, two or more announcers are paired, one performing most or all of the DJ duties, and between music sets engaging their partner(s) in banter, featuring jokes and comments on current events, frequently laced with satire and ridicule.

Internet Radio by Andrew Mitchell

ALL ABOUT ME: I am a mass communications major with an emphasis on television/radio at Southern Illinois University Edwardsville. My interests include video production, rock climbing, and volunteering.

ALL ABOUT INTERNET RADIO: Radio listeners have moved from standard AM or FM radio to new forms of radio like Pandora Radio, AccuRadio, and Live365. These new online formats play music based on the listener's favorite artists or genres. The stations do not require on-air personalities and are tailored to audiences based on personal tastes. While most stations play all types of genres, AccuRadio and Pandora have no classical music, and many of the sites don't have access to lesser-known indie artists. Those restrictions aside, many listeners are flocking to the stations because it gives them the chance to listen to a wide range of music without the commercials or the bands that they don't like.

. . . AND HOW DOES THIS AFFECT ANNOUNCING? New technology is geared toward improving efficiency, and in most cases this means reducing the human element. Because of these radio websites, jobs are being eliminated and replaced by computers and servers. I think the key to success in this medium is to provide the industry with talent that cannot be generated by a computer. It is also important to be flexible and multitalented. Knowledge will get you so far, and then you must have the passion and the drive to take you all the way. I admit that I like some aspects of web radio, but the thought of not having on-air personalities is disappointing.

Music radio features a great range of announcing styles, from rapid delivery to casual or laid back, but they're associated only with popular music. Announcers on classical music stations aren't included in this term, even though their work has much in common with that of DJs. This chapter discusses the work of the DJ, while the classical music announcer's role and qualifications may be found on the website for this text.

Figure 11-1
Morning drive-time partners usually feature a man and a woman, chosen because they relate well to one another, are competent, share a love for the type of music being offered, and enjoy great—and sometimes outrageous—senses of humor. *Courtesy of Celeste Perry, Dave Sholin, and KFRC.*

Music Radio Stations

Recorded music predominates on radio in the United States and Canada. There are more than 15,000 AM and FM radio stations in the United States, and most are all music or mixtures of music and talk. Nearly all popular music stations are FM; years ago, most AM stations gave up all-music formats because AM sound simply can't compete with FM. To survive, AM stations moved to all-talk, all-news, news/talk, agriculture, and sports, as well as religious and non-English-language broadcasting. Music on AM is represented by stations playing country, middle-of-the-road, gospel, and "oldies."

About 600 U.S. radio stations are ethnically oriented or broadcast in languages other than English. Many are all or mainly music. If you're qualified (or qualifiable) to announce on these stations, you may want to include them in your career plans.

Working Conditions

Small-Market Stations. As you begin your career, you'll likely find work at an underfunded small-market station with equipment that predates the digital revolution. You may work with music stored on cassette tapes and CDs, and commercials on tape carts (cartridges with one-quarter-inch tape that rewind and recue after each playing). During air shifts, you'll work in a combined announce booth and control room, called an on-air studio, and you'll perform the combined functions of announcer and engineer. This is called **working combo.** And you can expect to work a four- to six-hour air shift and perform other duties for additional hours each day.

At a small station, aside from your on-air work you may spend many hours performing other assigned chores: selling commercial time, writing and recording commercials, producing spots for local retailers, performing routine equipment maintenance, and/or reporting news and weather.

Duties likely will include reading or ad-libbing brief public-service announcements—often on a *community bulletin board* or *community calendar*—playing commercials and station IDs (on tape carts at some, and on hard disks, DAT, or programmable CDs at others), making entries in the program log, and, in some operations, especially on weekends and holidays, answering the telephone. Many music stations run contests and promotions, and as the on-duty DJ, you'll tease and then conduct the contests with phone-in callers. While doing all this, you're expected to be alert, witty, and personable.

If you begin your career this way, most likely your pay will be meager and your hours long, and you'll have no amenities such as health coverage or extra pay for overtime. But you should consider your job an apprenticeship, an opportunity to learn the basics of music radio from the ground up, learning by trial and error, acquiring skills and poise, and getting ready to move up when opportunities come your way.

This is but one scenario. Even if you begin your career at a small-market station, you may be asked to work with highly sophisticated computerized operations. The picture painted above of what you may face at a small station isn't always true and doesn't mention other possibilities. In the past, in terms of technology, equipment at smaller stations lagged decades behind that found at large and prosperous stations, but now sophisticated apparatus may be found at stations of every size. The twin factors of reduced equipment costs and the ability to operate stations with fewer employees combine to make technological upgrading economically attractive to station owners.

Major-Market Stations. If you're talented and lucky enough to become a popular drive-time DJ on a prosperous major-market station, your salary could be in six figures—or even above. High salaries generally are paid only to morning drive-time music announcers in large markets. Even announcers in major markets whose shifts are afternoon (both midday and afternoon drive times), evening, or overnight no longer draw the huge salaries they once commanded.

Whether working for a major- or a smaller-market station, your job will be demanding because you'll spend many hours a week in preparation. Successful DJs at both large and small stations spend considerable off-duty time each week preparing for their shifts (**showprep**), checking prep sites on the Internet, reading music trade magazines, and preparing informative or humorous pieces for their shows. Although most popular music radio stations, large and small, require DJs to

Figure 11-2
DJ Chuy "Chu-Dog" Gomez back-announces a music sweep on his urban contemporary station, featuring hip-hop and rhythm and blues. Chuy was born in Tepatitlan, Mexico. He received a 1995 Billboard award for Local Video Show of the Year. In addition to his afternoon drive-time shift on KMEL, Chuy hosts a weekly show broadcast in Japan, "All Japan Dance Top Ten." He studied broadcasting at the College of San Mateo, a community college. *Courtesy of Chuy Gomez and KMEL-FM.*

do their own engineering, an exception is usually made during morning drive time. At a "personality intensive" station—a station that features a very popular DJ or a team of announcers noted for their repartee—an engineer may operate the board and play music and sound effects.

Working at a Digital Radio Station

Just a few years ago, radio stations made considerable use of taped material, including audio cassettes, DAT (digital audio tape), and tape carts (cartridges). Today, most are digital operations and music, jingles, commercials, station promos, and similar material are recorded and stored on digital hard drives. The scenario that follows will give you an idea of how this may affect you if you work at a digital station—which, if you succeed as a music announcer, you certainly will. (Note: At some stations, you'll voice-track an entire shift's commentaries and be free to listen to your performance on your drive home or during a day at the beach.)

When you report for work at your station you're given scripts for the commercials you're to produce prior to your on-air shift. You enter a small production studio, where a digital workstation, complete with audio console and computer system, is available. You manipulate a track ball or mouse to activate the recorder and begin reading a commercial. As you speak, a "picture" of your voice appears on the video display monitor. It progresses across the screen from start to finish. After reviewing your performance, you select a music bed and mix it with your voice at the appropriate volume level.

With the aid of the track ball, you may edit any portion of the recording to eliminate or replace unwanted sounds, such as a stumble, a sneeze, or the wheeze of overaspirated intake breaths. Equipment at most audio workstations is set to apply **automatic gain control (AGC),** so when a reduced or barely audible sound is detected, your intake breath is increased in volume as the AGC "searches" for sound. To eliminate unwanted sounds, you locate on the computer screen the point at which the sound begins, press a key to mark it, then find the ending point and make a second mark. These marks "surround" the segment you're editing. A keystroke deletes the sound between the two marks.

Another option allows you not to delete but to exchange sounds. It permits you to rerecord one or more sentences, to place marks at the start and end of the unwanted sentence or sentences, and to simultaneously erase them and insert the preferred version.[2] Other features allow you to change the volume or the equalization of any portion of your recording or to remix the volume balance between the voice and the music bed. When you're satisfied with your edited commercial, you give it an identification name and number, and store it on a mass storage hard

Figure 11-3

DJ Carter B. Smith analyzes and comments on the day's stock market developments during afternoon drive time. His station features oldies, and its relaxed format permits DJs to engage in nonmusic topics of interest to listeners. The station's format appeals to mature listeners, many of whom tune in after the close of the stock market. The ability to make interesting and informative comments about topics aside from music is an asset to any popular-music announcer. *Courtesy of Carter B. Smith.*

---

[2] Recording and inserting portions of a commercial or other announcement is not recommended because it's nearly impossible to make them fit in with as much effectiveness as a spot that's done right in the first place; use this technique only when it's your only option!

disk.[3] You may produce between two and twelve commercials in a single day. On other days, when there are few commercials to produce, you may record promos for your station.

Later you'll enter the on-air studio, ready to start your shift. Before taking over from the DJ whose shift precedes yours, you begin your preparation. Working from a log prepared by the music director, you access the hard disk that stores the music library and select and stack in order the music cuts you'll play during your time on the air. You then move to a computer terminal, complete with keyboard, a track ball, and a video data monitor. A log, prepared by the traffic department, lists the commercials, station promos, and PSAs to be played during your shift, as well as the order and the precise times at which they'll be broadcast. Many of the commercials will have been sent to your station over high-quality telephone lines and then digitally reconstructed on a hard disk. Some commercials and nearly all of your public-service announcements (PSAs), jingles, and station promos were created in your production studio by you and your coworkers and then transferred from an audio console/video terminal system to the same mass storage disk that holds the agency-produced commercials. With the aid of the track ball, you select all stored cuts to be played and assemble them in the order in which they'll be broadcast. All program elements have been scheduled by the traffic department.

None of the recorded material is in your announce booth; it exists only on the computer in an adjacent room or even on another floor of the radio station building. As the time comes to play each program element—music, commercial, jingle—you use the track ball to find, the video screen to see, and the computer keyboard to select each segment. When it's time to play each program element, you press the "play" command, and the cut you've previously selected is sent to the audio console and out over the air.

While music is played, you may receive telephone calls from listeners. As you answer the phone, you inform callers that their calls will be recorded. If there's no objection, you'll then activate a recorder to make an audio record of the conversation. There are two reasons for recording these calls: The first is to preserve actual conversations to avoid problems later regarding prizes, prize winners, or other issues that could arise from misunderstandings; the second is to collect comments that later may be edited into sound bites and used in station promotions.

The scenario just presented for working at a digital radio station examines just one particular operating system. At some stations, DJs have before them a computer screen that lists, in order, every program element for the entire day as developed by the station's program or music director. As each program unit is activated, it's sent out over the air, and at its conclusion its listing on the computer screen moves up and off, to be replaced by the next element. Music and all other recorded materials are broadcast without assistance of the DJ. Interspersed are breaks that require the DJ to back-announce the songs played in a **sweep** (several songs played without interruption), give weather updates, comment on some item of interest or amusement, and, occasionally, read a commercial. When comments by

---

[3] The spelling *disc* is used for all sizes and speeds of records and in the term *disc jockey*. In all other applications, such as a mass storage medium, the spelling is *disk*.

the DJ are recorded in advance, the computerized system can enter the recordings as program elements. Announcers can be away from the station (for example, on a holiday), but their voices will be heard by their audience.

Now, the tough question: If equipment used at a digital station isn't available to you for practice, how can you prepare to operate it in the future? Your best and only choice is to focus on basics *because equipment has never produced an outstanding DJ!* First, develop your performance abilities and work for an on-air personality that brings out your best qualities; then learn operational skills, including audio engineering and computer operations. Most of the chapters of this text are devoted to assisting you in becoming an engaging performer; the following suggestions will assist you in developing technical skills:

1. Take at least one, and preferably two or more, courses in audio engineering. To be of practical use, the courses should include in-studio recording on multichannel recording consoles, mixing of multiple inputs, editing, use of board equalization, reverberation systems, graphic equalizers, limiters, overdubbing, and sound reinforcement. Although you may later on operate a board that requires little but the occasional pressing of busses (buttons) to open and close your announce mic, a comprehensive knowledge of board operation is necessary to perform the *production tasks* described in "Working at a Digital Radio Station."

Figure 11-4

Afternoon drive-time DJ Ray White teases upcoming songs on his FM station with a smooth jazz format. Ray became committed to music radio at the age of 15. "After my first visit to a local station, I was hooked on radio. And, I realized that the magicians on the air, much like the Wizard of Oz, were just regular people who had a knack for talking into a microphone—and a love for music." Ray majored in history and minored in communications at the University of Connecticut, Storrs. *Courtesy of Ray White.*

2. Most likely you're already proficient in advanced computer skills; but, if not, you should enroll in classes where you can learn both Macintosh and PC operations. You will enhance your employment opportunities if you also gain hands-on experience with major computing and editing programs such as Avid, Photoshop, DigiBeta, and, of course, Microsoft Word, AppleWorks, Microsoft Excel, and so forth.

As you choose your courses, remember that education for any sort of technical operation isn't limited by the specific equipment you use for practice. Learn what a board *does* and how it *operates*. If you have a functional knowledge of the board on which you practice, your understanding of audio recording, collecting, mixing, equalizing, and editing can be transferred quickly to boards you've never before seen or touched.

The development of your talent to make you an effective and compelling communicator should receive your highest priority. A sound working knowledge of audio engineering and computer operations should be your second goal.

Music at Independent Stations

Aside from cookie-cutter conglomerate stations with standardized and voice-tracked output, music at independent stations provides a range of opportunities for DJs. At stations where managers believe that people tune in for the music and not the voice of a DJ, most announcers are restricted to brief comments and a minimum of song identifications. At these very stations, in apparent contradiction to this notion, executives demand that morning drive-time DJs entertain their listeners with witty or wise chatter. DJs in other time periods must adhere to strict time limits for any impromptu remarks, "More Music, Less Talk" being their motto. This is discouraging to prospective DJs who know that their initial employment will be in non-prime-time hours, where they'll be unlikely to impress management or listeners with their repartee.

If the overall picture of music radio employment opportunities sounds discouraging, take heart. Good communicators, announcers who care about people and have ideas, values, and insights—and some good laughs!—to share will always find a place for their talents.

Steve Walker, a popular DJ whose comments on rapport are outlined in Chapter 5, sees present practices as only a blip in a continuing series of changes in music radio. He recognizes that automation has reduced the prominence of DJs, but he feels that this is a temporary state. He has this to say about availability and job security questions facing DJs:

Here are some thoughts on the fear of losing your job to a satellite or the dreaded hard drive. The bean counters that make these kinds of decisions will find it works some places but not others. I've been doing this for twenty-five years and have seen cycles where DJs went from talking and saying as much as they wanted as long as they didn't tick anyone off, to the "shut up and read the card" days when you were just a warm body.

Steve is convinced that, because most trends are cyclical, DJs will one day reclaim their prominent role in delivering not only music but making observations about life, events, people, and other topics. This is encouraging advice from one who's seen trends shift as capriciously, though not as frequently, as the daily weather.

The chapters on audio and video performance begin with discussions of audience rapport, and the comments quoted here from Walker, a successful and respected DJ, complete a three-way focus on that priceless commodity. The moral of this message from Steve Walker is to *work to become a compelling communicator, prepare yourself for success and expect to achieve it, and realize that you'll only "make it" if you truly want to build a relationship and make a positive difference in the lives of listeners.* You have to earn your success; you can become important only if you *deserve* to be important.

Alternative DJ Opportunities

If you're committed to a career in music announcing, you shouldn't focus only on radio station employment because there are other, related, job opportunities. **Mobile DJs** perform live in dance halls, as well as at birthdays, company parties, weddings, reunions, and similar festive occasions. **Karaoke** is a nationwide phenomenon that offers self-employment opportunities for those who have the personality to inspire audience participation and the ability to operate the required equipment.

Community radio stations are found in all fifty states, and offer opportunities for students and recent graduates to obtain on-air experience. All of these stations have several things in common: They are nonprofit; are dedicated to serving the needs of audiences within their signal range, usually a much smaller geographic area than commercial stations; and, most have but a few paid employees, with nearly all of the programming done by unpaid volunteers. Many community stations serve areas away from large cities, and reach listeners who are underserved by radio and television stations licensed in those cities.

Community radio stations are not further described in this chapter, because their programming is not limited to music radio. Opportunities for those planning careers in news, talk radio, sports announcing, consumer affairs, political reporting, or a host of special interest programs such as gardening, home improvement, health, exercise, and so forth, may find that community radio offers experience in their area of interest. An extended discussion of community radio may be found in Chapter 13, "Starting Your Announcing Career," beginning on page 311.

Mobile DJs

As a mobile DJ, Roy McNeill performs live in dance halls, at birthdays, company parties, weddings, reunions, and other festive events. He represents a large and growing number of music announcers whose entire audiences are both with and before them. Mobile DJs are sometimes referred to as "gigging DJs" because, instead of being steadily employed, they're booked for specific events, or gigs. The term *mobile* is appropriate because they offer their services within a certain radius—50, 100, 200, or more miles.

Some mobile DJs advertise their services in the Yellow Pages or on the Internet, while others sign on with a company that does much of their job-seeking work for them. One of the largest of these companies is Gigmaster, which represents DJs in all parts of the country. With Gigmaster, you're not under contract; instead, you pay to have your name, qualifications, experience, and other important details from a questionnaire placed on its website. Later, when a person in your area fills out a form asking for a DJ, your résumé and that of others will be sent. After that, it's up to you to sell yourself.

Roy McNeill wasn't thinking of his present career when he began acquiring the skills he now uses. He began playing guitar and piano at age 10, which eventually led him to songwriting and then to recording and editing his music. During four years in the Navy, he became an electronics technician. After his Navy service, Roy worked for no pay at various music recording studios, where he learned board operations, editing, and the sound qualities and characteristics of many types of professional mics. Working as a DJ for Virgin Records, he spent hours talking into the mic, which gave him confidence when speaking ad-lib to strangers.

Eventually, he decided to put his twin loves of music and performance together. He'd become aware of the field of mobile disc jockey work, so he bought the requisite equipment on credit, then starting searching for gigs on craigslist. After a few gigs, word of mouth took over. He still scans craigslist when business slacks off but expects soon to create his own website. Of course, not everyone can or will follow the

Figure 11-5
Roy McNeill prepares for a large wedding reception. He understands that playing music is not enough for success; mobile DJs must also entertain because being spirited, humorous, and responsive to their audiences is essential. Unlike on-air performers, who never see their listeners, mobile DJs must be alert and quickly sense and respond to cues they receive during the ongoing event. *Courtesy of Roy McNeill.*

same paths that led Roy to his present career, but collectively they offer examples of ways to prepare for mobile DJ work. You may want to check your state of preparation, then look for ways of adding to it the skills you'll need to become a mobile DJ.

Karaoke

Jan Lynch is a popular karaoke artist who's in business for herself. Most karaoke artists (KJs) are affiliated with companies that manage advertising, contracts, billing, and all other details, but Jan prefers to handle them herself.

Jan says of her work, "I've played every type of venue you can imagine, including parties, anniversaries, graduations, wedding receptions, Deseaños, and Bar and Bat Mitzvahs. I've also had interactive karaoke sessions with large conference groups and churches. And my favorite—a special education class once a month." Most of Jan's "gigs," though, are in restaurants/lounges, where karaoke is a weekly (and sometimes more frequent) feature.

Jan's investment in equipment is considerable and includes an amplifier/mixer of 400 watts and a single- (for backup) and triple-drawer karaoke player. She uses vocal speakers, which are smaller than conventional P. A. systems, because they're lighter. Additional equipment includes cordless and corded microphones, a playback monitor, and a full sound speaker (including mic) that faces the singer. She says, "It helps to hear what you are doing."

Music is a large expense because a karaoke performer must be prepared to play an incredible range of songs. She has four collections, plus "things I got here and there to get specific songs. Knowing the type of group you usually play to helps guide you to the types you go the heaviest on."

It's an advantage to be a competent singer, but it isn't a firm requirement. "What I think is most important is the way a show is conducted." Jan concludes her thoughts with this observation: "No real education is required for what I do, just trial and error and a need to sing and see that people have a good time. Training on equipment and setup would have been wonderful, but I struggled through on my own."

Figure 11-6

A karaoke session. Jan Lynch plays the music while a family joins in to sing the lyrics of songs that appear on the monitor before them. *Photo courtesy of Jan Lynch, and Sophia, Max, father John, and Katie Rose, who seems more interested in the audience than the music.*

Music Station Practices

At most popular-music stations, the program director develops a clock or wheel (often called a hot clock) that divides each hour of a particular time period into sixteen or more segments. Each segment specifies a certain activity for the DJ. In one segment, a sweep of music selected by the music director is played. In another, called a **stop set** or **spot set,** a commercial cluster is run. In yet another, a contest is announced, and in several segments weather updates are given. Music is categorized, according to the program director's concept of competitive programming, as instrumental, vocal, up-tempo, top 10, top 5, nostalgia, easy listening, and so on. Clocks used at stations with radically different music genres are similar, but categories of songs are geared to the style of music and overall "sound" of the station.

The days of DJs choosing the music they play are long over. Station managers set radio station music policy, and at major stations, a program director develops the play list. At medium- and smaller-market stations, the selections and

Figure 11-7

Popular-music stations often use a clock as a programming tool to ensure a balance of music, news, commercials, and features. This clock, which was created for the afternoon drive time, reflects the importance of frequent traffic updates. But clocks do more than manage what gets broadcast and at what times. When entered into a computer, a clock can be altered daily to keep listeners alert and competing stations confused.

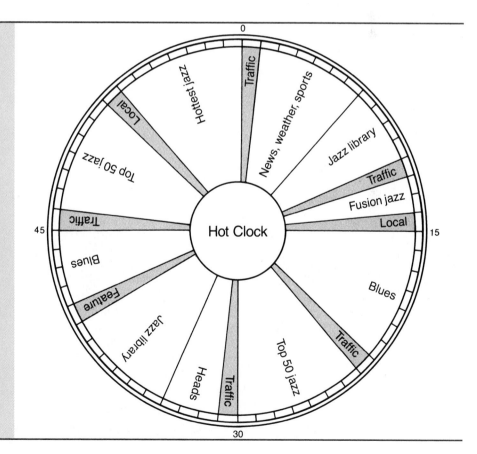

placement of songs may be made by a program director who likely has a regular air shift.

As a DJ on a larger station, you'll have some of the same problems and challenges as your counterpart on a small station. However, generally speaking, you'll have more help. A traffic department will have arranged your running log in the most readily usable manner, and the log will appear on a computer screen atop the audio console. The days of six-hour air shifts will be behind you, but show preparation and public appearances at fairs, parades, and similar events will extend your work time.

Regardless of variations, the technical and manipulative skills involved in DJ work can be acquired in a few weeks, assuming that you're computer literate. The challenge isn't merely being able to perform all of the routine duties well but to project an attractive and unique personality and to be energized and articulate during the few minutes each hour when you're in direct communication with your listeners.

SPOTLIGHT

Showprep Is Everything, and Everything Is Showprep

by Cosmo Rose

Showprep is an abbreviation of show preparation, and nearly all successful morning drive-time DJs believe that conscientious and regular showprep is what keeps audiences tuned in and makes the DJ stand out. In the Spotlight that follows, Cosmo Rose defines showprep and explains how he prepared for his morning drive-time show.

Cosmo Rose began his professional career at the age of 19 as a news anchor–reporter. After two years, he pursued his true interest, becoming a morning drive-time DJ on WJRZ-FM in Toms River, New Jersey. In 1996, he began the AlmostRadio Network, one of the first showprep sites on the Internet. Cosmo received his bachelor's degree in communications from Glassboro State College in Glassboro, New Jersey. In addition to his on-air hosting and showprep site management, he taught broadcasting courses at Cabrini College, Ocean County College, and Monmouth College, all in New Jersey.[4]

The title of this week's editorial is a phrase that I coined (I think I coined it, anyway) for a presentation my producer and I will make at a local university. The course is about showprep . . . the kind of course I wish had been offered at the school I attended and at the many schools where I was an instructor.

In today's radio climate, showprep is more important than ever. The competition for the best radio jobs is getting fierce as opportunities shrink. Only the best people will get on the air . . . and that's not only for high-profile shows like a.m. or p.m. drive time. Marginal talent doesn't really have a place in today's radio. That's why it's a

---

[4] Cosmo Rose, a music radio show host whose performances reflected both integrity and showmanship, succumbed to an incurable disease, sarcoidosis, in 2001 at the age of 36. He was the founder of AlmostRadio, a website devoted to helping disc jockeys around the world become better at entertaining and inspiring music radio listeners. His values (and sense of humor) were best reflected in his frequent editorials in AlmostRadio, where he stressed his respect for the audience, as well as the importance he attached to creativity, responsibility, and community service. Cosmo's wife, Marianne Rose, wrote, "His legacy lives in the projects he spearheaded, the people he helped, the friends he made, and the family he loved. Saying he will be missed is a vast understatement."

great idea to get our future broadcasters acquainted with good showprep habits.

Of course, as a great believer in showprep, it follows that I'm also a believer in "presentation" prep. I've spent the past few weeks outlining the types of showprep I do and how I do it. Rather than use this stuff on one class (which, of course, is honor enough), I figured I'd share it with you as well.

My first golden rule is spelled out in the title of this editorial: "Showprep Is Everything, and Everything Is Showprep." The first part was explained when I told you that good showprep is necessary to separate the good broadcasters from the mediocre. The second part refers to my belief that as entertainers (like stand-up comics), we are always preparing our shows. Many things that happen to us during the course of a day could potentially be used on the air as bits . . . or may give you an idea for a bit.

My second golden rule is that everyone who is successful is organized. Now, let me explain that I don't necessarily mean organized in the strictest sense, having a calendar, elaborate file system, and everything neatly in its place. But if you're successful, you most likely are at least an organized thinker when it comes to your chosen career.

Third golden rule . . . attitude makes a difference. As the job field narrows and the supply of radio applicants continues to grow, arrogance will be tolerated less and less . . . particularly at the hiring stage. After you start earning monster ratings, you may get away with a little more. However, that's a gamble too because ratings don't always stay high forever.

Those are the three rules that guide me through each workday and drive the level of showprep that I do. I've learned those rules mostly through either making mistakes or watching others making mistakes. It is via this same school of hard knocks that I also arrived at all the different types of showprep that exist . . . and there are probably many more than I use.

The first type of prep is vertical prep. In effect, this refers to looking at an individual day's show and planning it out break by break until every slot is filled. It is important to master this type of prep first because it will have the most immediate impact on the structure and presentation of your show.

The second type of prep is horizontal prep. At this level, you plan show ideas day by day . . . week by week. Here is where a calendar becomes most useful. If you get an idea for Easter, write it down on your calendar for one day during the week before Easter. At that point, you may not know what time you'll do the bit . . . you'll save that for vertical prep closer to the show date.

The last aspect of showprep I'll discuss is the sources of prep. My favorite source for prep is life experience or life stories. In my career I have found that I receive the greatest amount of feedback on those little life stories I tell about growing up, about my wife or daughter, or even about my cat. Those are the bits that listeners reflect back to me when they meet me at a live broadcast. And, the best part is, they can't effectively be stolen by anyone else. I am amazed at what about my show gets reflected back to me when I meet listeners out in public. It's never the goofy contest or the funny joke that I hear about. Instead, it's that little story I told about my daughter . . . or the funny thing my wife said. And as the listeners reflect this back to me, I realize they've probably told a few friends about it as well. There's the chatter component.

Now, sharing these types of stories may not make me that crazy, irreverent morning man in the eyes of my listeners, but it does make me human. Perhaps connecting with the audience on a human level can be equally as important . . . if not more.

A second major source of showprep is observation. Perhaps you've noticed a trend in TV commercials or a plethora of potholes in your town . . . whatever. Chances are your listeners have noticed it too . . . or at least will come around to your way of thinking.

The third source of prep is the most readily available: prepackaged prep. This is in the form of prerecorded comedy bits and song parodies, magazines, weekly radio newspapers, and e-mailed publications. There are also many sharing networks and computer bulletin board services that provide prep ideas for broadcasters.

A fourth source for showprep is your local newspaper. By being up on what's going on, you'll avoid becoming a generic morning show that could be playing anywhere in the country.

The final source of prep is: the moment. Many times we'll be planning one thing for our show when we get a call from a listener who introduces a topic so compelling, we're forced to shift gears. Or perhaps a side comment by a cohost will send you in an interesting direction. Being attuned to those opportunities when they present themselves can often yield some of the best shows of one's career.

Popular-Music Station Formats

Music stations vary from those that play one narrowly defined type of music to those playing a broader spectrum. The style of music featured by a station is called its **format.** Music stations describe their formats in a number of ways. A country-music station may call itself "modern country," and a station playing rap, hip-hop, soul, and R&B may classify itself as "urban" or "urban contemporary."

During the 1970s and 1980s, most popular-music station formats fit into one of a number of clearly defined categories. In the 1990s, two developments made it more difficult to categorize music stations. Some stations became quite diversified in the music they played, while others became more narrowly focused. To illustrate: Many country stations no longer confined themselves to songs that were clearly of the country genre, enlarging their scope (and, they hoped, their audiences) by playing pop songs with a broader appeal, as well as pop classics recorded by country artists. At the same time, the once clearly defined category of adult/contemporary (AC) splintered into more focused formats by stations that called themselves hot AC, soft AC, or urban AC, each with a distinct sound. Some stations played music that didn't fit any standard format, including contemporary religious; gospel-inspirational; and country-Spanish, sometimes designated ranchero.

What used to be a fairly stable mix of music formats across the country has splintered into so many sub-formats that describing them is both tedious and pointless. Moreover, music formats are constantly fragmenting. Spanish stations, for instance, are represented by Spanish AC hits, Spanish rock, Spanish CHR, Spanish classical, Spanish classic hits, Spanish easy listening,

Sound Bytes

You can access showprep sites by entering *show prep* on almost any search engine; among the dozens of hits, you'll be able to find some that offer a week or more of free access to their show-prep newsletters.

For a complete, updated list of URLs for this text-book, please see the accompanying CD.

Sound Bytes

CLASSICAL MUSIC

If you're interested in classical music, an entire section on this specialization may be found on the accompanying CD.

Spanish jazz, Spanish oldies, ranchero, romantica (soft AC), Spanish standards, and Tejano.

To demonstrate how difficult it is to categorize music formats today, sources for format statistics aren't in agreement as to the number of existent station formats, terms used for them, or abbreviations for each. *M Street Radio Directory* uses twenty-four categories of music formats; *Radio & Records (R&R)* uses thirty-three, including four categories of Christian popular music; and *Broadcasting & Cable Yearbook* lists thirty-three, including three not found in other listings: underground, hardcore, and new wave.

Music formats vary from region to region. Country stations are far more prevalent in the South than in the East. On the other hand, some formats, including adult contemporary, show nearly the same degree of popularity in all regions of the nation, ranging from 8 to 10 percent. In the American Southwest—which includes the area from California to Texas, as well as Cuban and Puerto Rican enclaves in the Northeast and Florida—so-called Spanish stations are extremely popular. "So-called" because the word *Spanish* is a misnomer—nearly all music played originates in Meso-America, with modifications in various regions to conform to local tastes and ethnicity. "Spanish" is appropriate only in the sense that the language heard is that of the announcers, audiences, and most commercials.

If you're serious about becoming a popular-music announcer, the most realistic way to focus your talents and your practice sessions is by monitoring on-air stations. You may have models in or near your community, so you should spend a good amount of time and effort sampling as many formats—and the announcing styles of each—as are of interest to you. If you live in a region where stations are not sufficiently comprehensive, there are several streaming audio services that will bring you stations from anywhere in the world, representing every genre of popular music that exists.

Announcing Styles

Many music stations—including those formatted as easy listening, adult/contemporary, country, or oldies—feature DJs with a conversational style of delivery, with a minimum of "chatter." On the other hand, hip-hop/rap/urban music stations often ask their announcers to offer a brash, irreverent, fast-paced delivery. Many Latino stations ask for a low-pitched, conversational, noticeably masculine style of delivery.

Because of the range of announcing styles on the air, you'd do well to practice a number of stylistic approaches to popular-music announcing. At the same time, it's important to be yourself. You must be able to project your individuality while speaking at different rates and levels of intensity.

Preparing for a Career as a DJ

In preparing for a career as a DJ, your highest priority must be to develop a compelling air personality. Beyond this, you must be able to use microphones correctly and to operate audio consoles and computerized workstations. Solid preparation

Checklist *Improving Your Popular-Music Announcing Style*

1. Become an authority on the type of music you intend to announce.
2. Work to develop an engaging and unique on-air personality.
3. Cultivate your sense of humor.
4. Learn to operate audio equipment efficiently.
5. Practice announcing for several types of formats.
6. Practice delivering commercials, PSAs, and station promos.
7. Perfect your ad-libbing skills.
8. Learn to match music and chatter to a specific station sound.

also includes skill in the use of all on-air studio equipment. It's of critical importance for you to become an authority on the type of music you intend to announce.

Concentrate on the sections in this book that discuss performance, interpreting copy, ad-lib announcing, commercial interpretation and delivery, news writing, news delivery, and interviewing.

Successful DJs have a well-developed sense of humor, usually of the off-the-wall variety. It's unlikely that anyone without a sense of humor can develop one after reaching adulthood, but it's possible to improve one's skills in almost anything, including comedy. An analysis of puns, jokes, and one-liners you find funny will tell you much about your sense of humor. It may be helpful to invent gags and test them on your friends. Most DJs demonstrate their sense of humor by making ironic or satirical ad-lib comments about current events and noteworthy people. Although a sense of humor is invaluable, it's equally important that you be willing to share yourself with your listeners, even when this means revealing painful or embarrassing experiences or minor problems in your life.

Disc jockeys also need considerable knowledge of music and musicians, including historical facts, trivia, and current developments. This is best gained by reading on a regular basis several trade magazines and newspapers. Among the most useful are *Billboard, R&R (Radio & Records)*, and a variety of tip sheets.

If you don't have an opportunity to do on-air work as a DJ, you can still practice introductions to recorded music and the kind of humorous chatter required of some DJs. Use the practice suggestions that end this discussion of DJs.

Before engaging in practice sessions, remember that all music stations work to achieve a particular sound. A station's sound is the result of a number of factors: the type of music played, the voices and personalities of the announcers, their energy level, the kinds of things they say, whether they speak over instrumental introductions or endings of songs, and the general pace of music and speech. Useful practice includes determining the specific sound you're attempting to achieve and the selection of music appropriate to that sound.

PRACTICE

➤ Honing DJ Skills

- In choosing music to introduce and play, choose performances you know and like. Look especially for music about which you can talk. You won't select your own music when working for a station, but it's good practice to begin with the easiest possible challenge.

- When you practice, actually play your songs, and play them all the way through. Pacing and mood demand that you and your music work together for a total impression.

- Practice headlining songs you'll play later. This is a realistic technique used to hold listeners who might otherwise switch to another station.

- Practice giving the name of the songs and their performers at the end of a sweep. All stations have policies on music identification, with most severely limiting IDs; and, while you'll have to conform to them, when you practice you should aim for communicating a maximum amount of information.

- Practice delivering commercials, ad-libbed public-service announcements, and station promos.

- Practice working with an audio console. You'll almost certainly be expected to operate your own console as a professional DJ.

- Practice performing intros. First, time the music between the start of the song and the start of the vocal. Then, work to introduce the number so that your voice stops just as the vocal begins or where there's a natural change in the music, as when the horn section begins. Although you may not appreciate DJs who talk over music, some stations require it.

- Practice ad-libbing about the music, the day's events, or ideas that intrigue you. You'll have little chance to ad-lib on a station with a tight format, but many stations will consider you for a job only if you're able to entertain in a spontaneous, ad-lib manner.

- Introduce songs ad-lib. Scripts (other than for commercials, some PSAs, and news briefs) aren't used by DJs.

- Avoid corny clichés. Try to develop your own announcing style. The creative expressions of popular DJs become the clichés of unimaginative and unoriginal announcers.

For information on job seeking, see Chapter 13. Above all, remember that there are jobs available if you're well trained, have native talent, and are willing to begin at a modest salary, work hard, and move to any geographic location.

PRACTICE

➤ Tracking Rate of Delivery of DJs

Make audio recordings of several popular-music announcers, each chosen to represent a different sound: the first from a low-key noncommercial station; the second, a fast-paced CHR station; the third, a country station; the fourth, an AC station; and the fifth, any station not listed in the first four, but one in which you have an interest. Play back each recording and make a typescript of any portion of the DJ performance, the longer the better. Count the number of words delivered in the time span. Compare rates of delivery according to types of stations.

Chapter 12

Sports Announcing

Chapter Outline

Before Committing Yourself . . .

Enthusiasm is a great motivator, but because the road to success as a sports announcer can be rocky, it's appropriate to consider the advice of those who've "been there, done that."

Among sports announcers, no one performed in more places, called a greater variety of sports, and succeeded at a higher level than Russ Hodges. Lead announcer for seven major-league baseball teams, including the Yankees and Giants (New York and San Francisco), he also announced football, televised boxing matches, horse racing, hockey, polo, golf, and nearly every other major and minor sport. His broadcasting career spanned forty-one years, from 1929 to 1970. In an interview shortly before his death, he gave this advice:

> First, to succeed you must love sports and broadcasting and fully commit yourself to both. Second, you must truly believe that you will succeed. Third, you must prepare yourself educationally for a different career just in case you're one of the ninety-five out of one hundred who don't succeed in sports broadcasting.[1]

These words of advice are deceptively simple, but if you think each of them through you'll find that they raise questions that should be considered, not only at this moment, but at every stage of your progress toward a life as a sports announcer.

Most announcers who succeed at a high level spend years of preparation before achieving success; nowhere is the struggle seen more clearly than in sports broadcasting. The field is extremely competitive and demands years of dedicated effort before there's any likelihood of significant return.

To become a successful sports announcer, you must have a passion for your work. You'll need it because sports announcing can be a stressful and exhausting way of life. You may find yourself traveling with a team, living out of a suitcase, putting in long hours, eating in restaurants and fast-food outlets, but even worse, grabbing bites of unappealing cold sandwiches during breaks between innings or during time-outs. You'll also be away from your family for extended periods. Only enthusiasm for your work and a supportive family can sustain you in such a job. Even sports reporters who don't travel outside their immediate geographical area work long hours and seldom have a day off.

---

[1] Russ Hodges was far more than a sports announcer. He aided the careers of many rising play-by-play announcers, formed close relationships with Hall of Famers in every sport, and never spoke an unkind word about anyone, even sportscasters who could be considered his rivals. Before retiring, he spent many hours with me, eager to pass on to users of *Television & Radio Announcing* his encyclopedic knowledge of play-by-play announcing. He described a career in sports broadcasting in these words: "It's the best life I can imagine, the best for all who want to spend their lives among the world's greatest athletes, those who want to experience the drama of exciting competition nearly every day." As insignificant as my gesture may be, I dedicate this chapter to the memory of Russ Hodges.

Sports announcing includes *sports reporting, play-by-play coverage,* and *play analysis.* Most established sports announcers devote themselves to one or two of these specialties, but nearly all beginners must become competent at all three. Interviewing sports figures and delivering commercials are additional challenges that must be managed well to succeed.

The Entertainment and Sports Programming Networks (ESPN and ESPN2) broadcast a wide range of sports events. ESPN covers traditional mainline sports such as football, basketball, baseball, golf, hockey, and tennis, but to fill its many hours of daily cablecasting, it also televises bicycle racing (the *Tour de France,* for example), rodeos, billiards, volleyball, horse show-jumping, bodybuilding championships, roller hockey, surfing, waterskiing, gymnastics, hydroplane racing, and even tractor-pulling contests.

In addition to ESPN, many regional radio and television sports networks offer employment to sports announcers. The Fox Sports Network has twenty-six regional sports networks, stretching from New England to Arizona, and from Florida to the Pacific Northwest. Fox also partners with Comcast Cable in several markets.

Working Conditions of Sports Announcers

As a sports announcer, you'll work for a radio or television station (perhaps both), for a broadcast or cable network, for an athletic team, or as a freelance announcer. Your working conditions, responsibilities, and income are determined by your affiliation.

Figure 12-1

Before, during, and after the game, sports announcers spend hours researching team and player histories, statistics, and interesting sidelights. Play-by-play announcer Bill King goes over his detailed stat book just before the start of a baseball game.
Courtesy of Bill King and the Oakland Athletics.

Sports announcers who cover games for major networks, whether play-by-play, analysts, or reporters, are generally at the top of the salary range and have the least strenuous schedules. They seldom broadcast more than one game a week and, even when they add reporting duties to their schedules, they're responsible for only a few minutes of sports news a day.[2] Sports announcers for national or regional cable systems are also well rewarded, but their work schedule is heavy: They may find themselves calling several games each week during basketball, football, hockey, and baseball seasons.

Sports announcers who work for athletic teams have the most strenuous but also the most exciting and fulfilling jobs. As an employee of a professional sports team, you'll travel with the club. You'll owe loyalty to your employer, even though you may sometimes find it difficult to reconcile your judgment with that of your boss. Nearly all team owners require sportscasters to advertise special-promotion days and push ticket sales, which is to be expected, while others demand that their play-by-play sportscasters openly root for their team. Some ask their announcers to favor their team but to do so with discretion. A few owners make no demands on their play-by-play staff but expect announcers as well as all other members of the organization to remain loyal to the team, especially when the team is on a losing streak. Even when working for the most genial or detached owner, you won't have as much freedom as does a reporter who works for a newspaper, or a radio, television, or cable operation.

Most sports announcers fill a variety of professional roles. The simplest combination is doing play-by-play baseball during its long summer season, and basketball, football, or hockey during the fall or winter. Other sports announcers combine five days a week of sports reporting for a station with weekend play-by-play reporting of college sports.

If you become a sports announcer, you'll probably begin at a small-market radio station doing some sports announcing along with other duties, such as reading hourly news reports or performing as a DJ. If you succeed, you may move into full-time sports reporting and play-by-play announcing. Another career path is to move to a larger-market station or, perhaps, to move from radio to television.

If you become a full-time sports reporter or play-by-play announcer for the electronic media, your work schedule and job description might well conform to one of the following models.

Sports Reporter for an All-News, Network-Affiliated Radio Station in a Major Market. You're responsible for several live reports during your daily shift. Your popularity has brought you supplemental responsibilities, including speaking before youth groups, at fan gatherings, service club luncheons, and so forth. Occasionally, when an important news story involves athletes or teams in your area, you prepare a report for your network.

Your work schedule is extremely demanding. Aside from the effort of working a six- to seven-day week, you constantly keep up with developments in all major

---

[2] Network announcers, of course, broadcast more frequently during postseason playoffs and championship games.

sports at amateur and professional levels. You spend hours each week reading the sports sections of several newspapers, *Sporting News, Sports Illustrated,* and other specialized publications. You're asked to speak at team receptions and banquets, news conferences, and civic functions. You schedule yourself to cover as many sports events as possible, do postgame interviews for your daily sports reports, and deliver some actualities live to your station shortly after a game has ended. You record interviews with the star (or, occasionally, the goat) of a game on a small digital recorder and edit and insert them into your reports. You also make notes as you watch the game so you can give a firsthand review, complete with actualities recorded in the locker room, on the following day's reports.

Sports Director for a Network Owned and Operated (O & O) Television Station. As sports director for an O & O television station, you prepare sports news for the daily 6:00 p.m. and 10:00 p.m., or 11:00 p.m., newscasts. You view and edit recorded sports action, select sports photos sent by wire services, and write two three- to five-minute segments for daily newscasts. You spend much of your time attending sports events with a camtech—unless you work solo and do the recording yourself. Pregame and postgame interviews with players and coaches comprise a good portion of your nightly sportscast. On some weekends, you spend hours at the station watching games on network television. You select key plays you may want to use on the air and dub them off. A three-hour game may provide you with as much as thirty minutes of dubbed action from which you'll choose a maximum of three minutes for each of your two sports segments.

Your day's work leaves little time for moonlighting. You attend three to five sports events each week watching events firsthand and recording interviews. You

Figure 12-2
Sports reporter Steve Bitker delivers his reports ad-lib, working from notes jotted down just prior to airtime. Steve studied journalism at San Diego State University and later received a degree in sociology at the University of California, Berkeley. *Courtesy of Steve Bitker and KCBS, San Francisco.*

spend early afternoons covering sports stories, accompanied by a camtech. You arrive at the station at 3:00 p.m., which leaves you less than three hours in which to view or review all available recordings, make selections, review sports news from the wire services, write your script, and prepare for your on-air performance during the 6:00 p.m. news. Between the 6:00 p.m. and the late-night newscast, you eat dinner, prepare for your second sportscast, and review sports scores as they come in from the wire services. Your workday ends after the late-night news but begins early the next day. You spend mornings arranging interviews, reading several sports magazines and sports sections of newspapers, and, perhaps, answering requests for information about the life of a sports reporter sent by high school and college students who would like to have your job.

Sports Director for a Small- or Medium-Market Radio Station. You focus on high school, college, and minor-league sports. You work for the station and for the A or AA baseball team whose games are broadcast over a three-station network. When not on the road with the team, you're involved in many local sports events:

- Doing play-by-play of the most important high school and college football and basketball games[3]
- Gathering reports from a group of students you've recruited and trained to phone in ongoing scores of games not being broadcast
- Play-by-play announcing of home football games for a nearby university
- Providing several brief sports reports each day for the hourly five-minute newscasts
- Acting as spotter for play-by-play sportscasters when university events are regionally telecast

And, as time allows, you do play-by-play reports of newsworthy local sports events such as tennis and golf tournaments; hockey and soccer championship playoffs; Little League, Babe Ruth, and Pop Warner championships; and track and field meets.

Sportscaster for a Television Network. You owe no allegiance to owners, managers, teams, or players. Your responsibility is to your viewers who expect accurate, balanced, and entertaining reports of each game. Because your continued success depends on perfection, you limit moonlighting and other commitments that would cut down on the hours of careful preparation necessary for a first-rate sportscast. Your schedule requires play-by-play work one day a week, which translates into a minimum of twenty-five baseball games during the season, plus preseason and postseason games, and sixteen professional football games, plus divisional playoff games and the Super Bowl.

---

[3] Popularity of high school and college games varies from place to place; hockey, baseball, soccer, tennis, swimming, and track and field are important to people in many parts of the United States and Canada.

This schedule adds up to nearly one game a week for the calendar year, depending on the duration of the playoffs. It's manageable because you're able to spend several days each week memorizing players by appearance, number, and position and you're able to rely on a professional support staff that includes a play and game analyst, a statistician, and (in the case of football) spotters. Your travel schedule is demanding, but you're able to return home for at least a portion of each week. Your high salary increases the number of hungry sportscasters coveting your job. This competition is reason enough for you to apply yourself constantly to perfecting and demonstrating your skills.

Sportscaster for a Cable Sports Channel. Your work is similar to that of a network sportscaster, but you call far more games each season. As is true of most sports announcers, you shift from one sport to another as seasons change. You work with a former star appropriate to the sport who adds "color" and interpretations and explanations of strategies.

Radio Play-by-Play Announcer for a Professional Major-League Baseball Team. You're employed jointly by a baseball organization and a radio station. In many respects, you lead a life similar to that of the athletes. You travel with the team, and the traveling secretary handles all details of transportation or lodging, which eases the stress of travel considerably. Throughout the season you broadcast on a regional radio network of as many as ten stations.

Including spring practice games and games rained out before the end of the fifth inning, but not including divisional playoffs or World Series games, you call about 170 games during the season. You work with a partner who calls between

Figure 12-3

Ed Farmer, lead radio announcer for the Chicago White Sox, began his baseball career as a pitcher, playing for the Cleveland Indians, Detroit Tigers, Baltimore Orioles, Chicago White Sox, Oakland A's, and Philadelphia Phillies. He moved from the field to the broadcast booth in 1991 and became lead play-by-play announcer in 2005. *Courtesy of Ed Farmer and the Chicago White Sox.*

two and three innings and provides anecdotal and statistical information throughout the game.

Play-by-Play Announcer for a Professional Minor-League Baseball Team. You call fewer games each season than your major-league counterpart, but both travel and play-by-play announcing are more rigorous. One of the ways underfunded minor-league teams manage to survive is by economizing on travel. Buses are used for travel whenever possible. The team remains in each town for four days, and you may call five games during the visit.

Play-by-Play Announcer for a Professional Football Team. Your working life is quite different from that of a baseball, basketball, or hockey announcer. Not counting preseason and postseason games, your team plays sixteen games each season, usually a week apart. You may broadcast on both radio and television, determined by the scheduling of a regional television network or a cable sports network.

Play-by-Play Announcer for a University Football Team. You call about twelve games each season, assuming funds are available for you to go on road trips with the team. Most universities offer free transportation to away games on charter flights but don't furnish per diem money. If a radio station, the university, and one or more advertisers put together a commercial package for broadcasting an entire season, your full travel expenses are met.

Play-by-Play Announcer for a Professional Basketball Team. You're part of a four-person announcing staff. You and your partner do television play-by-play, while radio coverage is provided by the two other members of the team's broadcasting staff. The season runs from October through April, during which each team plays eighty-two games. You spend half the season on the road, (with stays in each city of but one day.) During each month, you may travel to as few as seven or as many as ten cities.

Play-by-Play Announcer for a Professional Hockey Team. Your traveling and broadcasting schedule is nearly identical to that of your basketball counterpart. Your team plays eighty games, not counting preseason and playoff games. A typical road trip involves five matches in five cities spread over twelve days. Your friends who do play-by-play for minor-league hockey teams call fewer games each season, but they must endure more demanding travel schedules.

Interviewing Athletes

Interviews are an important resource for nearly all sports reporters. Chapter 8 will help you develop a general approach to interviewing. This section offers additional comments directed at sports reporting.

As a sports announcer, you'll generally interview players, coaches, managers, trainers, and owners. Your interviews usually take place at a sports event or a news conference. Pregame and postgame interviews are common to all sports. As you prepare for an interview, keep some of these questions in mind:

- What is the overriding significance of the game to be played or just concluded?
- Is there an interesting one-on-one player matchup?
- Is there something unique in the playing ability or game strategy of the person you interview?
- Has an athlete been on a hot or cold streak?
- Is there an unusually important or interesting game coming up?
- Is there any information about trades or free agents that might be newsworthy?

Interviews with athletes can be frustrating. The code of the locker room demands that athletes—other than wrestlers, boxers, and some professional tennis players—be modest about their own accomplishments and praise their teammates or opponents, regardless of their true feelings. Moreover, athletes are preoccupied before a game and exhausted afterward. Finally, the noise and confusion in dugouts and locker rooms and on the playing field can make sensible, coherent conversation difficult.

When interviewing sports stars, keep the following points in mind:

- *Assume that your audience is interested in and capable of understanding complex, precise discussions about training and techniques.* Avoid asking superficial, predictable questions. Your audience probably already knows a lot about the sport and the athlete and wants to find out more. Followers of tennis, golf, and Olympic performances such as gymnastics, diving, and equestrian events are less tolerant of superficial interviews than are most other sports fans. They've come to expect precise analytical comments, and they feel cheated if interviews with participants don't add to their understanding of complexities and strategies. Basketball and football have complex offenses and defenses, and fans have been educated to understand and appreciate detailed information about them. Baseball, one of the most subtly complex of all major sports, is seldom explained or discussed in an enlightened fashion through interviews, but you should not be discouraged from reaching for answers to complex questions.

- *Work up to controversial or critical questions with care.* If you ask a big question without any preliminaries, you're likely to get a routine statement "for the record" from athletes and coaches. Sports figures are interviewed so often that most of them can supply the questions as well as the answers. They tend to rely on safe explanations for most common questions. If you want more, lead up to big questions with a sequence of less controversial ones. If you begin an interview with a football coach by asking whether the coach approves of a trade recently made by the club's owners, the coach is naturally going to say "yes" and avoid elaborating. Begin instead by talking about the team and its strengths and weaknesses. Move to a question about the playing abilities of the newly acquired player. Ask specific questions about the player's strong and weak points. Finally, ask the coach to explain how the loss of the player who was traded away will affect the team. A coach will seldom criticize the decisions of the club's owners, but you'll have a better chance of getting more than a vague response if you don't ask the big question straight out. Give your guest a chance to comment informatively as well as loyally.

A warning: Don't use a roundabout approach to the big question if your intent is (or appears to be) *entrapment*. It's not only unfair but could make it more difficult to obtain cooperation in the future.

- *Get to know the athletes you're likely to be interviewing.* Knowing the athletes will help you to assess the kinds of questions they can and can't handle. Many sportscasters and some reporters travel with teams, visit locker rooms, and are invited to opening-day parties, victory celebrations, and promotional luncheons. If you have such opportunities, use them to become acquainted with the athletes who attend.

A warning: It's important to maintain a professional relationship to avoid becoming too subjective—or even obligated—to an athlete.

- *Listen to conversations among athletes and coaches.* A good way to discover what athletes and coaches think is timely and important is simply to listen to their conversations. Though time pressures sometimes require you to enter into these conversations to come up with a story or anecdote for your program, you can often learn more by listening. If you're lucky enough to have meals with athletes and be accepted in clubhouses or locker rooms, try to be a silent observer. You'll be amazed at the spontaneous insights that will emerge.

Again, a warning: Don't use your familiarity or friendships with sports figures to warp your judgment or betray a trust. In other words, don't make excuses for the poor play of an athlete because you have a warm relationship, and don't report things said to you or overheard by you that should remain confidential.

Editing Considerations

When interviewing for later editing into actualities, know in advance whether your questions will remain on the recording. This consideration is important because the questions you ask and the answers you receive must be guided by the way you'll later edit them. The following question and answer would be difficult to use if the question were not included in the actuality when broadcast:

QUESTION: You were in foul trouble early tonight. Do you think the refs were blowing a quick whistle?

> **ANSWER:** Well, I guess we had a little difference of opinion on that. I thought they were overeager. Talk of the possibility of some revenge for the last game probably had them uptight.

Without the question, the answer makes little sense. Of course, you could delete the question and write a lead-in that serves the same purpose:

> **LEAD-IN:** I asked Matty if he thought his early fouls came because the refs were blowing a quick whistle.

This approach works, but it would've been better if you and Matty had understood at the outset of the interview that you needed complete statements that could stand alone without your question. In that event Matty's response might have begun like this:

> **MATTY:** I got into foul trouble early, and I think the reason might have been . . . .

Sports Reporting

At small-market radio and television stations, the title *sports reporter* is synonymous with *sports director* because only prosperous stations can afford the services of more than one specialist. Radio sports directors are usually responsible for both live and recorded reports. They also prepare guidelines to be followed by news anchors who report in-progress scores and final results.

Television sports reporters are less likely to do double duty as reporter and director than are their radio counterparts. It's common to find three or more sports specialists at television stations: a sports director, who may or may not appear before cameras, and two or more reporters who prepare and deliver sports reports during regular newscasts. Typically, one sports reporter does the Monday to Friday newscasts, and the second reporter works weekends. Both cover sports events with camtechs and prepare recorded material for the sports segments of the station's newscasts.

The Television Sports Reporter

As a sports reporter for a local television station, you may find yourself preparing and delivering three features daily—for the 5:00 p.m., 6:00 p.m., and 10:00 p.m. or 11:00 p.m. newscasts—plus a recorded feature for weekend broadcasts. In another common arrangement, one reporter performs for the 5:00 p.m. news and the second is featured on the 6:00 p.m. and late-night newscasts. The first reporter does weekend sports.

As a sports reporter for a medium- or major-market television station, you can expect to have these resources available to you:

- A camtech for recording sports action and pregame and postgame interviews
- Recordings of complete sports events
- Sports video from a parent network
- Video from a television station with which you have a reciprocal agreement
- Digital photos and video from professional and college athletic organizations
- Sports news and photos from the Associated Press (AP) or ESPN
- Sports magazines and sports section of newspapers
- Press information kits and media guides from all major professional and university athletic organizations
- A telephone–audio recorder setup that allows you to make recordings of telephone interviews

The Associated Press provides nonstop coverage of sports, including detailed information on Major League Baseball (MLB); all other major professional sports, all major college sports, the Olympics, professional golf and tennis; and everything from Alpine skiing to wrestling and bowling.[4] The Associated Press also produces comprehensive information about sports through text, audio reports, video streaming, and photos and graphics. Written material (text) is sent under two services for radio stations: *SportsPower,* which includes wire copy, ongoing scores, audio sound bites, and correspondent reports; and *Sportspower Max,* which duplicates the offerings of SportsPower and adds air-ready scripts.

For television stations, *AP Television NewsPower* covers national and international sports stories, as well as sports news localized to each subscriber's state and two adjacent states. The *AP TV Wire* sends in-depth print-style stories. *AP Television Headlines* offers brief notes in print. Television stations may also subscribe to AP's international news video service, *Associated Press Television News* (APTN). Eighty-three bureaus located in sixty-seven countries send international and regional sports stories. The Associated Press also offers *AP GraphicsBank,* which includes more than 160,000 images, including "great moments in sports."

Team media guides are your best sources of detailed information. The guides outline each player's sports career; give statistics for individuals, the team, and the

---

[4] In addition to the abbreviation *MLB* for baseball, other sports are similarly abbreviated: *NHL* for National Hockey League, *NBA* for National Basketball Association, *WNBA* for Women's National Basketball Association, *NFL* for National Football League, *NFC* for National Football Conference, *AFC* for American Football Conference, *MLS* for Major League Soccer, *PGA* for Professional Golfer's Association, and *LPGA* for Ladies Professional Golf Association.

team's opponents; and include each player's photograph to make recognition easier. The won–lost records of every coach or manager who ever served the team and the performance leaders through the years who lead in many different categories are also noted. Both statistics and significant facts are included to help give your narrative a sense of authority.

Your job consists, first, of collecting, selecting, editing, and organizing available materials into a cohesive, action-oriented package for each of the evening's newscasts and then writing an entertaining and informative script. One of your tasks is to log significant plays as you watch games on television. The log is later used to edit the major plays for insertion into your reports.

Using essentially the same bank of visual materials and sports news items, you must prepare as many as three different sports reports each day. The trick is to organize and write your reports to avoid unnecessary repetitions. Many of your viewers will see two of your nightly reports, and a few will see all three, so all reports must provide fresh information for addicted fans. (Of course, a truly spectacular play may be shown on all three reports. Die-hard sports fans may actually stay up late to see it one more time!)

You'll be under constant pressure from your sports director to make your reports more visual. Because you're reporting on television, they'll obviously be "visual." What the director wants is a great deal of illustrative material (recorded inserts, even still photos) to avoid using the kind of shots some television producers sarcastically refer to as *talking heads*. You may feel that a series of recorded shots may be more confusing than enlightening or that some important stories should be narrated directly into a taking camera, but your judgment isn't the deciding factor.

When writing voice-over copy to accompany "play action" inserts, always try to match words and pictures cohesively. On television, when words and pictures don't match one another, the sound tends to fade from the viewers' awareness. Confine your remarks to the few essential comments needed to enhance understanding of what the viewers are seeing.

The Radio Sports Director

As sports director for a medium- or major-market radio station, you have many of the same responsibilities as your television counterpart. You produce several fast-moving sports reports each day, generate material to be broadcast after you've left the station, and establish and supervise station policy concerning sports. This last responsibility includes preparing an instruction sheet or manual for use by general or staff announcers. In the manual you indicate how sports bulletins are to be handled, how the sports news section of general newscasts is to be structured, and the order and the manner of reporting scores and the outcomes of games.

Depending on your geographical region, you might ask that a certain sport be given priority in reporting. In the Northeast, hockey often comes before basketball; in Indiana, basketball usually comes before baseball; and in Chicago, baseball almost always comes before tennis. If your town has a minor-league baseball team, you might ask that its scores be given priority over major-league results.

As a radio sports director, you're likely to use the following resources:

- A high-quality digital recorder on which you record interviews and news conferences for delivery during a live report. The recordings are also used for later editing and broadcasting on your regular sports reports. You may use a minidisk recorder for this and later dub your material to a digital recorder at the station for easy editing.
- Sports news and scores from news wire services. (See a listing of offerings from the Associated Press in the preceding section.)
- Audio feeds from wire services and perhaps from a parent network.
- Special wire-service sports features (listed earlier in this chapter).
- A specially adapted telephone for recording phone interviews.
- Press books and other sources of factual information from professional and university sports organizations.
- A variety of newspapers and magazines to which your station subscribes.

One of your most time-consuming jobs will be preparing the audio inserts for your broadcasts. This job includes gathering the recorded material, determining the items you'll use, writing a script to accompany the inserts, editing the excerpts, and dubbing the selected actualities to a storage system. Because radio reports demand extensive use of actualities, the procedures followed by one outstanding sports director, Hal Ramey of KCBS, San Francisco, are outlined here.

Ramey records his interviews without assistance. He attends many sports events and news conferences and conducts interviews for later review, selection, and insertion into his reports. He operates a Sony minidisk recorder for his interviews. During day football and baseball games, he presents his twice-an-hour sports reports live from the press box of the stadium, often incorporating actualities recorded prior to game time. His voiced reports are transmitted to his station digitally over an ISDN (Integrated Services Digital Network) telephone line.

When working at the station, Ramey arrives an hour or so before his first on-air report. He checks the sports wire and Internet sites to obtain information on games in progress, league standings, and other information appropriate to a given sport season. He then goes over the notes he made following his locker room interviews of the previous day. His notes list the following information for each interview:

- Computer markers where each actuality begins
- Name of the person being interviewed
- The in cue
- The out cue
- Length of the actuality
- A brief indication of the topic of the comments

Here's a typical note:

> 121 Fred Williams "I think we can" "be close" 15 secs "Win the pennant"

When preparing sports reports at the station, in addition to his own recorded interviews, Ramey uses audio feeds from CBS Radio Sports (*SportsFeed*) and the Associated Press as well as scores and sports reports sent to a desktop computer by the AP. A typical SportsFeed menu will outline twelve to twenty-five available cuts. Each cut is identified by number, the name of the speaker, the general subject of the comments, the length of the cut, and the out cue. Cuts are brief, averaging about fifteen seconds. Feeds are received and recorded automatically by computer, so it's a simple matter for Ramey to review them and make selections for inclusion in one of his ten live sports reports.

Ramey listens to the actualities and decides which to keep; on his computer he edits, labels, and stores those he plans to use. He then sketches a script for the actualities he's chosen and dubbed. At precisely fifteen and forty-five minutes past the hour, he goes on the air in the on-air studio to make his sports reports, usually incorporating up to four actualities in each.

Figure 12-4

Sports director and reporter Hal Ramey making one of his twice-hourly reports. Ramey attends numerous sporting events and records brief interviews with athletes, coaches, managers, and front-office personnel for later inclusion as actualities. *Courtesy of Hal Ramey and KCBS.*

Hal Ramey does ten two-minute live reports daily, for which he spends a minimum of eight hours preparing, and this does not account for special reports or weekend features. Oh, for the life of a sports reporter!

Student Voices

Technology in the Sports Stadium by Matthew T. McDermit

ALL ABOUT ME: My name is Matthew McDermit, and I am a communications major at Penn State University's Altoona College. I enjoy sports and recently completed an internship with the Baltimore Orioles. A highlight for me was working with the producers, announcers, and others to prepare game-day materials that were displayed on the scoreboard at Camden Yards.

ALL ABOUT TECHNOLOGY IN THE SPORTS STADIUM: Today sports stadiums are jam-packed with the latest technological entertainment devices. From play-by-play scoreboards to high-definition video boards, stadiums have become hosts for top-of-the-line entertainment equipment that's altering the role of the announcer. While serving as a production intern with the Baltimore Orioles, I had the chance to talk with the Orioles' public address announcer, Dave McGowan. McGowan stated that timing is everything when it comes to working as a P. A. announcer. The announcer and video board must work in sync. For this to happen, the control room and announcer must have constant communication, which ensures a good in-house show.

. . . AND HOW DOES THIS AFFECT ANNOUNCING? Although Internet radio and YouTube technology are threatening the need for announcers, it seems that stadium announcers are the one group not getting edged out by new electronics. True, they must learn to work with the new equipment, but that's not too hard with the rise of so many minor-league teams that offer great opportunities for amateurs to try their hand working with a Jumbotron and other technological devices. And then, with the right timing and development of a good, crisp delivery, skilled announcers might find sports-related work that could lead them to the major leagues.

Play-by-Play Announcing

Play-by-play coverage of football, basketball, hockey, soccer, and baseball games accounts for most of the many hours of sports reporting on radio and television. The person who calls the game, race, match, or event is known as the **play-by-play announcer,** even though sports such as track and field have no actual "plays." For many types of sports events, play-by-play announcers work with a play or game analyst, whose role is described in the next section.

As a sportscaster for a team that plays many games during a long season, you easily acquire the kind of information needed for intelligent ad-libbed commentary. Associating with league players makes player identification routine, and your involvement with a single sport gives you plenty of material for illuminating analyses and game trends.

As the play-by-play announcer at the highest levels of professional sports broadcasting, you have help from a broadcast staff and team management. Each broadcast day you're given a press information kit updating all relevant statistics. During the game, a sports wire such as SportsTicker, Inc., gives you the scores and details of other games. A full-time statistician may work with you, unearthing and bringing to your attention significant records or events you incorporate into your running commentary. An engineer continuously balances your voice with crowd sounds, adding drama to your narrative. When you telecast a game, you have instant replay to enrich the coverage. Even when doing radio play-by-play, watching a television replay gives you the information you need to tell your listeners that the game officials made a good, questionable, or incorrect call.

A famous athlete or former manager may be at your side giving evaluations and predictions that add another dimension to the broadcast. It's demanding work, but you have budget, personnel, and working conditions in your favor. However,

Figure 12-5

Like most of the athletes he reports on, Ken Korach came up through the "minors." He began play-by-play in 1981 with a minor league team, the Redwood Pioneers. After five years, he moved to the triple-A Phoenix Firebirds, then to the majors with the Chicago White Sox. He came to the Oakland A's in 1996 and became lead P-B-P announcer in 2006. *Photo courtesy of Ken Korach*

overlapping and ever-expanding seasons, as well as competition from single-sport specialists, require you to focus on no more than two, or possibly three, major sports.

When doing play-by-play for a smaller station you work a wide variety of games, ranging from high school to college and semipro, so your job is much more difficult. Rules of play may not be standardized, you may not know the players, and press information kits may not exist. You have little help and a meager budget.

Booth setups vary with the sport. Football usually demands the services of a team of four: play-by-play announcer, play analyst, and two spotters. When doing play-by-play, you sit between the two spotters, and the analyst sits next to one of the spotters. For high school, college, and some professional games, the analyst is likely to be quite familiar with the home team; the analyst's position is next to the spotter who points for the visiting team.

Spotting charts list both offensive and defensive players, but because football, especially at the professional level, is extremely complex, spotting charts lack adequate flexibility to cover offensive and defensive realignments. As play-by-play announcer, you concentrate on the handling of the football; spotters are responsible for showing changes in the lineups. For example, the defense spotter holds up five fingers to indicate a nickel defense, or the offensive spotter holds up three fingers to indicate three wide receivers in the game. In general, you use spotters for actions you can't see: It's your job to follow the football, so you leave other details of each play up to your spotters.

The booth setup for baseball can be as simple as one play-by-play announcer sitting with a remote mixer, a microphone, and an array of information sheets and scoring charts. Some radio and most television broadcasts are enhanced by adding two others to the team: a second play-by-play announcer and a game analyst who also may serve as statistician. The three-person team usually is positioned with the statistician to the right of the two play-by-play announcers. Typically, one announcer calls six innings, the other calls three. Before them are at least three cards or sheets of paper: two diagrams of the baseball field with the names of the defensive players of each team written in and score sheets for each team.

Another setup for baseball broadcasts calls for two announcers who take turns doing play-by-play and analysis, and sometimes an audio engineer who also serves as booth producer. More likely, though, the engineer, as well as the director and producer, is some distance away, usually in a remote trailer. The producer issues instructions to announcers and camera operators, including requests that the play-by-play team give ongoing scores, promote ticket sales for upcoming games, and interview important guests as they enter the booth.

The director decides on camera coverage and camera "takes" during the action and gives cues over the IFB for going to and returning from station breaks. The engineer adjusts audio volume, cuts from camera to camera on command, and plays commercials during breaks in the action. Another essential task sees the engineer recording the entire game, making notations of important plays, and cuing the cuts for playing in sequence during the postgame wrap-up.

Figure 12-6

Color commentator and basketball game analyst Steve Lavin enjoyed a distinguished career as head coach of basketball giant UCLA compiling a record of 145 to 78. He now makes regular appearances on ESPN's College GameNight, and provides color for prime-time college basketball games around the country on ABC Sports and ESPN. Steve developed his play-by-play skills as a high school student, sitting high in the cheap seats, calling games into a cassette tape recorder. *Photo courtesy of Steve Lavin.*

When calling baseball games, you must be able to score them accurately and quickly. Outs, scoring, unusually brilliant plays, errors, and other basic information are essential when recapping game action.

Basketball and hockey move so fast and have so few players that announcers have neither the time nor need for spotters. A name and position chart with pins indicating the players in the game at any given moment may be helpful at times; but there's generally little time to refer to it. On two-person announcing teams, the second announcer provides analysis (or color, on radio).

Boxing, golf, tennis, speed and figure skating, skiing, ski jumping, and gymnastics present no problems of competitor recognition. Spotting is unnecessary, and many of the complexities that make football, basketball, and hockey difficult to call, such as multiple players, complex offenses and defenses, and speed of action, aren't factors. However, all of these sports require in-depth knowledge, and fans expect reporters to have outstanding comprehension and judgment. It's standard practice for sports generalists to introduce, talk around, and summarize gymnastics, skiing, and skating, with the actual "play-by-play" provided by a former participant of the sport.

Boxing, golf, and tennis usually are covered by announcers who've competed in those sports, although occasionally competent calling is done by those who've made long and intense study of them. Announce booths may be lacking altogether at the sites of these sports; remote trailers take their place. At the opposite extreme, most notably for the Olympic Games, a highly sophisticated electronic center houses media coverage.

Practicing Play-by-Play Announcing

If you're a beginner, you should practice play-by-play announcing at every opportunity. Attend every sports event you can, not only major sports, but tennis, track and field, gymnastics, and skiing—anything that's recognized as a sport and is given radio or television coverage. Practice calling games or events into the mic of a digital recorder. Set your work aside until memory of the game has faded; then listen to see if your calling of the game painted a clear picture. Make note of any instances in which you find your reporting incomplete, unclear, tedious, or marred by numerous corrections and work to eliminate the flaws. In particular, note any *improvement*. Improvement builds confidence, and confidence guarantees further improvement.

It's difficult for a student of sports announcing to practice play-by-play for television. Practicing with an audio recorder will help prepare you for telecasting, but there are important differences in style, quantity of information given, nature of information provided, and availability of resources, including instant replay and graphic player identifications. Your firsthand introduction to the challenge of televised play-by-play will probably be served by observing others as they call games. If you can, obtain permission to be a silent and unobtrusive witness in announce booths during the telecasts of games in your area.

If you can't be in the booth, view games on television with a critical eye and ear. Record broadcasts of entire sports events. As you review them, make notes of your observations. Analyze moments of exceptionally competent—as well as incompetent—play-by-play narrative. Decide for yourself how much description is illuminating and learn to sense the moment at which announce booth chatter begins to reduce your enjoyment of the game.

Checklist   *Questions to Ask Yourself before You Enter an Announce Booth to Call a Game*

1. Is there anything unusual about this game?
2. Is either team or any player on a streak of any sort?
3. Are there any interesting rivalries in this matchup?
4. How might the weather affect the game?
5. Is there a home-team advantage?
6. How have these teams fared during the season and during the past few years?

Reflecting on these and similar questions should prepare you to call an interesting game.

Calling the Game

Arrive early the day of the game. Check starting lineups. If in doubt, check the pronunciation of players' names with press information personnel, assistant managers, or team captains. If possible, spend time with the players before the game; your effectiveness in describing the game will be enhanced by understanding how the players feel. Enter the booth long before game time. Lay out your spotting charts, scoring sheets, file cards of statistical and anecdotal information, and whatever notebooks or other materials you plan to use during the game. Examine your broadcast equipment. For both radio and television sportscasts, commercials, station promotions, and promotions of ticket sales are likely to be recorded before game time. This reduces pressure during the game and gives you many moments when you can take off your headset to make or read notes.

Plan ahead. Think about everything you'll need and make sure you have it with you when you arrive at the booth. Aside from the spotting charts, scoring sheets, and information cards, you'll need pencils, a pencil sharpener, erasers, pins for the chart, water or some other beverage, binoculars, and perhaps even an electric heater to keep your teeth from chattering!

If you and your analyst partner are new to one another, you may need to establish some simple hand signals to avoid confusion. A sportscast can be deadly for listeners if you and your partner continually interrupt one another or start speaking at the same time. The general rule is that the play-by-play announcer is in charge. You'll do most of the talking as plays unfold, while your partner will join in with appropriate comments after the action is completed. In baseball and football coverage, because there is time between moments of action, you may engage in a discussion but because such discussions should end as each new play is about to begin, raise a finger to signal that the conversation is over. Play analysts indicate they have a comment to make by raising a hand or slipping you a note. If you decide to allow the comment, you throw a cue by pointing an index finger when you come to the end of your own remarks. Analysts must complete their remarks well ahead of the moment when you must again pick up the play-by-play. Of course, hand signals (except for "you're on" cues) are unnecessary when sportscasters have worked together for long periods of time and sense when it's safe to interject comments.

When you call any game, keep several important principles in mind. First, believe that your chief responsibility is to your viewers or listeners. This translates into being completely honest in reports of the games you call. This belief will be difficult to hold to at times. Unreasonable owners, outraged players, and others who have a stake in your broadcasts may make irrational demands. In the long run, though, you'll prosper best if you have a loyal following of viewers or listeners who have faith in your integrity.

Second, remember that it's your responsibility to report, entertain, and sell. Your reporting must be accurate and fair. As an entertainer, you must attract and hold the fans' attention for up to three hours at a time; *entertaining* does not mean showing off your knowledge and opinions if they take away from the game. *Selling* means selling the sport more than the team. It means selling yourself as a credible reporter who communicates natural energy and objectivity but avoids forced enthusiasm.

Finally, avoid home-team bias. **Homers** aren't unknown to sportscasting, and some play-by-play announcers are famous for their lack of objectivity. The most important reason to avoid home-team bias is that it will blind you to the actual events taking place. Regardless of affiliation or loyalties, it's your responsibility to provide fans with a clear, accurate, and fair account of the game. This responsibility is more apparent if you do play-by-play for radio. Television fans can compare your work with what they see, but when you serve as the eyes of radio listeners, you have an obligation to report with objectivity, because your account is the listeners' total exposure to the event.

Additional Tips on Sportscasting

Some of these suggestions are appropriate to all sports; others apply to one or two.

Communicate the Important Events in a Game and Provide Interpretation when Appropriate. A game is more than a series of individual plays or events. Plays are part of a process that adds up to an overall pattern. If you're perceptive and deeply involved in the event, you'll be able to point out crucial plays and turning points immediately after they occur. It's your responsibility to grasp the significance of plays or incidents and then to communicate your awareness to viewers or listeners. You'll transmit significance not only by what you say but also by how you say it. Some critical situations will be apparent to any reasonably sophisticated fan, but at times you must be so tuned in to the game that your interpretation surpasses common knowledge.

When Doing Play-by-Play on Radio, Provide Listeners with Relatively More Information Than Is Necessary for a Telecast. Listeners need to know, for example, what the weather is like, how the stadium or court looks, how the fans are behaving, whether players are right- or left-handed (when applicable), the wind strength and direction, who's on first, how many yards for a first down, how many outs or minutes left in the game, and whether a particular play was routine or outstanding. Most important of all: *Repeat the score often, and always before going to a commercial and immediately after a commercial break.* You can't overdo this. Some sports announcers use a three-minute egg timer to remind them to mention the score (and other basic information) every time the sand has run through the glass.

When Doing Baseball Play-by-Play, Always Be Ready to Talk Intelligently and Entertainingly during Rain Delays. Baseball fans love baseball lore, and well-prepared announcers who can discuss historical aspects of the sport and provide a wealth of amusing or amazing anecdotes can make a rain delay the highlight of a game.

Never Make Events in a Game Seem More Important Than They Are. A dull game creates a natural temptation to entertain by exaggerating. Avoid this tendency.

Don't Overuse Sports Clichés. You can't avoid sports clichés entirely; there's a limited number of ways to describe things that happen over and over in a game. But unless frequent use of sports clichés is a part of your announcing persona, be conscious of clichés and try to avoid their overuse. Here are several overused sports expressions:

- In tonight's action
- Over in the NBA
- All the action is under the lights
- Was in complete charge
- He got all of it
- He was taking all the way
- Odds-on favorite
- Off to a running start
- Off to a shaky start
- Sparked the win
- Suffered a sixth setback
- Went the distance

These are all items worth communicating, so the challenge is to deliver the information without resorting to overused ways of expressing it.

Some familiar sports expressions are clear, direct, and uncomplicated and hardly can be improved on: *loaded the bases, gave up a walk, got the hat trick, was sacked, finished within one stroke of,* and *lost the decision.* In general, although you can't—and shouldn't—completely avoid clichés, improve the variety of your play-by-play delivery by using several ways of naming the same kinds of events or incidents.

Have Statistics in Front of You or Firmly in Mind before You Start to Talk about Them. If you make an error, you can easily correct it: "That's the fourth walk allowed by Rollins—hold it; it's the *third* walk." There's nothing wrong with making an occasional correction. If you repeatedly must make corrections, however, it becomes annoying.

On Television, Concentrate on Interpreting the Events and Adding Comments about Action Not Clearly Shown by the Camera. Television viewers don't necessarily see everything that a trained observer sees. Your commentary and instant replay can provide viewers with specific details that illuminate, instruct, and entertain.

When Doing Play-by-Play on Television, Avoid the Extremes of Too Much or Too Little Commentary. Avoid extraneous chatter that confuses and distracts viewers.

On the other hand, don't go to the opposite extreme and assume that viewers have been with you throughout the entire game and therefore know everything important that's occurred. From time to time, review key plays, injuries, and other pertinent facts.

When a Player Is Injured, Never Guess about the Nature or Severity of the Injury. If you consider it important to report on the details of the injury, send an assistant to the team trainer or physician. Inaccurate information about an injury can cause unnecessary worry for friends and family.

Don't Ignore Fights, but Don't Sensationalize Them. Hockey and football are often violent, and fights between players aren't uncommon. If you dwell on them, you may provoke both aggression by fans (thrown bottles, for example) and attempts by players to exact revenge.

If You're Not Sure about Information, Don't Guess. Wait as long as necessary to give official verdicts on whether or not a ball was fair or foul, a goal was scored, or a first down was made. Constant corrections of such errors are annoying to the fans.

Tell a baseball audience what inning it is as you give the score. Tell football, basketball, soccer, and hockey audiences which quarter or period it is and how much time is left. When you say that there are six minutes remaining, be sure to add "in the first half" or "in the game." Not all of your listeners have been with you throughout the entire game. Football audiences need to be reminded frequently who has the ball, where the ball is, and what down is coming up. It's all but impossible to give such information too often.

Give Scores of Other Games, but Never Allow Them to Interfere with the Game at Hand. When telecasting, remember that your viewers are being bombarded with information not only from you, the play analyst, and the camera coverage of the game but also from written information superimposed on the screen at the request of the director that show statistics, promote an upcoming program, or "tease" an after-game feature, such as "In the Clubhouse," or "The Fifth Quarter." Because of this overload, be careful not to further distract viewers from the game they're watching. Give scores of other games but be discreet. And, unless you're instructed to do so, don't give scores of other games during moments of high tension in the game you're calling.

Take Care of First Things First. Provide essential information before going into an analysis of the action. On radio, don't describe the double play until you've told the fans whether or not the player on third scored. In football, don't start talking about key blocks or sensational catches until you've indicated whether or not a first down was made on the play.

Don't Keep Telling Your Audience How Great the Game Is. If it *is* a great game, the events and the way you report them will speak for themselves. If it isn't a great game, no amount of wishful thinking will make it exciting. At the same time, as an unusually exciting game winds down, it *is* appropriate to express your honest emotions about the suspense of the game or the victory of an underdog.

If You Can't Immediately Identify a Player, Cover the Play without Mentioning Names and Give the Name When You're Sure of It. Here's a poor example of identifying players:

ANNCR: The ball is taken by Richards. . . . He's back in the pocket to pass. . . . He's being rushed. . . . He barely gets it away and it's intercepted by Pappas . . . no, I think it's Harrison. . . . He has it on the twenty-five, the thirty, the thirty-five and he's brought down on the thirty-seven. Yes, that was Pappas, the all-American defensive back.

This is a better example:

ANNCR: The ball is taken by Richards. . . . He's back in the pocket to pass. . . . He's being rushed. . . . He barely gets it away and it's intercepted on the twenty . . . back to the thirty, the thirty-five, and all the way to the thirty-seven. A beautiful interception by Charley Pappas, the all-American defensive back.

Learn Where to Look for the Information You Need. In baseball, watch the outfielders instead of a fly ball to see whether the ball will be caught, fielded, or lost over the fence. Watch line umpires to see whether a ball is fair or foul. In football, watch the quarterback unless you clearly see a handoff or a pass; then watch the ball. Let your spotters or analyst watch the defense and the offensive ends.

Don't Rely on Scoreboard Information. Keep your own notebook and record the data appropriate to the sport you're covering. For football, note the time when possession begins, the location of the ball after each play, the nature of each play, and the manner in which the drive ends. These notes will help you summarize each drive and will single out the most important plays. For baseball, keep a regular scoring chart and learn to read it quickly and accurately. For basketball, hockey, and soccer, rely on a statistician for data such as goals attempted and fouls and penalties assessed.

Give Statistics and Records. Baseball fans are always interested in batting and earned run averages, fielding percentages, strikeout records, and comparative statistics. Track and field followers are obsessed with distance and speed records. Statistics are only slightly less important to followers of football, basketball, soccer, hockey, and golf. Remember, though, that some statistics are of little value or interest, as in: "That was the seventh time this season that the Hornets were the first to score in the third quarter!"

Avoid Adopting Meaningless Catch Phrases. Perhaps the most prevalent and annoying habit of sports announcers is the interjection of the phrase *of course* into statements when the information being given isn't necessarily common knowledge, as in, "Wilson, of course, has run for over a hundred yards in each of his past seven games." Even when the information is widely known, *of course* adds nothing to most statements: "Fred McKinnon, of course, played seven years for the Pittsburgh Pirates before coming to the Mariners."

Eliminate or Control the Use of the Word Situation. With some sports announcers, nearly everything is a situation: "It's a passing situation," "It's a bunting situation." "It's a third-and-three situation." Constant repetition of this word can become very tiresome.

Use Background Sounds to Your Advantage. Most sports have moments of action that bring about an enthusiastic response from the crowd. The sounds of cheering fans can enhance your game coverage. Don't be afraid to remain silent at key times while the fans carry the excitement of the game for you.

When Working with a Play Analyst, Make Sure You and Your Partner Agree on the Pronunciation of Names That Could Be Pronounced in Different Ways. During a professional football telecast, the play-by-play announcer and play analyst pronounced the names of three players in different ways:

McMahon: (muk-MAN) versus (muk-MAY-un)

Lippett: (LIP-ut) versus (lih-PET)

Clayborn: (KLAY-born) versus (KLY-born)

These differences probably went unnoticed by most listeners, but as a professional you should first hear such differences and then discuss them with your partners with the hope of reaching an agreement. Although this isn't a major point, to be truly the best in your field demands that you correct even minor inaccuracies.

Checklist *Becoming an Effective Play-by-Play Announcer*

1. Communicate the important events in a game and provide interpretation when appropriate.
2. Provide a radio audience with more information than you would provide a television audience.
3. When doing television play-by-play, avoid the extremes of too much or too little commentary.

4. Never make events in a game seem more important than they are.
5. Don't overuse sports clichés unless you use them as an important part of your on-air personality.
6. Don't talk about statistics unless you have them in front of you or firmly in mind.
7. On television, concentrate on interpreting the events and adding comments about events not clearly shown by the cameras.
8. Be prepared to talk intelligently and entertainingly during periods of inaction, including rain delays.
9. When a player is injured, never guess about the nature or severity of the injury.
10. Don't ignore fights but don't sensationalize them.
11. If you're not sure about information, don't guess.
12. Repeat the score at frequent intervals.
13. Give scores of other games without neglecting the game at hand.
14. Provide essential information, such as yards gained or runs scored, before going into an analysis of the action.
15. Don't keep telling the audience how great the game is.
16. If you can't immediately identify a player, cover the play without mentioning names and give the name when you're sure of it.
17. Learn where to look for the information you need.
18. Don't rely on scoreboard information.
19. Give statistics and records.
20. Avoid adopting meaningless catch phrases.
21. Avoid overuse of the word situation.
22. Use background sounds to your advantage.
23. When working with a play analyst, reach an agreement on the pronunciation of names.

The Play Analyst

Play analysts interpret individual plays and overall strategies. They also provide information that helps listeners and viewers learn the finer points of a sport. Analysts are, without significant exception, former athletes or coaches of the sports they describe. Their in-depth knowledge allows penetrating analyses of ongoing sportscasts. Play and game analysis is highly specialized, and effective preparation requires considerable devotion to the sport itself.

Analysts provide information and interpretation that complement rather than duplicate what's offered by the play-by-play announcer. As an analyst, you must have a clear agreement about what to look for and how to report it. In football, you look for key blocks, tackles, and similar events of importance. In baseball, hockey, and basketball, you usually serve as a statistician and analyze the whole game rather than individual plays. In these sports, you'll see little or nothing that isn't seen by the play-by-play announcer, so you contribute information such as this:

> That was Ponce's twenty-first inning without giving up a walk.

> Garrett's forty-one points are a season high for him, but they're a long way from the record set by Wilt Chamberlain—he scored one hundred points in a game in 1962.

Hockey and basketball move so fast that opportunities for play analysis are limited. If interesting points are brought up at all, the play-by-play announcer usually introduces them. On the other hand, events in a baseball game proceed more slowly, allowing opportunities for analysts to explain the finer points of the sport.

The educational function of a play analyst is of great importance to those who care deeply about the sport being broadcast. In televised football games, play analysts use electronic "chalkboards" to draw the action and movements of a recently completed play. After viewing it and listening to the explanation, a reshowing of the play often helps us see things we hadn't noticed during real-time action. In the process we learn a bit more about the subtleties of the sport. The best analysts provide us with insights into the "structure" of a game as it progresses, pointing out that a particular play was a turning point, or that Team A, after falling behind by two touchdowns, made strategic defensive moves that are responsible for their regaining the initiative.

A baseball analyst—most often a former pitcher, catcher, or manager—can teach us much about the game of baseball. Two examples:

> **ANALYST:**   Jones just asked for a new ball. Not all baseballs are the same, and some just don't "feel right" to a pitcher. However, with two outs and the tying run on second, Jones most likely wants to throw a curve or a slider, and the ball he tossed back had flat seams. It's easy to throw a fastball with any baseball, but you want a ball with raised seams to help you throw a curve. And, of course, Chavez, being a

veteran, most likely knows that the next pitch he'll see will be a ball with a lot of motion on it. There's one complicating factor, though: Jones could have decoyed Chavez into assuming that a curve was coming by asking for a new ball.

ANALYST: Notice how, with runners on base, second baseman Washington will move right behind second base after every pitch. He wants to make sure that a return throw from the catcher to the pitcher doesn't go into center field. A bad return throw from a big-league catcher to his pitcher is a rarity, but first-rate ball players leave nothing to chance.

Gymnastics, figure skating, ice dancing, diving, and similar sports of a strongly aesthetic nature are almost always described by experts in the event. Analysis is the primary responsibility of the people who cover sports in which points are assigned by judges, because the vast majority of viewers have little precise knowledge of the pluses and the minuses of individual performances.

Here are a few tips for play and game analysts:

- Never repeat either exactly or by paraphrase what the play-by-play announcer has just said.
- Don't feel compelled to comment after every play of a football game or after every pitch of a baseball game. If you have nothing significant to report, remain silent.

Figure 12-7

Play analyst Chris Singleton works with White Sox lead play-by-play announcer, Ed Farmer. As is true of many—perhaps nearly all—analysts, Chris played several years in the majors, amassing an impressive knowledge of the game, players, baseball history, and much, much more. He started with the Houston Astros in 1990 and, after five trades and fifteen years, wound up his career with the Tampa Bay Rays. His chief responsibility is interpreting game strategies, explaining managerial moves, and relating interesting and humorous anecdotes. *Courtesy of Chris Singleton and the Chicago White Sox.*

- Be precise in the comments you make. "What a great catch" is neither useful nor informative. "Frick has just gone over the one-hundred-yard mark for the eighth time this season" is precise and useful.

- Do your homework on both teams. The play-by-play announcer will also have prepared, but in the heat of the game it may fall to you to remember facts or statistics forgotten by your partner. Make notes of key moments of the game.

- Your major contribution is to see the game with an objectivity not always possible for a play-by-play announcer. Look for the dramatic structure of the contest and report it when appropriate. Don't overdramatize, however.

- Never correct the play-by-play announcer on the air. If an important mistake has been made, write and pass a note. Listeners and viewers become uncomfortable when they sense conflict between members of an announcing team.

- A discussion between play-by-play announcer and analyst in which different points of view are expressed can be useful to fans. As long as the discussion is friendly—perhaps even amusing—there's no reason to avoid or prematurely terminate it.

- It may be difficult to maintain harmonious relations with your partner, but it's imperative. Fans appreciate listening to announcing teams that complement each other and work together to present the sports experience competently and completely.

- Be careful what questions you ask of your partner. Even the most competent veteran can draw a blank when concentrating on a game.

- Follow the rules set down by your play-by-play partner. You may have to ask for an opportunity to speak and then do so only when your partner gives you your cue. If your agreement with the play-by-play announcer calls for it, be prepared to make intelligent comments during time-outs and intermissions in basketball and hockey contests.

- Always be sure to end your comments before the next play begins.

- If you hope to become a professional sports announcer of any kind—reporter, play-by-play, analyst—you should build your own sports library and become knowledgeable about as many sports as possible. And remember—there's no substitute for practicing your skills!

SPOTLIGHT

The Key Is Preparation!
by Tommy Booras,
   Western Kentucky University

Professor Tommy Booras of Western Kentucky University believes that there's only one reason for undergoing the strenuous life of sports announcers: Love of the game! Aware that most who prepare for careers in sports broadcasting think only of the obvious rewards—describing games to thousands, associating with famous athletes, and becoming a celebrity—they likely overlook the hard work that goes into becoming and remaining a successful

Figure 12-8

Tommy Booras teaches broadcast production in the School of Journalism and Broadcasting at Western Kentucky University. An avid sports fan, he says this about his sports broadcasting manual, from which this spotlight was extracted: "The idea for my manual came from a performance class I was teaching in Texas. I had twenty students, and I wanted to use something in that class about doing play-by-play because all my research indicated there was not much available on the nuts-and-bolts of how to prepare for a game, keeping stats, and the like."

play-by-play announcer. His treatise on preparation is offered here to emphasize one important reality of sports broadcasting.[5]

Tommy Booras's play-by-play background was gained doing play-by-play for several high schools, as well as two seasons spent calling double-A baseball games with veteran Louisiana broadcaster "Freeway" Dave Nitz. He strongly advises students who want to enter sports broadcasting to take their opportunities wherever and whenever they can.

Contrary to popular belief, a play-by-play announcer doesn't just show up thirty minutes before game time, grab a soda and a program, and wait for the game to start. As in nearly every broadcasting job, there's more to it than meets the eye and ear. What you see isn't all that's there. The pregame ritual has three basic components that most experienced P-B-P announcers agree on:

Prepare, prepare, prepare!

There's no such thing as enough information, there can never be enough statistics, and you can never start early enough. A good play-by-play person does lots of homework. The gathering of insightful information on the players and coaches, the collection of meaningful statistics, and the ability to present them on the air combine to make an average broadcast a successful one. But the good P-B-P person doesn't feel the need or even the obligation to use every bit of information. The trick is to use the information you have at the right moment. Bringing up the extracurricular hobbies of a quarterback when his team is playing defense is not good use of information. Timing is everything in play-by-play. Information is essential, but using it at the right time is crucial.

Where do you get information? If it's a broadcast of a professional team, media relations departments compile more stats than a broadcast crew could ever use. These departments also create extensive media guides. Most of this information can be obtained through each team's website, and statistics are updated almost immediately after each game. The fortunate few who broadcast on the professional

[5] This excerpt is from a much more comprehensive treatise on sports announcing. His permission to reprint it here is acknowledged with sincere thanks.

sports level have no problem collecting whatever personal information and game statistics are needed. In addition, each league compiles its own statistics, and since league stats are considered official, it's a good idea to regularly consult the league's numbers.

Major college programs also fall in this category. Sports information departments are the lifeblood of the play-by-play announcer. Knowing the sports information director (SID) and the staff is an important element in keeping up with ever-changing information and statistics. It is the SID's job to make sure all media covering the game are updated and informed about players and statistics. As with the pros, major colleges utilize the Internet for current information and immediate statistical updates. The National Collegiate Athletic Association (NCAA) and the National Association of Intercollegiate Athletics (NAIA) also collect statistical information from each game, not to mention each individual conference's own numbers-gathering process.

But suppose you're broadcasting the local high school football games, and there are no media relations departments, no SIDs, no media guides, no websites, no central location for gathering statistics. Now what?

Now you must turn into a reporter.

Gathering statistics at the high school level is usually spotty, often unofficial, and always difficult to find. You'll have to do some legwork to collect enough information to use during the game. The first and most obvious place to start is with the coaches themselves. A phone call to the head coach is the initial contact. If it's possible, offer to meet the coach before practice. The head coach of the team you're broadcasting should give you as much information as you'll need, whether it's game stats or personal information on the key players. But you'll have to ask specific questions to get such information ("What about the halfback is unusual—does he have any hobbies? Is he a straight-A student? Does he volunteer his time somewhere?") Don't be afraid to ask the head coach these types of questions. Personal insight into the players can add a very personal and human element to a broadcast and gives the listeners a glimpse of these Friday night warriors they can't get anywhere else . . . except from you.

Of course, you expect complete cooperation from the coaching staff of the team you're broadcasting, but what about the other team? It's not unusual to run into a situation where the opposing team views you, the play-by-play announcer from the other team, as "the enemy." Coaches at every level are sometimes suspicious of outsiders, that is, people not associated with their program. This also includes the broadcasters. Scenario: The head coach of ABC High School is afraid he'll tell the P-B-P person from DEF High School something about ABC's offense and the P-B-P person will run straight into the coach's office at DEF High School and tell the coaches all about ABC's offense. Don't be totally surprised if you run into something similar to the "spy" theory. As the play-by-play announcer, you indirectly represent the team you're broadcasting for and, intentionally or not, players, coaches, and fans from the other side will see you as part of that team. You'll have your work cut out for you if and when you run into this type of dilemma. You'll need to assure the opposing coaches that you're not a spy, but a broadcaster, and all you're trying to do is get information on the other team so you can present a well-balanced and entertaining broadcast. You'll have to remind the opposing coaches that you work for the radio station airing the game, not the high school, and that you have no stake in the outcome of the game.

And that still might not be enough.

If you run into a wall from the opposing coaches, your next step is to contact local media outlets, such as the newspaper or the opposing P-B-P announcer, to get information from them. Small-town newspapers (daily, biweekly, or weekly) always have someone covering the local high school sports scene. Find out who he or she is, make the contact, and, hopefully, you'll get what you need. If the opposing high school has its own radio broadcast, it's always a good idea to introduce yourself to the play-by-play announcer. Perhaps the two of you could swap information on the teams, the best place to park, the booth setup at the stadium, a decent place to eat in town before and/or after the game, and so on. It never hurts to network with other media members. Be sure to return the courtesy, too.

By the way, if you're wondering when to start making these phone calls, the earlier the better. The Monday morning before a Friday night game is when the information-gathering process should start. It might take a couple of days to get through to a head coach. Don't expect a call back, either. Coaches rarely have the time or make the time to call a media member of an opposing team, so expect to make a lot of phone calls to the head coach's office. Be persistent. You might consider talking to other coaches on the staff, too. The offensive and defensive coordinators on a football team can give valuable insight into strategies and tendencies. They also get to know their players more closely than a head coach, so the coordinators, if they're willing, can provide personal information on a player the head coach might not know ("Watch our inside linebacker, number 55. He lives on a farm and wrestles bulls, so he's pretty strong and mean, too"). Remember: The head coach of any team isn't always the best source of information about that team. Coordinators and position coaches have as much knowledge, and sometimes more knowledge, than the head coach. The head coach also has other obligations (speaking engagements, personal appearances, media interviews) that the rest of the staff does not. The time element is always a factor with the head coach.

Bottom line: The earlier you begin your pregame informational gathering process, the better. You might need every minute you can devote to it.

But all the information and statistics in the world don't mean a thing unless you can access it during a broadcast. The majority of play-by-play broadcasters use what is called a spotter board. The spotter board contains names, positions, numbers, and whatever statistical facts are available for each player. In some cases, such as offensive linemen, there won't be any statistics. In these instances, height and weight are all that's available. For position players (quarterbacks, running backs, receivers), height, weight, yardage gained, yardage per carry or catch, and touchdowns are all traditional statistics football fans would want to know. Defensive players, such as defensive backs and linebackers, might only have takeaway statistics available (fumbles recovered, interceptions). Stats for basketball players would include field goal and free throw percentages, points per game, rebounds per game, and assists per game. Baseball statistics are plentiful; earned run average (ERA), batting average, home runs, runs batted in (RBI), fielding percentage, stolen bases, and so on. To know baseball is to understand that it is a game driven by statistics.

Side note: If you don't know how to keep a scorebook, learn quickly. A well-kept baseball scorebook can tell the entire game story with little or no embellishment from the broadcaster. Football drive charts and quarter-by-quarter (or half-by-half) scorebooks in basketball will give any play-by-play announcer a complete record of the game.

So, why do it?

If the life of a play-by-play announcer is this involved and time consuming, why pursue it as a career? Why would you be eager to make the extreme effort, the uncertainty, and the long years of apprenticeship with no guarantee of making the "big time"? If you ask most play-by-play announcers, they'll tell you they aren't in it for the money. That's good, because at the high school or small college level, financial rewards are few. In fact, for the hours required, the travel involved, the mental and physical hardships endured, the money-per-hour breakdown is usually less than the minimum wage. So if it's money you're after, seek employment elsewhere.

Then why do it? Why drive two to three hours or more, in your own car, for a few bucks, a green hot dog, a watered-down drink, to sit on top of a rickety old press box in a small, occasionally lit football stadium, a bandbox gymnasium, or a dirt patch with chalk lines, surrounded by fans who know more than you do, sound better than you ever could . . . and would trade places with you in a New York minute?

The love of the game!

 ## PRACTICE

➤ Play-by-Play Announcing

Using a battery-operated audio recorder, do play-by-play announcing for a baseball, football, basketball, or hockey game (or any other sport you prefer). Put the recording aside for a week or two and then listen to it critically. Are you able to visualize the game from the words you spoke and recorded?

 ## PRACTICE

➤ Getting Athletes' Names Right

Prior to an amateur sports event of any kind, obtain a list of players' names. Mark any whose pronunciation isn't obvious: You may be sure of the pronunciation of Smith but not of the preferred pronunciation of a player named Smythe. Depending on where you're allowed access, visit the locker room, the dugout, or other area where team executives may be found and ask for the pronunciation of names in question. As you're given the information, use your favored system of phonetic transcription (wire service, diacritics, or IPA) to denote correct pronunciation of names on the list.

Chapter 13

Starting Your Announcing Career

What Next?

So, at last you're ready for your first announcing job! If you've prepared for this step in a broadcasting program, it's likely you spent years looking ahead to your career but now find yourself suffering from an unusual anxiety, a strange feeling that strikes nearly all students at the point of graduation. "Am I *really* ready? Is there something I overlooked in my preparation? If I get a job, can I meet expectations? Maybe I should take another semester or apply to graduate school. If I do begin a job search, where do I *start?*" These feelings are common, although, of little comfort to you, it's worth pointing out that no one ever succumbed to graduation anxiety!

This chapter is designed to help meet your job search needs. It assumes you've had little or no paid experience as an announcer but feel you're ready for professional employment. Most information is also applicable if you've had some professional experience or if you received your training in internships, workshops, or through self-study.

If your objective is radio or television station employment, your goal may be in one or more of these categories:[1]

- Popular-music announcing (DJ)
- News reporting
- News anchor work
- News-related announcing as an environmental, consumer information, or entertainment news reporter
- Radio or television talk-show hosting
- Sports reporting and play-by-play announcing
- Weather reporting for radio, television, or cable

Aside from these broadcasting positions, there are careers in related fields, such as delivering radio or television commercials as a freelance performer. Good voices also are needed for documentary narration and informational programs on cable, including the *History Channel, Animal Planet, Arts & Entertainment,* the *National Geographic Channel, Discovery Channel, Travel Channel,* and so many more there's not enough space to accommodate them here. You also may find opportunities doing voices for cartoon characters or recording "talking books," as well as reading magazine and newspaper articles for the vision impaired.

But this is still a narrow list of employment possibilities. To make use of your talent, you may have to become inventive and move away from preconceived ideas of your need for career gratification; many opportunities exist aside from employment at stations, cable, or related organizations.

---

[1] A far more comprehensive list of announcing specializations may be found in Chapter 1.

Assuming you've benefited from the broad range of academic subjects you've studied outside your major field, your education may make you valuable to businesses or industries. With your liberal arts education and your abilities as a media performer, you should function well in any number of careers that call for articulate, confident communicators. True, some of the suggestions that follow may not excite you because they aren't what you've dreamed of. But if you contact some who work in these fields, you'll find many who've found fulfillment because the work is challenging, the pay is good, and they've found more security than is common in broadcasting.

Every year graduates of electronic communication programs are hired by businesses to make instructional audio and video recordings for employee training, including orientation for new employees, demonstrations and/or explanations of new products and technologies for salespersons already employed, and many other "in-house" applications. Media specialists are also hired to represent their company with information about nearly anything that's caught the attention of the news media, such as a product recall, a serious accident (an oil spill, mine cave-in), progress—or lack of it—during a strike, the status of a possible merger, or employee layoffs. Spokespersons also announce details of breakthrough products or furnish other information designed to keep the company before the public. Additional opportunities also exist for speakers representing nonprofit, people-serving organizations.

Another area of employment is found in state and federal government, where articulate speakers are needed. Here are a few such opportunities: giving nature talks in state or national parks, being the contact point between a police department or the highway patrol and the media, serving as media relations agents for elected public officials, and voicing audio and video presentations for visitors to city museums. In short, wherever there's a need for those with trained voices to reach out through live or recorded messages, there may be a place for you.

This chapter assumes that you've become capable, though not necessarily completely proficient, in the announcing specialization of your choice. As indicated in Chapter 1, merely taking a course or two in broadcast performance can't make you a competent journalist, sports reporter, or talk-show host. The information that follows assumes that you've supported your education with practice, that you've completed course work in the area of your specialization, and—ideally—that you've completed one or more internships.

PRACTICE

➤ Community Radio

Aside from broadcast and cable stations, exciting opportunities may be found in your neighborhood!

Scattered across the United States are more than 500 community radio stations, licensed by the Federal Communications Commission (FCC) to high schools, labor unions,

Figure 13-1

Lyons Filmer learned programming as a volunteer at nonprofit KPFA in Berkeley, California, from 1990 to 1999 in the women's public affairs and drama and literature departments. As a KWMR host, she shares a "Turning Pages" reading program and the music show, "The Celtic Universe." Photo courtesy of Lyons Filmer.

churches, towns, and community groups of all kinds. Some of these stations broadcast over the air, some are distributed by cable, and many of them stream over the Internet. Some are low-power FM stations (LPFM), restricted to a transmitter power of 100 watts or less. The rest are licensed as full-power stations. For those planning careers in broadcasting, community radio stations offer limitless opportunities for on-air experience.

One outstanding example of a full-power community radio station is KWMR, located in a rural area of Marin County, California. Operating at 230 watts power, KWMR broadcasts on 90.5 FM to the string of towns scattered around Tomales Bay and along the Pacific coast. KWMR also streams over the Internet and delivers many of its programs as a podcast. It is the emergency broadcasting station for West Marin, following FCC rules for the Emergency Alert System and working closely with the Marin County Disaster Council.

Lyons Filmer has been program director at KWMR since 2001. With support from the Programming Committee, she sets the program schedule and oversees the work of more than 100 volunteers. Program hours are roughly two-to-one music-to-talk. The talk programs reflect the concerns and interests of the people in West Marin. Topics include agriculture and the environment, politics and public affairs, health and spirituality, literature and the arts. Volunteer DJs on KWMR feature their own genre of music, which can range from retro rock, pop, hillbilly, honkytonk, reggae, music from the barrios, Celtic, or classical.

Figure 13-2

News producer Andrew Shaw, when he isn't on the air or out in the field gathering news and information, can be found at the news computer desk, writing scripts for his twice-daily news reports. Photo courtesy of Andrew Shaw.

Members of the local community create about 85 percent of the content that airs on KWMR. The rest is drawn from the pool of programs made available at no charge to community radio stations by networks like Public Radio International.

Andrew Shaw produces the news for KWMR. Shaw trained at KGNU in Boulder, Colorado, and moved to KWMR in 2005. His days are spent collecting the details of local stories and attending meetings of community groups. "Our radio station plays a key role in facilitating progress for passionate people," he said. "We also have the most fun." Shaw produces a program of local news called "The West Marin Report," which airs twice daily. He also produces "Epicenter," a roundtable discussion that explores local issues in depth.

While most of the opportunities at community radio stations are for volunteers, these stations are an excellent way to develop broadcasting skills. More information about community radio can be found on the website of the National Federation of Community Broadcasters, www.nfcb.org.

Preparing for Your Career

If you've decided that you want to be an announcer, you undoubtedly have many positive reasons. Being an announcer is an important job. Broadcasting and cable are exciting and dynamic fields. Electronic communication will unquestionably become more and more influential in coming years. Noteworthy rewards of fame and wealth await those who make it to—or near—the top of this profession. Finally, the opportunity to inform or entertain vast numbers of people is surely a powerful motivating force.

Before committing yourself to an announcing career, it's important that you make an honest assessment of yourself—of your strengths, your skills, your areas of specialized knowledge, your interests, and your values. No one can do this for you, but it's important that you make such an evaluation. Asking these questions should help clarify a number of things: What type of job or freelance work corresponds with my career interests and abilities? What type of work am I equipped to perform? What kinds of working conditions are necessary for me to receive job satisfaction? What salary will I need to support myself? And where am I willing or unwilling to live? Also ask yourself if you'll be comfortable in a field that offers little job security.

The Checklist presented on the following pages will help you assess your potential for success. It consists of questions that only you can answer. These questions are personal, and you needn't share your answers with others. For this self-assessment to be of value, it's imperative that you dig deeply and not settle for superficial answers. Undertake this self-assessment at various points during your student years and realize that your most valid answers will come at or near the end of your studies. And don't be unreasonably negative. No one expects a beginner to perform at the level of a veteran!

The time to begin preparing for that first job is while you're still in school. This is the time to start making connections that may someday pay off. As suggested in

Figure 13-3

Established news anchor Frank Somerville began his career while he was a student. In his senior year, Frank's internship at a small-market station turned into a paying position as a reporter and anchor. After two other jobs in larger markets, he became noon and evening anchor on KTVU, Oakland. He is seen here checking a monitor for details of a breaking story on CNN. His immediate job is to size up the story and write appropriate lead-ins. *Courtesy of Frank Somerville and KTVU.*

Chapter 1, you should join broadcast-related organizations such as *College Students in Broadcasting,* the *Association for Women in Communication, Inc.* (AWC), the *International Radio and Television Society–Alpha Epsilon Rho,* and the *National Black Media Coalition.* Students with a broadcast journalism emphasis may become members of the *Radio-Television Journalism division of the Association for Education in Journalism and Mass Communication, National Association of Hispanic Journalists, National Association of Black Journalists Online,* and *Society of Environmental Journalists.* Membership in the student category of the *Radio and Television News Directors Association* (RTNDA) is also available to you.

During your final two semesters in college, serve internships at the kinds of stations or other communication-related organizations where you'd like to work. *Important:* Ask for an internship only when you're ready to make a contribution at a particular firm; otherwise, you'll likely wind up stuffing envelopes or answering phones. And, because you may have little job-related knowledge to offer early in your educational program, you may make an unfavorable impression on those who may be in a position to hire you at a later time. However, when you're ready to help a business in some significant way, go for it, and give it all you have—your internship could very well turn into a job!

Checklist   Assessing Your Career Potential

As a Communicator in the Electronic Media

1. Do I truly have talent as a performer?
2. Is my voice adequate for the career I seek? If not, is it improvable through exercises and practice? Am I prepared to practice until the improvement has occurred?
3. (For television performance) Is my physical appearance appropriate for the kinds of positions I seek? If it is not, can my appearance be made acceptable or adequate through hair styling, makeup, and so forth?
4. Do I have an on-air personality that's engaging and unique?
5. What is there about me that makes me feel that I can succeed as an announcer?

As a Radio or Television Announcer

1. Am I willing to start at the very bottom of the ladder?
2. Am I willing to work for low wages?
3. Am I prepared to move anywhere at any time to further my career?

4. Can I live with the fact that any change in ratings, ownership, or format could cost me my job?
5. Do I perform well under pressure?
6. Does mic or camera fright currently interfere with my performance? If so, what are the chances that I can eventually bring this under control?
7. (For radio) Do I possess the technical skills necessary to operate audio equipment in an effortless and error-free manner?

As a Voice-Over Announcer for Commercials, Industrials, and Documentaries

1. Do I take direction well and respond quickly and sensitively to instructions?
2. Do I perform effectively under pressure?
3. Can I do a professional job of interpreting copy that requires accents, dialects, or character voices?
4. Am I prepared to live on an absolutely unpredictable and uncertain income?

As a Reporter or Anchor for Radio or Television News

1. Am I a quick judge of the newsworthiness of events as they happen?
2. Have I properly prepared myself to work as a journalist?
3. Can I remain reasonably detached at the scene of a wreck, fire, or other catastrophe in which people have been badly injured or killed?
4. Can I maintain my composure and deliver a coherent live report on location despite many ongoing distractions?
5. Have I adequately learned to operate basic items of audio and video equipment that I'll most likely use on the job?

As a Sports Reporter or Play-by-Play Announcer

1. Do I have a thorough grounding in all of the major sports, or am I a single-sport devotee?
2. Do I love sports enough to commit myself to becoming a sports announcer despite the scarcity of jobs and the stiff competition?
3. Am I willing to spend years of frequent travel, often being away from family and friends for weeks at a time?

As an Employee of an Organization Other Than Those Directly Related to Broadcasting

1. Has my preparation made me competent in announcer-related skills, including scriptwriting, audio and video equipment operations, editing, and presentations before audiences, as well as before mics and cameras?
2. Do I have the competency and interest to make a quick study of the basic operations of employers such as governmental agencies, nonprofit groups, or corporations?

Job-Hunting Tools

For most announcing jobs, you'll look for employment at radio or television stations, or independent production companies, including those associated with cable networks, in which case you'll approach them directly. If you're interested in commercial announcing and narrating, however, you'll most likely need to work through a talent agency. Whether you approach a station or talent agency, you'll need two things: a résumé with a cover letter and an audition recording.

Résumés

Your résumé is indispensable when you apply for a job in any announcing specialization. It lists in an abbreviated manner the most relevant facts about you. Employers can tell, almost at a glance, if you're appropriate for a vacancy or, at least, worthy of an interview. With so much at stake, the preparation of an attractive, factual, and to-the-point résumé is essential. Note, however, that *even the best résumé can't help you get a job if you aren't truly capable, dependable, punctual, and an asset to any employer*. The suggestions that follow assume that you have these qualities and that you deserve a position in broadcasting.

Before starting to prepare your résumé, visit the nearest career guidance or job counseling center. If you're a student, you'll probably find an office right on campus. If you're not attending school, you can still get help from job centers at almost any community college or four-year school. Some schools offer résumé-writing clinics regularly, sometimes for a small registration fee. Many college placement offices have free handouts on résumé writing. Arm yourself with as much information as you can find.

Although campus placement offices can help you with useful information on résumés, cover letters, and interviews, don't expect personnel in these offices to have all the answers. The field of broadcast performance is so specialized and so out of the ordinary that few career guidance counselors have firsthand in-depth knowledge of it.

Types of Résumés. Résumés are of two general types, plus a third that's a hybrid of those two. All provide some common items of information, including name, address, phone number, formal education, and references, but they differ in important respects. The first type, the **chronological résumé,** lists relevant

---

Figure 13-4

A chronological résumé lists employment information in reverse chronological order.

Mary Ann Williams
586 Poplar Avenue
Huntington, Kentucky 25704
(304) 555-6572

EMPLOYMENT

2005–Present   News reporter, WBRE-AM, Mount
Embree, Kentucky.
Cover local stories. Report live from
the field.
Produce news packages.
Specialize in education and the environment.

2000–2003   Paid news intern, WBRE-AM, Mount
Embree, Kentucky.
Collected and edited wire-service copy.
Rewrote news stories.
Maintained files.
Performed as weekend news anchor.

1999–2000   Volunteer reporter at local National Public
Radio station.
Wrote and voiced reports on school board
meetings, local election issues, and the
impact of growth on the local community.

HONORS

Dean's list, all semesters in college
President, College Students in
Broadcasting, 2004

employment in reverse chronological order. The second type, the **competency-based, or functional, résumé,** lists the applicant's areas of competency. The **hybrid,** or **combination, résumé,** as the name indicates, combines features of both the chronological and the competency-based résumés.

The chronological résumé is used by anyone with some professional experience. A sample of this type of résumé is shown in Figure 13-4.

The competency-based, or functional, résumé is your best choice if you're nearing graduation and looking for your first announcing job. Many graduating seniors can point only to the knowledge they've acquired in school, which includes skills learned on college radio and television stations, at public-access cable companies, or internships at commercial or public broadcasting stations. A chronological listing of part-time jobs held while in school, such as busing dishes or working in a car wash, isn't likely to impress a prospective employer. However, if you earned half or more of your living expenses while in school, state this, together with a brief list of jobs held. This tells a prospective employer that you're an industrious person who made a sacrifice to gain your education. If you've had bookkeeping, accounting, or sales experience, or if you're fluent in a language other than English, say so.

More important, point out that you can perform the duties required of a person in a particular announcing position. Specify, for instance, that you can operate all standard control-room or video equipment, that you can do audio or video editing, or that you can operate studio cameras and switchers. These and similar competencies serve as basic qualifications for entry-level positions. This is the thrust of a competency-based résumé, as the example in Figure 13-5 illustrates.

It's appropriate on a competency-based résumé to list positions you've held as a member of a college radio or television station staff and to provide information about work you've done as an intern. But it's *crucial* that you identify such work clearly. Applicants who make positions held on a campus radio station appear to have been held at a commercial station will be seen as misrepresenting their backgrounds. And those who try to pass off an internship as paid professional experience are written off immediately. No prospective employer would likely schedule an interview or review an air check with an applicant who seemed to be providing misleading information.

The hybrid résumé is useful for students who've had some professional experience either before or during school years and who've acquired knowledge and competencies also as a student. An example of a hybrid résumé is shown in Figure 13-6.

Tips on Preparation

Prepare more than one résumé, each with a different slant. For instance, as a graduate of a department of radio and television, you may want to apply for positions in both radio and television. The same résumé wouldn't be ideal for both. If you have two basic résumés—one for radio and one for television—you can further tailor each résumé to match your background and your interests with the requirements stated for the positions to which you're applying. Incorporate information

Figure 13-5

A competency-based, or functional, résumé presents the applicant's areas of competence.

Charles Gonzalez
1616 South M Street
Callison, New Jersey 08110
(609) 555-5456

EXPERIENCE

Intern at WBCD-AM and FM, an MOR station. Produced jingles and station IDs. Timed music cuts and produced filecards of basic information. Three years' experience as a DJ on the campus radio station featuring CHR and AOR music. Managed the station senior year. Served two years as the station's music director.
Worked two years as a stand-up comic at a local comedy club.

EMPLOYMENT

Manager of Callison Comedy Club, 1999–2001
Part-time sales associate, MusicLand, Callison, New Jersey, 2002–2004
Audio engineer at Genessee University student union for various performing groups, 2005–2006

EDUCATION

B.A. in Mass Communications, Genessee University, Fountain, New Jersey, 2006
Graduated with honors

REFERENCES

Ms. Gerri Boyd, Manager, Callison Comedy Club, Callison, New Jersey
Mr. Harry Freund, Manager, MusicLand, Callison, New Jersey
Professor Arthur Simons, Genessee University, Fountain, New Jersey

Figure 13-6
A hybrid, or combination, résumé gives both professional and academic achievements.

Ralph Wente
435 Livingston Street
Tacoma, Washington 98499
(206) 555-3790

OBJECTIVE

Entry-level position in television sports department

COMPETENCIES

Sports Knowledge

Thorough knowledge of sports officiating and scoring of gymnastics, diving, and other competitive sports. Six years' experience scoring baseball. Knowledge of football and basketball strategies.

Sports Experience

Played baseball (second base and shortstop), three years in high school and four years in college. Played football (running back) three years in college. Served as manager of the college basketball team for two years.

Other Competencies

Expert at both still and video camera work. Considerable skill in both on- and offline video editing. Two years' experience in writing copy for sports newscasts on campus television station. Bilingual in English and Spanish.

AWARDS AND HONORS

Dean's list, 2006–2008
Member and president of University Block T Club
(Sports Honor Society)
Valedictorian

EDUCATION

University of Tacoma, Washington, 2008, B.A., Broadcasting
Specialized in television performance, production, and writing for sports broadcasts.

REFERENCES

Professor Ray Marucci, Varsity Coach, University of Tacoma, Washington
Dr. Joyce Ntare, University of Tacoma, Washington
Dr. Bruce O'Hare, University of Tacoma, Washington

unique to each application by tailoring your competencies to those listed as required or desirable. You also can add station call letters, name of the city where it's located, or anything else that's pertinent and useful to make your résumé a perfect match.

In most instances, your résumé should be one page only. Although you may believe you have more than a page of information to disclose, prospective employers want to see your qualifications in the briefest form possible.

Your word-processing program may allow you to choose line spacing other than the traditional single, double, or triple spacing. For a résumé, single spacing is too dense and double spacing is too wasteful of page space. After creating your résumés as single-spaced documents, you should convert to a line spacing that makes the best visual impression and fits comfortably on a single sheet of paper.

In preparing your résumé, it's wise to make drafts and then ask a qualified person—a teacher of broadcasting, a person working in a career-guidance or job-placement center, or a broadcaster—to review and comment on them.

Omit from your résumé all of the following:

- *Height, weight, hair color, and eye color*—unless you're applying for an on-air television position or a job as an on-camera commercial performer for which your physical features are of importance. In this case, supply all pertinent physical information and include photographs.

- *Hobbies*—unless they add to your qualifications. Listing your collection of 1960s and 1970s Top 40 recordings could be important if you're applying for a position as a DJ on a station featuring hits of the past. Noting that you enjoy skateboarding or hiking is irrelevant.

- *Race, ethnic or national origin, gender, and physical condition*—It's against the law for employers to discriminate against job applicants on the basis of any of these facts or conditions. However, if you have a disabling physical condition that calls for special facilities or other considerations, mention this in your cover letter.

- *Your high school or college academic transcript*—unless it's requested. You may be asked to provide a list of courses you've taken that relate directly to a specific job, so keep your own list of courses you've completed, arranged by category.

Include information about the following in your résumé:

- *Your student record if it was exceptional*—For example, you may note that you were on the dean's list six semesters, that you graduated cum laude, or that you earned a 3.87 grade point average during your last sixty units.

- *Supplementary abilities that might be put to use at the station*—Include experience in sales, electronics, data processing, and audio production of commercials and features (including writing, recording, editing, and mixing). List the hardware (for example, Macintosh or PC) you can operate and the operating systems you're qualified to use.

- *Leadership positions*—such as student body officer, class president, commencement speaker, and so on.
- *Memberships in national associations that relate to broadcasting*—A list of important associations may be found on p. 428
- *Contributions to your community*—such as Little League coaching, charitable fund-raising, and similar activities.
- The ability to speak or read one or more languages—with an indication of the degree of your proficiency (bilingual, fluent, or conversant).

Career advisers are divided on the subject of references. Some suggest that you list four to six names, complete with titles and mailing addresses; others prefer a statement at the bottom, "References available on request." If you're applying to numerous potential employers, giving the same names could inundate those who are providing you with recommendations, so be selective. Choose your references wisely: Avoid close friends and family members. Use employers only if the employment was related to the job you're seeking and the former employer can verify your dependability, punctuality, honesty, or other qualities that would make you a good employee. Your best references may come from teachers and those who supervised your work in an internship or a paying job at a broadcast station. *Always obtain permission before listing anyone as a reference.* And when you do ask recommenders to send letters to potential employers, *always supply stamped and addressed envelopes.* Unless requested, don't use the Internet to ask questions of potential employers.

Your final draft should be printed, error-free, using a high-quality printer. Use a standard type font, such as Times, Helvetica (extended), or Geneva. Don't use a novelty font of any kind. Print size should be eleven or twelve point, unless your résumé will spill over onto two pages and you can find no information to shorten or eliminate. In this case, you may want to use ten-point size type. Try different fonts and different point sizes. You can select any size you wish but, before settling on type size, print a sample of lines from your résumé: What you see on your computer is not what appears on paper.

If you use a copying service, carefully check every detail before ordering numerous copies. Ask for twenty-pound bond paper. Have your résumés duplicated on white, off-white, or buff paper and use matching envelopes. Avoid garish or weird colors.

Finally, despite all of these suggestions about what to put in your résumé, if you find that you can't comfortably fit your information on one page, omit the least important points. If you must omit such items as community service, membership in organizations, leadership positions, or academic honors, you may put these on a supplemental résumé, included as a second sheet.

Photographs. It may be unwise to include a photograph when you apply for a position at a radio station or as a freelance voice-over performer. The physical appearance of those who do radio or voice-overs is totally irrelevant. The sound of your voice is all-important. A photograph adds nothing; it can in fact work against you if a potential employer thinks you don't "look like you sound."

On the other hand, photographs are essential when you apply for an on-air position in television. Send two or three photos that show you in different work environments. Photos may be black and white or in color and should be either five by seven inches or eight by ten inches. Don't send "artsy" photos, provocative poses, or graduation photos. The best photos are those taken while you're performing as a reporter, anchor, program host, or any other on-air role. You needn't spend a great deal of money on photos; producers and agents can see what they need to know by looking at high-quality snapshots. However, your photo's composition and what is depicted in it should have a professional look.

The Cover Letter. All résumés should be accompanied by a cover letter. This letter is perhaps as important as your résumé. It gives you an opportunity to stress some accomplishment or quality that makes you uniquely qualified for the job. It also allows you to say why you're interested in a particular station. The function of the cover letter is to persuade a prospective employer to read your résumé. The objective of the résumé is to influence the employer to listen to or to view your audition presentation; the goal of the demo is to gain an interview; the anticipated outcome of the interview is to obtain that job!

The nature of the cover letter will differ depending on whether you're applying for station employment or looking for an agent. Keep cover letters to station managers brief and to the point. Most such letters should contain four short paragraphs. The first tells the position to which you're applying and why you're applying to this particular station. The second paragraph gives brief details of your qualifications. The third refers to the accompanying résumé and audition demo and underscores the most significant points. The fourth paragraph requests an interview and states when you'll call to request it.

You can keep cover letters to agents quite brief because the audition demo counts for nearly everything. An opening statement of your qualifications and aspirations, a request that your demo be reviewed, and information as to how you may be reached are all you need to include. Cover letters should be an honest expression of *your* feelings, so don't look for a model cover letter to copy. If you can't clearly and effectively state your case in a cover letter, you may need to attend a résumé-writing workshop in which cover letters are discussed.

Never send a cover letter that's been duplicated by a copy machine. Résumés may be duplicated, but always create a separate cover letter for each person to whom you're sending a résumé. Compose your letter on a computer and have it printed by a letter-quality printer. Poor-quality computer-generated letters show sloppiness on your part and give the impression that they're being produced in quantity.

When composing your letter, use a ragged, not justified, right margin. Personalize each letter so that you

Sound Bytes

It is helpful to listen to audition demos of successful voice-over announcers. You can find such performances on the Internet.

Enter "voiceover announcers" on a search engine such as Google, and you'll find a number of sites that include samples of performances by professional announcers.

don't inadvertently give the impression that your applications are blanketing the nation: Address the employer by name and title and mention call letters, music format, news policy, or whatever's appropriate. Such details tell the reader that the letter in hand is the only one of its kind. Above all, your letter should be neat. *Proofread every letter carefully.*

Audition or Résumé Recordings. A recorded sample of your work is a must when looking for employment as an announcer. The sample, an **audition demo,** is needed when applying to a station or for work as a freelance voice-over performer. There are two basic types of performance demos; the first is a compilation of brief examples showing varied styles of announcing, and the second, an **air check,** is a sampling of your work culled from on-air performances. This is usually most effective because performing for an audience gives you a level of energy and a sound that's impossible to duplicate when recording for audition purposes.

Producing an Audition Demo

When applying for station employment, you may send an audition demo on CD-ROM (radio), DVD (television), or even a cassette audio- or videotape; while tapes may be considered obsolete for most uses, nearly every station maintains a few playback machines and will continue to do so for some time. However, because tapes may send a signal to potential employers that you're not up on modern technology, you should use them only if you have no possibility of producing CDs or DVDs.

A demo is basically a montage of samples of your performance skills. Long referred to as an **audition tape,** it's a selection of several brief pieces.[2] A typical three-minute CD-ROM or tape for a position as a DJ, for example, should feature five or six varied cuts:

1. A series of ad-libbed music intros (or back-announcing a music set)
2. Ten seconds of an upbeat commercial
3. An ad-libbed comment on some amusing event of the day
4. A piece teasing a contest or some similar station promotion
5. Ten seconds of an intimate and subdued commercial
6. A brief news story, read at a rapid rate
7. One or two ten-second PSAs

If your audition CD is going to an all-news station, it should present several short news stories of varying moods, plus at least one fifteen- or thirty-second commercial. A presentation demo for a position in sports should include samples of sports reporting, play-by-play, and play analysis. Gear your selections as specifically as

---

[2] Although tapes are now seldom used, the term *audition tape* continues in use at most stations to identify samples of announcing, as the term "disc jockey" has persisted even though DJs no longer play discs.

possible to the stations at which you'd like to work. If time permits, use the actual call letters of the station to which you're applying.

Air Checks

If you have samples of on-air performances, such as on a local public-access television or radio channel, a college station, or a closed-circuit campus setup, they can be the basis of a carefully edited and assembled recording.

Students often compile recordings from their media performance classes, or on news, entertainment, and information programs sent by their colleges' department of community relations to local broadcasters or cable companies. If you've retained a collection of your performances, select several minutes of your best work. For radio, limit your recorded material to no more than three minutes. And, because some station managers or news directors won't listen for the full three minutes, be sure to place your best work at the beginning.

Audio CDs and tapes are inexpensive to produce. Audio recording equipment available in most college departments of broadcasting is adequate for this purpose. Use only top-of-the-line audio cassettes or CDs and create professional-quality labels. Use only new tapes. Make sure that each label includes the call letters of the station to which it is being sent.

Because demos, like résumés, are both simple and inexpensive to make, it's important to make more than one version. Each music radio station has an established sound, an overall mood and spirit. If you're applying for an announcing position at a station that expects its announcers to display wit, warmth, and congeniality, the material you send must be quite different from that prepared for a station whose announcers are instructed to keep their comments brief and matter-of-fact. Also, one adult contemporary station may have a sound that differs considerably from a competitor's station in the same market. Study the sounds of stations in which you're interested and individualize your audition demos accordingly.

Similarly, news departments vary to some degree in preferred announcing styles, so make your application demo only *after* studying the style of each potential job opening.

If you can't use school equipment to record and edit your demo, find a recording studio that provides such a service. Audio recording studios are generally found only in or near larger cities, so you may have to travel to one if you live in a smaller community. The business listings in telephone directories include recording studios. Obtain price quotations from at least three studios before choosing one.

Independent video production companies may be found in every medium-to-major market. Some produce only studio-based audition recordings. Others will go into the field with you to cover some planned news event, such as a parade, a picket line, or a marathon. If you have a choice of production companies, try to find and select one that will include field reporting that's ad-libbed or ad-libbed from notes. Most production companies will provide some guidance, including suggestions for improving your appearance or your performance. Production companies usually charge by the day, with a one-day minimum, plus extra charges for editing the recording and making copies. You can expect to pay between $500 and $1,500 for a complete video presentation dubbed to DVD.

Figure 13-7

Student Jennie Jones, a broadcast and electronic communication arts major, introduces the music she plays on the campus radio station. The station, staffed and managed by students, features an alternative rock format. As Jennie opens her announce mic to comment on the music or promote a contest, a recorder is activated that produces a "skimmed air check"— a recording with only her comments, which she may use later when she applies for a DJ position. Other students at this station create sound stories, radio dramas, public-service announcements, and campus newscasts. *Courtesy of Jennie Jones and KSFS, San Francisco State University.*

Producing Demos for Review by a Talent Agent

Talent agencies require a different kind of demo. Most of the voice work you'll obtain through agencies will be for these specializations:

- Radio commercials
- Voice-over narration for television commercials (both radio and television commercials are called voice-overs by freelancers)
- Corporate videos (also called industrials)
- Documentary narration, promos for stations, and promos for radio and television specials
- Cartoon voicing

Cartoon voices require great versatility; at one time, you'll be asked to speak as a mature (and threatening) animal, such as a lion; at other times a chicken, kitten, cow, or squirrel. Aside from animals, you must be competent at an array of human voices such as a young, spoiled brat, an angry mother, or a tough cop. If you're good at accents, you may be asked to portray a Russian, an English man or woman speaking in both Cockeney and Oxford dialects, or Americans from the deep South, New England, or the upper Midwest. For your demo, make sure you offer only brief examples of cartoon voices that you do the best.

To become a freelance performer, you almost certainly will need an agent. Agents notify their clients when work that suits their talent is available. Agents help their clients prepare and record the audition for a specific job and negotiate payments with potential employers. Agents collect 10 percent of all payments earned, but effective agents more than earn their fee. If you decide to seek an agent, structure your first audition performance to persuade an agent to "take you on."

A presentation prepared for freelance work is different from that for radio station employment. Most important is that you demonstrate your ability to interpret copy. Unless you're convinced that your future lies in doing character voices or accents and dialects, you should concentrate on performing high-quality, imaginative, but basically standard, commercial copy. Select pieces that demonstrate a range of approaches—*thoughtful, concerned, upbeat, sultry, excited, laid back*, and so on. Do only ten to fifteen seconds of each. As you assemble the bits, arrange them in a sequence that shows contrast; begin with a soft sell, follow with a hard sell, and continue with samples of your entire range. The entire audition demo should run no longer than three minutes.

If you want to do character voices and your repertoire includes foreign accents or regional dialects, use samples of these in carefully selected bits of commercials. Put on your demo only those voices that you perform extremely well. Confine your voiced bits to ten to fifteen seconds each; take somewhat longer—for example, twenty to thirty seconds—to demonstrate your ability to do straight narration for industrials. In short, provide the agent with as great a range of vocal competencies as possible. Some freelance performers prepare as many as three different demos: straight commercial announcing, characters and cartoon voices, and narration for industrials.

If you're serious about a career as a freelance announcer, consider taking a workshop given by a professional performer. Many reputable freelance announcers conduct workshops with small groups of students that focus on skills needed for this work. Workshops sometimes cover only one or two weekends and usually culminate in the production and packaging of a presentation demo. To identify a potential coach, ask your instructors as well as professional announcers for suggestions. When contacting those who offer courses, ask for permission to sit in on a session before enrolling in a course. If you're satisfied that the instructor is capable, that the workshop is compatible with your needs, and that the cost isn't excessive, you could wind up with greatly enhanced performing abilities, as well as a professionally produced audition demo.

Other Tips Concerning Presentation Demos

Almost anyone can make an impressive demo if enough time and effort are spent preparing it. Working at it for several days, doing take after take, and then selecting only the best bits of your work and assembling them can result in a high-quality product. However, this approach is unrealistic because it likely will present a distorted image of your abilities; if it's your demo that gets you an agent or a job, you'll have to live up to its quality consistently. Make certain that your demo truly reflects what you can do under actual recording circumstances.

Don't send out demos that are hastily made, are made with inferior equipment, or were made before you attained your present level of ability. Poorly performed samples of your work will prejudice potential employers or agents against you.

Duplicate demos for voice performance, whether for radio station or freelance employment, on CDs. Be sure to listen to every dub you make, and listen all the way through; often stations receive demos with inaudible or distorted sections and immediately file them in the wastebasket. Include your identification both on the CD itself and on its plastic box.

Cell Phones, Answering Machines, and Pagers. When surveying broadcast announcers as to how they got their first job more than 85 percent responded that they happened to be "in the right place at the right time." In other words, they were immediately available when an opening arose. You can't, of course, be physically present at several radio or television stations at the same time, but you can be available at all hours—if you have a cell phone, an answering machine, a fax machine, an e-mail address, and a pager.

Cell phones are the most desirable of these communication devices, but they can't meet all of your job-related needs. When using an answering machine, make sure you have a businesslike message on it. A prospective employer will be turned off by a raucous, bawdy, or childish message. Don't use an answering system that requires callers to punch numbers according to a programmed series of choices—"If you want to leave a message for Allison, press 1 now," and the like.

E-mail and faxed messages, including requests for information not on your résumé, can be received by fax for later printing. If possible, have a dedicated line installed for your fax.

Mailing Address and Phone Number. Because you may be away at school and therefore without a permanent address, you should give some thought to the address and phone number you list on your résumé. For most job seekers, it's best to list only one address, one that will remain accurate for some time (that of your parents, perhaps). The telephone number given should be for the phone you use every day.

Sound Bytes

You can perform job searches on the Internet. *Broadcast Employment Services* offers a number of services under such categories as Master Station Index, Index, E-Resume Database, Freelance Directory, TV Forum, Situations Wanted, and Internship Database. Jobs in radio, television, cable, and film are included. A Broadcast Employment Services membership is free for a one-month period. Fees are charged for longer subscriptions, the cost determined by the length of membership, ranging from three months to five years. To subscribe, go to:

www.tvjobs.com/index_a.htm

For a complete, updated list of URLs for this textbook, please see the accompanying CD.

SPOTLIGHT

Surviving Career Changes

Fred LaCosse is a media performer whose career demonstrates the twists, turns, frustrations, and successes that are common to most people who spend years in broadcasting. Fred earned his undergraduate degree in humanities at a small liberal arts college in Indiana. He then went to graduate school at Northwestern University and majored in broadcasting. The university guaranteed him thirty hours a week on the air with the local educational television station. His response: "A dollar an hour! Wow! It was great experience. It was in the third market in the country!" Here is Fred's story:

Everything was live—it was before videotape. Fantastic experience! We were live from 4:00 p.m. to 7:30 p.m., back-to-back programs, three studios. I did that for two years while I was getting my master's degree. Then I got a job in Columbus, Ohio, at the NBC station as studio supervisor.

After two years in the army, Fred got a job as stage manager at Channel 11 in San Jose, California. After two years, he was promoted to the job of announcer–director:

I didn't want to do any air work, but I studied about six months—started doing voice-overs, reading anything into a tape recorder in an old shed. And I would go out there every morning for an hour or so and slooow-ly, slooow-ly, get better, almost tolerable. After about six months, I started improving, and I mean it was finally air-able.

After I was there about a year, they made me production manager. We finally got videotape, and every used-car dealer in the Valley wanted to cut commercials on videotape so

he could sit there on Thursday, Friday, or Saturday night and watch himself on television.

During my time there, I would fill in on occasion when some of the anchors would go on vacation. At that time we had a three-person news department. We had two people who could shoot and report, and one guy in Monterey, who would set the tripod, start the camera, go around the other side, and give his report. And he did wonderful stuff.

On the average day there, I'd go in about 11:00 a.m., play with the budget, meet with the boss, be concerned with union hassles. Then I'd produce the early newscast, go home and grab a quick bite, say "Hi" to my wife and kids. Come back and do the late newscast, then hang around 'til maybe 12:30 a.m. or so to finish up some paperwork. Those were long, long days. Then KRON called and asked, "Would you consider coming to San Francisco to anchor the news?" I wasn't sure, but I was willing to take a look. I was doing pretty well in San Jose at the same time, making decent dollars as a department head, but I decided to audition.

And what an audition! I auditioned with Jerry [an ongoing anchor]. I'd read a story, he'd read a story, I'd read a story, he'd read a story, and then we'd rap, ad-lib for thirty seconds just to see how the rapport was, how we'd jell. Jerry would bring up something, and I'd respond. Because that's what they wanted to find out—whether or not I could think on my feet, and how it worked, how it jelled. I was offered the weekend job, but it was $9,000 a year less than I was making in San Jose, and I couldn't do it. A lot of decisions you'll make along the line in your career make you wonder later: "What would have happened if?"

After four years in news in San Jose, I got another nod to come to San Francisco to audition. They set me up in the newsroom, and said: "Why don't you just prepare about three minutes' worth of copy?" I thought, "Great—I can at least read my own stuff." It's a lot easier to read your own stuff. So I wrote up about three minutes' worth of copy, maybe six or seven different stories, and went down to the studio with a stage manager and a camera operator. The stage manager cued me, and I read the copy and signed off and just sat there wondering what was going on. After about five minutes, the news director came in and said: "The station manager would like you to just sit there and talk about yourself, and how you feel about the news business for maybe five minutes or so."

Now, that's kind of interesting. That's when you learn whether or not you have that ability to keep it going. To think, to plan, and at the same time be talking. If you can develop that skill, if you happen to have it, it's amazing how much that will help you when you finally get into a situation when a heavy news story comes down and you've got to be out there at the anchor desk for an hour or two or three coordinating, gathering information, and trying to make it sound very smooth. That is not easy to do. Especially if you have the wrong producer telling you stupid things in your ear! So I talked for five minutes, telling how I felt about various things, and then I sat for about another ten minutes. Then the news director came down and said: "The manager would like to see you in his office."

I thought I'd probably blown the audition. As soon as I sat down, he said, "LaCosse, we'd like you to come to work for us." He could be a tough cookie, and I think in this first meeting he was establishing our relationship right then.

I spent the next four years anchoring the news. It was the most boring job I ever had in my life. The most boring job! I was in the fourth-largest market in the country. I'd come out of a situation where I was working twelve hours a day consistently. Working my head off but totally immersed in it. Now I come up here—fourth market—and all they'd let me do is anchor. And that is the most boring job in the business. It pays you five times as much money as any other job in the business, but it's boring.

Your primary job as an anchor is to be a journalist. The first hour and a half when I got to the station, I'd spend reading wire-service copy. I read about five different newspapers. You have to know what's going on. You have to read a lot, and you have to know how to spot the salient points. I took a speed-reading course in college, and it was invaluable to me.

After four years, the news director was replaced and another person took over and replaced me with "his man." Two years later, I replaced him. That's how this silly business works.

A few years earlier, during a strike, I had started a business. I coached business people on how to get their points across on television. Eventually it became so successful that I gave up anchoring altogether. After two years I was approached by a San Francisco television station to be a cohost on a morning talk and interview show. I did that for five years until a new owner cut the budget by 50 percent, fired half the producers and, at contract renewal time, reduced talent salaries by 50 percent. I went back to my business and lived happily ever after.

Finding Job Openings

Colleges and universities are sites of intensive recruiting activity every spring semester. That's the good news. The bad news is that *broadcasters* almost never appear on college campuses to interview prospective employees. However, this fact shouldn't discourage you. Media executives don't like to advertise job openings beyond the requirements of law. They're busy people, and they don't want to schedule interviews with dozens of job applicants. Many station executives, particularly those at smaller-market stations, make vacancies known to faculty members in college and university broadcasting departments and request that no more than three to five students be told of each opening. If you've gained the confidence and respect of a faculty member, ask to be notified of job openings in your field of interest.

Also, remember that jobs are available if you're willing to move to a small market, to accept an entry-level position, and to work for a subsistence salary. This is called *paying your dues*.

The long-established and accepted practice of underpaying and overworking novices in the field of broadcasting is deplorable; however, the fact remains that this is the way it was, is, and (most likely) always will be. If you're committed to becoming a successful radio or television announcer, chances are you'll have to begin at the proverbial bottom and gradually work yourself into better and higher-paying positions.

Announcements of job openings are published in trade magazines, including *Broadcasting & Cable* and *Radio & Records (R & R)*. In all areas of the country, *craigslist* includes position vacancy notices.[3] As with job listings in every field, the Internet is more current than any other source.

To find your first job, however, don't limit yourself to responding to ads for announcers. Most stations that advertise either can't find anyone willing to work at their station or are looking for people with at least a few years of appropriate experience. Announcing-position vacancies occur regularly at most stations, so you should apply to every station you consider to be a good starting point or a second step for you. Begin with stations in your own area, unless you have compelling reasons to leave.

Applying for a Position at a Station

When applying for a media performance position, no matter where you apply, what type of job you seek, or which medium you favor, there are many practices that apply to all. With a completed résumé and presentation demo—and, of course, your education and college broadcasting experience—you're ready to apply for an announcing job. This section is appropriate for those applying for DJ work, radio or television news reporting and anchoring, and sports reporting.

---

[3] The craigslist website provides notices of job opportunities not only in and around cities in the United States and Canada but in most cities of the world. Nearly all ads posted are for short-term employment, and many offer no pay but give you an opportunity for experience and exposure. Go to: www.craigslist.org/about/cities.html. Select the city, click on "jobs," then "film/tv/video."

Figure 13-8

Broadcast major Doug Brown stands as he reads the news on KSFS, a student radio station. The station sends its signal throughout campus and, via cable, to the city of San Francisco. The radio station has digital postproduction editing systems, Sony digital audio players, and digital special effects units. You can access the campus radio station at this website: www.ksfs.sfsu.edu. *Courtesy of Doug Brown and KSFS, San Francisco State University.*

Most first-time applicants for announcing positions should be able to follow these recommendations easily.

To apply for a job, obtain the names of the program directors of those stations where you'd like to work. Names of key station personnel are listed in *Broadcasting & Cable Yearbook,* which can be found at many libraries and at nearly every radio and television station. Before writing to a program director, however, use the Internet to confirm that the person listed is still with the station and in the same position. There's a great deal of movement of executives in the broadcasting industry.

Send a brief letter, a résumé, and your presentation demo or air check to each program director. In your letter, state that you'll call in a week to see if an interview can be arranged. Follow through with the telephone call but don't be discouraged if few or none of the station managers expresses interest in you. Even though announcing jobs are available, the number of persons applying for them far exceeds available positions. Perseverance is the most important quality a prospective announcer can possess.

If you live in a major or secondary market, it's unlikely that you'll be hired straight out of college as an on-air announcer. Therefore, be prepared to look for work in a smaller market. *Broadcasting & Cable Yearbook* can help you locate stations to which you may want to apply. It lists every radio and television station in the United States and Canada, indicates its signal strength (a clue to its audience size and therefore its economic standing), gives names of chief administrative personnel, and, for music stations, indicates the music format. All information in this yearbook can be updated on the Internet.

In addition to obtaining as much information as you can about a station to which you're applying, make sure you've actually watched or listened to it. It will be very awkward in an interview if you know little or nothing about the station. If a station to which you're applying is so far away from your home that you can't receive its signal, you likely will be able to view or listen to it over the Internet. It will be to your advantage if you can intelligently discuss details of the station's programming. If applying to a popular-music station, for instance, you should know its music format, the nature of the DJ's chatter (if any), whether the morning drive-time period makes use of two or more announcers, and so on.

For a position in television news, note when each day's newscasts are scheduled, their length, and number of on-air personnel used and number of reports from the field in each of them. If at all possible, make note of the appearance and style of all on-air announcers. Find out such basic details as: What is the typical length of a report from the field? Does the station work with a single anchor or coanchors? What news features (weather, traffic, skiing conditions, sports reports, business reports, and such) does the station provide?

There are several websites where you can find and print location maps and driving directions to a broadcast station or other business, including Google, Yahoo!, AAA, and MapQuest.

Interviewing for a Job

The job interview is critical in your pursuit of a position as a radio or television station performer. A general manager, station manager, or program director may be impressed with your credentials, your demo, and your résumé, but an interview is usually the final test that puts you to work—or sends you away.

Before seriously seeking a job, you may want to discuss career possibilities and job seeking with an executive at a station where you're *not applying* for work. This is called an **informational interview.** Almost any college teacher of broadcasting can guide you to someone (perhaps a former student) who'll be happy to spend time exploring your employment prospects. Ask the professional to review your résumé and discuss strategies for finding employment.

The suggestions and comments that follow are based on several assumptions: *that you truly are ready for the position you seek, that you'll honestly state your capabilities and competencies, and that you'll be able to back up your statements by performing effectively.*

Before you appear for an interview, practice being interviewed. A friend or an instructor may be willing to assist you and then critique your performance. Remember that an interview is not acting, but it *is* a type of performance.

When confirming an appointment for an interview by phone, don't ask how to find the station or where to park. To ask such questions is to give the impression that you can't find your way around.

Before going to another town for a job interview, take time to learn something about that community. Nearly every town and city in the United States has its own website, with much information about size, major industries, schools, and so forth.

When going to an interview, have with you all pertinent information about yourself that you might need to complete an application form. This includes: *Social Security number, driver's license number, dates of graduation, dates of starting and ending various jobs,* and *previous addresses.* Also bring a list of references in case you're asked for it.

Always be early for an interview but not too early; five to ten minutes ahead of your appointment is just about right. If you're being interviewed in an unfamiliar city or town, drive past the station sometime before the interview—preferably the day before and at the same time of day as your appointment. Not only will you learn the way to the station, but you'll also see how busy traffic is at that time of day and where to park.

Dress neatly and conservatively for your interview. Although some on-air radio performers dress casually, they're established and you're not. You'll probably be interviewed by a person who is essentially a business person, not a performer. Suits, sport coats, and ties are appropriate dress for men for interviews. Conservative dresses or suits are appropriate for women.

Be yourself. Don't try to act the part of the person you assume the interviewer is looking for.

Be frank about your strengths and accomplishments but take care not to come across as boastful.

Match your eye contact with the interviewer's. Most interviewers maintain strong eye contact, but if you meet one who doesn't, act accordingly. Eye contact isn't the same thing as staring. Take your cue from the interviewer. If the interviewer looks you in the eye, try to reciprocate.

Don't take chances by making small talk that might reveal ignorance. For instance, don't ask what tune is being played—it might be number one in that community. Don't venture opinions about broadcasting in general unless they're important to the point of the interview. You can hurt your cause by stepping on the toes of your interviewer.

Be careful to avoid traps. Some interviewers will lead job applicants along and make somewhat outrageous suggestions to see if the applicant is an unprincipled "yes" person. Don't be argumentative but think carefully before you respond to questions that seem off the wall.

Don't misrepresent yourself or your abilities in any way! Even if you obtain a job through an exaggeration of your capabilities, you won't have it for long.

Stay away from politics, religion, and sex. If the interviewer tries to lead you into any of these areas, politely avoid them.

Figure 13-9
When keeping an appointment for a job interview, present yourself in the most attractive manner possible. Dress neatly and conservatively for an interview. Although some on-air radio performers dress casually, they're established, and you're not. *Photo Courtesy of David Hatton and Dina Ibrahim.*

The law forbids discrimination on certain grounds. Interviewers can't require you to reveal information such as your national origin, religion, and physical condition. If you refuse to divulge such information, do it as tactfully as possible.

Although you're under pressure during a job interview, try to be relaxed, warm, open, and relatively energetic. Help the interviewer to enjoy spending time with you. Don't, however, try to entertain by taking over the interview by telling stories, anecdotes, or jokes.

Be ready to answer any questions the interviewer may have regarding your résumé. Also, be prepared to tell your life story—in an abbreviated form, of course. This might include where you were born, where you grew up, schools attended, significant travel, relevant job experience, and where you're headed in your career. (*But* be careful about this one: You might talk your way out of a job if you indicate that you see it is step toward better things.)

During an interview, find opportunities to ask questions. Most people like to believe they have something of value to communicate. If you feel comfortable doing so, ask the interviewer for advice. You may or may not get the job, but you'll certainly get some tips from an experienced person and make that person feel your respect.

Mention your favorable opinions about the station, its sound, and its on-air personnel. This isn't the time to tell the interviewer what you don't like about the station or any plans you may have for changing things.

Never try to gain the sympathy of the person interviewing you by complaining about your problems. People will hire you for one or more of these reasons: (1) They believe you can help them or make them look good, (2) they believe you can make money for them, or (3) they need someone and think you're the best applicant. You'll never be hired because a station executive feels sorry for you.

You may be asked to do an audition after an initial interview. You've already sent in an air check or audition demo, but this is an on-the-spot, under-pressure audition, and it can be nerve wracking and threatening. If you're truly prepared and well suited for an on-air position, this is your opportunity to really show off! The important point is that you should go into each job interview with the attitude that you will succeed. If you do, you'll always be prepared for an on-the-spot audition.

If you're asked to audition, you may be given scripts full of words that are difficult to pronounce, sentences that feature plosive and sibilant sounds, announcements that contain foreign words and names, or a script that requires you to read 190 to 200 words a minute. Practice in advance of job interviews for these and similar possibilities.

If you're taken on a tour of the station, make note of the equipment being used and be prepared to state whether or not you can operate it. When you're introduced to engineers, people in sales and traffic, on-air announcers, and others, show genuine interest in them and what they're doing. If you feel no such interest, you're probably applying to the wrong station.

If you smoke, avoid it totally while you are at the station. Even if your host is a smoker, others who are influential at the station may take offense. It's all right to accept an offer of coffee, tea, or a soft drink, but under no circumstances should you accept an offer of an alcoholic beverage.

Toward the end of the interview—especially if it's gone well—look for an opportunity to ask about salary and benefits. However, make sure that what's gone before in the interview tells you that such queries are appropriate. It's important for you to know whether health, dental, and vision plans are offered and how long you must be employed before they take effect, but if your instincts warn you against asking, you'll have a chance to discuss these matters if and when you're contacted with a job offer. A good interviewer will generally bring this up without your asking, but you can't count on it. Almost without exception, the salary of a first-time station employee is abysmally low, so be prepared for that.

As soon as possible after your interview—preferably on the same day—send a thank-you note to your interviewer. Write only what you truly feel; exaggerations are transparent to any seasoned station manager.

Joining a Union

To work at a unionized station or to perform freelance at a high professional level, you'll be obliged to join a union. The two unions for performers are the American Federation of Television and Radio Artists (AFTRA) and the Screen Actors Guild (SAG). Generally speaking, AFTRA represents performers who work live on radio or television or whose performances are recorded to an electronic storage medium. SAG represents those who perform on film. Radio and television station and network announcers usually belong to AFTRA. Freelance performers as a rule belong to both.

Joining a performers' union can be tricky. Acceptance by SAG requires that you've worked as a film performer; the catch is that you aren't likely to be employed as a film performer unless you already belong to SAG! A way around this dilemma is to join AFTRA, which doesn't require previous professional employment. After you've gained experience as a member of AFTRA, you'll be eligible for membership in SAG.

Going Where Your Career Takes You

If you live in a major or secondary market, you may have to leave for a smaller market to obtain that first job—unless, of course, you're willing to accept an entry-level job as a receptionist, a courier, or a clerk in the mail room. A few graduating seniors are so talented that they move directly from school to an on-air position at a medium-market or, occasionally, even a major-market station. For most, though, a career begins by moving to a smaller market where there's less competition and, usually, lower pay. Most radio and television stations in markets of more than 200,000 hire only on-air performers who've gained experience and moved up through the ranks in smaller markets.

"Going to the sticks" is a negative and self-defeating phrase for gaining initial employment in a smaller market. It implies that moving to and working in a small town are unfortunate necessities for most beginning broadcast performers. This attitude carries with it a feeling of contempt for life and work in markets outside major metropolitan areas. It also implies that, after suffering for several years in some sort of rural purgatory, all will be well if the individual is able to "move up" to a larger market. There are several good reasons for shunning this attitude.

First, by starting your career in a smaller market you can begin your on-air work at once, thereby accelerating your growth as a performer. Unlike those who start at a major-market station as a receptionist or a runner, you don't have to wait for that break that may never come.

Second, life as a broadcaster in a small town can be deeply fulfilling. If you're effective, you'll develop a following that sees you not only as a *person* but also as a member of the community. Knowing that you're able to help your region in significant ways through public-service work can be rewarding. Putting down roots, becoming a contributing member of society, and participating in town events can regularly confirm the fact that you do make a difference!

Salaries do tend to be lower in smaller markets, and many stations are nonunion. But the cost of living is lower, so your standard of living might actually be higher in a small town than in a large city.

A final reason for avoiding a negative attitude about a small market is that people who do the hiring are quick to spot condescension. Would you hire applicants who acted as though they were making a sacrifice to come to work for you?

This chapter is designed to help you find entry-level employment at a radio or television station. Most of the suggestions are applicable to other kinds of employment—doing voice-overs, industrials, and other freelance work, for example. However, there are several things this chapter can't provide. It can't give you talent, good work habits, or the perseverance required for success in the world of broadcasting. Remember that the jobs are out there, and you can obtain yours if you have performance skills, are reliable and hardworking, and have a strong drive to succeed.

Preparing a Scannable Résumé

Prepare a résumé that's consistent with today's technology and a job could be just a mouse click away. Many leading businesses now use electronic applicant tracking systems that scan résumés into a computer system that searches for and extracts important information necessary to qualify you for a job. Knowing this can help you prepare a résumé that computers can scan and read.

A scannable résumé has standard fonts and crisp, dark type and offers plenty of facts for the artificial intelligence to extract: The more skills and facts you provide, the more opportunities you have for your skills to match available positions. A scannable résumé is like a traditional résumé: You focus on format and content. When preparing your résumé, use the tips in the following Checklist.

Checklist *Format Tips to Prepare Your Scannable Résumé*

1. Submit a clean original and use a standard-style résumé.
2. Avoid an unusual format, small font sizes, graphics or lines, print that's too light, or paper that's too dark, all of which make it difficult for the computer to read your résumé.

Tips to Maximize the Scannability of Your Résumé

1. Use white or light-colored paper printed on only one side.
2. Provide the clearest possible print original.
3. Use standard typefaces (for example, Times, Helvetica, or Geneva).
4. Use a font size of eleven or twelve points.
5. Avoid fancy treatments.
6. Avoid vertical and horizontal lines, graphics, and boxes.
7. Avoid two-column formats that look like newspapers or newsletters.

Content Tips to Maximize "Hits"

1. *Use enough key words to define your skill, experience, education, professional affiliations, and so forth.*
2. *Describe your experience with concrete words rather than vague descriptions.*
3. *Use more than one page if necessary.*
4. *Use jargon and acronyms specific to your industry.*

Additional Tips

1. *When sending a résumé, send it as an attachment through the Internet because it always produces the best quality. In addition, when you send your résumé via e-mail, use plain text in ASCII (American Standard Code for Information Interchange) format.*
2. *Avoid faxing, unless specifically asked to do so. Even the best fax reproduction isn't the best quality.*

PRACTICE

➤ Drafting Your Résumé

Write a résumé following the guidelines and examples given in this chapter. Bring copies for your instructor and, if appropriate, for each class member to discuss and compare.

PRACTICE

➤ Checking Out the Job Scene

Visit your nearest career-guidance center and obtain any available handouts on résumés, job interviews, and other information that may help you find that first job. Find a current issue of *Broadcasting & Cable* magazine and compile a list of advertised job openings for on-air talent. Note the geographical areas in which the greatest number of openings exist and note the areas of specialization most in demand.

Appendix A

Scripts to Develop Performance Skills

This appendix offers you many scripts for practice. The first section is made up of narrative scripts, including essays and "impressions" — a type of essay that explores inner feelings and is therefore especially effective on radio. While some of these audio pieces may seem unrelated to what you hear on radio, they have considerable value as preparation for voice-over performances for television and film documentaries. Unlike brief news stories, interviews, or commercials, their length and complexity ask you to read, study, and then come up with an interpretation that blends the many elements of the script into a cohesive whole, into a story that moves listeners along a path from start to completion.

There are more commercials and PSAs in this appendix than all other categories combined. The reason? Commercials are more diverse—and therefore present more varied challenges than any other type of broadcast material. Their range of styles, concepts, accents, and character types demand that their interpreters tell a complete story in fifteen to sixty seconds. Many commercials, unlike narratives, are dramatized, usually in a two-person dialogue, so the requirement of announcer as actor is invoked.

After working with these challenges, you may want to turn to the Internet for more practice copy. There you can choose only scripts that excite you and serve your particular needs. After locating several essays, for example, you can print, read, and record your favorites. And, with a system such as RealPlayer or QuickTime, you can listen to scripts read by their authors. Television commercial scripts may be found at: www.geocities.com/tvtranscripts/comm/.

Solo Narrative Scripts

Essays

Radio and television essays are personal statements that represent the feelings or opinions of their authors, and they most often are narrated by their creators. Generally speaking, essays don't deal with hard news, and they need not be timely. The purpose of most essays is to explore a situation, a tradition, or a movement and to present it with analysis and a personal point of view. Essays may be serious, tongue-in-cheek humorous, or anger driven.

In Flanders Fields

J. Michael Travis

This past April, I had the fortune to travel to Belgium on business. I sell

German lager, but my boss sent me to Flanders on a probing mission.

Survey the country, seek out ales, evaluate them, and file a report. An old friend of mine had come to Belgium eighty-two years earlier on a probing mission; he had not come to drink ale.

We entered the country via Armentières, France. Armentières, of song and legend, on a day the Belgian countryside looked like a landscape in an old master's painting; the sky a study in gray, the first meadow-flowers had just arrived, apple blossoms filled the air, and spring tripped north again for the year.

Many years before as a child I had marveled as my father's dear friend Dutch Rikks told me tales of his years on the Western Front, a soldier of the Great War. Dutch was called Dutch because his friends in Alabama could not pronounce Deutsch. Yes, Dutch Rikks was a German landser, a Hun, one of the bad guys. The stories Dutch told were usually about "boys just about your age" (I was 12 at the time), and how Dutch and his friends survived the storm of steel. These were not tales of combat, they were lessons of live and let live, and how much like each other the opposing soldiers were, until the whistles blew.

One day Dutch made me promise to visit his friends in Belgium. In my innocence I asked Dutch, "Where do your friends live in Belgium?" His reply hit home on this early morning forty years later: "They are in the German cemetery near Iper, they lie in Falnderen, in the fields. Please go see them, tell them I miss them and I love them. Michael, they are good men."

My traveling companion is no stranger to death. John is a Marine and has seen the elephant more times than P. T. Barnum. No more than ten kilometers into Belgium John grabbed my arm and said: "There are dead men here, thousands of them." He is right, more men could die in a week on the Western Front than in all of my friend's wars combined. Shortly, we began to see soldiers' graves marked by simple white crosses. These are cemetery plots that were only partially filled, and John related: "Dressing stations, these poor bastards almost made it to the hospitals before they died." Our journey continues, and the cemetery plots began to fill and become larger as we approach the front. Crosses row on row that mark the spots of dead soldiers in a forgotten war. Our travels have now brought us to this remote part of the world where many years ago the nations of Europe fought to the death in the fields of Flanders for all the right reasons.

Poperinge, Belgium: It is morning and a farmers' market in the town square greets us with a variety of cheeses and produce second to none. During the war, Poperinge was behind the English lines, an area of rest and relaxation—if you discount the errant artillery round falling into the town, or the square, where deserters were executed at dawn. Across the square we find a café packed with local farmers drinking ale at 6:30 a.m. After we down a couple of liters, the bartender, a strikingly lovely red-head, asked: "Are you going to the battlefields in Iper?" "Yes," I said. "Do you have kin there?" "Friends," I replied. "There are not many Americans there," our hostess commented. I told her we were going to see friends in the German cemetery.

You could have heard a pin drop in the café. I told my story about my promise to Dutch, and our lovely hostess made a quick recovery: "They are all the same now. It is good you have honored your promise and have come to see them. The German boys don't get many visitors."

In Flanders fields, there are numerous cemeteries for the various nationalities buried there, marked by crosses and the occasional Star of David. In truth the crosses and stars mark but a few spots where the dead reside. Many lie in graves, but just as many were atomized to a red mist by high explosives. Others are resurrected each year as rains of spring, and the farmers' plows bring them into the waking world for one last visit.

While visiting Dutch's friends in the brooding yet beautiful German cemetery, it dawned on us that Flanders is not a monument to a war, but it is a shrine dedicated to peace. This was the war to end all wars, a war so terrible no one would dare to unleash hell upon the earth ever again. But people forgot, and eighteen years later, an even more horrible conflict swept peace away, and with it the idea that the last war on earth had been fought. As I reflect on our journey, our nation is on the brink of yet another conflict in a faraway land. Daily we hear the cry of "we are going to war." The trouble is "we" are not going to war. The nation never goes to war. It can be at war, but it is our children who go to war. Not the president, not the politicians, and surely not those shrill voices on the radio serving up a ration of hate and intolerance disguised as patriotism. No, it is the young men and women who are bound by honor and duty, who will serve and die. War is like a poisonous drug, to be used sparingly. Even when there is no other alternative, it is lethal, and humans grow too fond of it.

Yet there in Flanders fields, the ideal remains that peace is possible. Young men and women don't have to leave their countries to destroy one another only to become the residents of lonely graves, in lands far away, in monuments to forgotten wars, remembered only by a few loving relatives and friends. On the eve of conflict, I wish more people could see the crosses in Flanders fields; it just might change some minds and save some lives.

Impressions

An impression is an essay that explores inner feelings and is quite personal. While it differs from other essays only in its degree of "shared privacy," it's useful to consider an impression separately because the mood conveyed and the degree of self-involvement are of a different order. One way of expressing this is to say that, while all impressions are essays, not all essays are impressions.

Well-written "impressions" will help you appreciate the rich (and seldom used) potential of the aural medium of radio. The only broadcast service through which you're likely to hear such works is noncommercial radio, including PBS and community radio stations.

Impression

Karen Fremont

MUSIC: Bach Prelude—fade in and under

I can't imagine a life without music. Ever since I was 3 years old I was banging away on the piano and learning songs from my mother. As I grew older, she nurtured my interest and gave me the opportunity to have private music lessons. She was in the church choir at St. John's Episcopal church and had close friends who were music teachers. That choir was full of life. People with such passion for music filled the group, and the anthems were always outstandingly beautiful. But not one of them had the passion quite like my teacher, Timothy Eaton.

MUSIC: fade out

We called him Tim. It was so much less teacher-sounding than Timothy. He could play any instrument and make it sound as if he'd been playing it all his life. His voice was smooth and pure, with a clarity that really made you feel the words he sang. He taught me piano, flute, and voice, but I always thought the singing was the most fun. I'll never forget the day he suggested we sing a duet. It was my favorite song: "Somewhere Out There," from the movie *An American Tail.*

We practiced this song over and over again. He played the piano and sang his parts with such grace and beauty as my 11-year-old voice struggled to keep up. I was so excited to get the chance to perform this song at the recital we had coming up, and it was the only thing I cared about practicing. Finally, I was performing a song I'd heard on the radio! It was a big deal. My family and friends were all supposed to come to the recital, and I couldn't wait for them to hear it.

After a period of time that seemed eternal, it was the day of the recital. I wore my favorite red dress and black patent leather shoes. I called all my friends to make sure they were coming. We arrived at the church and I was starting to get really nervous. My stomach was fluttering around and I was getting too short of breath, but Tim said, "Don't worry, you're going to nail this song. I'm right here with you." My admiration and respect for him told me he was right, but it was so hard to catch my breath! But then my time came to stand up in front of everyone and sing with Tim, and I was ready for it.

And boy, did I sing with Tim. We totally let go, alternating verses and locking in our harmonies as we flowed through the song. I didn't feel nervous when I was up there with him. I felt free as the notes rang from our throats. We sang as if we were never going to sing again. At the end, the applause and cheers from the room echoed so loudly in my ears I could barely hear Tim tell me what a good job I had done. With tears in his eyes he hugged me, and he was so proud of me I could feel it in his embrace. And at that moment, we were the only two people in the room.

That downstairs choir room at St. John's Episcopal church is still ringing with music, but Tim's voice no longer resides there. He was diagnosed with AIDS shortly before that recital and became very sick in the years to come. If it wasn't for him and his faith in me, I'm not sure where I'd be today. He taught me how to play, how to sing, but he also taught me how to really feel the music I put forth. He showed me that life can be lived to the fullest without reaching the age of 40, as he surrounded himself with music and love. He made me realize that I can pursue my dream, my dream of becoming a performer and sharing my gift with the world. The last time I saw Tim he was directing a professional chorale, and his powerful and graceful movements reminded me of that day. That day we sang our hearts out, with the words: "When the night wind starts to sing a lonesome lullaby, it helps to think we're sleeping underneath the same big sky."

Timothy Eaton died on December 22, 1996. I know he would be proud that I never stopped making music. I miss him a lot, and I wish he could see me now. But our song reminds me that "somewhere out there, if love can see us through—then we'll be together, somewhere out there, out where dreams come true."

MUSIC: fade in ending of "Somewhere Out There."

Cheek to Cheek
Michael Morla

It was 1:45 in the morning (sounds of a crowd in a bar . . . music under mellow rock music). She took one last sip of her Long Island and asked me if I wanted another drink . . . I said, "it's too late, the bartender's already announced the last call for alcohol" . . . she whimpered and leaned her head on my shoulder . . . the butterflies started to fly around my stomach . . . I gently pushed her away from me . . . she kept repeating how drunk she was . . . then the DJ played the last song of the night (R-Kelly, "Feeling on Your Booty" . . . music under) she then held my hand . . . the kind of holding couples would do . . . fingers interlocking . . . she held my hand tight and led me to the dance floor . . . for one moment I felt so lucky . . . here I was with a beautiful girl . . . the kind of girl who turns heads wherever she goes . . . and she was holding me . . . a guy who is totally opposite from her in looks . . . she pulled me close to her . . . we started to move to the rhythm of the beat . . . we were cheek to cheek . . . her skin next to mine. I held my head back to look at her and her eyes were closed . . . but she had a smile . . . as the song ended . . . (music stops) . . . she grabbed my hand again . . . I pulled away and told her I had to use the bathroom . . . she said she'd wait for me in front . . . (sounds of a crowd).

As I walked outside the bar I couldn't find her . . . I felt nervous . . . maybe I should have told her to wait for me in front of the bathroom . . . all of a sudden I see her with a group of guys across the parking lot . . . one big guy had his arm around her . . . suddenly I felt a little animosity . . . but I just stood there looking cool . . . she was the center of attention . . . I just stared from afar and admired how beautiful she was . . . then she saw me . . . she politely told the guys that she had to go . . . the guys responded and said "where are you going?" . . . she didn't answer but instead walked directly toward me . . . she greeted me with a hug . . . and suddenly the butterflies were flying again . . . we started to walk to my car . . . I grabbed her hand . . . this time I'm leading her . . . as we got closer to my car I noticed a lot of people driving by looking at us . . . (sounds of cars driving by) . . . cars honked at us . . . she waved . . . I had to put a frown on my face . . . I had to show these guys that I was her man.

We finally arrived at her place . . . as I walked her to the door she was laughing . . . asking me if she looked okay. I took her keys and opened the door and noticed that her roommate was on the couch sleeping . . . I told her to keep quiet . . . I shut the door behind me . . . I dragged her up the stairs to her bedroom and laid her down . . . her eyes were closed . . . but I knew she was awake because she kept a smile . . . I unzipped her boots and took them off . . . she suddenly got up and asked me if her feet stank . . . we both laughed . . . she again closed her eyes and leaned her head on my chest . . . I pushed her to the bed softly . . . but when I got up she grabbed my hand and begged me to stay . . . I told her that I had to leave but she sat up and gave me a hug . . . so I laid down with her. The bed was small—only a twin size—so we had to stay close together . . . after a few minutes I tested her . . . I slowly got up but she grabbed me . . . and said "please don't leave me." Then she held me . . . I lay down with her, cheek to cheek . . . a feeling of chills ran through my body . . . the butterflies were flying . . . I thought about how close we'd danced that night . . . how every guy was looking at me with envy as she led me to the dance floor . . . how she was the center of attention . . . how beautiful she was . . . but most importantly I thought about me and her . . . how I was her best friend . . . a friend who was there for her through all her problems . . . a friend who made her laugh when she was down . . . a friend who was different . . .

a friend she trusted . . . and that's all I ever was to her . . . a best friend . . . a tear came down my cheek to her cheek . . . as if she was crying too . . . but she wasn't . . . she was so beautiful . . . she had her eyes closed with a smile on her face . . . I kissed her on the cheek . . . we held each other tight . . . she was happy . . . she had a best friend to hold that night . . . but I was sad . . . I didn't have a girlfriend to hold . . . It's been a year now and that night has faded away . . . I'm still alone, and now she's with somebody else . . . a lot of guys told me that I should have gone for it . . . but I have no regrets . . . the choices we make dictate the lives we live . . . and I know I'm a good person with a good heart. Even though she was never my girl-friend, I'll always cherish the friendship we had . . . I'm probably the only guy strong enough to keep a beautiful girl like that as a friend . . . but at least I had that one night . . . a night when we slept cheek to cheek . . .

About the Rooms
Midei Toriyama

On a rainy, quiet afternoon, I leave the window slightly open to allow the air to stream into the room. I hold a cup of hot raspberry tea in my hands, feeling the warmth and enjoying the aroma. I feel the movement of air on my cheek—the combination of the cold air from the outside and the warm steam rising from the tea cup. I am completely relaxed in this com-fortable room where silence gently lies. With a sense of great apprecia-tion, I lie down in the heart of solitude, thinking how lucky I am to be the resident of a room with such good vibrations.

Every room has a different atmosphere that cannot be seen but only sensed with the surface of my skin; they call this "intuition." When I look for a place to live, the room has to have some kind of impression or impulse that welcomes me. I don't know if there are many people who share this feeling; however, I feel it when my senses respond to the frequency of the room—the vibration of the molecules of the airwaves. I believe there is a congeniality between the room and the resident. I can feel it when the room likes me. When I don't feel it in a room, I will not be living there for long. I once had a room with no feeling of the vibration. At that time I was forced to find a place to live as quickly as possible. I was visiting here from another city to look for a place, but I did not have much time. All I had was a couple of days, which was not sufficient to find the best place. After miles of walking to look at many different places, I finally ended up with a two-bedroom flat near the Geary Theatre. However, although the place was nice and actually pretty, with a huge living room and a high ceiling, a spacious kitchen, and cozy bedrooms, I did not receive the feeling. I compromised because of the limited time that I could spend.

I moved in but lived there just for a few weeks. Something did not feel right, and I was again thrown into the middle of town to look for "room to rent" signs.

Fortunately it did not take me long to find the next place. That time I knew I was getting the place even before I got to the door of the room; I could feel it while I was going to the stairs. I remember I was so excited to open the door that my hand was shaking. The room did welcome me in an obvious way. I heard every part of the room—the ceiling, the walls, the windows, and the floors—all giving a shout of joy to have me in. As soon as I opened the door I felt a big pressure of air on my whole body.

The room was full of wind; there was a whirlpool of air, and I was wrapped within it. It felt as though invisible tentacles were crawling over my body to identify me. I was welcomed.

I lived there for a whole year. When I moved out of the room I left a little wish for the next resident-to-be for their good time in this room where I packed pounds of memory in numbers of boxes. I loved the room, and I could tell the room as well appreciated my residency.

Then I was drawn to this present place nearby the ocean. It may be just a sentiment of my own; however, I think the space or rooms can sense the resident's feelings. I do not know how and why, but for some reason I hear something that space radiates. And it does change its atmosphere. After the absence of a few days, I can always tell the change in the air. It smells different. To me, it seems like it is complaining of my absence. The space is alive, I believe, and it needs to be communicated with in some way. We are likely to be insensitive to this kind of matter and treat it without respect. What if there is a spiritual thing involved? We don't know, but how can we be so sure that no such thing is present?

On a rainy day, on such a quiet afternoon, I comfortably sit in the room with a cup of tea in my hands. I hear the silence with my eyes closed. Slowly, the aroma of raspberry tea expands in the room. I open my eyes and smile, experiencing the same feeling of tentacles which crawled on me in that old room with the feeling of the wind. It was also a rainy, quiet day, just like this.

One more essay. It reaches inside its author, and comes to a conclusion from which we all can learn and benefit.

Missed Opportunities

Ben McLintock

We've all got things that we regret in lives.

Especially missed opportunities.

When we look back at those kinds of things, the act of reminiscence can be very bitter.

When they say hindsight is twenty-twenty, boy they aren't kidding.

This is a big regret in my life that I wish to share with you.

Throughout the course of your life, your family, more often than not, is a constant.

They're always there, and you can't pick them.

Like my dad says, "You can pick your friends, but you can't pick your family."

This constancy can be a double-edged sword, though.

While it can provide a sense of permanence, it can also lead to the mistaken assumption that they will always be there.

When you're 13, you think that your family members will be there forever.

The reason I bring this up is because when I was 13, my grandfather, my mother's father, was diagnosed with lung cancer.

Three months later, he died from complications caused by it.

I still remember the last time I saw him.

He was a tall man, with a great, booming voice.

That day I don't remember him talking much louder than in a soft whisper.

I didn't know it at the time, but the reason my parents took me and my sister down to see him was because they knew he wouldn't be alive much longer.

When I look back on my memories of him, my regret as a young man is that I never really got to know my grandfather.

I don't really blame myself.

After all, I was only 13, and we all know that the priorities of adolescents differ greatly from older people.

Sure, I saw him at family get-togethers and camping trips, but I have to ashamedly admit that I don't really know the person behind the title of grandfather.

I know that he was kind, and he had a laugh you could hear a mile away.

But as far as talking with him, finding out what he was like, I never did that.

Now that chance is forever denied to me.

It's amazing how we can interact with people for years and years and never truly know much about them.

When I was ready to go to college, my big dilemma was figuring out where I was going to live.

When my dad's parents, who lived in the college town, said they would be glad to have me live with them while I went to school, I jumped at it.

It was a great opportunity, if anything else because they laughed at me when I asked them how much they wanted me to pay them a month.

Now I see it as an even greater gift, one I'm glad I've not squandered.

I missed the chance to get to know my Mom's dad, but here was the perfect opportunity to get to know my other grandfather.

Living with your grandparents has its own unique set of drawbacks, but I wouldn't trade it for any dorm room or apartment in the world.

I get to see them on nearly a daily basis and know what they're really like outside the weekend visits and holiday cheer.

I feel lucky not only because I had this chance, but because I saw it for what it was and took advantage of it.

I'm old enough to realize that my grandparents won't always be there, and one day, all I'll have of them are memories.

One thing I've learned in life is that it's not often you get second chances to do certain things.

I feel very lucky to have gotten the chance to live with them.

It has given me the chance to build up memories of them that will last me the rest of my life after they're gone.

Treasure your family.

Take the time to see them.

Take the time to talk with them.

Life has a way of moving all too fast, and when you're young, it can be hard to put on the brakes and take a look at those around you.

But it's important to do just that.

Sound Bytes

Now that you've seen a few examples, you're encouraged to use the Internet to find other narrative scripts to use for further development of your interpretive abilities. Richard Rodriguez, Clarence Page, Anne Taylor Fleming, and Roger Rosenblatt are highly respected commentators, and their works can be accessed and printed through the PBS website:

www.pbs.org/newshour/essays-dialogues.html

For a complete, updated list of URLs for this textbook, please refer to the accompanying CD.

I missed my chance to get to really know one of my grandparents.

I'm glad I had enough sense to not make the same mistake with my other ones.

Radio Commercials

Scripts for Solo Delivery

These commercials were written for delivery by a single performer. Nearly all can be performed effectively by persons of either gender and of any age. In some, an introduction, tag, or other addition is made by a second voice, but the main message of each commercial is delivered by one performer.

Peaches & Cream

TITLE:	"Boutiques"
LENGTH:	60 seconds
BY:	Mia Detrick

ANNCR: This is . . . . . . from Peaches & Cream with some highly significant facts about shopping in our boutiques; first of all you'll find an extraordinary selection of jeans, tops, sweaters, and dresses. We buy from 138 different manufacturers, so you can find just what you want . . . and you don't have to pay a lot of money. Of the 138 different lines we carry, 137 of them are inexpensive; and the other one, we keep in the back room. Furthermore, at Peaches & Cream you don't have to deal with uppity salesladies who are snotty to you because you aren't flashing a large wad of bills. All of our salesladies are especially selected for their easygoing, personable dispositions . . . and, besides; none of them are on commission this is a very important fact. Lastly, nobody at Peaches & Cream has a perfect body, to make you feel fat. There is a Peaches & Cream in Sausalito and in Mill Valley. If you haven't heard about Peaches & Cream, you had better hurry down before we get famous and lose our humble charm.

AGENCY:	Donn Resnick Advertising
CLIENT:	Lincoln Health Source
LENGTH:	60 seconds
TITLE:	"Take Charge"
MUSIC:	LINCOLN HEALTH MUSIC

ANNCR: How long are you going to live?

How well are you going to live?

Knowing which habits and behaviors can hurt your health and making a few changes for the better can make a real difference. For instance, lifestyle choices like smoking, unhealthy diet, lack of exercise, and alcohol abuse can lead to serious illness. Yet all these factors are under your control. So, by making a few changes—by taking charge—you can lead a healthier, happier life. The Health Source, John C. Lincoln Hospital's resource center, has the latest information on how your lifestyle affects your health and the important changes you can make. We're easier than a library, give you more information than a magazine, and we're free.

The Health Source is one more way Lincoln Health is making a difference in people's lives. To take charge of your lifestyle, call me, at 555-6356. That's 555-6356.

LINCOLN MUSIC ENDS

AGENCY:	Annette Lai Creative Services
CLIENT:	Celebration Coffee
LENGTH:	60 seconds
MUSIC:	"CELEBRATION," by Kool and the Gang—Instrumental

ANNCR: Tired of the same weak coffee every morning, America? Well, wake up to CELEBRATION! The new freeze-dried instant from International Cuisines. Made from the choicest Celebes (SELL-uh-beez) beans from Indonesia. A unique roasting process allows the beans to retain their rich and natural taste. Because of CELEBRATION'S deep flavor, you use less. An eight-ounce jar makes twice as many cups as the same-sized jar of the leading brand. With the fast-paced life you lead, CELEBRATION gives you the freshly brewed taste of coffee without the wait. And, it's not just for mornings—CELEBRATE all day with CELEBRATION. Made from the finest Celebes beans and deep-roasted to perfection, perfectly brewed, and quickly freeze-dried to retain their priceless flavor. That's the secret of CELEBRATION. And, for those who like a deep-flavored coffee without caffeine, try 97 percent caffeine-free CELEBRATION. Come on, America—it's time to CELEBRATE!

AGENCY:	Millar Advertising, Inc.
CLIENT:	Andre's International Bakery
LENGTH:	60 seconds
ANNCR:	Hot, fresh breakfast rolls, glistening with melting butter! Croissants (krah-SAHNTS) and café au lait (kahf-AY-oh-LAY). Raisin bran muffins to go with your poached eggs. Andre's has these delicacies, and they're waiting for you now. For afternoon tea, Andre suggests English crumpets, served with lemon curd. Or scones and pomegranate jam. For after-dinner desserts, how about baklava (bahk-lah-VAH), the Persian delicacy made with dozens of layers of paper-thin pastry, honey, and chopped walnuts? Or, if your taste runs to chocolate, a German torte (TOR-tuh)? These and dozens of other international delights are created daily by Andre and his staff. Made only of pure and natural ingredients—Grade A cream and butter, natural un-refined sugar, pure chocolate and cocoa, and imported spices. For mouth-watering pastries, it's Andre's International Bakery. We bring you the best from the gourmet capitals of the world. Visit Andre's today! In the Corte Madera Shopping Center. Andre's!

Dramatized Radio Commercials

Several commercials for two or more performers are presented here to help you work on characterization, teamwork, and timing. Most of these spots are humorous, and their comic effectiveness is dependent on your ability to simultaneously project an off-the-wall delivery while remaining completely believable to your listeners. Slight exaggeration is called for in most instances, but avoid becoming too extreme or farcical. If listeners feel that you're play-acting, you'll fail to communicate such subtle qualities as gullibility ("Research Lab") and slight annoyance and petulance ("Mona Lisa").

Eric Poole, writer–producer of the first spots in this section, describes himself as "head creative guy of Splash Radio, a commercial production company with nearly fifty Clio, Sunny, New York Festival, and London International Festival awards." These commercials demonstrate his understanding of the "Theatre of the Mind" potential of radio, as well as a wild but disciplined sense of humor.

AGENCY:	Splash Radio
CLIENT:	Frosty Paws
PRODUCT:	Intro
TITLE:	"Research Lab," as produced
SFX:	FOOTSTEPS
MAN:	And this is our motivational research center . . .
GUY:	Wow . . .
MAN:	Where we do all our doggie treat research.
GUY:	Doggie treat?
MAN:	Yeah, dogs are capable of much more than you think.
GUY:	Really?
MAN:	Oh, yes. They've just never had the right motivation.
GUY:	Oh.
MAN:	What does your dog do?
GUY:	Well, he rolls over, plays dead . . .
MAN:	Exactly. Now in here . . .
SFX:	DOOR OPEN, PIANO, TAP DANCING

VOICE:	Okay, girls, big finish!
GUY:	Dogs tap dancing?
MAN:	Yeah, they want the new frozen treat for dogs, Frosty Paws.
GUY:	Frosty Paws?
MAN:	It's like ice cream for your dog. Now in here . . .
SFX:	DOOR OPEN, JAZZ COMBO PLAYING
GUY:	A jazz quartet!
MAN:	You should hear Muffin's tenor sax solo.
GUY:	Wow.
MAN:	We've found dogs will do anything for Frosty Paws. And over here . . .
SFX:	DOOR OPEN, TYPEWRITERS
GUY:	Secretarial school?
MAN:	Typing, dictation, and shortpaw.
ANNCR:	Unleash your dog's potential with Frosty Paws, the world's first frozen treat for dogs. There's never been anything like it. It's full of protein, vitamins, and minerals. And unlike real ice cream, it won't upset your dog's stomach.
SFX:	DOOR OPEN, MUSIC UP
MAN:	And this is our malt shop.
GUY:	Lotta dogs eating Frosty Paws.
MAN:	Uh huh. Smart as they are, they still think it's ice cream.
ANNCR:	Frosty Paws, the world's first frozen treat for dogs. New in your grocer's ice cream freezer. Go fetch some today.

AGENCY:	Splash Radio
CLIENT:	Wisconsin Dental Association
PRODUCT:	Checkups
TITLE:	"Mona Lisa," as produced
MUSIC:	ITALIAN CLASSICAL THEME UNDER

MONA: Gee, Leonardo, I'm really excited about you painting my portrait.

LEONARDO: So am I, Mona. You're gonna make me famous.

MONA: Ah, you DaVinci boys, such flatterers.

LEONARDO: Okay, sit down on this marble slab and smile.

MONA: Okay.

LEONARDO: (A BEAT) Mona . . .

MONA: Yeah?

LEONARDO: You're not smiling.

MONA: I know.

LEONARDO: I can't paint a world-famous portrait that'll hang in the Louvre if you don't put on a happy face.

MONA: This is as happy as it gets.

LEONARDO: Look, just say "cheese."

MONA: I can't.

LEONARDO: What do you mean, you can't? I got a career riding on this picture.

MONA: It's my teeth.

LEONARDO: Your teeth?

MONA: I didn't get regular checkups as a kid, so now I'm paying for it.

LEONARDO:	Let me see.
MONA:	No!
LEONARDO:	Open your mouth!
MONA:	Lay off, DaVinci, or I'm calling Mister Lisa.
LEONARDO:	Maybe you oughta call a dentist.
MONA:	Maybe I oughta call Van Gogh.
LEONARDO:	Not with those ears.
ANNCR:	Today's dentistry is more than just filling cavities. Your regular dentist cares about your teeth for the long term, too. And keeping your teeth healthy now can save you lots of money down the road. Get the picture?
MONA:	Can't you just pretend I'm smiling and draw in some teeth later?
LEONARDO:	Oh, forget it. Just sit there with that dumb blank expression.
MONA:	It's mysterious.
LEONARDO:	Yeah, who's gonna buy that?
ANNCR:	Call your regular dentist for your six-month checkup now. A reminder from the Wisconsin Dental Association. And smile.

CREATION AND PRODUCTION:	Chuck Blore & Don Richman, Inc.
CLIENT:	AT & T
LENGTH:	60 seconds
CATHIANNE:	(ON PHONE) Hello.

DANNY:	Uh, hi. You probably still remember me. Edward introduced us at the seminar . . .
CATHIANNE:	Oh, the guy with the nice beard.
DANNY:	I don't know whether it's nice . . .
CATHIANNE:	It's a gorgeous beard.
DANNY:	Well, thank you, uh, listen. I'm gonna, uh, be in the city next Tuesday and I was, y'know, wondering if we could sorta, y'know, get together for lunch?
CATHIANNE:	How 'bout dinner?
DANNY:	Dinner? Dinner! Dinner's a better idea. You could pick your favorite restaurant and . . .
CATHIANNE:	How 'bout my place? I'm my favorite cook.
DANNY:	Uh, your place. Right. Sure. That's great to me.
CATHIANNE:	Me too. It'll be fun.
DANNY:	Yeah . . . listen. I'll bring the wine.
CATHIANNE:	Perfect. I'll drink it.
BOTH:	(LAUGH)
DANNY:	Well, OK, then, I guess it's a date. I'll see you Tuesday.
CATHIANNE:	Tuesday. Great.
DANNY:	Actually, I just, uh, I called to see how you were and y'know, Tuesday sounds fine!
SOUND:	PHONE HANGS UP (YELLING) Tuesday . . . AHHHA . . . she's gonna see me Tuesday. (FADE)
SUNG:	REACH OUT, REACH OUT AND TOUCH SOMEONE

AGENCY:	Cunningham & Walsh, Inc.
CLIENT:	Schieffelin & Co.
LENGTH:	60 seconds
ANNCR:	Once again, Stiller and Meara for Blue Nun.
ANNE:	Hello, I'm Frieda Beidermyer, your interior decorator.
JERRY:	Oh, yes, come in. This is my apartment.
ANNE:	Don't apologize.
JERRY:	Huh?
ANNE:	They didn't tell me you were color-blind. Plaid windows?
JERRY:	I want decor that makes a statement about me, that exudes confidence, savoya fair. Where do we begin?
ANNE:	The Last Chance Thrift Shop. Everything's gotta go.
JERRY:	Everything?
ANNE:	Everything.
JERRY:	These are mementos my parents brought back from their honeymoon.
ANNE:	They honeymooned in Tijuana?
JERRY:	You noticed the terra-cotta donkey?
ANNE:	I noticed. Out.
JERRY:	So, where do we start?
ANNE:	We start with a little Blue Nun.
JERRY:	I want my apartment converted, not me.
ANNE:	No, Blue Nun white wine. It'll lend you some style.
JERRY:	I never tried Blue Nun.

ANNE: You have so much to learn, my naive nudnick. Blue Nun tastes terrific.

JERRY: I want good taste.

ANNE: That's why you can get Blue Nun by the glass or by the bottle at swank bars and restaurants.

JERRY: Gee, style, confidence, and taste. Will Blue Nun do all that for me?

ANNE: It's a bottle of wine, honey, not a miracle worker.

ANNCR: By the glass or by the bottle, there's a lot of good taste in Blue Nun. Imported by Schieffelin (SHIFF-uh-lin) & Company, New York.

AGENCY:	Shmosie Advertising
CLIENT:	Rosario's Coffee Roastery
LENGTH:	30 seconds
BY:	Karen Fremont

SFX: FAMILY BUSTLING AROUND GETTING READY FOR THE DAY

MAN: (FRUSTRATED) Honey, where's the coffee?

WOMAN: It's right in the cupboard, where it always is.

MAN: I don't see it.

WOMAN: That's because you're looking for the store brand bag! I went to Rosario's Coffee Roastery and got their Arabian Mocha from Yemen!

MAN: And how much did they soak you for that?

WOMAN: Only $7.99 a pound! They have weekly specials, like Jamaican Blue Mountain for only $12.99 a pound and Bourbon Santos from Brazil for just $11.99 a pound. And I picked up a new gold coffee filter for only $12.95!

MAN: Affordable gourmet? My sweet little bargain shopper! You did it again!

WOMAN: (SUGGESTIVELY) Anything for you!

ANNCR: Sale lasts from August 30th to September 15th. Rosario's Coffee Roastery—Mainfield—on the corner of Chapman and Pixley. Come see why everyone is brewing Rosario's Coffee.

CLIENT: Rosario's Coffee Roastery
OCCASION: Regular Weekly Specials
TITLE: "Fall in Love"
BY: Debbie Thompson

SFX: CHILDREN'S VOICES CHATTERING

ANNCR: (MALE WITH CALMING, SEXY VOICE) Do you remember the first time you fell in love?

SFX: DRAMATIC ROMANTIC MUSIC

ANNCR: Remember that incredible electrical charge that surged through your veins . . . it was so predictable. It drove you wild every time you saw her. Yeah, I know exactly what those feelings are like because I have them even now. I'm not talking about my first grade girlfriend, but something even more exquisite.

SFX: WAVES ON A SANDY BEACH. GENTLE WIND BLOWING THROUGH PALM TREES. COFFEE POURING INTO CUP

ANNCR: I'm talking about Jamaican Blue Mountain, the world's rarest and most unique coffee.

SFX: ROMANTIC MUSIC. WOMAN SNIFFING A CUP OF HOT COFFEE. SHE REACTS TO SMELL

ANNCR: Experience that rich island taste. Smell that distinct aroma that makes it truly unique. Jamaican Blue Mountain coffee is found only on the sun-drenched island of love and at Rosario's Coffee Roastery on the corner of Chapman and Pixley in Mainfield. Fall in love again. Jamaican Blue

Mountain is on sale August 30 through September 15. Also try our other exotic blends from around the world. Whatever you do, don't let love pass you by. Rosario's Coffee Roastery: gourmet coffees at grocery-store prices. Come visit us today.

Character Voices and Accents

No suggestions on how to affect accents or develop unusual character voices are given because written instructions are of little help. Audio recordings of professional announcers performing all sorts of character roles are available on the Internet and may be obtained through a program such as RealPlayer or QuickTime. Some audiovisual departments and learning resource centers have recorded performances that may guide your efforts.

As you work with these scripts, make recordings and listen critically to the results. If you aren't truly outstanding at doing a particular voice, abandon it in favor of others that you can do with authority.

The Pitch "Artist"

The commercial that follows is an example of a type of commercial that is, fortunately, rarely heard. Nevertheless, it will afford you an opportunity to see if you can perform it in sixty seconds without slurring or stumbling. The commercial contains 221 words.

AGENCY:	Client's Copy
CLIENT:	Compesi's Meat Locker
LENGTH:	60 seconds
ANNCR:	How would you like to save dollars, while serving your family the best in beef, pork, chicken, and lamb? Sounds impossible? Well, it isn't, if you own a home freezer and buy your meats wholesale at Compesi's Meat Locker. Hundreds of families have discovered that it actually costs less to serve prime rib, steaks, and chops than it does to scrimp along on bargain hamburger and tough cuts. The secret? Buy your meat in quantity from Compesi's. Imagine—one hundred pounds of prime beef steaks and roasts for less than $3.00 a pound! Save even more by purchasing a quarter of a side. With every side of beef, Compesi's throws in twenty pounds of chicken, ten pounds of bacon, and a leg of spring lamb—absolutely free! If you don't

own a freezer, Compesi's will get you started in style. Buy any of their 300-pound freezers, and Compesi's will give you a freezer full of frozen food free! Meat, vegetables, even frozen gourmet casseroles, all free with the purchase of a new freezer. Prices for freezers start at $399, and terms can be arranged. Beat the high cost of living! Come into Compesi's and see which plan is best for your family. Compesi's has two locations—in the Lakeport Shopping Center, and downtown at 1338 Fifth Street.

Low-Pitched Voice

IN-HOUSE:	KGO-TV
TITLE:	"3:30 Movie, Creepy Creature Tease"
MUSIC:	"THE DAY TIME ENDED"

ANNCR: (STING ON "NIGHT") Hello. Afraid of those creepy things that go bump in the night? Well, I wouldn't watch Channel 7's *3:30 Movie* because we've got a whole week of creepy creatures.

SFX: LOUD FROG

Monday, it's Ray Milland and his giant (SFX) *Frogs*. (SLIGHT PAUSE) Tuesday, Hank Fonda is all wrapped up in *Tentacles*.

SFX: MALE SCREAM

Wednesday, it's back to those old days, with prehistoric creatures in *The People Time Forgot*.

SFX: ELEPHANT TRUMPET, BACKWARD

Thursday, little gnomes (NOMES) are after a luscious young wife in *Don't Be Afraid of the Dark*. (SFX: WOLF HOWL) Finally, Friday—if you haven't had enough—it's a submarine full of snakes in *Fer-de-Lance*. Creepy Creatures starts Monday on Channel 7's *3:30 Movie*.

SFX: WOLF HOWL

High-Pitched Voice

AGENCY:	Annette Lai Creative Services
CLIENT:	Allison's Pet Center
LENGTH:	60 seconds
MUSIC:	INSTRUMENTAL VERSION OF "RUDOLPH, THE RED-NOSED REINDEER" UP AND UNDER TO CLOSE

ANNCR: (HIGH-PITCHED AND ELFLIKE) Hi! I'm Herman, one of Santa's helpers. Rudolph would have been here, too, but he's getting the light bulb in his nose replaced right now. We're inviting you to Allison's Pet Center for their annual and spectacular Christmas sale! Every year, kids send letters to Santa asking for puppies and kittens, monkeys and mice—and, to top it off, some ask for aquariums, too! Can you imagine what the back of Santa's sleigh looks like? Come on, give Santa a break! I don't want to babysit all those animals and fishes until Christmas Eve—I want to go back to building dollhouses! Come to Allison's and save on household pets and presents for your pets. Get a head start on your Christmas shopping. The sale starts on Saturday and runs through Christmas Eve. Allison's is located at the corner of Fulton and North Streets, in Petaluma. And, a Meow-y Christmas and a Happy New Year from Allison's Pet Center!

British Accent (Oxford)

AGENCY:	Ammirati & Puris, Inc.
CLIENT:	Schweppes Mixers
LENGTH:	60 seconds
SFX:	WINTER SOUNDS (RAIN, SLUSH, ETC.)

BRITISH VO: Leave it to American ingenuity to take a rather bleak time of year and transform it into a season full of quaint but cheerful holiday traditions.

SFX: HOLIDAY MUSIC

And leave it to British ingenuity to impart a rare sparkle to these festivities—Schweppes.

For example, when feasting until immobilized on an oversized bird, Schweppes Club Soda, bursting with Schweppervescence, makes a lively dinner companion. Your ritual of cramming as many people as possible into a department store elevator, meanwhile, inspires a thirst only Schweppes Ginger Ale with real Jamaican ginger can quench. And while transfixed to the telly watching a group of massive, helmeted chaps smash into one another, what could be more civilized than Schweppes Tonic Water with essence of lime and Seville oranges? And while many of your holiday traditions seem quite curious to us, we certainly toast their spirit. And suggest you do the same, with the purchase of Schweppes. The Great British Bubbly.

Regional Accent

This commercial for Egg McMuffin asks for a Southern accent. As you interpret it, avoid going too far into caricature. Your listeners should be entertained by the unique vocabulary and regional allusions, while forming a positive attitude toward the product.

AGENCY:	McDonald & Little Advertising
CLIENT:	McDonald's
PRODUCT:	Egg McMuffin
LENGTH:	60 seconds
TITLE:	"Breakfast Is a Big Thing"
ANNCR:	You know, down in Willacoochee where I hail from, breakfast is a big thing with grits and fried steak of lean and all, but the other day I had a different kind of breakfast. I went to a McDonald's store. It was right after 7 in the morning, and they were cooking breakfast like I never saw. They take this

muffin, it's not like biscuits, I suppose it's what people over in England sop syrup with, cause it's called an English muffin. But they take this foreign muffin and heat it up, and flat dab on it they put a yard egg, and this bacon that's more like ham, but they call it Canadian bacon. And right there on top of all of it they put a piece of cheese. And I'm telling you that it sure is mighty delicious. I never did have breakfast before that you could hold in your hand. But that would be kinda messy with grits.

Transylvanian Accent

AGENCY:	Scott Singer
CLIENT:	Partytime Novelties
LENGTH:	30 seconds

ANNCR: (SCARY MUSIC) (BELA LUGOSI IMITATION) Good evening. You are probably expecting me to say that my name is Count Dracula and that I am a vampire. Do you know what makes a vampire? Do you really? It's not the hair—bah! greasy kid's stuff! It's not the cape, made from your sister's satin bedsheets. No! It's the fangs that make the vampire. Now, you too can have the fangs. Dress up for parties—frighten the trick-or-treaters on Halloween. These plastic marvels fit over your regular teeth, but once there—you'll be the hit of the party. Amaze and delight your ghoul friend. It is so much fun! I know. So, send for your fangs today. Send $2.98 to FANG, Box 1001, Central City, Tennessee. Or dial toll-free: 800-DRA-CULA. Order before midnight tonight. That's an order!

Spanish Pronunciation

AGENCY:	Smith and Steiner, Advertising
CLIENT:	Su Casa
LENGTH:	60 seconds

MUSIC: MEXICAN HARP, UPBEAT TEMPO, IN AND UNDER TO CLOSE

ANNCR: Ole, Amigos! (oh-LAY ah-MEE-gos) Su Casa (soo KAH-sah) means "your home," and that's how Ramona wants you to feel when you visit her at San Antonio's most elegant Mexican restaurant, Su Casa. Ramona features the most popular dishes from Mexico, including enchiladas verdes or rancheros (en-chil-AH-das VEHR-days or rahn-CHAIR-ohs), chile con queso (CHEE-lay kahn KAY-so), and chimichangos (chee-mee-CHANG-gos). But, Ramona also has special family recipes that you won't find anywhere else. Try pescado en concha (pess-KAHD-o en COHN-chah), chunks of sole in rich cream and cheddar cheese sauce, served in scallop shells. Or scallops La Jolla (lah-HOY-uh), prepared with wine, lemon juice, and three kinds of cheeses. Or baked swordfish manzanillo (mahn-zah-NEE-oh). See Ramona today, where her home is your home. Su Casa!

German Accent

The two award-winning commercials that follow feature Dieter (DEET-er), a German imported-car salesman. These commercials were improvised, so the scripts were actually typed after the fact.

AGENCY: Young & Rubicam

CLIENT: Lincoln-Mercury Dealers

LENGTH: 60 seconds

TITLE: "Dieter 5"

DIETER: Pull over and help me, please, my car is . . .

WEAVER: Hi, Dieter.

DIETER: Hello, Mr. Weaver.

WEAVER: Having a little trouble with that fine European sedan, huh?

DIETER: Having a little lunch.

WEAVER: Yeah, the hood's up.

DIETER: Heating my bratwurst on the engine block.

WEAVER: It must be done; it's smoking.

DIETER: It's smoked bratwurst.

WEAVER: Hmm, some kind of hot purple liquid's dripping out of there.

DIETER: Smoked fruit punch.

WEAVER: Uh huh, you know I haven't had any trouble since I traded in that car you sold me for this Mercury Cougar, Dieter.

DIETER: Mercury Cougar, it's a very fine car.

WEAVER: Oh, it's a lovely car, Dieter.

DIETER: Could you give me a ride in the Mercury Cougar to the mechanic?

WEAVER: Oh, I want to give you more than a ride, Dieter. I want to give you a push.

DIETER: I don't want a push.

WEAVER: Get in the car, Dieter.

DIETER: My car is moving.

WEAVER: Turn the flashers on. I want people to see this.

DIETER: Let me get in there.

WEAVER: Clear the way.

DIETER: (LOUDLY OUT THE CAR WINDOW) He's not pushing me; I'm pulling him!

ANNCR: The Mercury Cougar. Compare the performance with luxury European imports. Compare the styling with the luxury European imports. Even before you compare the price.

WEAVER: Okay, Dieter, you're on your own.

DIETER: Wait, this isn't a service station; it's a Lincoln-Mercury dealership.

WEAVER: Think about it, Dieter.

ANNCR: The Mercury Cougar. See your Lincoln-Mercury dealer today, at the sign of the cat.

AGENCY: Young & Rubicam
CLIENT: Lincoln-Mercury Dealers
LENGTH: 30 seconds
TITLE: "Dieter/Law"

DIETER: Mr. Weaver. I have something for you.

WEAVER: What is this, Dieter, a flyer? Are you having a sale?

DIETER: It's a subpoena. I'm suing you.

WEAVER: Suing me? For what?

DIETER: I'm no longer just Dieter Eidotter, car salesman. You're dealing with Dieter Eidotter, third-week law student.

WEAVER: What is this? "Defamation of car"?

DIETER: You told people that Mercury Cougar was better looking than the car I sell.

WEAVER: It's a fact.

DIETER: It's an opinion.

WEAVER: "Alienation of affection?"

DIETER: Well, the people who found out that the Mercury Cougar costs one-half as much as the car I sell don't come into the showroom anymore.

WEAVER: You're blowing more smoke than one of those diesels you sell.

DIETER: Oh, now you're into the murky legal area of libel, and slander, and torts.

WEAVER: What's a tort?

DIETER: Well, right now, it's a chocolate cake. But when I find out what it is . . .

WEAVER: You're not even a real lawyer. I don't have to put up with this. Here is what I think of this thing, right back at you!

DIETER: This could be second-degree littering, Mister.

ANNCR: The Mercury advantage. Compared to the imports, Mercury gives you more style, more features, more for your money. See your Lincoln-Mercury dealer.

Public-Service Announcements (PSAs)

The campaign "Child Abuse" was created by advertising agencies as a pro bono contribution to the National Committee to Prevent Child Abuse. This and many other PSA campaigns are coordinated, produced, and distributed by the Advertising Council, a private, nonprofit organization of volunteers. Since 1942, the Ad Council has been the leading producer of public-service advertising in the United States. In 1996, it generated more than $700 million worth of free advertising time.

The Advertising Council, Inc.
CHILD ABUSE PREVENTION CAMPAIGN
For: National Committee to Prevent Child Abuse
:30 LIVE RADIO COPY—"Before It Starts"

For years, child abuse has been a problem to which there were few answers. But now, there's an innovative new program that can help stop the abuse before it starts. A program that reaches new parents early on, teaching them to cope with the stresses that lead to abuse. It's already achieving unprecedented results. To learn how you can help where you live, call 1-800-CHILDREN. Because the more you help, the less they hurt. Call 1-800-CHILDREN today. A public-service message from the National Committee to Prevent Child Abuse and the Ad Council.

CHILD ABUSE PREVENTION CAMPAIGN

"TESTIMONY":	30 MUSIC UNDER ENTIRE SPOT
WOMAN:	I first met Jane right after Jonah was born.
ANNCR:	Now there's a revolutionary new approach to stopping child abuse before it can start.
WOMAN:	She said it was normal for new mothers to get frustrated. She taught me when to take a minute for myself.
ANNCR:	By reaching new families early on, this program teaches them how to cope with the stresses that lead to abuse. But we need your help where you live. Call 1-800-CHILDREN, 1-800-CHILDREN. A public-service announcement brought to you by the National Committee to Prevent Child Abuse and the Ad Council.

CLIENT:	The Boys and Girls Clubs of Jackson
LENGTH:	30 seconds (Children's spot #2)
BY:	Karen Fremont, Joseph Travis
SFX:	A HIP-HOP BEAT—UP AND UNDER
ANNCR:	(KID'S VOICE): Can you hear that beat? I made it at the recording studio at the Boys and Girls Club. They have an awesome studio and a lot of other stuff too, like digital photography, filmmaking, and theater projects. They also have cool art programs with drawing, mural painting, and printmaking. I can make all kinds of things at the Boys and Girls Club that I can't do at home, and it's a lot more fun than just hanging out watching TV after school. It's only five dollars to be a member, and it'll get your parents off your case for sure. Check out their website at bgcj.org. My friends and I did, why don't you?
ANNCR:	(WOMAN'S VOICE): The Boys and Girls Clubs of Jackson. A positive place for kids.

CLIENT:	Dance Palace Community Center
LENGTH:	30 seconds
BY:	Gregory DeMascio
SFX:	TRUMPET FANFARE. THE SOUND OF A PARADE APPROACHING
WOMAN:	What a beautiful day in downtown Point Reyes!
MAN:	It's the Dance Palace Parade!
MUSIC:	BOB WILLS, WESTERN SWING
WOMAN:	The costumes of the Western dance class are so lovely!
MUSIC:	JAPANESE FLUTE AND TEMPLE BELLS
MAN:	Wow! The yoga class is stretching in formation.
SFX:	EXCITED CHILDREN'S VOICES. DRIBBLING BASKETBALLS
WOMAN:	The after-school kid's group is weaving in and out of the CPR class!
MAN:	It's amazing what you can do at the Dance Palace.
WOMAN:	And it's easy to join. For information, call 663-1075.
MAN:	or visit their website, www.dancepalace.org.
SFX:	FADE UP PARADE SOUNDS. HOLD BRIEFLY, AND SLOWLY FADE OUT

CLIENT:	Dance Palace Community Center
LENGTH:	20 seconds
BY:	Gregory DeMascio
SFX:	THE ECHO OF FOOTSTEPS IN A LARGE, EMPTY BUILDING, WALKING TOWARD US. THEY STOP
ANNCR:	(FLAT VOICE, WITH ECHO) A building is nothing but a hollow, lifeless shell.

SFX: THE ECHO OF FOOTSTEPS WALKING AWAY, (CROSS FADE TO) PARTY SOUNDS. MURMURING VOICES. CHILDREN PLAYING. LAUGHTER. MUSIC (UNDER FOR)

ANNCR: (WARM VOICE) Until it's filled with people like you.

ANNCR: (SFX OUT) Join the Dance Palace Community Center. For information, call 663-1075. See you there.

CLIENT: Amigos de las Americas
LENGTH: 60 seconds

ANNCR: Are you a teenager, 16 years or older? Are you looking for the adventure of a lifetime? Why not check out Amigos de las Americas? Amigos is a non-profit organization with chapters in cities all over America. Amigos spend the school year studying Spanish and paramedic work and spend the summer working in a Latin American country. What do Amigos do? Well, last year Amigos administered over 230,000 dental treatments to 60,000 children. They gave over 90,000 immunizations for polio and other diseases. And, they tested over 22,000 people for tuberculosis. Amigos work in rural areas and big city slums. They are not on vacation. Assignments in Panama, Ecuador, Paraguay, and the Dominican Republic, among others, call for dedicated, caring young people. If you think Amigos is for you, write for information. The address is: 5618 Star Lane, Houston, Texas 77057. Or use the toll-free number: 1-800-555-7796. Amigos!

Television Commercials

Only a handful of television commercials is provided here. Nearly all television commercials, whether produced by large advertising agencies or small-market stations, require special effects, animation, or elaborate sets, which generally are unavailable to students. Computerized digital-effects equipment manipulates images in a number of dazzling ways, and announcers, aside from those in dramatized sketches, are limited most often to voice-over delivery. In many commercials, an announcer may be seen briefly at the outset, and then perform as an unseen voice-over narrator. To practice television commercial delivery, you may want to adapt some of the radio commercials for direct, on-camera presentation.

AGENCY:	Kim & Sons
PRODUCT:	Street Beat
BY:	Andrew Kim
LENGTH:	60 seconds
CAMERA 1: MCU	ARE YOU TIRED OF THE SAME OLD HIP-HOP TV SHOWS, PLAYING THE SAME OLD MUSIC VIDEOS DAY AFTER DAY? ARE YOU FED UP WITH MAINSTREAM RAP SNEAKING IN TO TAKE OVER OUR RADIOS AND TV STATIONS? DO YOU WISH THERE'D BE A SHOW THAT PLAYS ALL TYPES OF HIP-HOP?
CAMERA 2: CU	WELL, YOUR WISHES AND DREAMS HAVE FINALLY BEEN ANSWERED. *STREET BEAT*, A NEW AND FLAVORFUL HIP-HOP TV SHOW, HAS BEEN HATCHED TO EXPOSE ALL TYPES OF HIP-HOP TO THE PHOENIX AREA. *STREET BEAT* SOCKS OUT EVERY SUNDAY EVENING AT MIDNIGHT ON THE NEW TV 8, OR CHANNEL 43 FOR OUR CABLE USERS.
CAMERA 1: 3/4 SHOT	FROM OLD SCHOOL, TO BACKPACKER, TO HYPHY, AND TO MAINSTREAM, *STREET BEAT* BLASTS OUT ALL THESE INNOVATIVE TYPES OF HIP-HOP MUSIC. *STREET BEAT* REACHES OUT TO THE GREATER PHOENIX AREA. SO DON'T BE SURPRISED WHEN YOU SEE THE CAST HITTING THE STREETS, CONCERTS, AND PARTIES TO FIND OUT WHAT YOU THINK ABOUT THE MANY PRESENT-DAY HIP-HOP ISSUES.
CAMERA:	SUNDAYS AT MIDNIGHT ON THE NEW CHANNEL 8. REAL HIP-HOP FOR REAL HIP-HOP HEADS. PEACE.

NOTE: Although written for radio, the AP/PM spot could easily be converted to televison, with great opportunities for some good acting!

BY:	Eric Poole, Splash Radio
CLIENT:	Kresser Stein Robaire
PRODUCT:	AM/PM Mini-Markets
TITLE:	"All Out"
SFX:	STORE AMBIENCE
GUY:	Hi, welcome to AM/PM.
MAN:	Thanks. I heard about your new Rib-B-Q sandwich . . .
GUY:	Yeah, flame-broiled pork smothered in spicy barbeque sauce on a sesame seed bun . . .
MAN:	With toppings you can add *yourself* . . .
BOTH:	(TOGETHER) For just 99 cents . . .
MAN:	And I'd like one, please.
GUY:	(FLATLY, DEFINITIVELY) We're all out.
MAN:	You're all out?
GUY:	Yep. Nada. Zip. Zero.
MAN:	But they're only here for a limited time.
GUY:	I'm really sorry.
MAN:	(DISAPPOINTED) Okay, well, thanks anyway.
SFX:	FOOTSTEPS AWAY, THEN SUDDENLY STOP
MAN:	Hey, what was that?
GUY:	(MOUTH FULL) What?
MAN:	I saw you take a bite of something.

GUY: (DEFENSIVELY, MOUTH STILL FULL) It was nothing.

MAN: (SUSPICIOUS) You sure? It looked like a big sandwich.

GUY: Positive.

MAN: Well, okay.

SFX: TWO OR THREE FOOTSTEPS, THEN STOP SUDDENLY

MAN: There! You did it again!

GUY: (MOUTH FULL AGAIN, DEFENSIVE) What?

MAN: You took another bite. You've got a Rib-B-Q sandwich back there, haven't you?

SFX: (BARELY ABLE TO GET THE WORDS OUT) No, I swear!

MAN: We'll see about that. There's the manager. Excuse me, sir . . .

SFX: FOOTSTEPS

BOSS: (CHEWING, MOUTH STUFFED) Yes?

MAN: (HE REALIZES THEY'RE ALL IN ON IT) Oh, for crying out loud . . . I . . .

ANNCR: Introducing AM/PM's mouth-watering new Rib-B-Q sandwich . . . just 99 cents, with toppings you can add yourself. But you'd better hurry . . . before the employees get 'em all.

BOSS: (MOUTH FULL) Anybody got a napkin?

ANNCR: At participating AM/PM's for a limited time. Price is suggested, actual prices may vary. Fill up for less at AM/PM.

AGENCY:	Backer & Spielvogel, Inc.
CLIENT:	Quaker
PRODUCT:	Celeste Pizza
LENGTH:	30 seconds

SUPER: Guiseppe Celeste (Fictitious Little Brother)

GUISEPPE: I need your help. My big sister, Mama Celeste, she make a great crust for her pizza. But was Guiseppe's idea. I say, "Mama, you make perfect sauce, perfect toppings, make a perfect crust." *She* do it. But *I* think it. So my picture should be on the box, too, no? Which you like? (HOLDS UP PICTURES) Happy—"Hey, I think of great crust!"? Or serious—"Yes, I think of great crust"? Or it could be bigger? (HOLDS UP HUGE PICTURE)

ANNCR VO: Celeste Pizza. Delicious crust makes it great from top to bottom.

AGENCY: In-house
CLIENT: Madera Foods
LENGTH: 60 seconds

VIDEO	AUDIO
OPEN ON ANNCR STANDING BEFORE CHECKOUT STAND.	**ANNCR:** I'm here at Madera Foods checking up on the specials you'll find here this weekend.
CUT TO PRODUCE SECTION. ANNCR WALKS INTO FRAME. ANNCR PICKS UP A GRAPEFRUIT.	There are excellent buys in fresh fruits and vegetables. Like extra fancy Indian River ruby red grapefruit, three for ninety-nine cents.
ANNCR POINTS TO LETTUCE.	Or iceberg lettuce for seventy-nine cents. And, don't overlook the relishes—green onions or radishes, two bunches for eighty-nine cents.
CUT TO MEAT DEPARTMENT. ANNCR WALKS INTO FRAME.	Meat specials include rib roast at three-sixty nine a pound, all lean center-cut pork chops at two seventy-nine a pound, and lean ground chuck at only one ninety-nine a pound.

CUT BACK TO CHECKOUT STAND.	And, here I am, back at the checkout stand. Here's where you'll really come to appreciate Madera Foods. Their low, low prices add up to a total bill that winds down the cost of living. So, pay a visit to Madera Foods this weekend. Specials are offered from Friday opening to closing on Sunday night. Madera Foods is located in the Madera Plaza Shopping Center.
CUT TO ANNCR OUTSIDE FRONT ENTRANCE.	
DISS TO MADERA FOODS LOGO.	Hours are from 9:00 a.m. 'till 10:00 p.m., seven days a week.
SLIDE. HOLD UNTIL CLOSE.	See you at Madera Foods.

AGENCY: Sherman Associates, Inc.
CLIENT: Bayview Health Club
LENGTH: 60 seconds

VIDEO	AUDIO
OPEN ON MCU OF TALENT.	Get ready! Swimsuit season is almost here! Now's the time to shed those excess pounds and achieve the body you know is hidden somewhere within you.
ZOOM OUT TO MEDIUM SHOT.	The Bayview Health Club will help you find the possible you. Bayview is a complete fitness club.
CUT TO STILL PHOTOS OF EACH FEATURE AS IT IS MENTIONED.	We offer day and evening classes in weight training, aerobic and jazzercise dance, full Nautilus equipment, tanning, Jacuzzi, and sauna facilities.

CUT TO MCU OF TALENT.	In addition, we sponsor weight-reduction clinics, jogging and running programs, and health and beauty seminars, with a supportive staff to coach you in every facet of personal health care. Bayview is tailored for you—the modern man or woman—and, for this month only, we're offering new members an introductory price to join: Just half price! That's right, a 50 percent reduction during the month of April.
CUT TO MCU OF TALENT.	So, call now for a tour of our facilities. Meet the staff, and chat with satisfied members. Bayview Health Club, in downtown Portland. Join now. Don't lose time—instead, lose that waist, with a 50 percent reduction in membership costs.
MATTE IN ADDRESS AND PHONE NUMBER.	Find the hidden you, and be ready for the beach! Bayview Health Club: we're ready when you are!

And, here's a public-service announcement for television.

CLIENT: Boys and Girls Clubs of Jackson	
BY: Joseph Travis, Karen Fremont	

VIDEO	**AUDIO**
MONTAGE OF STREET SCENES	**SFX:** SOUNDS OF LOUD URBAN STREET, CARS, TRUCKS: AND HORNS, KIDS YELLING

	ANNCR: Ever wondered what all those kids do after school? Many of them end up here, on the streets of Jackson, where they face serious conflicts as they struggle to hold their own.
MONTAGE: VOLUNTEERS WITH KIDS.	There's a place for these kids, the Boys and Girls Clubs of Jackson. **SFX:** CROSSFADE STREET SOUND WITH SONG "GREATEST LOVE OF ALL" **ANNCR:** The Boys and Girls Clubs offers a better way to spend after-school hours.
KIDS PLAYING BASKETBALL.	Your help is always needed. Just a little help from you will give kids opportunities to explore who they are.
STAFF AND KIDS MAKING MUSIC.	You can volunteer to work with kids one-on-one or make a donation. For more information log on to bgcj.org or call 334-2852.
DANCE CLASS, DISS TO KIDS TAKING PICTURES.	Children are our only hope for a better world, and with your help, we like to think that anything's possible.
KIDS HUGGING VOLUNTEERS.	The Boys and Girls Clubs of Jackson, a positive place for kids.

Appendix B

Phonetic Transcription

As an announcer, you face unique and challenging problems in pronunciation. In reading news and commercials, you'll frequently encounter words of foreign origin, and you'll be expected to read them fluently and correctly. As a newscaster, you'll be expected not only to pronounce foreign words and names with accuracy and authority but also to know when and how to Americanize many of them. Although British announcers are allowed to Anglicize categorically, you would be seen as odd or incompetent if you said *don KWIKS-oat* for *Don Quixote* or *don JEW-un* for *Don Juan,* as they do.

Because English pronunciation is subject to few general rules, English is one of the most difficult languages to learn. In Spanish the letters *ch* are always pronounced as in the name *Charles;* in American English *ch* may be pronounced in the following ways:

sh as in *Cheyenne*

tch as in *champion*

k as in *chemist*

two separate sounds, as in the name *MacHeath*

There are many other examples. In the sentence "I usually used to find this useful," the letter *s* is sounded differently in the words *usually, used,* and *useful.* The letter *a* is pronounced differently in the words *cap, father, mate, care, call, boat,* and *about.* Similar variations are seen for all other vowel sounds and most consonants as well. For example, *th* is pronounced differently in *Thomas, thought,* and *then; r* is pronounced differently in *run, fire,* and *boor.* Letters may at times be silent, as in *mnemonic, Worcester,* and *Wednesday.* At other times, and for no logical reason, a word is pronounced correctly only when all letters in it receive some value, as in *misunderstood* and *circumstances.* The letters *ie* are sometimes pronounced *eye,* as in *pie,* and sometimes *ee,* as in *piece.* Two words with almost identical spellings, such as *said* and *maid,* can have quite different pronunciations. In short, the only constant in spoken American English is variation.

The whole problem of English pronunciation was reduced to its most obvious absurdity by George Bernard Shaw, who wrote *ghoti* and asked how this manufactured word was to be pronounced. After all attempts had failed, Shaw revealed that it was to be pronounced *fish*: the *gh* to be pronounced *f* as in *enough,* the *o* to be pronounced *ih* as in *women,* and the *ti* to be pronounced *sh* as in *motion.*

Of course, common words don't cause pronunciation problems. But try to determine the correct pronunciation of the following words—some quite familiar, others less so—according to your knowledge of language and any rules of pronunciation you may have learned:

quay	flaccid
dais	mortgage
interstices	gunwale

medieval   forecastle

brooch   egregious

cliché   phthisic

Now look up the correct pronunciation of these words in any standard dictionary. After checking the pronunciation, you'll agree that no amount of puzzling over them, and no rules of pronunciation, would have helped.

Correct American and Canadian pronunciation of English not only is inherently illogical but also changes with time and common usage, generally tending toward simpler forms. It is becoming more and more acceptable, for example, to pronounce *clothes* as *kloz*, to leave the first *r* out of *February,* and to slide over the slight *y* sound in *news* so that it becomes *nooz.*

If you have difficulty pronouncing words whose spelling offers little help, you may be doubly perplexed by American personal names and place names derived from foreign originals. As a sportscaster, for example, you can't assume that a player named Braun gives his own name the correct German pronunciation, *Brown,* because he may pronounce it *Brawn* or *Brahn.* If, as a sportscaster, you tried to pronounce every foreign-derived name as it would be pronounced in the country of origin, your audience would wince every time you failed to use the established pronunciation.

American place names present the same problem. In Nebraska, *Beatrice* is pronounced *bee-AT-riss.* In South Dakota, *Pierre* is pronounced *PEER.* In California, *Delano* is pronounced *duh-LAY-no.* In Kentucky, *Versailles* is pronounced *ver-SALES.* In Georgia, *Vienna* is pronounced *vy-EN-uh.* In the Southwest, Spanish place names are pronounced conventionally neither as the Spanish original nor as they seem to be spelled. For example, in California, the *San* in *San Jose* is pronounced as in *sand* rather than as Spanish speakers would pronounce it (as in *sonnet*), and *ho-ZAY* is used rather than the Americanized *jo-ZAY* or the Spanish *ho-SAY.*

Because the only standard for pronouncing place names is the common practice of the natives of the region, you must be on guard to avoid error. All American and Canadian communities have special and capricious ways of pronouncing the names of streets, suburbs, nearby towns, and geographic landmarks. Radio and television announcers who are new to an area and offend listeners consistently with mispronunciations may not be around long enough to learn regional preferences. Los Angelenos pronounce *Cahuenga* as *kuh-WENG-uh,* and in San Francisco, *Gough* Street is pronounced *GOFF.* In Arkansas, *Nevada* County is pronounced *nuh-VAY-duh.* In Georgia, *Taliaferro* County is pronounced *TAHL-uh-ver.* Bostonians may not care if you mispronounce *Pago Pago* (correctly pronounced *PAHNG-go PAHNG-go*), but they will be annoyed if you pronounce *Quincy* as *KWIN-see* rather than *KWINZ-ee.*

It's not surprising that the problems inherent in the pronunciation of American English have given rise to various systems of phonetic transcription. Two of these systems are outlined here, and the third—the International Phonetic Alphabet—is discussed at length.

Wire-Service Phonetics

Several news agencies provide radio and television stations with news stories, sending the stories via satellite and telephone lines to computer terminals. When a word or a name that might cause pronunciation problems is transmitted, that word often is phoneticized—given a pronouncer—as in the following example:

> **(Sydney, Australia)** The island nation of Vanuatu (Vahn-oo-AH-too)—formerly New Herbrides (HEB-rih-deez)—was hit today by a strong earthquake.

Pronouncers are useful, but you shouldn't rely on them completely. They're sometimes ambiguous and occasionally inaccurate. A few sounds defy accurate transcription. Wherever possible, check pronunciations in dictionaries, atlases, or other appropriate sources.

All of the symbols of wire-service phonetics appear in Table B-1, arranged in the same order in which they appear in the International Phonetic Alphabet. (Because we're dealing with speech sounds, alphabetic arrangement has no relevance.) Key words have been chosen for clarity; therefore, most are commonplace. Two symbols are sometimes given for a single sound. For example, the second vowel sound listed, *I*, works well for the word *impel*, but *IH* works better for *bituminous*. If this word were transcribed as *bi-TOO-muh-nus* instead of *bih-TOO-muh-nus*, a reader might pronounce the first syllable as the English word *by*.

With a little practice—and some ingenuity—you can make wire-service phonetics into a useful tool. The consonants are easiest to learn because most of them represent only one sound; the symbols *T, D, S, Z,* and *M,* for instance, can hardly cause confusion. Other consonant sounds need two letters to represent them: for example, *TH* (THIN), *CH* (CHAT), and *SH* (SHOP). One symbol, *Y,* is used for two sounds, one a consonant and the other a diphthong. As a consonant, it appears in the word *yeoman* (YO-mun); as a diphthong, it represents an entirely different sound, as in *sleight* (SLYT). The symbol TH is the most troublesome, for it represents the initial sounds in *think* and *then.* Context can help in some instances but not all. It works for *hearth* (HAHRTH), but not *calisthenics.* Anyone seeing KAL-is-THEN-iks might read THEN as the common English word, and this is not the correct sound.

Some vowel sounds are a bit troublesome, but they can be differentiated usually by their contexts. The letters *OO,* for example, stand for vowel sounds in *food* and *poor,* which are not, of course, the same. Here is how context can help distinguish between them:

> buoy (BOO-ee)   boorish (BOOR-ish)

In these examples, the words *boo* and *boor* tell which sound to give *OO.*

TABLE B-1 Symbols of Wire-Service Phonetics

Symbol	Key Word	Phonetic Transcription
Vowels		
EE	*believe*	(bih-LEEV)
I or IH	*impel, bituminous*	(im-PELL), (bih-TOO-muhn-us)
AY	*bait*	(BAYT)
E or EH	*pester, beret*	(PEST-er), (beh-RAY)
A	*can*	(KAN)
AH	*comma*	(KAH-muh)
AW	*lost*	(LAWST)
O	*host*	(HOST)
OO	*Moorhead*	(MOOR-hed)
OO	*pool*	(POOL)
ER	*early*	(ER-lee)
UH	*sofa*	(SO-fuh)
Diphthongs		
Y	*lighting*	(LYT-ing)
AU	*grouse*	(GRAUSS)
OY	*oiling*	(OY-ling)
YU	*using*	(YUZ-ing)
Consonants *		
TH	*think*	(THINGK)
TH	*then*	(THEN)
SH	*clash*	(KLASH)
ZH	*measure*	(MEZH-er)
CH	*church*	(CHERCH)
J	*adjust*	(uh-JUST)
NG	*singing*	(SING-ing)
Y	*yeoman*	(YO-mun)

*The consonants *P, B, T, D, K, G, F, V, S, Z, H, M, N, L, W,* and *R* are pronounced as in English and therefore are not listed. The symbol *G* is always as in *green*, never as in *gene*.

It isn't for common words that wire-service phonetics were developed. Here are some typical words that might be given pronouncers by a wire service:

Beirut (bay-ROOT)   Sidon (SYD-un)

Bayreuth (BY-royt)   Coelho (KWAY-lo)

Clio (KLY-oh)   Ojai (O-hy)

TABLE B-2 Sources for Correct Pronunciation of Personal Names and Place Names

Category	Source
Names of persons	The individual featured in the story; failing that, members of the family or associates
Foreign names	Appropriate embassy or consulate
Foreign place names	*American Heritage Dictionary*
State or regional place names	State or regional historical societies or the state police or highway patrol
Names of members of legislatures	Clerk of the legislature

Schuylkill (SKUHL-kill)   Yosemite (yo-SEM-ih-tee)

Faneuil (FAN-uhl)   Hamtramck (ham-TRAM-ik)

Obviously, your use of such phonetic transcription will be reserved for the few names and words in your copy that require you to turn to a dictionary, gazetteer, or similar reference work. Table B-2 offers suggested sources for correct pronunciations in several different problem categories.

At times you'll have to read a news story for which no pronouncers are given. When time permits, you should look up difficult or unfamiliar words in a dictionary and do your own transcribing of them, as in this example—done easily and quickly on a word processor:

(**Nashville, Tennessee**) Medical researchers today revealed a study showing that as few as two cups of coffee can cut the blood flow to your brain by 10 to 20 percent. Dr. William Wilson, assistant professor of psychiatry at Vanderbilt University, and coauthor of the study, said: "While the blood-flow reduction does not seem severe enough to cause problems in normal individuals, it is unclear whether it may increase the risk of transient ischemic (iz-KEE-mik) attacks and cerebral infarctions (seh-REE-bruhl in-FAHRK-shunz) in high-risk individuals or those recovering from cerebrovascular (seh-REE-bro-VAS-kyu-ler) accidents."

Wire-service phonetics work well in this example, but there are times when the system will not work. There is simply no foolproof way to use the twenty-six letters of the English language to represent more than forty speech sounds. Furthermore, the wire-service system doesn't include symbols for most foreign speech sounds that don't occur in English. In the past, teletype machines were limited to the same symbols found on an ordinary typewriter. Today's computers, however, could be programmed to reproduce any symbol desired, so the time may come when additional pronunciation symbols will be added to the twenty-six letters now in use.

A good starting point would be to add these symbols from the International Phonetic Alphabet:

[ð] for the initial sound in *then*

[ʊ] for the vowel sound in *good*

[ə] for the unstressed vowel sound in *above*

Diacritical Marks

Dictionaries use a system of phonetic transcription that features small marks placed above the vowels *a, e, i, o,* and *u,* along with a few additional symbols for sounds such as *th* in *thin* and *zh* in *vision.* The *American Heritage Dictionary* uses these symbols:

ă	pat	ā	pay	âr	care	ä	father	oi	boy
ĕ	pet	ē	be					ou	out
ĭ	pit	ī	pie	îr	pier			hw	which
ŏ	pot	ō	toe	ô	paw				
ŏŏ	took	ōō	boot						
th	thin	*th*	this						
ŭ	cut	ûr	urge						
zh	vision								
ə	about								

Diacritical marks are not completely standardized; there are variations from dictionary to dictionary. The *American Heritage Dictionary* uses seventeen symbols to indicate the vowel sounds of the English language. *Webster's Collegiate Dictionary,* on the other hand, uses more than twenty. If you decide to use diacritical marks to indicate correct pronunciation on your scripts, it's important to adopt one system of marks and stick with it. Going from one dictionary system to another could be very confusing.

The system of phonetic transcription used in dictionaries has at least three important limitations. First, diacritical marks are rather difficult to learn and to remember. The publishers of most English-language dictionaries recognize this fact and place a guide to pronunciation on pages throughout the book. A second disadvantage is that diacritical marks were not designed for use by oral readers. The marks are small and vary only slightly in their configurations. When accuracy under pressure is demanded, diacritical marks often fail to meet the test. A final limitation of the method of transcription used in dictionaries is that the key words used may vary in pronunciation from area to area. To learn that *fog* is pronounced as *dog* may tell some Texans that *fawg* rhymes with *dawg* and a Rhode Islander that *fahg* rhymes with *dahg.*

Some modern dictionary publishers have developed rather sophisticated pronunciation guides. They have eliminated some ambiguity through the use of more standardized key words. Fairly extensive discussions of pronunciation, symbols to indicate foreign speech sounds not heard in the English language, and a few symbols from more sophisticated systems of phonetic transcription have been added.

The International Phonetic Alphabet

The International Phonetic Alphabet (IPA) was devised to overcome the ambiguities of earlier systems of speech transcription. Like any other system that attempts to transcribe sounds into written symbols, it is not totally accurate. It does, however, come closer to perfection than any other system. Like diacritics, the IPA uses key words to indicate pronunciation, so if you speak with a regional accent (other than so-called standard broadcast speech), you may have difficulty making the IPA work for you.

The International Phonetic Association assigned individual written symbols to all speech sounds of the major languages of the world. Whether the language is French, German, or English, the symbol [e] is always pronounced *ay* as in *bait*. Speech sounds not found in English have distinct symbols: For example, [x] represents the sound *ch* in the German word *ach*, and [y] represents the sound *u* in the French word *lune*.

The IPA is not difficult to learn, but few professional announcers use it or have even heard of it. Most broadcast announcers get by with wire-service phonetics or diacritics, but those who want to excel in certain areas of news or sports announcing (international coverage) should learn and continue to practice with the IPA. Announcers at the Winter Olympics in Lillehammer, Norway, for example, were asked to pronounce the names of competitors from a great many nations, including Wang Xlulan of China, Ivar Michal Ulekleiv of Norway, Bernhard Gstrein of Austria, Mitja Kunc of Slovenia, and Eva Twardokens of the United States. It is unlikely that any announcer present knew the rules of pronunciation for all languages represented, so a good ear and an efficient system of phonetic transcription were necessities. The need for an effective system of transcription is also important for classical music announcers.

This appendix presents a detailed exposition of the IPA. With the help of the IPA, you can learn the principles of French, German, Spanish, and Italian pronunciation. The Appendix on Foreign Pronunciation can be found on the accompanying CD.

The IPA is a system for encoding the correct pronunciation of problem words, allowing efficient and accurate retrieval. The IPA may seem formidable at first, but it's actually easier to learn than the system of diacritical markings used in dictionaries. You'll find many uses for the IPA, and if you intend to enter the field of broadcast performance, you should make a sincere effort to learn it. Because spoken language is the communication medium used by announcers, mastery of any aspect of human speech will benefit your work.

Although it is true, as noted, that a small number of professional announcers use the IPA, all would benefit from knowing and using it. Those who do not know the IPA usually use wire-service phonetics, adding symbols of their own as necessity demands. Such a system can handle most of the pronunciation problems that arise in a day's work, but it fails often enough to warrant being replaced by a more refined and accurate system.

The IPA has several advantages:

- It's an unvarying system of transcription in which one symbol represents only one speech sound.
- Every sound in any language, however subtle it may be, is given a distinctive symbol.
- Once the correct pronunciation of each sound is learned, there's almost no possibility of error because of regional dialect.
- The IPA is the most nearly perfect system of describing human speech sounds yet devised.

The IPA is used by music departments to teach lyric diction, both for English and foreign languages; speech departments use the IPA to teach dialects. Unfortunately, the IPA is seldom taught to those intending to become broadcast announcers, even though a knowledge of the IPA could spare announcers many embarrassing moments.

The *NBC Handbook of Pronunciation* (New York: HarperCollins, 1991) transcribes names of persons and places using IPA symbols. Many foreign language dictionaries and texts use the IPA to indicate correct pronunciation. *A Pronouncing Dictionary of American English,* by John S. Kenyon and Thomas Knott (Springfield, Mass.: G. & C. Merriam, 1953), transcribes exclusively into the symbols of the IPA. Both it and the *NBC Handbook of Pronunciation* are excellent sources of correct pronunciation of American and foreign place names and the names of famous composers, authors, artists, scientists, and political figures.

As is true of any system that connects speech sounds to symbols, the IPA defines each sound in terms of its use in a particular word. For example, the sound of the IPA symbol [i] is pronounced like the vowel sound of the word *bee.* This poses no problem in instances in which the key word is pronounced uniformly throughout the United States and Canada, but a distinct problem arises when there are regional variations in the pronunciation of a key word.

In learning the IPA, keep in mind that the speech sounds and the key words used in describing them are as in "Standard American" or "standard broadcast" speech. As stated in Chapter 4, deviations from this style of speaking are not substandard *unless* speech sounds are so distorted as to make comprehension a problem. While this chapter does not put forth "Standard American" as the only or best way to pronounce American English, it's necessary to use it to teach the IPA system of transcription. The system developed by the International Phonetic Association is based on speech sounds as formed by those who speak "what is vaguely called standard speech" (Kenyon and Knott, in *A Pronouncing Dictionary of American English*). The authors make it clear that "standard speech" is that spoken by most network announcers. If you live in a region of the United States or Canada where Standard American is not spoken, you may experience some difficulty in learning the IPA symbols. If, for example, you live in the southeastern United States, and you pronounce the word *bait* as most Americans pronounce *bite*, then the key words used to explain the IPA may confuse you.

Use of the IPA will be reserved for the occasional word in your copy with which you're unfamiliar. After determining pronunciation by referring to a source—one suggested in Table B-2, or by other means that work for you—you can render it into IPA symbols directly above the unfamiliar word in your script. With practice, you should be able to read your script, problem word and all, with little chance of stumbling.

Here's an illustration of how this appears on a script:

['kɪmbḷtən]

The mayor of the small North Carolina town of Kimbolton said today that he is skeptical about reports of flying saucers above his community.

A glance at *A Pronouncing Dictionary of American English* shows that Kimbolton is pronounced *Kim-BOLT-un* [kimˈboltṇ] in the Ohio community of that name, but in the town of the same name in North Carolina it is pronounced *KIM-bul-tun* [ˈkɪmbḷtən]. The correct pronunciation of the name of a town may seem of slight importance to some, but to a professional announcer it's a matter of pride to be as accurate as time and resources permit.

IPA symbols represent vowel sounds, diphthongs or glides, and consonants. This appendix covers only the sounds in American speech.

Remember that the IPA is used to transcribe *sounds*. Pronounce the word as you transcribe it, breaking it down into its component sounds. In transcribing the word *broken*, for example, say to yourself the first sound, *b*, then add the second, making *br*, then the third, forming *bro*, and so on. Because one sound in a word may condition the sound that precedes or follows it, you should use an additive system, rather than one that isolates each sound from all others. Note, however, that this advice is meant for those in the early stages of learning to use the IPA. With practice and growing proficiency, you'll be able to transcribe almost without conscious effort.

Vowel Sounds

Vowel sounds are classified as front vowels and back vowels, depending on where they are formed in the mouth. The front vowels are produced through vibrations of the vocal folds in the throat and are articulated by the tongue and teeth near the front of the mouth. The back vowels are produced in the same manner but are articulated by the tongue and the opening in the rear of the mouth.

The Front Vowels. The front vowels are summarized in Table B-3. Note that [a] is pronounced *aah*, as in the word *bath* as pronounced in parts of the northeastern United States. This sound is not usually heard in Standard American Speech, but the symbol must be learned because it is a part of two diphthongs to be considered later.

If you pronounce each of these key words in turn, beginning at the top of the table and running to the bottom, you will find your mouth opening wider as you move from one sound to the next. As your mouth opens, your tongue is lowered and becomes increasingly relaxed.

The two front vowels [i] and [ɪ] require some elaboration. If you look in some American dictionaries, you may be surprised to discover that the final sounds of words such as *busy* and *worry* are given the pronunciation [ɪ], as in *ill*. Now there can be no doubt that in Standard American, as well as in the speech of most other sections of the country, these words have a distinct *ee* sound. Kenyon and Knott, in *A Pronouncing Dictionary of American English,* take note of this fact but indicate that minor variations in the pronunciation of this sound are too complex to pin down. Like many other American dictionaries, Kenyon and Knott's work uses the symbol [ɪ] for words in which the sound may actually be either [ɪ] or [i]. Thus they arrive at the pronunciation [ˈsɪtɪ] (SIH-tih) for *city.* Though it is doubtful that many Americans actually pronounce the word in this manner, most Americans do pronounce the final sound in the word somewhere between a distinct [ɪ] and a distinct [i].

It's worth repeating at this point that the essential purpose of the IPA is to help you transcribe words whose pronunciation may be unknown to you. The examples used here and throughout this chapter are included to make the IPA clearer to you, not because of any assumption that you actually have problems pronouncing words such as *busy* or *city.*

TABLE B-3 IPA Symbols for the Front Vowels

Vowel Sound	IPA Symbol	Key Word	IPA Transcription of Key Word
"ee"	[i]	*beet*	[bit]
"ih"	[I]	*bit*	[bɪt]
"ay"	[e]	*bait*	[bet]
"eh"	[ɛ]	*bet*	[bɛt]
"ah"	[æ]	*bat*	[bæt]
"aah"	[a]	*bath*	[baɵ]*

*Eastern United States and British pronunciation only.

TABLE B-4 IPA Symbols for the Back Vowels

Vowel Sound	IPA Symbol	Key Word	IPA Transcription of Key Word
"ah"	[ɑ]	*bomb*	[bɑm]
"aw"	[ɔ]	*bought*	[bɔt]
"oh"	[o]	*boat*	[bot]
"ooh"	[ʊ]	*book*	[bʊk]
"oo"	[u]	*boot*	[but]

The Back Vowels. Table B-4 presents the back vowels.[1] If you pronounce each of these vowel sounds in turn, you will find your mouth closing more and more and the sound being controlled at a progressively forward position in your mouth.

The Vowel Sounds *er* and *uh*. Only two other vowel sounds remain, *er* and *uh*, that cause some trouble for students of phonetics. Consider the two words *further* and *above*. In *further*, two *er* sounds appear. Pronounce this word aloud and you will detect that, because of a stress on the first syllable, the two *ers* sound slightly different. The same is true of the two *uh* sounds in *above*. Because the first syllable of this word is unstressed and the second is stressed, there is a slight but definite difference between the two sounds. The IPA makes allowances for these differences by assigning two symbols each to the *er* and *uh* sounds:

[ɝ] for a stressed *er*, as in the *first* syllable of *further* [fɝð'ɚ]

[ɚ] for an unstressed *er*, as in the *second* syllable of *further* [fɝðɚ]

[ʌ] for a stressed *uh*, as in the *second* syllable of *above* [əbʌv]

[ə] for an unstressed *uh*, as in the *first* syllable of *above* [əbʌv]

The unstressed *uh* sound is given a special symbol and name—[ə], the **schwa vowel.** Naturally, in a one-syllable word with an *uh* or an *er* sound, the sound is stressed. For this reason, in all one-syllable words, both *er* and *uh* are represented by their stressed symbols:

bird [bɝd]   church [tʃɝtʃ]   sun [sʌn]   come [kʌm]

Certain combinations of sounds may be transcribed in two ways, either of which is as accurate as the other. The word *flattery*, for example, may be transcribed either

---

[1] The English language has many words with unsounded letters, such as the final *b* in the key word *bomb* in Table B-4. You may experience an unconscious tendency to include these in phonetic transcriptions. You should remember, however, that you are transcribing *sounds*, not letters, and should disregard all letters not sounded in a word.

TABLE B-5 IPA Transcriptions for American English Diphthongs

Diphthong	Pronunciation*	Key Word	IPA Transcription of Key Word
[aɪ]	A rapid combination of the two vowels [a] and [ɪ]	*bite*	[baɪt]
[aʊ]	A rapid combination of the two vowels [a] and [ʊ]	*how*	[haʊ]
[ɔɪ]	A rapid combination of the two vowels [ɔ] and [ɪ]	*toy*	[tɔɪ]
[ju]	A rapid combination of the two vowels [j] and [u]	*using*	[juzɪŋ]
[ɪu]	A rapid combination of [ɪ] and [u]	*fuse*	[fɪuz]
[eɪ]	A glide from [e] to [ɪ]	*say*	[seɪ]

*Note the subtle difference in the sounds of the diphthongs [ju] and [ɪu].

['flætəˑi] or ['flætəri]. The difference in the way [ɚ] and [ər] are pronounced is imperceptible to most ears.

Diphthongs. A diphthong is a combination of two vowel sounds, pronounced with a smooth glide from one sound to the other. If you say the *ow* of *how,* you will notice that it cannot be completed without moving the lips. There is no way of holding the sound of the entire diphthong; you can hold only the last of the two vowels of which it is formed. The diphthong in *now* is actually a rapid movement from the vowel [a] to the vowel [ʊ].

The diphthongs of American English are summarized in Table B-5. Note that the vowel [e], as in *bait,* is actually a diphthong, because its pronunciation in a word such as *say* involves a glide from [e] to [ɪ]. In other instances—in the word *fate,* for example—the [e] is cropped off more closely. Because it changes according to the context, the [e] sound may be transcribed either as a pure vowel, [e], or as a diphthong, [eɪ]. It will be found both ways in various dictionaries and other works using the IPA.

Consonants

With only seven exceptions, the IPA symbols for consonant sounds are the same as the lowercase letters of the English alphabet. The consonants are therefore fairly easy to learn.

In general, consonants may be classified as either voiced or unvoiced. If you say aloud the letters *b* and *p,* adding the vowel sound *uh,* to produce *buh* and *puh,* you will notice that each is produced in exactly the same way, except that *b* involves phonation (a vibration of the vocal folds) and *p* is merely exploded air, with no phonation at all. Because most consonants are related this way, they are listed here in their voiced–unvoiced paired relationships rather than alphabetically:

[p] is exploded air with no phonation, as in *poor* [pʊr].

[b] is a phonated explosion, as in *boor* [bʊr].

[t] is exploded air with no phonation, as in *time* [taɪm].

[d] is a phonated explosion, as in *dime* [daɪm].

[k] is exploded air with no phonation, as in *kite* [kaɪt].

[g] is a phonated explosion, as in *guide* [gaɪd].

[f] is escaping air with no phonation, as in *few* [fɪu].

[v] is escaping air with phonation, as in *view* [vɪu].

[θ] is escaping air with no phonation, as in *thigh* [θaɪ]. It is similar to the consonant [f] but has a different placement of the tongue and lips. The Greek letter theta is its symbol.

[ð] is escaping air but with phonation, as in *thy* [ðaɪ].

[s] is escaping air without phonation, as in *sing* [sɪŋ].

[z] is escaping air with phonation, as in *zing* [zɪŋ].

[ʃ] is escaping air without phonation, as in *shock* [ʃak].

[ʒ] is escaping air with phonation, as in *Jacques* (French) [ʒak].

[tʃ] is an unvoiced, or unphonated, combination of [t] and [ʃ]. It is pronounced as one sound, as in *chest* [tʃɛst].

[dʒ] is a voiced, or phonated, combination of [d] and [ʒ]. It is pronounced as one sound, as in *jest* [dʒɛst].

The following consonants have no pairings:

[h] is an unvoiced sound, as in *how* [haʊ].

[hw] is an unvoiced sound, as in *when* [hwɛn].

[m] is a voiced sound, as in *mom* [mam].

[n] is a voiced sound, as in *noun* [naʊn].

[ŋ] is a voiced sound, as in *sing* [sɪŋ].

[l] is a voiced sound, as in *love* [lʌv].

[w] is a voiced sound, as in *watch* [watʃ].

[j] is a voiced sound, as in *yellow* ['jɛlo].

[r] is a voiced sound, as in *run* [rʌn].

Some Common Consonant Transcription Problems. A few consonants are potential sources of confusion and deserve special consideration.

The word *fire* is pronounced usually [faɪɚ] in the United States and Canada but is transcribed frequently as [fīr] by the authors of dictionaries and phonetics texts. The problem here is that the *r* sound in a word such as *run* is really quite different from the *r* sound in the word *fire;* that is, the *r* sound differs depending on its position in a word. There is another difference: The *r* in *boor* is different from the *r* in *fire,* even though both are in the same position in the word and follow a vowel sound. This difference stems from the fact that it's easy to produce [r] after the vowel [ʊ] but difficult to produce [r] after the diphthong [aɪ]. If you transcribe *fire* in the conventional manner as a one-syllable word—[fīr]/FYR/[faɪr]—you must be careful, because the word can be spoken only with two syllables—/FY/ and /ER/ (fi) and (er) [faɪ] and [ɚ].

Another potential source of trouble is the plural ending. Years of conditioning have taught us that most plurals end in an *s,* though in actuality nearly all end in a *z* sound—*brushes, masters, dozens, kittens,* and so on. Make certain, when transcribing into IPA, that you do not confuse the two symbols [s] and [z].

The common construction *-ing* tends to make one think of a combination of [n] and [g] when transcribing a word like *singing.* Some students mistakenly transcribe this as ['sing,ging]. In IPA a distinct symbol, [ŋ], is used for the *ng* sound. The correct transcription of *singing* is ['sɪŋɪŋ]. Another common error is to add [g] after [ŋ]. To do so is incorrect.

The symbol [j] is never used to transcribe a word like *jump.* The symbol [dʒ] is used for the initial sound in names such as *Jack and George* and in the word *just.* The symbol [j] is always pronounced as in *young* [jʌŋ], *yes* [jɛs], and *William* ['wiljəm].

Note that many of the consonants change their sounds as they change their positions in words or are combined with different vowel sounds. You have already seen how the *r* sound does this. A similar change takes place in the *d* sound. Notice it in the first syllable of the word *dazed.* Because the initial *d* is followed by a vowel sound, [e], the *d* is sounded. But when the *d* appears in the final position of the word, it is merely exploded air and is only slightly different from the sound a *t* would make in the same position. The only way the final *d* could be sounded would be if a slight *schwa* sound were added.

Syllabic Consonants. Three of the consonants, [m], [n], and [l], can be sounded as separate syllables without a vowel sound before or after them. Though the word *button* may be pronounced [bʌtən], in colloquial speech the [ə] sound is often missing, and the word is represented [bʌtn̩]. In such a transcription, the **syllabic consonant** is represented by a short line under the symbol. Here are transcriptions for a few other words using syllabic consonants:

hokum ['hokm̩]   *saddle* ['sædl̩]   *apple* ['æpl̩]

Accent Marks

Polysyllabic words transcribed into IPA symbols must have accent marks to indicate the relative emphasis to be placed on the various syllables. The word *familiar* has three syllables, [fə], [mɪl], and [jɚ]. In Standard American the first of these syllables receives little emphasis, or stress; the second receives the primary emphasis; and the third receives about the same degree of emphasis as the first.

The IPA indication of primary stress in a word is a mark ['] *before* the syllable being stressed.[2] In the word *facing* ['fesɪŋ], the mark indicates that the first syllable is to receive the **primary stress.** If the mark is placed below and before a syllable, as in *farewell* [ˌfɛr'wɛl], it indicates that the syllable is to receive **secondary stress.** A third degree of stress is possible, but no mark is provided—this is an unstressed sound.

The word *satisfaction* will clarify the stressing of syllables. A continuous line drawn under the word indicates the degrees of stress placed on the syllables when uttering them:

sæt   ɪs   fæk   ʃən

It can be seen that there are three rather distinct degrees of emphasis in the word. This word would be transcribed [ˌsætɪs'fækʃən]. The primary mark is used for the syllable [fæk] and the secondary mark for the syllable [sæt]; there is no mark on the two unstressed syllables, [ɪs] and [ʃən]. Because secondary stress varies from slightly less than primary stress to slightly more than the unstressed syllables in a word, the secondary accent mark is used for a wide range of emphases, although it is used only once per polysyllabic word.

The following list of related words (related either in meaning or in spelling) shows how accent marks are used in IPA transcriptions to assist in representing the correct pronunciation:

consequence ['kɑnsə,kwɛns]	*consequential* [ˌkɑnsə'kwɛnʃəl]
overalls ['ovɚ,ɔlz]	*overwhelm* [ˌovɚ'hwɛlm]
interim ['ɪntɚɪm]	*interior* [ɪn'tɪriɚ]
mainspring ['men,sprɪŋ]	*maintain* [men'taɪn]
contest (n.) ['kɑntɛst]	*contest* (v.) [kən'tɛst]
Oliver ['ɑlɪvɚ]	*Olivia* [o'lɪviə]
invalid (sick person) ['ɪnvəlɪd]	*invalid* (not valid) [ɪn'vælɪd]

Because the schwa vowel, [ə], and the vowel [ɚ] are by definition unstressed, they need no further mark to indicate stress. Because the vowel sounds [ʌ] and [ɝ]

---

[2] Note that this practice is the opposite of dictionary phonetic transcription. In which the stress mark comes at the end of the stressed syllable.

are by definition stressed, they, too, need no additional mark when they appear in a transcribed word. For example, the words *lover* [lʌvɚ] and *earnest* [ɝnəst] are transcribed without accent marks of any kind.

PRACTICE

> ➤ Phonetic Transcription

For additional practice, transcribe any of the passages of this book into IPA symbols. When you have acquired some degree of proficiency with the IPA, begin transcribing from the daily news any names and words with which you are unfamiliar. Gazetteers and dictionaries will give you correct pronunciations of unfamiliar words. To find the correct IPA transcriptions of unfamiliar words, use *A Pronouncing Dictionary of American English* or the *NBC Handbook of Pronunciation*.

Summary of the IPA

For handy reference, all of the IPA symbols used to transcribe Standard American speech are listed in Table B-6. Examples of words whose phonetic transcriptions contain each symbol are also given in the table.

TABLE B-6 IPA Symbols for Sounds of Standard American

IPA Symbol	Key Word	Other Words
Vowels		
[i]	*beet* [bit]	*free* [fri]
		peace [pis]
		leaf [lif]
		misdeed [mɪsˈdid]
		evening [ˈivn̩ɪŋ]
[ɪ]	*bit* [bɪt]	*wither* [ˈwɪðɚ]
		pilgrim [ˈpɪlgrɪm]
		kilowatt [ˈkɪləwɑt]
		ethnic [ˈɛθnɪk]
		lift [lɪft]
[e]	*bait* [bet]	*late* [let]
		complain [kəmˈplen]
		La Mesa [ˌlɑˈmesə]
		coupé [kuˈpe]
		phase [fez]

(continued)

TABLE B-6 IPA Symbols for Sounds of Standard American *(continued)*

IPA Symbol	Key Word	Other Words
[ɛ]	*bet* [bɛt]	*phlegm* [flɛm] *scherzo* [ˈskɛrtso] *Nez Perce* [ˈnɛzˈpɚs] *pelican* [ˈpɛlɪkən] *bellicose* [ˈbɛləˌkos]
[æ]	*bat* [bæt]	*satellite* [ˈsætḷaɪt] *baggage* [ˈbægɪdʒ] *campfire* [ˈkæmpˌfaɪr] *Alabama* [ˌæləˈbæmə] *rang* [ræŋ]
[ɝ]	*bird* [bɝd]	*absurd* [əbsɝd] *early* [ɝli] *curfew* [kɝfju] *ergo* [ɝgo] *hurdle* [hɝdḷ]
[ɚ]	*bitter* [bɪtɚ]	*hanger* [hæŋɚ] *certificate* [sɚˈtɪfəˌkɪt] *Berlin* [bɚˈlɪn] *flabbergast* [ˈflæbɚˌgæst]
[ɑ]	*bomb* [bɑm]	*body* [ˈbɑdi] *collar* [ˈkɑlɚ] *pardon* [ˈpɑrdṇ] *padre* [ˈpɑdre] *lollipop* [ˈlɑliˌpɑp]
[ɔ]	*bought* [bɔt]	*fought* [fɔt] *longwinded* [ˈlɔŋˈwɪndɪd] *rawhide* [ˈrɔhaɪd] *Kennesaw* [ˈkɛnəˌsɔ] *awful* [ˈɔfḷ]
[o]	*boat* [bot]	*closing* [ˈkloziŋ] *Singapore* [ˈsɪŋgəpor] *tremolo* [ˈtrɛməlo] *odor* [ˈodɚ] *Pueblo* [ˈpwɛbˌlo]
[ʊ]	*book* [bʊk]	*looking* [ˈlʊkɪŋ] *pull* [pʊl] *took* [tʊk]

IPA Symbol	Key Word	Other Words
		tourniquet ['tʊrnɪˌkɛt]
		hoodwink ['hʊdˌwɪŋk]
[u]	*boot* [but]	*Lucifer* ['lusɪfɚ]
		cuckoo ['kuˌku]
		losing ['luzɪŋ]
		nouveau riche [nuvo'riʃ]
[ʌ]	*sun* [sʌn]	*lovelorn* ['lʌvlɔrn]
		recover [ˌrikʌɚ]
		chubby ['tʃʌbi]
		Prussia ['prʌʃə]
		hulled ['hʌld]
[ə]	*sofa* [sofə]	*lettuce* ['lɛtəs]
		above [əbʌv]
		metropolis [ˌmə'trapḷɪs]
		arena [ə'rinə]
		diffidence ['dɪfədəns]

Diphthongs

[aɪ]	*bite* [baɪt]	*dime* [daɪm]
		lifelong ['laɪf'lɔŋ]
		leviathan [lə'vaɪəθən]
		bicycle ['baɪˌsɪkḷ]
		imply [ˌɪm'plaɪ]
[aʊ]	*how* [haʊ]	*plowing* ['plaʊˌɪŋ]
		endow [ˌɛn'daʊ]
		autobahn ['aʊtoˌban]
		council ['kaʊnsḷ]
		housefly ['haʊsˌflaɪ]
[ɔɪ]	*toy* [tɔɪ]	*toiling* ['tɔɪlɪŋ]
		oyster ['ɔɪstɚ]
		loyalty ['lɔɪḷti]
		annoy [ə'nɔɪ]
		poison ['pɔɪzn̩]
[ju]	*using* ['juzɪŋ]	*universal* [junə'vɝsḷ]
		euphemism ['jufəmɪzm̩]
		feud [fjud]
		refuse [rɪ'fjuz]
		spew [spju]
[ɪu]	*fuse* [fɪuz]	
[eɪ]	*say* [seɪ]	

(continued)

TABLE B-6 IPA Symbols for Sounds of Standard American *(continued)*

IPA Symbol	Key Word	Other Words
Consonants		
[p]	*poor* [pʊr]	*place* [ples] *applaud* [əˈplɔd] *slap* [slæp]
[b]	*boor* [bʊr]	*break* [brek] *about* [əˈbaʊt] *club* [klʌb]
[t]	*time* [taɪm]	*trend* [trɛnd] *attire* [əˈtaɪr] *blast* [blæst]
[d]	*dime* [daɪm]	*differ* [ˈdɪfɚ] *addenda* [əˈdɛndə] *closed* [klozd]
[k]	*kite* [kaɪt]	*careful* [ˈkɛrfəl] *accord* [əˈkɔrd] *attack* [əˈtæk]
[g]	*guide* [gaɪd]	*grand* [grænd] *aggressor* [əˈgrɛsɚ] *eggnog* [ˈɛg,nɔg]
[f]	*few* [fɪu]	*finally* [ˈfaɪnḷi] *affront* [əˈfrʌnt] *aloof* [əˈluf]
[v]	*view* [vɪu]	*velocity* [vəˈlɑsəti] *aver* [əˈvɚ] *love* [lʌv]
[θ]	*thigh* [θaɪ]	*thrifty* [ˈθrɪfti] *athwart* [əˈθwɔrt] *myth* [mɪθ]
[ð]	*thy* [ðaɪ]	*these* [ðiz] *although* [,ɔlˈðo] *breathe* [brɪð]
[s]	*sing* [sɪŋ]	*simple* [ˈsɪmpḷ] *lastly* [ˈlæst,li] *ships* [ʃɪps]
[z]	*zing* [zɪŋ]	*xylophone* [ˈzaɪlə,fon] *loses* [ˈluz,ɪz] *dreams* [drimz]

IPA Symbol	Key Word	Other Words
[ʃ]	shock [ʃak]	ashen [æʃən] trash [træʃ]
[ʒ]	Jacques [ʒak]	gendarme [ˈʒanˈdɑrm] measure [ˈmɛʒɚ] beige [beʒ]
[tʃ]	chest [tʃɛst]	checkers [ˈtʃɛkɚz] riches [ˈrɪtʃɪz] attach [əˈtætʃ]
[dʒ]	jest [dʒɛst]	juggle [dʒʌgl] adjudicate [əˈdʒudɪˌket] adjudge [əˈdʒʌdʒ]
[h]	how [haʊ]	heaven [ˈhɛvən] El Cajon [ˌɛlˌkəˈhon] cahoots [ˌkəˈhuts]
[hw]	when [hwɛn]	Joaquin [hwɑˈkin] whimsical [ˈhwɪmzɪkl̩]
[m]	mom [mɑm]	militant [ˈmɪlətənt] amusing [əˈmjuzɪŋ] spume [spjum]
[n]	noun [naʊn]	nevermore [ˌnɛvɚˈmɔr] announcer [əˈnaʊnsɚ] sturgeon [ˈstɚdʒən]
[ŋ]	sing [sɪŋ]	English [ˈɪŋglɪʃ] language [ˈlæŋgwɪdʒ] pang [pæŋ]
[l]	love [lʌv]	lavender [ˈlævəndɚ] illusion [ɪˈluʒən] medial [ˈmidil]
[w]	watch [wɑtʃ]	wash [wɔʃ] aware [əˈwɛr] equestrian [ɪˈkwɛstriən]
[j]	yellow [ˈjɛlo]	William [ˈwɪljəm] Yukon [ˈjukɑn]
[r]	run [rʌn]	Wrigley [ˈrɪgli] martial [ˈmarʃəl] appear [əˈpɪr]

American English Usage

Appendix Outline

To be an announcer is to be a user of words, and serious students of announcing will undertake a careful study of their language—English for most in the United States; English and French for Canadians; and Spanish, Chinese, German, Polish, Russian, or Tagalog, for instance, for those who intend to broadcast in a non-English language. Learning about language means engaging in several different but related studies. It means making a lifelong habit of using dictionaries. It means becoming sensitized to nuances of language and seeking the precise, rather than the approximate, word; changing your vocabulary as changes in our language occur; cultivating and practicing the art of plain talk. And it means perfecting your pronunciation.

This appendix is designed for those who will speak on English-language stations, and it considers usage from the standpoint of the broadcast announcer.

Top professional announcers use words with precision and manage to sound conversational while honoring the rules of grammar. Regrettably, though, some broadcast announcers are far from perfect and commit errors in usage daily. During a two-week period, broadcast announcers made the following mistakes:

- "The White House press secretary claimed that the Iraqi dictator had flaunted every resolution passed by the United Nations." The spokesperson meant *flouted*. To *flaunt* is to "exhibit ostentatiously." To *flout* is to "openly defy."

- "That's like shooting ducks in a barrel." The announcer has confused two clichés—"shooting fish in a barrel" and "shooting sitting ducks."

- ". . . and this poor old guy was trodding along the street, looking for aluminum cans." The word is *trudging* and is the past participle of *trudge*. The announcer may have meant *plodding*, but it's unlikely that the intended word was *trotting*.

- "And, while Debbie's marriage was floundering on the rocks . . . ." To *flounder* is to stumble or lurch. The correct word is *founder*, a term used for a ship in danger of sinking.

- "And _____ is the latest state to reintroduce corpulent punishment." *Corpulent* means "excessively fat." The announcer meant *corporal*, a euphemism for physical punishment. Even a skinny person might receive corporal punishment.

- "The secretary of state reportedly will visit South America late this summer." There are many kinds of visits—long visits, brief visits, surreptitious visits—but no one can make a reported visit. The announcer meant "It is reported that the secretary of state . . . ."

- "Coach Washington has done a great job of gerrymandering his team in light of its injuries." The sports reporter meant *jury-rigging*, a term for coping with problems by improvising temporary solutions. To *gerrymander* is to draw voting district boundaries in such a way as to give an advantage to the political party that drew them.

- "The jury's verdict culminated a case that had dragged along for seven months." The verdict may have concluded the case, but the case culminated in a verdict.

- "And the Oakland A's are on a pace to set a new, all-time record!" By definition, when a record is set it is both new and all-time. This is a rare case of double redundancy.
- "The violinist transcended the audience to a state of rapture." The announcer meant *transported*, not *transcended*.

American English is a dynamic, ever-changing language. Although change is slow during periods of relative stability, it never ceases. During times of upheaval, whether political, economic, technological, or social, changes in our language take place rapidly. World War II, for example, created many new words, among them *blitz, fellow traveler, fifth column, radar,* and *quisling.* Operation Desert Storm brought us *SCUDS, stealth bombers,* and *smart bombs.* Many terms from the world of computers have been added to our language, including *byte, modem, RAM, ROM,* and *hacker.* And the Internet gave us *webcasting, podcasting, cyberspace, streaming radio, URL,* and *browser,* among dozens of other terms. In time, new inventions and events will cause new—or recycled—words to be learned and used. As a professional announcer, it's imperative that you remain alert to changes in our language.

Usage Guidelines

Jargon and Vogue Words

Every profession and social group has a private or semiprivate vocabulary, and some words and phrases from such groups enter the mainstream of public communication. It is useful and enriching when expressions such as *gridlock, agribusiness, software,* or *hostile takeover* (the world of business) are added to the general vocabulary. As an announcer, you should guard against picking up and overusing expressions that are trite, precious, deliberately distorting, or pretentious. Here are a few recent vogue words and phrases with translations into plain English (slightly facetious in some cases).

From the Military	
de-escalate	To give up on a lost war
balance of power	A dangerous standoff
nuclear deterrent	The means by which war can be deterred when antagonistic nations possess enough nuclear weapons to destroy the world
debrief	To ask questions of someone
collateral damage	Dead civilians
friendly fire	The accidental killing of soldiers by their comrades

From Government

at home and abroad	Everywhere
nonproliferation	Monopolization of nuclear weapons
disadvantaged	Poor people
Department of Human Resources Development	The unemployment office
decriminalize	To make legal
dehire	To fire an employee

From Academe

quantum leap	A breakthrough
de-aestheticize	To take the beauty out of art
dishabituate	To break a bad habit
microencapsulate	To put into a small capsule
found art	Someone else's junk
megastructure	A large building

One of the most offensive speech habits of recent years is tacking the suffix *-wise* onto nouns that create awkward words:

- Culturewise, the people are . . .
- Foodwise, your best buy is . . .
- National-security-wise, we should . . .

Such clumsy errors are made by those who don't know any better and by others who've found such usage an easy way to avoid more complex sentence structure. The suffix *-wise* does, of course, have a proper use in words such as *lengthwise* and *counterclockwise*.

Redundancies

To be **redundant** is to be repetitive. Redundancy can be a useful tool for reinforcing or driving home a point, but most often redundancy is needless repetition. *Close proximity* is redundant because *close* and *proximity* (or *proximate*) mean the same thing. A *necessary requisite* is redundant because *requisite* contains the meaning of *necessary.* Spoken English is plagued with unnecessary redundancy, so be on guard and use repetition only when it serves a purpose.

Develop a keen ear for redundancies. Recognizing errors in usage is the first step toward avoiding them.

Here are some redundancies heard far too often on radio and television:

Phrase	Why It's Redundant
an old antique	There can be no such thing as a new antique.
both alike, both at once, both equal	*Both* refers to two people or things, and *alike at once*, and *equal* all imply some kind of duality.
completely surround, completely abandon, completely eliminate	To *surround*, to *abandon*, and to *eliminate* are done completely if they're done at all.
cooperate together	To *cooperate* means that two or more operate *together*.
divide up, end up, finish up, rest up, pay up, settle up	All of these are burdened by unnecessary *up*s.
equally as expensive	If something costs what another thing does, then inevitably their costs are equal. (The correct form is *equally expensive* or *as expensive as*.)
exchanged with each other	An exchange is necessarily between one and another.
general consensus	*Consensus* means "general agreement."
I thought to myself	Barring telepathy, there is no one else one can think to.
joint partnership	*Partnership* includes the concept of *joint*.
knots per hour	A *knot* is a nautical mile per hour, so *per hour* is redundant.
more preferable	Use this phrase only if you're comparing two preferences.
most outstanding, most perfect, most unique	A thing is outstanding, perfect, or unique, or it isn't. There are no degrees of any of these qualities.
Sahara Desert	*Sahara* means "desert."
serious crisis	It's not a crisis unless it's already become serious.
set a new record	All records are new when they're set.
Sierra Nevada mountains	*Sierra* means "rugged mountains."
still remains	If something *remains*, it must be there *still*.
totally annihilated	*Annihilate* means "to destroy totally."
true facts	There can be no untrue facts.
visible to the eye	There's no other way a thing can be visible.

Clichés

A **cliché** is an overused expression or idea. Many clichés are **similes,** a figure of speech in which two essentially unlike things are compared—"Frank was strong as a bull." Other clichés are merely overused expressions, such as "without further ado" or "none the worse for wear." It's important to detect trite catch phrases or overused similes that may have invaded your vocabulary and then to eliminate them. Memorable speakers and writers are noted for the avoidance of common-place expressions, as well as for their language skills in evoking the mood, character, or the ambiance of a particular place.

Most popular clichés were once innovative and effective. They became clichés by being overused and, in many instances, misapplied by people who weren't aware of their original meanings. In a recent postgame interview, a sports reporter made this comment: "With Pete having a sprained ankle, and you playing with a broken toe, it seems that you guys played the game with your hearts on your sleeves." The term *hearts on your sleeves* is a cliché, but that's not the only problem. The phrase is from the days of chivalry (knighthood) and means "openly showing your love" for a lady. The reporter apparently intended to say something like this, "You guys are all heart." (Another cliché, by the way. . . !)

Many clichés reflect our rural past. We say he was "mad as a wet hen," "fat as a pig," "stubborn as a mule," "silly as a goose," "strong as an ox," and similar expressions. Though not all clichés are similes, most similes in common use are clichés. Most of these animal similes have been learned by rote and are used by people who've never associated with creatures of the barnyard. Most of us should replace these expressions with similes that reflect our own experiences.

Good use of language demands that we think before we fall back on the first cliché that comes to mind. Commonly used clichés include these:

- *hustle and bustle*
- *first and foremost*
- *at any rate*
- *at this point in time*
- *to make a long story short*
- *stop on a dime*
- *by and large*
- *the phone was ringing off the hook* (few of today's telephones have *hooks*—or *ring,* for that matter!)
- *quick as a flash* or *quick as a wink*
- *quiet as a grave* or *quiet as a tomb*
- *dead as a doornail*
- *dry as a bone*

- *cool as a cucumber*
- *hungry as a bear*
- *fresh as a daisy*
- *at the end of the day,* or *when all is said and done,* meaning *eventually*
- *pushing the envelope* This term comes from mathematics, specifically as used in airplane design, and has no precise definition when used in conversation.

The effectiveness of these clichés and dozens more like them has simply been eroded by endless repetition. Good broadcast speech isn't measured by the ability to produce new and more effective images, but quite often creative expression can make for memorable communication. See what a little thought and time can do to help you use language creatively. How would you complete the following similes to make novel and effective images?

as awkward as _____

as barren as _____

as deceptive as _____

as friendly as _____

as quiet as _____

as strange as _____

In addition to overworked similes, many other words and phrases have become hackneyed through overuse. Many clichés can be heard on daily newscasts. If you intend to become a news reporter or newscaster, you should make a careful and constant study of words that have become meaningless and replace them with meaningful synonyms.

Many speakers and writers use clichés without knowing their precise meaning. In doing so, it's easy to fall into error. For example, the adjectives *jerry-built* and *jury-rigged* sometimes become *jerry-rigged* or *jury-built* when used by people unaware that the first adjective means "shoddily built" and the second is a nautical term meaning "rigged for emergency use."

It's also important to avoid incorrect quotations from or allusions to works of literature. Here are a few examples of this type of mistake:

- The phrase "suffer, little children" or "suffer the little children" has been used recently to mean "let the little children suffer." The original expression, in the King James Bible version of Mark 10:14, is "Suffer the little children to come unto me." In this context, *suffer* means "allow": "Allow the little children to come unto me."
- "Alas, poor Yorick, I knew him well." This is both corrupt and incomplete. The line from *Hamlet,* Act V, scene i, reads: "Alas, poor Yorick! I knew him, Horatio: a fellow of infinite jest."
- The misquotation "Music hath charms to soothe the savage beast" is an inelegant version of a line from the play *The Mourning Bride* by William Congreve. The original version is "Music hath charms to soothe the savage *breast.*"

- The all-too-familiar question "Wherefore art thou Romeo?" is consistently misused by people who think that *wherefore* means "where." It means "why." The question asks, *"Why* are you Romeo?" not *"Where* are you, Romeo?"

These are but a few of many common misquotations. As a broadcast announcer, you should check original sources routinely. Excellent sources for checking the accuracy of quoted phrases are *Bartlett's Familiar Quotations* and the *Merriam-Webster Book of Quotations,* available in print and also on compact disc. Use a quotation if it truly belongs in your work. When in doubt, skip the cliché—even correctly cited clichés are still clichés.

Latin and Greek Plurals

When you discuss media, a term that includes broadcasting, cable, and print media, be meticulous in using *medium* for the singular and *media* for the plural. Radio is a *medium.* Radio and television are *media.* We can speak of the *news media* but not of *television news media.* If people who work in broadcast media don't practice correct usage, no one else will, and the incorrectly used plural *media* will take over for the singular form.

Data is another Latin plural that is misused commonly as the singular, as in "What is your data?" This sentence should be "What *are* your data?" The sentence "What is your *datum*?" is correct if the singular is intended.

Many other words of Latin and Greek origin are subject to similar misuse. Here are some of the more important of these (note that in the singular form the Greek words end in *-on* and the Latin words end in *-um*):

Singular	Plural
addendum	addenda
criterion	criteria
memorandum	memoranda
phenomenon	phenomena
stratum	strata
syllabus	syllabi

Words that refer to graduates of schools are a more complicated matter, for both gender and number must be considered:

- Female singular—*alumna:* "She is an alumna of State College."
- Female plural—*alumnae,* pronounced *uh-LUM-nee*: "These women are alumnae of State College."
- Male singular—*alumnus:* "He is an alumnus of State College."
- Male plural—*alumni,* pronounced *uh-LUM-ny*: "These men are alumni of State College."

- Male and female plural—*alumni,* pronounced the same as the male plural: "These women and men are alumni of State College."

Solecisms

A **solecism** is a nonstandard or ungrammatical usage. It's related to a **barbarism** (a word or phrase not in accepted use), and both should be avoided by broadcast announcers. Surely you don't need to be told that *ain't* is unacceptable or that educated speakers don't use *anywheres.* In early childhood we all pick up substandard words and phrases, but they survive to plague us if we don't become aware of them. These include the following:

- *Foot* for *feet,* as in "She was five foot tall." Five is more than one, and it demands the plural *feet:* "She was five feet tall." (No one would say that a person is "five foot, six inch tall.")
- *Enthused over* for *was enthusiastic* about.
- *Guess* as a substitute for *think* or *suppose,* as in "I *guess* I'd better read a commercial."
- *Expect* for *suppose* or *assume,* as in "I *expect* he's on the scene by now."
- *Try and* for *try to,* as in "She's going to *try and* break the record."
- *Unloosen* for *loosen,* as in "He *unloosened* the knot."
- *Hung* for *hanged,* as in "The lynch mob *hung* the cattle rustler." *Hung* is the past tense of *hang* in every meaning other than as applied to a human being. Correct usages are "I *hung* my coat on the hook" and "He was *hanged* in 1884."
- *Outside of* for *aside from,* as in "*Outside of* that, I enjoyed the movie."
- *Real* for *really,* as in "I was *real* pleased."
- *Lay* and *lie* are problem words for some speakers of English. *Lie* is an intransitive verb (it does not require a direct object) meaning "to recline." It's used correctly in the following examples:

  Present tense: "I *lie* down."

  Past tense: "I *lay* down."

  Past participle: "I had *lain* down."

- *Lay* is a transitive verb (requiring a direct object) that means "to place."

  Present tense: "I *lay* it down."

  Past tense: "I *laid* it down."

  Past participle: "I had *laid* it down."

  Hens *lay* eggs, but they also *lie* down from time to time. A parent can *lay* a baby on a blanket and then *lie* next to her.

Words Often Misused

Hopefully, reportedly, and *allegedly* are among several adverbs misused so pervasively and for so long that some modern dictionaries now accept their misuse. Adverbs modify verbs, adjectives, and other adverbs. In other words, adverbs tell us how something happened. In the sentence "He runs rapidly," *rapidly* is the adverb, and it *modifies* the verb *runs*. The adverb tells how he ran.

Hopefully means "with hope" or "in a hopeful manner." To say *"Hopefully,* we will win" is not the same as saying "We hope we will win." The former implies that *hope* is the means by which we'll win. *Hopefully* is used correctly in these sentences: "She entered college hopefully"; "He approached the customer hopefully."

There is no proper use of *reportedly.* This quasi-adverb is of recent origin and doesn't stand up to linguistic logic because there's no way to do something *in a reported manner.* To say "He was *reportedly* killed at the scene" isn't the same thing as saying "It's *reported* that he was killed at the scene." "He was *reportedly* killed" means that he was killed *in a reported manner.*

The adverb *allegedly* is misused widely, and a detailed discussion of its misuse may be found in Chapter 9, "Radio News."

Adverbs such as *hopefully, reportedly,* and *allegedly* represent a special problem to announcers. Should you go along with conventional misuse? One argument in favor of doing so is that everyone understands what's meant. An argument against it is that widespread misuse of adverbs undermines the entire structure of grammar, making it increasingly difficult for us to think through grammatical problems. Because any sentence can be spoken conversationally without misusing adverbs, it's to be hoped that you'll use adverbs correctly.

Other words often misused are discussed in the following paragraphs:

Don't say *anxious* when you mean *eager. Anxious* means "worried" or "strained" and is associated with anxiety.

Connive, conspire, and *contrive* are sometimes confused. To *connive* is to "cooperate secretly in an illegal or wrongful action." To *conspire* is to "plan together secretly"; one person cannot conspire, because a conspiracy is an agreement between two or more persons. To *contrive* is to "scheme or plot with evil intent"; one person is capable of contriving.

Contemptible is sometimes confused with *contemptuous.* Contemptible is an adjective meaning "despicable." *Contemptuous* is an adjective meaning "scornful" or "disdainful." You may say "The killer is *contemptible*" or "He is *contemptuous* of the rights of others."

Continual and *continuous* are used by many speakers as interchangeable synonyms, but their meanings aren't the same. *Continual* means "repeated regularly and frequently"; *continuous* means "prolonged without interruption or cessation." A foghorn may sound continually; it doesn't sound continuously unless it's broken. A siren may sound continuously, but it does not sound continually unless it's going off every five minutes (or every half-hour or every hour).

Convince and *persuade* are used interchangeably by many announcers. In some constructions either word will do. A problem arises when *convince* is linked with *to,* as in this incorrect sentence: "He believes that he can *convince* the Smithsonian directors to give him the collection." The correct word to use in this sentence is *persuade. Convince* is to be followed by *of* or a clause beginning with *that,* as in "I could not *convince* him *of* my sincerity" or "I could not *convince* him *that* I was honest." The sentence "I could not *convince* him to trust me" is incorrect. In the following sentence, heard on a network newscast, *persuade* should have been used: "He did not know whether or not the president could *convince* them to change their minds."

Distinct and *distinctive* are not interchangeable. *Distinct* means "not identical" or "different"; *distinctive* means "distinguishing" or "characteristic." A *distinct* odor is one that cannot be overlooked; a *distinctive* odor is one that can be identified.

Emanate means to "come forth," "proceed," or "issue." You may say "The light *emanated* from a hole in the drape." Note that only light, air, aromas, ideas, and other such phenomena can emanate. Objects such as rivers, automobiles, or peaches cannot emanate from mountains, a factory, or an orchard.

Farther and *farthest* are used for literal distance, as in "The tree is *farther* away than the mailbox." But *further* and *furthest* are used for figurative distance, as in "*further* in debt."

Feasible often is used interchangeably with five other words: *possible, practical, practicable, workable,* and *viable.* These words should be differentiated by people who want to be precise in their use of American English.

- *Feasible* means "clearly possible or applicable": "The plan was *feasible*" or "Her excuse was *feasible.*"

- *Possible* means "capable of happening": "It is *possible* that the plan will work."

- *Practical* refers to the prudence, efficiency, or economy of an act or thing: "This is a *practical* plan" or "He is a *practical* person."

- *Practicable* means "capable of being done": "The plan is hardly *practicable* at this time." Note that *practicable* never refers to persons.

- *Workable* means "capable of being worked or dealt with": "The plan is *workable.*" Note that *workable* implies a future act.

- *Viable* means "capable of living, growing, or developing": "That is a *viable* tomato plant." Recently, *viable* has replaced *feasible* in many applications. You should avoid using this overworked word. If you remember that it's derived from the Old French *vie* and the Latin *vita,* both of which mean "life," it's unlikely that you will speak of "*viable* plans."

Implicit means "implied" or "understood"; *explicit* means "expressed with precision" or "specific." "He made an *implicit* promise" means that the promise was understood but was not actually stated. "His promise was *explicit*" means that the promise was stated very clearly.

To *imply* is to "suggest by logical necessity" or to "intimate"; to *infer* is to "draw a conclusion based on facts or indications." You may say "Her grades *imply* a fine mind" or "From examining her grades, I *infer* that she has a fine mind." Avoid the common practice of using one of these words to mean the other.

Libel meant originally "any written, printed, or pictorial statement that damages by defaming character or by exposing a person to ridicule," but libel also includes words spoken over the air, especially when read from a script. *Slander* means "the utterance of defamatory statements injurious to the reputation of a person." *Defamation* is a more general term meaning both libel and slander.

A *loan* is "anything lent for temporary use"; to *lend* is to "give out or allow the temporary use of something." *Loan* is a noun, and *lend* is a verb. You may say "She applied for a *loan*" or "He *lent* me his rake" or "Don't *lend* money to friends." Avoid using loan as a verb, as in "Don't *loan* money to friends."

Oral means "spoken." *Verbal* means "of, pertaining to, or associated with words." *Aural* means "of, pertaining to, or perceived by the ear." *Verbal* is less precise than *oral,* because it can mean spoken or written. For this reason, the phrase "*oral* agreement" rather than "*verbal* agreement" should be used if the meaning is that the agreement wasn't written. Although *oral* and *aural* are pronounced the same, they're used in different senses: "She taught *oral* interpretation" but "He had diminished *aural* perception."

People (not *persons*) should be used in referring to a large group: "*People* should vote in every election." *Persons* and *person* should be used for small groups and for individuals: "Five *persons* were involved" and "The *person* spoke on the telephone." A *personage* is an important or noteworthy person. A *personality* is a pattern of behavior. It's technically incorrect to call a disc jockey a **personality,** even though the term has wide acceptance.

Most dictionaries indicate that *prison* and *jail* can be used interchangeably, but strictly speaking, a *jail* is maintained by a town, city, or county, whereas *prisons* are maintained by states and the federal government. *Jails* generally confine prisoners for periods of less than a year; *prisons* or penitentiaries are for people with longer sentences.

Repulsion is the act of driving back or repelling; *revulsion* is a feeling of disgust or loathing. Do not say, "His breath *repelled* me," unless you mean that his breath physically forced you backward.

Reticent means "silent"; *reluctant* means "unwilling." Don't say "She was *reticent* to leave" when you mean "She was *reluctant* to leave."

Rhetoric is the art of oratory or the study of the language elements used in literature and public speaking. Rhetoric isn't a synonym for *bombast, cant,* or *harangue. Rhetoric* is a neutral term and should not be used in a negative sense to mean empty or threatening speech.

A *robber* unlawfully takes by violence or intimidation something belonging to another; a *burglar* breaks into a house or store to steal valuable goods. Although both actions are felonies, they're different crimes, so *robber* and *burglar* shouldn't be used interchangeably.

Xerox is the trademark of a corporation that makes copying machines. The company specifies that *Xerox* is the name of the company or, if followed by a model number, a specific machine. A photocopy made by that or any other machine is not "a Xerox."

This review of common usage errors is necessarily limited, but it may be adequate to alert you to the problem. If you habitually make errors such as those described here, you should undertake a study of English usage.

Deliberate Misuse of Language

As an announcer, you'll at times have to read copy that's ungrammatical, includes poor usage, or requires deliberate mispronunciation. Here are a few examples: "So, buy _____! There's no toothpaste like it!" If there is no toothpaste like it, the advertised product itself doesn't exist. The correct expression is "There's no *other* toothpaste like it." In "So, gift her with flowers on Mother's Day!" the word *gift*, which is a noun, has been used ungrammatically as a transitive verb. You can *give* her flowers on Mother's Day, but unless all standards of grammar are abandoned, you can't *gift* her. When you are asked to commit these and other errors as an announcer, what should you do?

You may resent the advertising agency that asks you to foist poor examples of American speech or pronunciation on the public. Although some errors in usage are made by copywriters through ignorance, don't assume that all copywriters are unaware of correct standards of grammar or pronunciation. Many of the mistakes in their copy are deliberate. Poor grammar, many advertising copywriters believe, is more colloquial and less stilted than correct grammar. Poor usage causes controversy, and to attract attention is to succeed in the primary objective of any commercial message.

You may be obliged to make deliberate mistakes when they're requested of you, and this is a problem because your audience will assume either that the mistake is yours or that the poor usage or mispronunciation actually is correct! You should use language properly in all broadcast circumstances that you control. When you're asked to read ungrammatical copy exactly as it is written, you should, if possible, ask the writer or the agency if it can be changed.

This appendix ends as it began, with a brief compilation of some usage errors heard on radio and television. The sentences that follow have one thing in common—all are incorrect:

- "The owner of the destroyed house was nonplused about it." This would seem okay except that in the accompanying sound bite the owner said, "Well, it could've been worse." The owner, then, actually was *nonchalant*, rather than *nonplused*.

- "So much for the wisdom of political pundents." This blunder was heard several times during a recent political campaign. The correct word is *pundit*, derived from the Hindi *pandit*, meaning a learned person.

- "The Bears were hoping to cash in on their field position, but that point is now mute." The word is *moot*, which, in this usage, would mean "irrelevant."

- ". . . and, for music lovers, this Saturday night at 8:00 the Opera Guild stages the Mozart opera, *The Marriage of Figuroa.*" "Figuroa" is a major thoroughfare in Los Angeles, named after an early Californian. The announcer meant *The Marriage of Figaro.*

- ". . . and, when the storm came in, it rained unrelentlessly for the next eight hours." The unnecessary *un* canceled out *relentlessly,* so according to the reporter, it didn't rain much at all! (Beware of unnecessary *uns* that literally say the opposite of what was intended, as in "*unloosen* the knot.")
- ". . . so, it's important for the inspectors to sift through the chafe." The announcer meant *chaff,* a word referring to the outer coating of grains removed during threshing. To *chafe* is to "irritate by rubbing."
- "A barge with a large wench is on its way to the scene of the accident." It's unlikely that even a *huge* wench could lift a truck from the bay. The word the announcer meant is *winch,* a stationary hoisting or hauling machine.
- "They [the 49ers] have been top-heavy, passwise to runwise." This statement, made during a football broadcast, combined jargon (tacking -*wise* onto nouns) with an expression ("top-heavy") that isn't a good substitute for "lopsided," "unbalanced," or "disproportionate."

This list of errors in usage is brief, but it illustrates the kinds of mistakes made by professional speakers who should be providing models of correct speech. If you make mistakes such as these or if you confuse *who* and *whom, shall* and *will, like* and *as,* and *which* and *that,* this appendix should serve as notice that you should undertake a serious study of American English. The suggested resources in Appendix D include several works on American English usage that should be a part of every announcer's library.

Appendix D

Suggested Resources

Ⅰn the broad field of electronic communication some practices undergo constant change, while others are more permanent. Production and programming are the most vulnerable to change; voice improvement—for example—is far less transient. Accordingly, this bibliography lists many books that discuss recent developments in the field of electronic communication, as well as other works that treat less short-lived aspects of our field. To bring this down to specifics, a ten-year-old book on television lighting is not listed here because the move from camera pick-up tubes to digital signal processing dramatically reduced lighting requirements. On the other hand, twenty-year-old texts on voice improvement, articulation, interpretation, and interviewing are listed because the information contained in them is not time bound. While a number of the latter are no longer in print, they're likely to be found in your school's library because many are timeless classics.

In addition to the works listed here, check the Index for websites that will lead you to many sources of information and practice material. As you know, the Internet undergoes changes daily, so use it regularly to search for updated works.

Chapter 1: Announcing for the Electronic Media

Rivers, William L., Schramm, Wilbur, and Christian, Clifford G. *Responsibility in Mass Communication,* 3rd ed. New York: Harper & Row, 1980. (out of print)

U.S. Department of Labor. *Occupational Outlook Handbook.* Published periodically. Available in U.S. Government bookstores and most college libraries.

Chapter 2: The Announcer as Communicator

Blythin, Evan, and Samovar, Larry A. *Communicating Effectively on Television.* Belmont, CA: Wadsworth, 1985. (out of print)

Follett, Wilson. *Modern American Usage: A Guide.* Edited by Jacques Barzun. New York: Hill & Wang, 1998.

Chapters 3 and 4: Voice Analysis and Improvement and Pronunciation and Articulation

Anderson, Virgil A. *Training the Speaking Voice,* 3rd ed. New York: Oxford University Press, 1977.

Cooper, Morton. *Change Your Voice, Change Your Life.* North Hollywood, CA: Wilshire Book Co., 1996.

Modisett, Noah F., and Luter, James G. Jr. *Speaking Clearly: The Basics of Voice and Articulation,* 4th ed. Edina, MN: Burgess, 1998.

Morrison, Malcolm. *Clear Speech: Practical Speech Correction and Voice Improvement,* 3rd ed. Stoneham, MA: Heinemann,1997.

Rizzo, Raymond. *The Voice as an Instrument,* 2nd ed. New York: Odyssey Press, 1978. (out of print)

Sprague, Jo, and Stuart, Douglas. *The Speaker's Handbook,* 5th ed. San Diego: Harcourt Brace Jovanovich, 1999.

Stone, Janet, and Bachner, Jane. *Speaking Up: A Book for Every Woman Who Talks.* New York: Carroll & Graf, 1994.

Utterback, Ann S. *Vocal Expressiveness.* Chicago: Broadcast Voice Series, Bonus Books, 1992.

Utterback, Ann S. and Freedman, Michael G. *Broadcast Voice Handbook: How to Polish Your On-Air Delivery.* Los Angeles: Bonus Books, 2005.

Wells, Lynn K. *The Articulate Voice: An Introduction to Voice and Diction.* Boston: Allyn & Bacon, 2003.

Chapters 5 and 6: Audio & Video Performance

Ehrlich, Eugene H., and Hand, Raymond Jr. *NBC Handbook of Pronunciation*, 4th ed. New York: HarperCollins, 1991. (out of print)

Hawes, William. *Television Performing: News and Information.* Stoneham, MA: Focal Press, 1991.

Malandro, Loretta A., et al. *Nonverbal Communication*, 2nd ed. New York: McGraw Hill, 1989.

McConkey, Wilfred J. *Klee as in Clay*, 3rd rev. ed. Lanham, MD: Madison Books, 1992. (out of print)

Chapter 7: Commercials and Public-Service Announcements

Alburger, James. *The Art of Voice Acting: The Craft and Business of Performing for Voice-Over.* Burlington, MA: Focal Press, 2007.

Cronauer, Adrian. *How to Read Copy: Professionals' Guide to Delivering Voice-Overs and Broadcast Commercials.* Chicago: Bonus Books, 1990.

Douthitt, Chris. *Voiceovers: Putting Your Mouth Where the Money Is.* Portland, OR: Grey Heron Books, 1976.

Fridell, Squire. *Acting in Television Commercials for Fun and Profit*, updated ed. New York: Crown, 1995.

Kenyon, John S., and Knott, Thomas A. *A Pronouncing Dictionary of American English.* Springfield, MA: G. & C. Merriam Company, 1953. (Long out of print, but you most likely will find it in your school library.)

McCoy, Michelle, and Utterback, Ann S. *Sound and Look Professional on Television and the Internet: How to Improve Your On-Camera Presence.* Chicago: Bonus Books, 2000

Morrison, Malcolm. *Clear Speech: Practical Speech Correction and Voice Improvement.* Portsmouth, NH: Heinemann, 2001.

Peacock, James. *How to Audition for Television Commercials and Get Them.* Chicago: Contemporary Books, 1982. (out of print)

Quinn, Sunny. *Put Your Mouth Where the Money Is: How to Build a Successful Radio and TV Voiceover Business.* Jupiter, FL: Airwave Publications, 1998.

Saulsberry, Rodney. *Step Up to the Mic: A Positive Approach to Succeeding in Voice-Overs.* Tomdor Publishing, 2007.

Saulsberry, Rodney. *You Can Bank on Your Voice: Your Guide to a Successful Career in Voice-Overs.* Agoura Hills, CA: Tomdor Publishing, LLC, 2007

Searle, Judith. *Getting the Part: Thirty-Three Professional Casting Directors Tell You How to Get Work in Theater, Film, Commercials, and Television.* New York: Limelight Editions, 1995.

See, Joan. *Acting in Commercials,* 2nd ed. New York: Watson-Guptill Publications, 1998.

Chapter 8: Interview and Talk Programs

Brady, John Joseph. *The Craft of Interviewing.* New York: Random House, 1997.

Cohen, Akiba A. *The Television News Interview.* Newbury Park, CA: Sage Publications, 1987. (out of print)

Chapters 9 and 10: Radio News and Television News

Cremer, Charles F., Keirstead, Phillip O., and Yoakam, Richard D. *ENG: Television News* (McGraw-Hill Series in Mass Communication), 3rd ed. New York: McGraw-Hill, 1995.

Fang, Irving. *Television News, Radio News,* 4th rev. ed. St. Paul, MN: Rada Press, 1985. (out of print)

Gans, Herbert J. *Deciding What's News: A Study of CBS Evening News, NBC Nightly News, Newsweek and Time.* New York: Random House, 1989.

Goldstein, Norm, ed. *The Associated Press Stylebook and Libel Manual,* rev. ed. New York: Dell Publishing, 2000.

Graber, Doris A. *Processing the News,* 2nd ed. Lanham, MD: University Press of America, 1994. (out of print)

Hewitt, John. *Air Words: Writing for Broadcast News,* 2nd ed. Mountain View, CA: Mayfield, 2001.

Killenberg, George M., and Anderson, Rob. *Before the Story: Interviewing and Communication Skills for Journalists.* New York: St. Martins Press, 1989.

MacDonald, R. H. *A Broadcast News Manual of Style,* 2nd ed. New York: Longman, 1994.

Shipley, Kenneth G., and Wood, Julie McNulty. *The Elements of Interviewing.* San Diego, CA: Singular Pub Group, 1997.

Chapter 11: Music Announcing

Apel, Willi. *Harvard Dictionary of Music,* 2nd ed. Cambridge, MA: Bellnap Press, 1969.

Crofton, Ian, and Fraser, Donald. *A Dictionary of Musical Quotations.* New York: Schirmer Books, 1989.

Cross, Milton. *New Milton Cross' Complete Stories of the Great Operas.* New York: Doubleday, 1955. (out of print)

Fresh, DJ Chuck. *How to Be a DJ: Your Guide to Becoming a Radio, Nightclub, or Private Party Disc Jockey.* Boston: Thomson Course Technology, 2004.

Keith, Michael C. *The Radio Station,* 7th ed. Stoneham, MA: Focal Press, 2006.

Lieberman, Philip A. *Radio's Morning Show Personalities: Early Hour Broadcasters and Deejays from the 1920s to the1990s.* Jefferson, NC: McFarland & Co., 1996.

Weigant, Chris. *Careers as a Disc Jockey.* New York: Rosen Group, 1997.

Chapter 12: Sports Announcing

Gunther, Marc, and Carter, Bill. *Monday Night Mayhem: The Inside Story of ABC's Monday Night Football.* New York: William Morrow, 1988. (out of print)

Madden, John. *One Size Doesn't Fit All and Other Thoughts from the Road.* New York: Villard Books, 1988.

Smith, Curt. *The Storytellers: From Mel Allen to Bob Costas: Sixty Years of Baseball Tales from the Broadcast Booth.* Foster City, CA: IDG Books, 1995.

Smith, Curt. *Voices of the Game: The First Full-Scale Overview of Baseball Broadcasting,* updated ed. New York: Simon and Schuster, 1992. (out of print)

Chapter 13: Starting Your Announcing Career

Ellis, Elmo I. *Opportunities in Broadcasting Careers,* rev. ed. Lincolnwood, IL: VGM Career Books, 2005.

Pearlman, Donn. *Breaking into Broadcasting.* Chicago: Bonus Books,1986.

Reed, Maxine K., and Reed, Robert M. *Career Opportunities in Television, Cable, and Video,* 4th rev. ed. New York: Facts on File, 1991.

Appendix E

Suggested Internet Resources

Chapter 1: Announcing for the Electronic Media

United States Bureau of Labor Statistics:

www.bls.gov/oco/ocos087.htm

Talent agencies:

www.futurecasting2000.com/agency.htm
www.pozproductions.com/agtmainp.htm
www.beaweb.org/directories.html

The Association for Women in Communication, Inc.:

www.womcom.org/

National Broadcasting Society/Alpha Epsilon Rho

www.nbs-aerho.org

The Radio and Television News Directors Association (RTNDA):

www.rtnda.org/

The National Association of Black Journalists:

www.nabj.org/

Society of Professional Journalists:

www.spj.org

National Association of Hispanic Journalists:

www.nahj.org/

Society of Environmental Journalists:

www.sej.org

The Radio-Television Journalism Division of the Association for Education in Journalism and Mass Communication:

www.aejmc.org

The American Society of Newspaper Editors (ASNE) Statement of Principles:

www.asne.org/kiosk/archive/principl.htm

Chapter 2: The Announcer as Communicator

Audition performances by professional announcers can be accessed via:

www.ozvoxaudio.com
www.voiceprofessionals.com

Chapter 3: Voice Analysis and Improvement
Chapter 4: Pronunciation and Articulation

The University of Virginia Library contains a vast collection of the works of major British and American poets:

www.etext.lib.virginia.edu/britpo.html

Chapter 5: Audio Performance

Radio essay and commentary scripts from National Public Radio's News-Hour with Jim Lehrer:

www.pbs.org/newshour/essays-dialogues.html

Chapter 6: Video Performance

Drew's Script-o-Rama contains scripts of complete television dramas, both serious and comic:

www.script-o-rama.com/

Chapter 7: Commercials and Public-Service Announcements

The Television Transcript Project includes commercial scripts arranged by category—for instance, headache remedies and restaurants:

www.geocities.com/tvtranscripts/
www-gap.dcs.st-and.ac.uk/~history/BiogIndex.htm

Chapter 8: Interview and Talk Programs

CNN contains transcripts of interviews with current newsmakers, as well as transcripts of programs such as *CNN Sunday, Crossfire, Inside Politics, Reliable Sources,* and *Your Health:*

www.cnn.com/TRANSCRIPTS/

Chapter 9: Radio News
Chapter 10: Television News

To obtain printouts of up-to-the-minute news copy, go to:

www.fullcoverage.yahoo.com/

Chapter 11: Music Announcing

To learn more about club or mobile DJs, go to a search engine (Google, Alta Vista), enter "disc jockeys," and click "go" or "search."

To learn more about show preparation for music announcers, visit the following website:

dir.yahoo.com/News_and_Media/Radio/Show_Preparation/

Chapter 12: Sports Announcing

Much information on sports announcers and brief biographies of sports play-by-play announcers, commentators, program hosts, reporters, and play analysts may be found by simply entering "sports announcers" on Google.

Chapter 13: Starting Your Announcing Career

You can perform job searches on the Internet. Broadcast Employment Services offers a number of services under such categories as Master Station Index, Index, E-Resume Database, Freelance Directory, TV Forum, Situations Wanted, and Internship Database. Jobs in radio, television, cable, and film are included:

www.tvjobs.com
www.amfmjobs.com

There are several Internet services that you can access and then print maps and detailed driving instructions from your address to that of a particular radio or television station, including MapQuest, Google, and Rand McNally.

Glossary

Popular music format abbreviations are not standardized. For example, "oldies" is listed as OL and "country music" is designated as CW by *Broadcasting and Cable Yearbook; Radio and Records* (R&R) lists these formats as OLD and CTY. Both abbreviations are given in this glossary.

Most terms in this glossary appear in the text. Other terms are included because they are used commonly in broadcasting and may be encountered by anyone entering the broad field of electronic communication.

AAA   Adult alternative music. A radio station music format featuring eclectic Rock.

abstraction ladder   S. I. Hayakawa's term for the fact that several terms usually are available for the same phenomenon, some precise and some abstract.

A/C or AC   Abbreviation for *Adult Contemporary*, a popular music category.

accent   The way words are pronounced, usually determined by the regional or national background of the speaker. Everyone has an "accent," because the term simply means the way we sound words.

account executive   A person who sells broadcast time for a radio station or an agency.

actuality   A radio news report featuring someone other than broadcast personnel (politician, police inspector, athlete, or eyewitness) who provides an actual statement rather than one paraphrased and spoken by a reporter.

ADC   Adult contemporary music. A radio station music format featuring soft-to-moderate rock, ballads, and current hits.

ad-lib   (noun, verb, or adj.) and **ad lib** (adverb) To improvise and deliver spontaneously.

affricates   Speech sounds that combine a plosive (release of air as in saying the letter *p*) with a fricative (friction of air through a restricted air passage as in saying the letter *s*); an example is the *ch* sound in *choose*.

AH   Abbreviation for *adult hits*, or *hot adult contemporary*, a popular-music category.

air check   An audition tape, usually a portion of an actual broadcast. Also called a *presentation tape*.

allusion   An indirect but pointed, or meaningful, reference: "He is as subtle as Dirty Harry" is an allusion.

alveolus   The upper gum ridge.

ambient noise   Unwanted sounds in an acoustical environment (such as air conditioners, traffic noises, airplanes).

ambient sounds   Normal background sounds that do not detract from the recording or the program and may even add to the excitement of the broadcast (such as crowd sounds at a sports event).

American Federation of Television and Radio Artists (AFTRA)   The union made up of radio and television announcers whose work is either live or taped.

anchor   The chief newscaster on a radio or television news broadcast.

announcer   Anyone who speaks to an audience through an electronic medium: radio or television transmission over the public airways, cable or other closed-circuit audio or video distribution, or electronic amplification, as in an auditorium or a theater. Announcers include newscasters, reporters, commentators, sportscasters, narrators, "personalities," disc jockeys, program hosts, and people who deliver commercial messages (as contrasted with those who act in dramatized commercials).

AP   Abbreviation for *adult alternative*, a popular-music category.

AR   Abbreviation for *album rock*, a popular-music category.

articulation   The breaking up of vocal tones into recognizable sounds we call words. You can articulate words without phonation; you do so whenever you whisper.

articulators   The speech organs that create speech sounds, chiefly the jaw, tongue, and lips.

AS   Abbreviation for *adult standard*, a popular-music category.

ASNE   Abbreviation for *American Society of Newspaper Editors.*

aspirate   To release a puff of breath, as in sounding the word *unhitch*. Overaspiration results in a popping sound when sitting or standing close to a microphone.

assignment editor   The station news executive who gives assignments to reporters, writers, and videographers.

attitude   An announcer's position or bearing, made up of mindset, stance, point of view, and beliefs; similar to mood, but going deeper and connoting a relationship between the announcer and persons being addressed.

audience demographics   See *demographics.*

audience rapport   A bond between performer and audience, based on a feeling of mutual respect and trust.

audio console   The control board that receives, mixes, amplifies, and sends audio signals to a recorder or a transmitter.

audiotape cartridge   A cartridge of 1/4-inch audiotape that plays, rewinds, and cues itself.

audition demo   A recorded sample of your work as an announcer. There are two types of audition demos: the first, a compilation of brief examples showing varied styles of announcing; the second, an air check, is a sampling of your work culled from on-air performances.

audition tape   Common term for a recording of a job applicant's performances. Auditions may actually be recorded on media other than tape, including CDs. Also called a *résumé recording*.

automatic gain control (AGC)   A device that automatically regulates the volume to maintain a consistent level.

AWRT   Abbreviation for *American Women in Radio and Television*.

barbarism   A blunder in speech; similar to a solecism.

barter   The exchange of airtime for goods or services.

BB   Script symbol for *billboard*, used to indicate to an announcer that an upcoming feature or event should be promoted.

BEA   Abbreviation for *Broadcast Education Association*.

beat check   Using a telephone to search for and tape news stories from a list of agencies, including the FBI, police and fire departments, local hospitals, the weather bureau, and airport control towers; also called the *phone beat*.

bed   See *music bed*.

bending the needle   Causing the swinging needle of a VU or VI meter or an audio console to hit the extreme right of its calibrated scale, indicating to the operator that the volume of the sound being sent through the console is too high.

BG   Abbreviation for *black gospel*, a popular-music category and **BG** script symbol for "background," referring most often to background music.

BGS   Black gospel music. A radio station music format featuring African-American gospel music.

bidirectional   The pickup pattern of a microphone that accepts sounds from two of its sides.

bilabial   Sounds articulated primarily by both lips, for example, the consonants *p* and *w*; also called *labial*.

billboard   To promote an upcoming feature or event on the air.

billing log   The name given by the sales and business departments to a radio station's program log; a listing, in sequence, of each element of the broadcast day, including commercials.

blocking   Instructing performers in a television production as to when and where to stand, walk, and so on.

BLU   Blues music. A radio station music format featuring classic blues.

board   In radio, an audio console; in television news operations, a large Plexiglas sheet on which the elements of a newscast are entered throughout the day.

board fade   A lowering of the volume on an audio console, usually to the point of losing the sound altogether.

boom   Short for "audio boom," a device for moving a microphone without allowing either its operator or the mic to be seen on the television screen. Most booms are mounted on movable dollies and have controls for moving the microphone in or out, up or down, or sideways. Television camera cranes are sometimes called booms.

boosting   Strengthening an audio signal by means of an amplifier.

box graphic   Pictures and words, contained in a rectangle, that illustrate a news story being delivered. The graphic usually is seen in the upper right or upper left of the television screen.

brain   The computer used to program an automated radio station; also called a *controller*.

BTA   Abbreviation for *best time available*.

bulletin   Sports news stories issued by the Associated Press. Bulletins include blockbuster trades, deaths of noteworthy athletes, and pennant and World Series clinchers.

bulletin font   The oversized type produced by a printer or typewriter that prints scripts for television news broadcasts.

bumper   The device used to move a television program from one element to another, as in a transition from the program to a commercial or from one segment of the program to another.

buttons   Allow you to open and close your announcer mic, to open and close the intercom or talk-back mic, and to open a mic in the newsroom for feeding out a news bulletin.

calling the game   Giving a play-by-play description of a sports event.

camera consciousness   The awareness on the part of a performer of the capabilities and limitations of the television cameras.

camtech   An abbreviation of "camera technician," a term used at many stations in place of the outmoded "cameraman."

cardioid   A type of microphone pickup pattern that is heart-shaped.

cart   Short for "audiotape cartridge"; a loop of tape encased in a plug-in cartridge that automatically recues.

carted commercials   Commercials dubbed to audiotape cartridges.

carted music   Music selections transferred to audiotape cartridges. Most music stations have switched to digitally recorded play machines.

carting   The act of dubbing, or recording on, an audiotape cartridge.

cart machine   An electronic audio device that records and plays back (or sometimes only plays back) material for broadcast.

cart with live tag   A commercial that begins with a recorded announcement, often with musical background, and ends with a live closing by a local announcer.

chain   A group of broadcast stations owned by one company or by a network.

channel selector switch   A control on an audio console that enables the operator to select from two or more inputs.

character generator (CG)   An electronic device used for creating titles, bar graphs, and many other graphics for the television screen.

cheating to the camera   Positioning oneself to create the impression on screen of talking directly to another person, while presenting a favorable angle to the camera.

CHR or CH   Abbreviations for *contemporary hit radio*, a radio station music format that features the current top rock hits, sometimes interspersed with a few golden oldies; also known as *top 40.*

chroma-key   An electronic system that makes it possible for one television scene to be matted in behind another. Chroma-keying is used to show a slide or some other graphic aid behind a news anchor, for instance. Blue is generally used for chroma-key matting.

chronological résumé   A résumé that presents basic information on work experience in chronological order.

CLA   A radio station music format featuring classical music.

clichés   Overused and worn-out expressions.

clock   See *hot clock.*

CLR   A radio station music format featuring classic rock music of the 1960s, '70s and '80s.

club (or mobile) DJs   DJs who perform live in dance halls, as well as at birthdays, company parties, weddings, reunions, and similar festive events. Club DJs represent a large and growing number of music announcers whose work is not broadcast.

cluster   Two or more radio commercials played without intervening comment or program material; also called *commercial cluster* or *spot set.*

CLX   Classic hits music. A radio station music format featuring a blend of rock and pop music of the late '60s through the early '80s.

CNN   Abbreviation for *Cable News Network.*

coanchors   Two or more announcers who share the role of chief newscaster on a radio or television program.

cold copy   A script not seen by an announcer until the moment to read it has arrived.

color   Comments made by a member of an announcing team to add an extra dimension to a live broadcast, usually consisting of human-interest anecdotes and informative, amusing, or unusual facts.

combination résumé   A résumé that combines features of a competency-based and a chronological résumé; also called a *hybrid résumé.*

combo operator   A radio disc jockey who does his or her own engineering.

commercial cluster   See *cluster.*

commercial sweep   A series of radio commercials played without intervening program material.

communicaster   Used by some radio stations to identify the host of a telephone call-in show.

community billboard, community bulletin board, community calendar Representative names for segments of airtime devoted to brief public-service announcements.

community radio stations   Radio stations found in all fifty states. They are non-profit; are dedicated to serving the needs of audiences within their signal range — a much smaller geographic area than that of commercial stations — and, most have but a few paid employees, with nearly all of the programming done by unpaid volunteers.

compact disc (CD)   A small optical disc on which digitally recorded music is stored.

competency-based (or functional) résumé   A résumé that stresses the skills an applicant possesses.

compressor   An electronic device that keeps a sound signal within a given dynamic range.

computerized information systems   All systems that feature computerized operations, including video editing, character generator operations, billing logs, and so forth.

condenser microphone   A type of microphone that features a diaphragm and an electrode as a backplate.

console   An audio control board.

consumer affairs   A term used in broadcast stations to identify a reporter who covers news stories that involve health issues, product warnings, and other issues that affect the general public.

continuity book   A loose-leaf compilation of radio commercials in the order they are to be read or introduced (if on tape) by the announcer on duty; sometimes called *copy book*.

continuity department   See *traffic department*.

continuity writers   Writers of broadcast scripts other than news scripts.

controller   The computer that controls the programming of an automated radio system; also called the *brain*.

cooperative commercials   Commercials used on both radio and television, whose cost is divided between a national and a local advertiser.

copy book   See *continuity book*.

copy sets   Multipart forms, complete with one-use carbon papers, used widely in television newsrooms to create as many as six duplicate scripts of a program.

corporate media   See *industrial media*.

correspondents   Reporters stationed some distance away from their stations or network headquarters.

cover letter   The letter written to accompany a résumé or an audition tape.

cover shot   A television shot that gives a picture of a medium-to-large area. On an interview set, a cover shot would include both interviewer and guest(s).

CR   Abbreviation for *classic rock*, a popular-music category.

crank up the gain   To increase the volume of sound going through an audio console.

crescendo   An increase in the volume or intensity of an announcer's voice.

cross fade   Manipulating the volume controls of an audio console so that one program sound fades out while another simultaneously fades in.

crossplug   A pitch made by a disc jockey or talk program host to promote another program on the same station.

CTY   A radio station music format featuring a variety of current country music hits.

CU   Television script symbol for *close-up*.

cue box   Small speaker in an audio control room or on-air studio that allows an audio operator to hear program elements as they are being cued up or previewed; sometimes called a *cue speaker*.

cue cards   Cards used in television to convey information or entire scripts to on-camera performers.

cumes   Short for *cumulative ratings*, which indicate the number of people listening to or viewing a particular station at a given time.

cutaway shots   Reaction shots, usually of a reporter listening to a newsmaker, recorded at the time of an interview and later edited into a package to avoid jump cuts at points in the report where parts of the speaker's comments have been omitted.

cut sheet   In radio, a listing that indicates how to edit one or more cuts from an audiotape to a tape cartridge; in television news operations, a form on which information about taped material is entered during editing by videotape engineers.

CW or C/W   Abbreviations for *country*, a popular-music category. Despite the *W*, the format is referred to simply as "country."

CZ   Abbreviation for *classic hits*, a popular-music category.

daypart   A term used by music radio stations to identify specific portions of the broadcast day, which may be *dayparted* into morning drive time, afternoon drive time, midday, nighttime, and overnight.

debriefing log   A record kept by radio and television stations of information about the performance of guests and the degree of audience interest in them.

decrescendo   A decrease in the force or loudness of an announcer's voice.

de-essing   The process of using a compressor to reduce sibilance.

delegation switch   A switch on an audio console that allows its operator to send a signal to a selected channel.

demographics   The profile of an actual or intended audience, including information on age, sex, ethnic background, income, and other factors that might help a broadcaster attract or hold a particular audience.

denasality   A quality of the voice due to speaking without allowing air to pass through the nasal passage.

depth of field   The area in front of a camera lens in which every thing is in focus.

design computer   A device for making television graphics. Most feature a keyboard, a monitor, an electronic tablet with stylus, and a menu of effects that it can produce.

Desk   A name used for the assignment editor in broadcast news operations.

diacritical marks   The marks used by dictionaries to indicate pronunciation.

diacritics   Marks added to letters of the alphabet to indicate a particular pronunciation. For example, a straight line, added above the letter "e" indicates that the sound is pronounced as in the first syllable of "easy."

diaphragm   The muscular membrane that separates the stomach from the lungs.

diction   Same as *articulation* and *enunciation*.

digital audio tape (DAT)   One medium (a compact disc and a hard storage disc being others) for storing and later playing digitally recorded sound.

digital cartridge machine (DCM)   A tape player that records and plays digitally recorded sound.

digital video effects (DVE)   Special effects produced by equipment that changes an analog video signal to digital, making it possible to manipulate images in many creative ways.

diphthongs   Speech sounds that consist of a glide from one vowel sound to another; for example, the *oy* sound in the word *joy*.

disc jockey   The person who identifies the music and provides pertinent comments on a popular-music radio station.

DJ   Abbreviation for *disc jockey*, sometimes spelled *deejay*.

donut commercial   A commercial with a recorded beginning and end, and live material read by a local announcer in the middle.

double out   A term used in radio production to warn an engineer that a speaker repeats the out cue in a particular tape. A sports coach, for example, may say "early in the year" both in the body of his comments and at the end of the cut; the warning *double out* is given so that the engineer will not stop the cart prematurely.

drive time   Hours during which radio stations receive their highest audience ratings, usually 6 to 10 a.m. and 3 to 7 p.m.

drugola   The acceptance of illegal drugs in exchange for such favors as promoting a recording produced by the supplier of the drugs.

dubbing   Transferring audio- or videotaped program material to another tape; also, recording another person's voice onto the soundtrack to replace the voice of the person who is seen on the screen.

DVE machine   A device that can turn a video picture into a mosaic, swing it through space, make it shrink or grow in size, and achieve many other visually interesting effects.

dynamic microphone   A rugged, high-quality microphone that works well as an outdoor or hand-held mic; also known as a *pressure mic*.

earprompter   A small earpiece worn by a performer, used to receive instructions from a producer or director. Also called *IFB*.

ear training   Developing a sensitivity to sounds, especially spoken words, and the ability to detect even slight variations from accepted standards of pronunciation, articulation, voice quality, and other aspects of human speech. Ear training is an essential part of voice improvement.

easy listening formula   A system for judging the clarity of a script that is to be broadcast.

EFP   Abbreviation for *electronic field production*.

egg-on-face look   The strained look of a performer who is trying to hold a smile while waiting for the director to go to black.

elapsed-time clock   A clock that shows how much time has been used up, rather than time remaining, in a broadcast segment.

electronic applicant tracking systems   Systems that scan résumés into a computer system that searches for and extracts important information necessary to qualify you for a job.

electronic field production   Any kind of videotaping using minicams and portable recorders and done on location.

electronic news gathering   Producing news reports for television in the field, using the same kind of portable equipment employed in electronic field production.

electrostatic microphone   An alternative term for a *condenser mic*.

ELF   Abbreviation for *easy listening formula*.

Emergency Alert System (EAS)   The FCC's replacement for the Emergency Broadcast System, a program that requires certain broadcast stations to notify the public in case of an emergency such as a tornado, forest fire, or toxic spill.

ENG   Abbreviation for *electronic news gathering*.

enunciation   Same as *articulation*.

equalizer   A system that automatically controls sound by selecting frequencies to emphasize or to eliminate.

equal time   A provision of the Communications Act that requires broadcast licensees in the United States to provide time on an equal basis for legally qualified candidates for office.

ESPN   Abbreviation for *Entertainment and Sports Programming Network.*

ET   A script symbol for "electrical transcription," which was an early term for a certain type of phonograph record, now used for any kind of disc recording.

extemporaneous   Comments prepared in advance but delivered without a script or notes.

EZ   Abbreviation for *easy listening,* a radio station music format that features primarily instrumental versions of popular songs.

FA   Abbreviation for *fine arts–classical,* a radio station music format that features classical music, opera, theater, and culture-oriented news and talk.

facsimile transmission   Abbreviated as *fax,* the transmission of images or printed matter by electronic means.

fact sheet   An outline of information about a product or an event from which a writer prepares a script for a commercial or public-service announcement.

fade out   Using a *fader* or *potentiometer* to gradually reduce the sound until it no longer can be heard. The same term is used for the fading to black of a video signal.

fader   A control on an audio console enabling an operator to increase or decrease the volume of sound going through the board.

fairness doctrine   A former policy of the FCC that required broadcast licensees to devote airtime to the discussion of public issues.

FCC   Abbreviation for *Federal Communications Commission.*

feature reporter   Reporter who writes, edits, and announces soft news stories that engage audiences with stories that move, entertain, amuse, and/or illuminate.

Federal Communications Commission   The governmental agency that oversees broadcasting and other telecommunications industries in the United States.

feedback   A howl or squeal created when a microphone picks up and reamplifies the sound from a nearby loudspeaker.

fidelity   Faithfulness to an original sound, as in a recording of a live music performance.

field reporter   A radio or television reporter who covers stories away from the station, as contrasted with anchors who perform on a news set.

field voicer   A report from the field, sent live to a station by a reporter.

flaring   Flashes on the television screen caused by reflection of studio lights or sunlight off some shiny object, such as jewelry.

format   (1) A type of script used in television, usually a bare script outline; (2) the type of programming provided by a radio station (for example, an MOR format);

(3) the layout of a radio or television script, or the manner in which dialogue, sound effects, music, and other program elements are set forth on the page.

freelance   An announcer or other media performer who works without a contract or a long-term appointment.

freeze   To remain motionless, usually at the end of a television scene.

fricatives   Sounds created by the friction of air through a restricted air passage; an example is the sound of the letter *f.*

future file   A set of thirty-one folders (one for each day of the month) holding information about coming events so that they may be considered by an assignment editor for news coverage.

gaffer's tape   The tape used to hold cables in place in television studios. (A *gaffer* is the chief electrician on a motion picture set.)

gain   The degree of sound volume through an audio console.

gain control   A sliding vertical fader or rotating knob used to regulate the volume of sound through an audio console.

General American   The speech of educated citizens of the Midwest and Far West of the United States and of most of Canada; also called "broadcast speech" and "Standard American Speech."

general-assignment reporter   A radio or television reporter who does not have a regular beat or assignment.

glide   In speech, a rapid movement or *glide* from one vowel sound to another, as in the *oy* sound in the word *joy.* Also called a *diphthong,* pronounced *dif-thong.*

glottal consonant   The letter *h,* when uttered without vibration of the vocal folds.

glottal stop   A speech sound produced by a momentary but complete closure of the throat passage, followed by an explosive release of air.

graveyard shift   Working hours that extend from midnight until 6:00 a.m.

HAC   Hot adult contemporary music. Same radio station music format as *ADC,* adult contemporary.

hand signals   Signals developed to communicate instructions to performers without the use of spoken words.

happy talk   A derogatory term for a newscast featuring news personnel who ad-lib, make jokes, and banter with one another.

hard copy   The printed copy of the output of a computer or word processor.

hard news   Important stories that are usually unanticipated by a broadcast news department.

hard-sell commercial   A commercial that is characterized by rapid vocal delivery, high volume, and excessive energy.

headline   To *tease* upcoming music selections on a radio show.

headlines signal   A hand signal given by an announcer to tell the engineer that headlines will follow the news item currently being read.

headphone jack   A receptacle on a tape recorder or audio console for connecting a headset.

hemispheric   The pickup pattern of a microphone that accepts sounds within a half globe.

hitting marks   Moving to an exact spot in television performance, usually indicated by tape placed on the floor or on the ground.

homers   Sports play-by-play announcers who show an obvious bias for the home team.

horizontal spots   Radio commercials scheduled at about the same time across the days of the week.

hot change   Words created by a character generator that jump from one word or phrase to another on the television screen.

hot clock   A wheel used by music, satellite, and news radio stations to schedule program elements. At popular-music stations, the hot clock indicates the types of music to be played during a typical broadcast hour (up tempo, golden oldie, current hit, and so on.), and indicates precisely when local insertions (commercials, weather reports, or local news) may be made. News station hot clocks specify the timing of headlines, news stories, weather and traffic reports, commercials, and other program components; also called the *clock* or the *newswheel*.

hybrid (or combination) résumé   A résumé that combines the features of a chronological and a competency-based résumé.

hypercardioid   A microphone pickup pattern.

I & I   Script symbol for "introduce and interview."

IDs   Brief musical passages used to identify an upcoming sports report, business report, or other feature; also called *sounders* or *logos*.

impromptu   A performance delivered with little or no preparation and without a script.

in cue   The recorded words that open a segment of an interview that will be dubbed and used as part of a report.

industrial media   Audiovisual presentations made for (and often by) corporations, government agencies, and similar entities and intended for internal use, usually for training purposes; usually referred to as "industrials."

industrials   See *industrial media.*

inflection   The variation of the pitch of a human voice.

infomercial   *Informercials* typically are half-hour television sales pitches, with two or more announcers demonstrating such products as exercise machines, hair restorers, cooking equipment, fishing equipment, and beauty aids.

informational interview   A conversation with an experienced broadcast executive for the purpose of gaining information about job-seeking.

input selector switch   Control on an audio console that allows more than one program input (several microphones, for example) to be fed selectively into the same preamp.

interdental   A speech sound made with the tongue between the upper and lower teeth: for example, the *th* sound in *thin.*

International Phonetic Alphabet (IPA)   A system of phonetic transcription that employs special symbols to denote pronunciations.

interruptable foldback (IFB)   A miniaturized earphone worn by news reporters, anchors, and sportscasters. Instructions and cues are given over the IFB by producers and directors.

in the mud   Expression used when the volume of sound going through an audio console is so weak that it barely moves the needle of the VU meter; the needle is said to be *in the mud.*

in the red   Opposite of in the mud, *in the red* is the term used to describe sounds that are too high in volume. Other terms for this are *bending the needle* and *spilling over.*

intro   Abbreviation of *introduction,* also known as a *lead-in.*

jargon   The specialized vocabulary of a group such as computer technicians, athletes, military personnel, or a particular ethnic group.

JAZ   Abbreviation for a radio station music format featuring jazz music.

jazz   A radio station format featuring mostly instrumental traditional and smooth jazz.

jock   Short for *disc jockey.*

jump cut   A noticeable "jump" in the television picture when a portion of taped material has been edited out.

JZ   Abbreviation for *jazz,* a popular-music category.

karaoke   A performance in which recorded instrumental music is played, while audience volunteers sing the vocal parts before an audience.

keys   Images, usually lettering, keyed into a background image by a *character generator*.

labial   A speech sound made primarily with the lips; for example, the sound of the letter *p*.

labiodental   A speech sound requiring the lower lip to be in proximity to the upper teeth. Labiodental sounds are associated with the letters *f* and *v*.

larynx   The part of the body connecting the trachea (or windpipe) and the pharynx (the area between the mouth and the nasal passages) and containing the vocal folds.

lavaliere microphone   A small microphone clipped to the dress, tie, or lapel of a performer.

lead-in   The opening phrases of a taped or live report or the words used by a reporter to introduce a taped actuality or voicer. Also know as an *intro*.

lead-out   The closing phrases of a taped or live report or the words used by a reporter in adding a conclusion to a taped actuality or voicer. Also known as an *outro*.

level indicator   A device that shows graphically the amount of volume being sent through an audio console or to an audio- or videotape recorder.

libertarian theory   A theory concerning the media that maintains that except for defamation, obscenity, or wartime sedition there should be no censorship of the news whatsoever.

light-emitting diode (LED)   A device that indicates audio volume through the activation of a series of small lights.

limiter   In audio operations, a device that limits the output volume, regardless of the strength of the input volume.

liner notes   Notes prepared by a radio station executive, from which a disc jockey will promote a contest, an upcoming feature, or another disc jockey's show; sometimes called "liner cards."

lingua-alveolar   A speech sound made with the tip of the tongue (or lingua) placed against the upper gum ridge (or alveolus): for example, the sound of the letter *t*.

linguadental   A speech sound made with the tongue between the upper and lower teeth: for example, the initial sound in *thin*.

linguapalatal   A speech sound made with the tip of the tongue nearly touching the upper gum ridge: for example, the sound of the letter *r*.

linguavelar   A speech sound made when the rear of the tongue is raised against the soft palate (or velum) and the tip of the tongue is lowered to the bottom of the mouth, as in sounding the letter *k*.

lip synch   Matching, or synchronizing, the movement of the lips with the speech sounds of the performer. This is achieved automatically with video equipment, but is difficult when dubbing one performer's voice to the lip movements of another who is seen on-screen.

live coverage   Reporting on a story as it happens, most often from the scene of the event.

local marketing agreement (LMA)   In this practice, two or more radio stations enter into an arrangement in which they share facilities, staff, and equipment and, in some instances, even a frequency.

log   A listing of the order of elements to be delivered during a newscast, or the songs and other program components (commercials, news breaks) at a music radio station.

logo   An aural or visual symbol used to identify a program, product, company, or similar entity. The famous CBS eye is the logo for that network. An aural logo is also called a *sounder*.

looping   The dubbing of one person's voice onto the soundtrack of a tape to replace the voice of the person who is seen on the screen.

MA   Abbreviation for *modern adult/contemporary*, a popular-music category.

MAC   Modern ADC (adult contemporary) radio station music format that blends current modern rock music with slightly older rock music.

major market   A city or metropolitan area with a potential viewing or listening audience of more than 1,000,000.

market   The reception area of a radio or television station, classified as major, secondary, or smaller.

marking copy   Making notations on scripts as reminders of when to pause or to stress a word or phrase or to show phonetic transcriptions of difficult words.

marks   Positions for television performers, usually indicated by small pieces of gaffer's tape on the floor of the studio or on the ground at an exterior location.

master pot   A control of an audio console, capable of raising and lowering simultaneously all sounds going through the board; *pot* is short for *potentiometer*.

matte in   To combine electronically two pictures on the television screen without superimposing one over the other; see also *chroma-key*.

menu   A listing of stored information available for retrieval through a computer workstation. Menus are tailored to the needs of news directors, reporters, play-by-play sports announcers, and talk-show hosts, among others.

message design and testing   The process of determining in advance the objectives of a given program and then rating its degree of success after it is performed.

mic fright   A fear of performing in front of a microphone.

mic input   A jack (a socket) that accepts a cord from a microphone into a device, such as a recorder.

microcasting   Same as *narrowcasting.*

microphone consciousness   An awareness of the capabilities and shortcomings of microphones.

minicam   A small, lightweight, portable television camera and its associated equipment.

minidoc   A short documentary, usually produced as a series for a radio or television news program.

minus out   To eliminate the announcer's voice from the sound relayed back from a satellite to the announcer's IFB so that the 1-1/2 second delay will not confuse the announcer.

mixer   An audio console.

MLB   Abbreviation for *Major League Baseball.*

mobile DJs   Mobile DJs perform live in dance halls, as well as at birthdays, company parties, weddings, reunions, and similar festive occasions. They usually have a setup that allows for the playing of vinyl records, CDs, or music from a hard drive.

MOD   A contemporary hit radio station format that focuses on modern rock.

moiré effect   A wavering or shimmering of the picture on a television screen, due to patterns of small checks or narrow stripes on performers' clothing.

monaural   A sound system featuring only one loudspeaker.

monitor pot   A control on an audio console enabling the operator to adjust the volume of sound coming from a monitor speaker without affecting the volume of sound being broadcast or recorded.

monitor select switch   A switch on an audio console used to selectively monitor program and audition outputs.

monitor speaker   A speaker in an audio control room that enables the operator to hear the material being broadcast or recorded.

mood   A state of mind or emotion projected by a performer. Some typical moods are gloomy, joyous, cynical, elated, and festive. See also *attitude.*

moonlighting   Working at odd jobs, usually at night, while holding down a permanent position.

morgue   A collection of magazine and newspaper clippings, organized by topic and used for gathering background information for news stories and interviews.

MOS   Script abbreviation for "man-on-the-street interview." (Despite efforts to avoid gender-specific references in broadcast terminology, this term is still used. A gender-neutral alternative is *vox pop*.)

multidirectional microphone   A microphone that can be adjusted to employ more than one pickup pattern.

multievent recorder/player systems (MERPS)   Audio/video computerized electronic cart machines. MERPS's memory and storage capacity permit it to perform a variety of functions once done by a cumbersome master reel.

multi-images   A digital video effects device that changes the video signal from analog to digital; one of many options that DVE equipment offers is that of *multi-imaging*, splitting the screen into sectors, with each section containing a different visual image, or repeating the same video information in each cell.

musical IDs   Musical logos that identify a program or a program segment.

music bed   The musical background of a radio commercial, usually laid down before voices are added.

music sweep   Several music recordings played back-to-back without interruption or comment by the DJ.

muting relays   Devices that automatically cut off the sound from a monitor speaker when an announce mic in the control room is opened.

NAB   Abbreviation for *National Association of Broadcasters*.

narrowcasting   Programs not intended for large, heterogeneous audiences.

nasality   A quality of the voice due to allowing air to exit through the nose, rather than the mouth, when speaking.

nasals   Speech sounds that employ nasal resonance, such as *m, n*, and *ng*.

National Public Radio (NPR)   A network of noncommercial radio stations, established by the Corporation for Public Broadcasting.

NBA   Abbreviation for *National Basketball Association*.

news script   The copy from which news anchors work. News scripts may be seen by anchors as hard copy or as electronically generated copy seen on a prompter.

newswheel   News station *newswheels* or *hot clocks* specify the timing of headlines, news stories, weather and traffic reports, commercials, and other program components; also called the *clock*.

NFL   Abbreviation for *National Football League*.

NHL   Abbreviation for *National Hockey League*.

nonverbal communication   That part of a person's communication with others that does not involve speech, such as gestures, facial expressions, and so on.

NR   Abbreviation for *New Rock*, a radio station music format that features modern rock.

O & O   Abbreviation for *owned and operated*; refers to radio or television stations owned and operated by a parent network.

off hours   The portion of a broadcast day, usually late night and very early morning, when the audience is least likely to be tuned in.

off mic   Persons are said to be *off mic* when they speak outside the ideal pickup pattern of a microphone.

OL   Abbreviation for *oldies*, a popular-music category.

OLD   Oldies music. A radio station music format that features popular music of the '50s, '60s, and '70s. Current popular music is played only in rare exceptions.

omnidirectional   A microphone pickup pattern in which all sides will accept sound signals.

on-air studio   The studio in which radio DJs and news anchors perform.

on-air talent   Persons who perform on radio or television. The term usually is associated with music station announcing, but reporters, anchors, and voice-over performers also are *on-air talent*.

opening up to the camera   Positioning oneself at a slight angle from a second person to present a favorable appearance to the camera.

optimum pitch   The pitch at which a speaker feels most comfortable while producing the most pleasant speech sounds.

orbiting spots   See *rotating spots*.

out cue   The words that conclude a recorded and carted program segment, alerting an announcer that the carted segment has come to its conclusion. When editing audiotaped interviews or statements, an out cue indicates the final words spoken in a given segment, and tells the editor (usually the reporter) where to electronically or manually "cut" the tape.

outro   A lead-out at the end of a radio or television news report, such as an actuality or a wrap.

overmodulation   Excessive volume that distorts an audio signal.

package   (1) A complete news report prepared by a field or special-assignment reporter, needing only a lead-in by an anchor; (2) a series of programs marketed to television stations as a unit.

panic button   A control that allows a producer to cut off obscene or defamatory comments by a caller on a telephone talk show.

panoramic potentiometer   A volume control that allows an operator to change the volume balance between two audio channels.

pan pot   Short for *panoramic potentiometer.*

payola   The accepting of money in return for playing certain songs on the air.

pay-per-view   Cable television offerings, such as new movies or sports events, for which viewers are charged a fee beyond their monthly cable service cost.

peripheral vision   The ability to see out of the corners of the eyes, to see a hand signal, for example, without looking at the person giving it.

personal attack, personal attack rule   A *personal attack* is a verbal attack, made during a broadcast, on "the honesty, character, integrity or like personal qualities" of another person. The *rule*, set forth by the Federal Communications Commission, requires broadcast licensees to notify those who are attacked and to inform them as to the ways in which they may reply.

personality   A term sometimes used for a DJ, program host, or other popular entertainer.

pharynx   The area between the mouth and the nasal passages.

phonation   The term referring to speech sounds produced by the vibration of the vocal folds.

phone beat   See *beat check* or *phone check.*

phone check   Using a telephone to search for and gather news stories from a list of agencies, including the FBI, police and fire departments, local hospitals, the weather bureau, and airport control towers; also called the *phone beat* and *beat check.*

phoneme   The smallest unit of distinguishable speech sound.

phone screener   A person, usually a producer or assistant producer, who receives telephone calls from listeners or viewers who want to talk with a program host and who attempts to eliminate calls from people who are obviously cranks or drunks or are too-frequent callers.

pickup   The term *pickup* is used in at least three ways in voice-over recording work. If you stumble or slur a word, you are expected to pause, say "pickup," pause again, and begin reading from the beginning of the sentence in which you stumbled. A *pickup session* is a recording session in which specific lines, recorded at an earlier session, are deemed unusable and must be recorded again. *Pickup* also refers to picking up one's cue—in other words, speaking more closely on the heels of a line delivered by another performer.

pickup arm   The arm on a turntable that contains the stylus; also called the *tone arm.*

pickup cartridge   The pickup cartridge on an audio turntable contains a stylus and a mechanism that picks up vibrations on a phonograph record and transduces the vibrations into electrical energy.

pickup pattern   The three-dimensional area around a microphone from within which sound is transmitted most faithfully, also referred to as the *polar pattern.*

pickup session   See *pickup.*

pitch   The property of a tone that is determined by the frequency of vibration of the sound waves. For humans, the slower the vocal folds vibrate, the lower the pitch of the voice.

pitch "artist"   A type of announcer whose style is reminiscent of sideshow barkers and old-time medicine shows.

platform speech   An exaggerated style of speaking, featuring overly precise articulation and a distinct "British" sound.

play analyst   An announcer, usually a former star athlete, who works with a play-by-play announcer, providing insight and analysis of a game.

play-by-play announcer   A sportscaster who describes the action of a game.

playlist   Music approved by radio station management for playing at stipulated times.

plosive   A speech sound manufactured by the sudden release of blocked-off air. In English, the plosives are *p, b, t, d, k,* and *g.*

plugola   The free promotion of a product or service in which the announcer has a financial interest. (Reading or playing commercials that have been paid for is not illegal, even when the announcer has an interest in the product being advertised.)

polar pattern   See *pickup pattern.*

political correctness (PC)   A concept with a range of meanings but confined in this text to *language* that is sensitive and appropriate, as opposed to that which is hurtful or demeaning.

polydirectional   A pickup or polar pattern that can be adjusted to operate with more than one pickup pattern. Same as *multidirectional.*

popping   The sound made when a plosive is spoken too closely to a sensitive mic.

postmortem   A meeting held after a broadcast to discuss what worked, what did not, and why.

postproduction   Editing and other electronic manipulation of audio or videotapes after they have been recorded.

pot   Short for *potentiometer.*

potentiometer   A volume control on an audio console.

preamplifier   An electronic device that boosts the strength of an audio signal and sends it to the program amplifier; often shortened to "preamp."

preparation   The development of skills to help you be heard and appreciated by broadcast audiences.

presentation tape   An edited recording of an on-air performance. Also called an *aircheck.*

press kit   An organized body of printed information prepared by political parties, law enforcement agencies, or sports teams, among others, for reporters, sportscasters, and others who may find such kits useful as they plan their stories or prepare for play-by-play coverage.

pressure microphone   A rugged professional microphone that features a molded diaphragm and a wire coil suspended in a magnetic field; also called a *dynamic microphone.*

pressure zone microphone (PZM)   A type of microphone that eliminates time lags between direct and reflected sounds.

primary stress   The syllable in a spoken word that receives the emphasis. In the word *primary*, the first syllable receives the primary stress.

prime time   That part of the broadcast day during which the radio or television audience is most likely to be tuned in.

production console   An elaborate audio console with features not found (or needed) on on-air studio boards, including equalization and other signal processing options.

production studio   A radio studio in which music is dubbed from discs to carts or DAT, station promos are recorded, and other program elements requiring a sophisticated audio setup are produced.

program amplifier   An electronic device that collects, boosts, and sends sounds to a transmitter or tape recorder.

program log   A listing of all commercials, public-service announcements, and program material broadcast by a station.

promo   Short for "promotion"; any prepared spot that promotes viewing or listening to a station or a program broadcast by the station.

prompter   Any of several machines that display a script before a broadcast performer; also called "prompting devices" or "teleprompters" (however, TelePrompTer is the brand name of one prompting system).

pronouncer   The phoneticized pronunciation for a word or name included on wire-service copy.

pronunciation   A way of speaking words. The particular accent used by persons in sounding words.

prop   Short for "property"; any article other than sets or costumes used in a television production.

property   An object that a performer holds, displays, or points to.

PT   Abbreviation for *preteen*, a radio station music format featuring music, drama, or readings that focus mostly on a preteen audience.

public-service announcement (PSA)   A radio or television announcement that promotes a charitable or nonprofit organization or cause.

Q & A session   Question-and-answer session; a brief on-air discussion of a news story between an anchor and a reporter in the field.

raw sound   Recorded or live sounds from the site of news stories that add to the "reality" of reports. Raw sounds include those of foghorns, crickets chirping, jet aircraft flying overhead, people chanting, and the sound of marching bands at a parade.

RB   Abbreviation for *R&B/urban*, a popular-music category.

RC   Abbreviation for *religious/contemporary*, a radio station music format featuring modern- and rock-based religious music.

RCK   Rock music. A radio station music format that plays mainstream rock, with a mix of current hits and recent hits from the archives.

real time   Whether live or recorded, *real time* refers to performances that are unedited and heard or seen by an audience exactly as they are or were performed.

recurrent   A term used in music radio to indicate selections that are just off the playlist.

redundancy   Repetition of ideas or words or phrases, which is sometimes appropriate, as in repeating a telephone number to be called, and sometimes excessive, as in the term "joint partnership."

reporter   A person who reports news stories that occur away from a radio or television station; some categories are *field, general-assignment,* and *special-assignment reporters.*

resonance   The intensification of vocal tones during speech as the result of vibrations in the nose and cheekbones.

résumé   A written statement that includes work experience, qualifications, educational background, and interest areas, often submitted with employment applications.

reveal   Words or phrases produced by a character generator and "revealed" one at a time on the television screen to match the points being made by an announcer.

ribbon microphone   A sensitive, professional microphone that has a metallic ribbon suspended between the poles of a magnet; also referred to as a *velocity mic.*

rip and read   To take news copy directly from a wire-service and read it on the air without editing it, marking it, or prereading it.

robotic cameras   Television cameras programmed to move to predetermined positions without individual human operators.

roll   Words or phrases produced by a character generator and moved from bottom to top on the television screen.

rotating potentiometers   Knobs on an audio console that are turned clockwise or counterclockwise to raise or lower the volume of sound; see also *vertical fader*.

rotating spots   Commercial announcements whose time of broadcast varies throughout the week; also called *orbiting spots*.

rotating table   The "table" on a record player that holds a disc and spins while a pickup stylus transmits sound from its grooves to another destination, such as a speaker or an audio console.

RTNDA   Abbreviation for *Radio and Television News Directors Association*.

rule of three   A theory that the impact of a statement is diluted by going beyond three words or phrases in a sequence.

running log   A listing of the times at which every program element will be broadcast by a radio station. Also known as a *run sheet*.

run of station (ROS)   A system of scheduling radio commercials on a random basis at available times.

run sheet   A run sheet, or *running log*, follows the established format of a news radio station and indicates the times at which headlines, features, time checks, commercials, and other newscast elements will be played. The log may be on sheets of paper, on a computer screen, or on both.

SA   Abbreviation for *soft adult contemporary*, a popular-music category.

SAC   Soft adult contemporary music. A radio station music format that plays only the softest contemporary pop recordings and soft-sounding pop records from the '60s and '70s.

SAT PIC   Abbreviation for "satellite picture," a view of Earth's weather sent from a satellite.

SB   Abbreviation for *soft urban contemporary*, a popular-music category.

scannable résumé   A résumé specially formatted for scanning by a potential employer.

scener   A live or taped radio news report on a breaking event.

schwa vowel   In phonetic transcription, the *schwa* vowel represents an unaccented *uh* sound, as the last syllable in *sofa*. It is transcribed as an inverted *e*, depicted as [ə].

Screen Actors Guild (SAG)   The union for those actors and announcers whose work is filmed (as opposed to taped).

search engines   World Wide Web indexing and searching systems, such as Alta Vista, Yahoo!, Lycos, and Google. Users select a search engine and enter a key word(s) to locate websites with information they seek.

secondary market   An area with a potential broadcast audience of between 200,000 and 1,000,000 viewers or listeners.

secondary stress   Multisyllabic words usually have different degrees of stress, as in the word *secondary*. SEC receives primary stress, ON is unstressed, DAR receives secondary stress, and Y is unstressed.

segue   To broadcast two elements of a radio program back-to-back without overlap or pause. The first sound is faded out, and the second is immediately faded in. The script symbol is *SEGUE*.

semivowels   Speech sounds similar to true vowel sounds in their resonance patterns. The consonants *w, r,* and *y* are the semivowels.

separates   The term used by the Associated Press for individual sports stories.

set   Two or more songs played back-to-back without intervening commentary by the DJ.

SFX   Script symbol for *sound effects.*

SGS   Southern gospel music. A radio station music format featuring gospel music and spirituals that have a country music base.

shopping channels   Television channels devoted to the showing and selling of products. Viewers may make purchases by telephone or email.

showprep   The abbreviation for *show preparation.*

sibilance   The sound made when pronouncing the fricatives *s, sh,* and sometimes *z.* Excessive sibilance is exaggerated by sensitive microphones.

signature   Same as a *logo* or *ID.*

simile   A figure of speech in which two essentially unlike things are compared, as in "a meal without salad is like a day without sunshine."

simulcast   The simultaneous broadcasting of the same program over an AM and an FM station or over a radio and a television station.

situationer   In most television news operations, news directors, producers, reporters, directors, and other key members of the news team meet to discuss and plan upcoming newscasts. A list of available stories, called a situationer, is handed out, and the stories are discussed one by one as decisions are made as to what stories to cover, who is to gather each report, and the order in which the stories will be broadcast.

slate   An audio and/or visual identification of a taped television program segment that is included at the beginning of the tape and provides information about the segment—its title, the date of recording, the intended date of showing, and the number of the take.

slip start   A method of starting a cued-up phonograph record by allowing the turntable to rotate while the operator's hand holds the disc motionless and then releases the disc.

slug commercial   A hard-hitting commercial, usually characterized by high volume, rapid reading, and frenetic delivery.

slug line   The shortened or abbreviated title given to a news event for identification purposes.

smaller market   An area with a potential audience of fewer than 200,000 viewers or listeners.

social responsibility theory   A theory concerning the media that charges journalists with considering the potential consequences of their coverage of the news.

soft news   News stories about scheduled events, such as meetings, briefings, hearings, or news conferences, that lack the immediacy and urgency of hard news.

soft-sell commercial   A commercial that features restrained announcer delivery and (usually) a melodious musical background.

solecism   A blunder in speech.

SOT   Script symbol for *sound on tape.*

sound bite   A brief statement made on-camera by someone other than station personnel; equivalent to an actuality on radio.

sounder   A short, recorded musical identification of a particular radio program element, such as a traffic, sports, or weather report; also referred to as an *ID* or *logo.*

sounds   Recorded statements introduced as part of radio news stories. Sounds include actualities, wraps, sceners, and voicers.

special-assignment reporter   A radio or television reporter who specializes in one aspect of news gathering, such as crime reporting, politics, environmental issues, or news from a particular geographic area.

speech personality   The overall quality of a person's voice, which makes one instantly recognizable to friends when speaking on the telephone.

spilling over   Another expression for bending the needle.

spot   Another term for a commercial.

spot set   A cluster of commercials played one after the other.

SS   Abbreviation for *Spanish*, a radio station music format featuring music from Latin America.

Standard American Speech (or Standard American Dialect)   That manner of pronouncing words used by educated persons in the Midwest and Far West of the United States and Canada.

stand-up   A direct address made to a camera by a television reporter at any time within a news package, but almost always for the closing comments.

stash   A term used for songs that are not on a radio station's current playlist but are occasionally played.

station ID   Short for *station identification.*

station logo   A symbol, either aural or visual, by which a station identifies itself.

status-conferral function   The concept that the media of radio and television confer exalted status to those who appear on them.

STD   Adult Standards music. A radio station music format featuring American popular standards mixed with soft popular music, mainly vocal.

stereo   A two-or-more-speaker sound system. Abbreviation of "stereophonic."

sting   Abbreviation of "stinger," a sharp musical chord used to highlight a transition or draw attention.

stop set   A cluster of commercials played one after the other.

streaming audio (radio)   Playing and announcing music over the Internet.

stringer   A freelance reporter who is paid only for stories chosen and used by a station's news department.

studio cards   Cards used in television to convey information or entire scripts to on-camera performers.

stylus   The needle part of a tone arm pickup cartridge.

super   Short for *superimposition*, the showing of one picture over another on the television screen.

supercardioid   A microphone pickup pattern used chiefly in television boom mics. Also called *hypercardioid.*

sweep   The playing of several songs consecutively, without intervening comment by the DJ.

sweetening   Electronically treating music during recording and in postproduction to improve the sound quality.

switchable   A microphone that features a switch that changes the pickup pattern of the mic. Also called *multidirectional* and *polydirectional.*

switcher   (1) The video console that allows an operator to cut, dissolve, and perform other electronic functions; (2) the title given to the person who operates such a console.

switches   Allow you to open and close your announce mic, to open and close the intercom or talk-back mic, and to open a mic in the newsroom for feeding out a news bulletin.

syllabic consonant   The consonants *m, n,* and *l,* which can be sounded as separate syllables without a vowel sound preceding or following them. In phonetic transcription, the word *saddle* can be transcribed as [sædl], with the line under the letter *l* indicating that it is sounded as a separate syllable.

tag   To make closing comments at the end of a scene or program segment.

takes   Any number of attempts to record a program segment successfully.

taking a level   A procedure in which performers, prior to going on the air or being recorded, speak into a microphone at the volume level they will use during the show. This enables an audio engineer to establish the optimal volume level.

taking camera   In a multi-camera television production, the camera that is "on" at a specific moment.

talent   A word often used to describe radio and television performers other than news personnel. "Talent" actually refers to a quality or a possession, rather than to individuals, but the term has taken hold and likely will be with us forever.

talk-back microphone   The mic located in a control room that allows the audio operator to speak to people in other production areas, such as studios or newsrooms.

talking head   A derogatory term for a television shot featuring a close-up of a speaker addressing the camera.

talk station   A radio station, usually an AM station, that features a number of talk and telephone call-in shows daily.

tally light   A red light mounted on the top of a television camera that, when lit, indicates the *taking camera.*

tape cart   A cartridge of $\frac{1}{4}$-inch audiotape that rewinds and that recues itself.

tape cart players   Machines that play quarter-inch audiotapes that are looped inside a cartridge and that automatically rewind as they are played.

target audience   The intended audience for a program or a commercial.

tease   A brief promotion of a program or an upcoming segment of a program.

telegraphing a movement   A subtle indication by a television performer who is about to move, stand, or sit. Directors and camera operators need such warnings to follow movements effectively.

tempo   A speaker's rate of delivery.

tight shot   A close-up shot.

time code   A means of marking each frame of a videotape for later editing.

time-delay system   A means of delaying material being broadcast live (such as a radio call-in talk show) to permit intervention if someone uses profanity or makes other unacceptable comments.

tone arm   The device on a turntable that holds the pickup cartridge and its stylus. The stylus "rides" the grooves of a record and converts the vibrations into electrical energy.

toss   To turn the program over to a coanchor, a weather reporter, or an other member of the broadcast team with a brief ad-libbed transitional statement.

total audience plan (TAP)   A system for distributing commercial messages over three or more dayparts.

trachea   The windpipe.

traffic department   The personnel at a broadcast station who schedule the placement of commercials.

transduction   The conversion of sound waves into electrical energy.

trash television   Television talk shows that regularly use intimidation, obscenity, vulgarity, and controversial and unsubstantiated statements to attract an audience that seeks cheap thrills.

turntable   The "table" on a record player that holds a disc and spins while a pickup stylus transmits sound from its grooves to another destination, such as a speaker or an audio console.

UAC   Urban AC (adult contemporary) music. A radio station music format that features the softest contemporary rhythm & blues music mixed with soft R&B music of previous years.

unidirectional   A microphone pickup pattern in which sound is accepted from only one direction.

unphonated   Speech sounds that don't employ vibrations of the vocal folds, as in the plosive sounds *p, b, t, k,* and *g.*

unvoiced consonants   The consonants of spoken English that do not involve the vibration of the vocal folds. Examples are *p, t, k,* and *f.*

unvoiced sounds   Sounds made with no vocal vibration, as when saying "shhhh."

UOL   Rhythm & blues oldies music. A radio station music format featuring soul and R&B records of the '60s and '70s from black-oriented stations.

uplink   A transmitter that sends a signal to a satellite and is often part of a mobile van.

URB   Urban contemporary music. A radio station format that plays a blend of current R&B, rap, hip-hop, and dance music.

urgent   Sports news story issued by the Associated Press. Urgents include no-hitters, major firings of coaches and managers, and important breaking stories.

uvula   The small area of tissue suspended from the rear of the soft palate.

variable equalizer   A filter that enables an audio console operator to eliminate undesirable frequencies, such as those associated with scratches on a record.

velocity microphone   See *ribbon microphone*.

velum   The soft palate.

vertical fader   A sliding lever on certain audio consoles that is moved up or down to raise or lower the volume of sound.

vertical spots   Radio commercials scheduled at various times on a given day.

videotape recorder   Any of several types of electronic recording devices that record and store picture and sound for later playback or editing.

VI meter   Short for *volume indicator meter*, which registers the volume of sounds through an audio console.

virgule   A slash, used by some announcers to indicate a pause when marking broadcast copy for delivery.

viscous damping   The tone arm of a record player uses a silicone fluid in a hydraulic mechanism to prevent it from making sharp or sudden movements. The fluid is *viscous*, and the *damping* acts as a restraint.

vitality   The enthusiasm and high energy level of a performer.

vocal folds (vocal cords)   A part of the speech mechanism that vibrates to generate sounds. The rate of vibration determines pitch, and the amount of energy behind the vibration determines the volume of a sound produced.

vocalized pauses   Sounds, such as *er* or *uh*, uttered by some speakers to cover what otherwise would be silence as they search for a word or a thought.

voiced consonants   The consonants of spoken English that require the vibration of the vocal folds. Examples are *b, d, g,* and *v.*

voiced sounds   Speech sounds made by vibration of the vocal folds (frequently called vocal cords.)

voice-overs   Taped performances in which the announcer is not seen.

voice quality   The way your voice sounds, including such characteristics as resonance, thinness, timbre, nasality, huskiness, and tone.

voicer   A carted report from a radio news reporter.

voice tracking   A practice in which a single announcer's voice is heard on dozens of radio stations across the U.S.

volume   In audio terms, *volume* or *amplitude* refers to the relative strength (magnitude) of a sound signal.

vowel   A pure phonated tone that can be held indefinitely without moving the articulators: for example, the sound *ah* in *father.*

vox pop   Abbreviation of *vox populi,* Latin for *voice of the people.* Newscasts often feature brief expressions of opinion elicited from passersby. The term *man on the street* (MOS) is seldom used for such collections of opinion because of its gender bias.

VTR   Abbreviation for *videotape recorder.*

VTR SOT   Abbreviation for *videotape, sound on tape.*

VU meter   Short for *volume unit meter,* a part of an audio console that shows, by means of a swinging needle, the volume of sound going through the board.

web browser   A tool that allows users to find sites on the Internet. Popular browsers are Microsoft Internet Explorer, Netscape Navigator, and Mozilla Firefox.

wheel   See *hot clock.*

wild spots   Radio commercials guaranteed by a station to be played at some point within a designated block of time.

windpipe   The windpipe, also called the *trachea,* is a tube, slightly longer than four inches, that extends from the larynx to the lungs.

wipe   An electronic effect in which one picture appears to push another off the television screen.

wire-service phonetics   Symbols used to illustrate sounds. They were designed at a time when teletype machines were limited to capital letters only. An apostrophe was used to indicate the syllable to be stressed, as in (SILL'-UH-BUHL).

WNBA   Abbreviation for *Women's National Basketball Association.*

woodshedding   The careful study, marking, and rehearsing of broadcast copy before performance.

working combo   Performing both announcing and engineering functions for a radio broadcast.

wowing   The distorted sound when a record or tape is run at an incorrect or inconsistent speed.

wrap   A recorded report from the field in which a radio news reporter provides a lead-in and a lead-out, *wrapped around* an actuality; also called a *wraparound.*

WX   Script symbol for "weather report."

XAC   Spanish adult alternative music.

XRA   Spanish ranchero music.

XST   Spanish standards music.

Index

Credits